WESTCOUNTRYMAN

WESTCOUNTRYMAN

A life in farming, countryside, cricket and cider

Anthony Gibson

CHARLCOMBE BOOKS

Charlcombe Books
e-mail: stephen.chalke@hotmail.co.uk
tel: 07968 138122

First published 2021

ISBN: 978 1 9996558 8 4

Printed and bound in Great Britain by
CPI Antony Rowe, Bumpers Way, Chippenham SN14 6LH

For my family: past, present and future

Previous books by Anthony Gibson

West Country Treasury
A Compendium of Lore and Literature, People and Places
with Alan Gibson (1989)

A Celtic Odyssey
(2009)

Of Didcot and the Demon
The Cricketing Times of Alan Gibson
(2009)

With Magic in my Eyes
West Country Literary Landscapes
(2011)

Gentlemen, Gypsies and Jesters
The Wonderful World of Wandering Cricket
with Stephen Chalke (2013)

The Coloured Counties
Literary Landscapes of the Heart of England
(2017)

Somerset's Summer
(2019)

Also as co-writer:

From Wiveliscombe to Whitehall
A Farmer's Life
by Fred Elliott (2011)

Rosey
My Life in Somerset Cricket
by Brian Rose (2019)

For details of which of these books are still available and how to order them,
visit **www.anthonygibsonbooks.co.uk**

Contents

Preface

Writing an autobiography is, by definition, the ultimate in self-regard and egotism, and for that I apologise in advance. My justification (or possibly excuse) is that I have in the course of my life and career been at the centre of any number of crises, controversies and major events, in farming especially, and am thus able to offer a perspective on those events which others who have lived through them may find interesting.

My 36 years in the NFU were nothing if not eventful! Politically we had EEC entry and transition to the Common Agricultural Policy, the 1974 beef crisis, the imposition of milk quotas and the various subsequent reforms of the CAP, each of which had profound effects on the farming community in the West Country and beyond. In the countryside we moved from damaging conflict between farmers and conservationists to a constructive accommodation in which I am proud to have been able to play some small part. Climatically we endured the 1976 drought, the 1978 blizzard, the sea flooding along the North Somerset coast of 1981 and a series of damaging flood events on the Somerset Levels, from the most recent of which, in 2013-14, a new and long overdue model of flood prevention and water management has evolved.

And then there were the two great animal health crises of the last half century: BSE, which threatened to destroy the UK livestock industry, and the 2001 outbreak of Foot and Mouth Disease, which shook the rural community in the South-West to its foundations. In both of those traumatic episodes I didn't just have a front-row seat but, for better or for worse, was one of the lead actors.

My career has not, however, been entirely taken up with disasters and crises. I have been fortunate enough to have been able to give a helpful shove to some of the most positive developments in the consumer market, like the growing demand for local food, real ale and artisan cider. I am particularly proud of the way in which Taste of Somerset and Taste of the West, at the births of both of which I acted as midwife, have been trail-blazers in the local food revival.

If crisis dogged my footsteps during my time with the NFU, the opposite has been true of my career as a cricket scorer, reporter and commentator for the BBC, in which I was fortunate enough to have been able to witness great games, like the 1975 World Cup final, and describe great innings, like Viv Richards' 322 and Graeme Hick's 405. And if most of my past ten years or so as a commentator on Somerset cricket has been marked by heroic failure, I was at least on the microphone at Lord's in 2019, for the Royal London One-Day Cup triumph.

This book is much more about the professional life of Anthony Gibson than my personal life, but I hope that the early chapters will give readers some idea of where I came from, just as the chapter on my brother Andrew will, I hope, shed some light on the single most tragic event of my life and its impact on me.

In writing the book, I have sought to be honest, accurate, generous and fair. Considering the events I have been involved in, and the strong feelings they inevitably evoked, I seem to have made remarkably few enemies over the years, in any sphere, and it was certainly never my intention to use this book to settle such old scores as remain outstanding.

Finally I really ought to apologise for the length of the book. But then again, I suppose it is my good fortune to have had so much to write about. I hope you enjoy reading about my life as much as I – for most of the time – have enjoyed living it.

Thanks and Acknowledgements

I am very grateful to Phil Bowern, editor of the Western Morning News, for the photographs which he kindly dug out of the archives, and to my old friend Wesley Wyatt for the photograph of some of the sheep he lost in the 1978 blizzard.

Particular thanks go to Stephen Chalke, for his invaluable help and guidance with the text and the photographs and for allowing this book to be published under his imprint. No author could be more blessed in his publisher than I have been with Stephen.

1

In the blood

I was born in the Totnes maternity hospital on the Plymouth Road, an austere and utilitarian building which looks every inch the workhouse it had once been. I was a happy, healthy and, as it would turn out, very lucky baby. Fate had dealt me a good hand. I was fortunate in where I was born, in the beautiful South Hams; in when I was born, in 1949 at the height of the post-war baby boom; and blessed above all in my parents.

My father Alan and mother Olwen had met at Oxford; he an undergraduate reading history at Queen's; she having been evacuated to Oxford from Westfield College, part of the University of London, reading English; both highly intelligent, strikingly attractive and strong-minded in the liberal tradition. No wonder I gurgled contentedly in my pram.

My father's family were Durham miners on his father's side, Durham seafarers on his mother's. His father Norman was one of 13, all brought up at Tudhoe, just outside Spennymoor. He was sent down the pit at 12, survived being gassed towards the end of the First World War and, despite having had little in the way of a formal education, taught himself enough to win a place at Spurgeon's College, to train as a Baptist Minister. I have no personal recollection of him for he died of stomach cancer when I was still a baby but, from everything I have heard or read, he was a good, kind, generous, deeply religious man, much loved by his congregations at, in turn, Attercliffe, Ilkley, Leyton, Falmouth and, finally, Totnes. If there is one of my forebears from whom I like to think the better part of me has been inherited, it is my grandfather Norman.

My father's mother, Jenny, or Nana as we always called her, was a very different kettle of fish. She was a Welch, a reasonably well-to-do family of South Shields sea-farers. Being sailors, they had a fondness for alcohol, sometimes to excess, particularly on the part of Jenny's father. This turned her implacably against the demon drink, not a drop of which can ever have crossed her lips. Nor Norman's, for that matter, certainly not after he had met Jenny, who made up for her physical frailty in the ironclad strength of her religious convictions. Whether Norman's abstinence was similarly a reaction to the drinking habits of his mining family, I don't know, but it wouldn't be in the least bit surprising. At any event, they were determined that young Alan should not be tempted. He loved to recall how, as a boy, his mother would make him hold his nose and run past any pubs they came across, so as to avoid even a sniff of the devil's brew. This did not work out as Alan's parents had intended. He drank his first pint of beer at the Rising Sun in West Bagborough in his last term at Taunton School and, after that, never looked back!

For all that, his strict Dissenting upbringing left a deep impression on my father. Growing up, he was every bit as religious as his parents and had every intention of becoming a Baptist minister himself, until he went to Oxford and his horizons broadened. Even so, he still became a fine preacher, much in demand among the chapels of South Devon and Cornwall. But the contrast between the way he felt he ought to be living his life and the often boozy, libidinous reality created a tension in his conscience which, by his own admission, was a major factor in the mental problems which haunted his later years.

But we are getting ahead of ourselves. At Oxford my father was something of a star. During his four years there he became President of the Queen's JCR (effectively the college student union), President of the University Liberal Club, cricket correspondent for the university magazine Isis and, briefly, President of the Oxford Union. The relevant entry in the Union's 'List of Former Officers' for the Hilary term of 1945 reads 'President: NAS Gibson*' (his first name was Norman, which he never used) – the asterisk denoting 'elected but did not hold office owing to war service or other causes'. In my father's case, the 'other causes' were his arrest, by the military police, for having failed to turn up for a medical examination ("for what seemed to me the very good reason that I had the chance to meet CB Fry"), by which he had hoped to avoid being called up on account of a weak chest.

Shortly afterwards, his Union Presidency notwithstanding, he found himself in the army, a circumstance he endured for the next two years "spent almost entirely in hospital" before returning to Oxford for a final year. He took a First and might have become a don but when a job came up as an itinerant lecturer on local history with the Workers Educational Association, under the aegis of the University College of the West of England, soon to become the University of Exeter, he took that. It meant that he could live with his parents, get married and travel around the South Hams villages which he had already come to love.

My mother came from a not dissimilar background, albeit one that was almost entirely Welsh, to the extent that my maternal grandparents were always referred to as 'Nain' and 'Taid' (pronounced Nine and Tide). I say 'almost entirely Welsh' because mother's paternal grandmother, Ellen, had been an illegitimate child, adopted by a family called Jacques, and family tradition had it that her father had been an Irish railway gangmaster who had come to North Wales to help build the line from Bangor to Bethesda.

Ellen was certainly quite a character, known for her intelligence, her cooking and for her mood swings, which, when she was on a high, would lead her into gigantic spending sprees. According to my mother's cousin Eluned, Ellen, when in the mood, would dress up like a duchess and "parade down Bethesda High Street in splendid hats and other finery" – much to the dismay of her husband, William Thomas, who had to pick up the bills. William was a foreman at the local slate quarry, but he had been born the son of a farmer, another William, at Tyn y Clwt just outside Bethesda on the Bangor Road. So, bearing in mind my subsequent career, it is reassuring to know that there is at least some farming blood in my veins, thanks to my great-great-grandfather, as well as a drop or two of the Irish, courtesy of the visiting railwayman.

My mother's father, Daniel Thomas, was the youngest of five. He grew up to be another extraordinarily gifted man, winning a bardic chair for his Welsh verse at the Bethesda Eisteddfod in 1909 when he was only 19. He took a degree in history from the University of Wales at Bangor (as it was then), became a teacher but then was badly wounded on the Somme. He and my grandmother Ruth met, probably in Bangor, where her father William Hughes had been born and brought up, back before the war.

Not until three years after the war did they marry, by which time both were teachers: Daniel at Tetbury in Gloucestershire, Ruth in Portsmouth. From Tetbury he moved to Dursley before finishing his career at St David's College in Bristol. With his glasses, his dark suits and his hair slicked down, he could be a slightly forbidding, austere, buttoned-up presence, belying the warmth, wit and passion of his poetry. My mother wrote of him, long after his death: "He was a very fair man and a natural disciplinarian who never needed to raise his voice or his hand. I loved him dearly but was always a little in awe of him. I often wish that I had been able to talk to him about his life before he died ... but as I grew up and married things became very difficult."

Nain's father, the Rev William Hughes, was, by all accounts, another fine man. Born in Bangor into a family which originated in Anglesey, his ministry took him to Crewe, Keighley, Hebden Bridge, Golborne, Ashton-in-Makerfield, Great Broughton in Cumbria and finally Nantwich. He was a tall, handsome, evidently athletic man, whose great joy was riding around the country on his bicycle, visiting villages, churches, historic monuments and beauty spots. As a young man he would think nothing of cycling from Keighley back to Bangor, to see his family, and at the age of 58 he cycled the 300 miles from Cockermouth to Tetbury in three days, to visit my grandparents.

Not long afterwards, he swapped his push bike for a motorcycle and it was on that that he met his end, killed when a lady driver pulled out onto a main road in Nuneaton without seeing him until it was too late. It was a tragic end to a life well lived. But I am glad to say that, four generations down the line, my son George has inherited the Reverend William's love of cycling.

His obituary in the Cheshire Guardian vividly describes the sort of man he must have been: 'He had lived his life at full speed and gave out his whole energy in every cause in which he was interested. His enthusiasm was unbounded once his mind was made up. He hated half-measures. He possessed the valuable knack of infecting others with his own enthusiasm for a cause.'

Maybe I've inherited some of that, as well.

William and his wife had two daughters, my grandmother Ruth and her younger sister Mennai (who, like a good many on both sides of my family, suffered serious mental problems). By the time I came to know Nain, as we always called her, she had turned into a rather prissy woman, dumpy, silver-haired, occasionally kindly but more often disapproving, either of my mother, my brother and myself or, most of all, my father, whom she could not abide – and the feeling was mutual!

But she must have had plenty about her in her younger days, for she was one of the very first female undergraduates at Manchester University, and by the time she and Dan finally married, in 1921, she was senior geography mistress at a big school in Portsmouth. She also, rather later, made national headlines by proposing a motion at the Women's Institute's Annual Meeting in the Albert Hall, praising the nutritional qualities of fresh milk to the skies and urging it be made more widely available to schoolchildren. So she and I do have something in common!

In researching my family history, I have just discovered something that my mother must have kept from me all her life: that, according to her 'Baby Record', completed by her parents, she had an older sister, Branwen, born on May 8, 1923 and dying the next day, which would be my birthday many years later. Perhaps that's why she never mentioned it. My mother would herself go on to have a still-birth, about a year after I was born. She would have been called Angela.

One oddity about my mother's upbringing was that, despite both her parents' families and most of their friends and neighbours having Welsh as their first language, she could barely speak a word of it. The explanation hints at a certain snobbishness, which my mother certainly did not inherit. Welsh was the language of the common people, you see. Olwen was destined for greater things. She must speak only English. It was a shame. I am proud of my Welsh ancestry and often wish that I knew more of the language than just 'Nain' and 'Taid'.

So there you have my ancestral ingredients. Plenty of brains on both sides, ditto religion and teaching. Self-motivation as well, to climb the social ladder from relatively humble origins – coal-mining in the case of my father's family, slate-quarrying in my mother's – to positions not just of respectability but of considerable respect: in Norman's case as Baptist Minister, in Dan's as a senior master at Dursley Grammar School.

There was never much money in either family, but both sets of parents made big sacrifices, in the Gibsons' case to send Alan off to Taunton School (which he hated at first but came to enjoy) and in the Thomas's to send my mother on a Governors' Scholarship to Clifton High School for Girls for her sixth-form years. She was an outstanding pupil, a school prefect and head of School boarding house, described by her headmistress as 'an able girl, with a facility for doing things well and also an artistic side to her nature which has shown in her love of music and acting'. The love of music I have inherited, and maybe some acting skill as well! From there she won an Open Exhibition to study English at Westfield College, part of the University of London, in 1941. Politically both families were Liberal, not actively so but from deep conviction. As teachers or Baptist ministers to a man and a woman, they were all not merely accustomed to speaking persuasively in public, but very good at it, so that was in my genes as well. And hardly a drop of drink between them!

One other thing that my grandfathers had in common was a love of cricket. I don't think either of them was particularly proficient at playing the game, but both followed it with a passion. In 'Growing up with Cricket' my father recalls how, after church at Ilkley on Sunday, all the talk was of cricket:

> *At the end of morning service, as we gathered by the doors for a chat,*
> *my father's sermon was less discussed than how Yorkshire were doing.*
> *The biggest stir I can remember in that pleasant town was when*
> *Herbert Sutcliffe came to play in a match there.*

Both father and son would remain faithful to Yorkshire for the rest of their lives, although they did come to have a soft spot for Essex as well. Norman's next move was to Leyton, and the manse was just across the road from the cricket ground where Essex played most of their home games in the 1920s and early 30s. Both he and Alan were able to witness some memorable cricket from the balcony of the house, none more so than that famous day in 1932 when Herbert Sutcliffe and Percy Holmes put on 555 before the first Yorkshire wicket fell, a partnership that is still a record for any wicket in first-class cricket in England.

I'm not sure which team Taid supported. Probably his adopted county of Gloucestershire, with the likes of Wally Hammond, Tom Goddard and Charlie Parker in their ranks. His moment of cricketing glory came in 1938, when the Australians under Bradman were the touring side. The Sunday Express offered a bat signed by the entire Australian squad for the best cricketing limerick submitted by a reader. My grandfather won it – not undeservedly, I would suggest – for the following:

> *His skill lies in spin, not celerity;*
> *Left-handed, he bowls with dexterity.*
> *He knows how to flight 'em,*
> *To tempt Don to smite' em.*
> *His name, yes in truth, it is Verity!*

I still have the bat and the newspaper cutting. How proud he must have been.

There is one other thing to be said about the influence of my worthy, strait-laced grandparents, and that is the effect they produced on my father and mother and thus, indirectly, on me. So far from following in their parents' footsteps, both, when they reached a certain age, rebelled. Nor did either have a close sibling to keep their wilfulness in check. My father's sister, Marjorie, died of gastro-enteritis whilst still a baby, while my mother's brother, Robin, was completely different in temperament and outlook. It was not that he lacked intelligence or talent. He read history at Aberystwyth and became, in time, an even more distinguished teacher than his father, finishing his career as headmaster of a big school in Exeter. But he never married and never really managed to escape the clutches of his mother, whose favourite child he had always been. This served only to inflame my mother's rebelliousness, and brother and sister were never close.

Sharp-eyed readers will already have observed that there is one aspect of my genetic make-up which is conspicuous by its absence, and that is any West Country element. I may have been born in Devon, but I was certainly not bred there. I am a sort of Geordie/North Waleian cross. Had I been a sheep, I would have been a Cheviot X Welsh Mountain – not the most obvious combination but lacking nothing in hybrid vigour!

Returning to my parents, I think my mother would say if she were still alive that she was as much in thrall to her handsome, charming, brilliant but decidedly erratic fiancé as she was in love with him. Throughout his adult life he would fly into a towering rage at the slightest provocation and even at this early stage in their relationship his passions would sometimes overflow into violent arguments, coupled with threats of suicide. I know that there were times when she yearned for a less tempestuous relationship, but he was her first boyfriend and I don't doubt she dreaded the consequences were she even to hint at leaving him. So, loyally, she stuck by him, even to the extent of travelling alone, halfway across the country, in the wartime black-out to visit him in a military hospital at Catterick. It is my good fortune that she did.

After taking her degree in English in the summer of 1945, my mother found a job teaching in a run-down, anarchic boys school at Buxton in Derbyshire – another episode in her life effectively dictated by my father, who was stationed nearby. She may have been fresh out of university and decidedly unversed in the wicked ways of the world, but my mother never lacked for toughness and resourcefulness, or indeed for a degree of cunning when it was required. She has written a delightful short account of her time there and of how she recruited the biggest and roughest boy in each class to act as her 'champion':

> *My own class was a third form (14-15 year-olds), one of the most difficult stages in school life, and there I had a champion called Boardman – short, thickset and as tough as old boots. He instructed me to wait down the corridor while he sorted things out. I tried not to hear the shouts and the bangs and the ominous thumps while this*

process was under way. Then he would appear in the door and beckon me – "All right now, miss" – and in I would go. "Good morning boys," I would say, as they reluctantly and shamefacedly got to their feet – apart from one or two who seemed to be lying in the gangway where they had fallen. "Got us bukes, miss?" was the next question, and so the lesson would begin.

My mother taught at Buxton for a year before taking a job at Torquay Girls Grammar School, an establishment which could hardly have been more different – "an academic, all-girls school presided over by a very old-fashioned headmistress who was pretty innocent of the ways of the world". She was there for just over two mostly happy years, handily placed for Totnes and marrying my father in August 1948. I was born almost exactly nine months later.

2

Sparkwell

So much for the ingredients that went into the making of the young Anthony Alan Gibson. I have never been quite sure how much of a person's character is determined by nature (one's genes) and how much by nurture (one's environment and upbringing), but it is fair to say that I was as well-blessed in the latter as in the former, certainly in my early years.

Until I was two, we lived under the same roof as my father's parents in an apartment in Fleetwood House, a prominent and rather ugly villa overlooking Totnes station and the river Dart, which served as the manse. I could see the keep of Totnes Castle out of the window of my bedroom, which my father, in a sudden fit of domesticity, had painted a dazzling shade of 'sunshine yellow'. Not that I can recall looking out of the window, you understand. The memory is owed to later visits.

However, my two earliest memories are from Fleetwood House, either when we were living there or, more probably, a couple of years afterwards. The first is of being taken by my grandmother on the little train that ran its way joltingly up the Dart valley to Ashburton (the fact that it was just the two of us suggests that it may have been when my mother was looking after my brother as a baby). Happily, thanks to the volunteers of the South Devon Railway, the line still operates, and I have travelled on it several times with two of my granddaughters, Hermione and Darcy, evoking happy memories of that distant excursion. The other is of espying what I took to be a large and luscious grape on Nana's kitchen table. On grabbing it and greedily biting in, I discovered it to be a pickled onion! I have never much liked onions since.

My brother Andrew – Chippy, as we always called him, on account of his being a 'small sausage' and thus a chipolata – was born in July 1951, shortly before we bade our farewells to Fleetwood House and moved to Sparkwell, a rather plain but very friendly little village about eight miles north-east of Plymouth, on the edge of china clay country. My father was by now on the staff of the BBC in Plymouth, working as a General Programme Assistant, so the move suited him well. It also suited my mother, who had become more and more uncomfortable and unhappy under the same roof as her saintly, sanctimonious, Sabbatarian mother-in-law. There wasn't even the benign presence of grandpa Norman to sweeten the pill, for he had died of stomach cancer the previous year, at the age of just 60.

The new Gibson abode was a wing of a substantial Edwardian house, which we rented from the owners, Clive Crowley and his wife Gladys. Captain Crowley, as he was always known, was ex-Royal Navy, a touch eccentric and liked a drink. In 1952, about a year after we'd moved in, my father was despatched to Seale-Hayne near Newton Abbot by the BBC, in one of those enormous black Humbers that carried the recording equipment in those days, to cover the Devon County Show, which that year was held jointly with the Bath and West and Royal Shows, making it a very special event, graced by the young Queen Elizabeth, no less. Not having lived at Fursdon for very long, my father acceded to Captain Crowley's suggestion that he come along for the ride. It turned out to be a distinctly bumpy one. The good Captain made the very most of the hospitality on offer, got himself roaring drunk, all the time making the very most of being 'with the BBC, doncha know'. He fell fast asleep on the way back to Plymouth and, according to family legend, had to be carried unconscious from the car when they finally reached home.

In front of the Crowleys' section of the house stretched a large area of grass, which neither the Captain nor his wife was particularly keen on cutting with the hand mowers, which were all they had. So one day the Captain decided on a plan. He would hitch the two mowers to the back of his Morris Minor, which he would drive, with Gladys steering the mowers from behind, one in each hand. Unfortunately the Captain rather let his enthusiasm run away with him, setting off down the grass at a great rate and then applying the brakes sharply when the time came to turn around, accelerating the mowers like a sling-shot. Gladys, who had been hanging on like grim death, could do nothing as one mower swung out violently to the right, the other to the left. "Clive, Clive," she could be heard calling desperately, as her grip gave way, leaving her prostrate on the grass, one mower among the chickens and the other in the shrubbery. It was one of the great moments of my childhood.

I have nothing but happy memories of Fursdon. The house stands at the eastern end of the village of Sparkwell, in a triangle bounded by the Cornwood Road to the north and the lane to the ancient farm of Baccamore to the south. There were laurels to climb in at the back of the house, a good-sized lawn in front for early games of cricket and football and plenty of handsome trees in what we called 'the woods', against both roads and at the apex of the triangle where the two roads met. All around was unspoilt Devon countryside, with Dartmoor just a few miles up the road, Harford Moor being a favourite destination on a Sunday afternoon.

We had two big tabby cats, Adam and Arnold, and a Welsh terrier called Judy, who sadly didn't long survive the move from Totnes. My mother was at home to look after her two boys. My father was doing well at the BBC, producing programmes like the original radio soap-opera 'At the Luscombes' (in which I made my radio debut at the age of four) and 'Speak Your Mind', broadcasting on all manner of subjects and even being given his own record request programme called 'What's Your Fancy', the forerunner to 'Good Morning', of which more anon. There were underlying tensions in the relationship between my parents, often involving his mother, but I had become accustomed to my father's occasional drunken rages and, as a family, we were as happy in those Fursdon years as at any time.

I am not one of those fortunate autobiographers, like Laurie Lee or Winifred Foley for example, who can recall every detail of their time at village school, even to the point of offering up pungent sketches of the characters and foibles of their teachers and classmates. In truth I could not name a single one of my contemporaries at Sparkwell Village School. Later in life I did get to know well a man who had been at the school at the same time as me, John Hoskin, now a successful and distinguished farmer on the Duchy of Cornwall estate in Dorset. But he was a few years older than me and lived on a farm at Venton at the other end of the parish, so I doubt if our paths ever crossed at the time.

I do remember our two teachers: Mrs Paddon, the head-mistress, a smartly turned-out, slightly starchy lady who took the senior of the two classes; and crinkly-haired, warm-hearted Miss Ricketts who looked after the five to eight year olds. We did have paper and pencils rather than slates and chalk, but my impression is that the teaching was fairly basic. When we left Sparkwell and moved to Derriford in 1957, when I was eight and spent a single, unhappy term at Crownhill Primary School, I discovered to my shame and mortification that I was the only child in the class who could not do joined-up writing.

The food I do remember. It was horrid. Pig's liver and fatty bacon boiled in grey, oniony sludge was the worst of it, braised heart not far behind. For 'afters', we had tapioca, or stodgy spotted dick with custard with skin on it, or maybe blancmange, all equally unpleasant. We all spoke with strong South Devon accents – us boys referring to the girls as "they liddle mayuds" – and it was, I think, a happy school in which children from all sorts of different backgrounds rubbed along happily together.

One other memory which I cherished for years about Sparkwell Village School was that I had first gone there in the depths of winter, on my own, had found the school shut on account of deep snow and had made my way home again. It seemed to me to exemplify how tough and self-reliant children were expected to be in those post-war years, in sharp contrast to the molly-coddling which subsequent generations enjoyed.

But when I reminded my mother of this a few years back, she insisted it was rubbish, a product entirely of my imagination. I had first gone to school at the start of the autumn term 1954 and she had taken me herself. And I don't doubt for a moment that she was right about that, not least because there could have been no reason for me starting in January, although the memory of having once walked to school through the snow and finding it closed does still stubbornly persist.

As my brother and I grew older, we began to explore the surrounding countryside. The big area of woodland to the south of the village, which we called 'Beechwood' (more correctly, Tin Wood, I believe), was a particular favourite. There were two made-up tracks running through it, but Chippy and I had our secret paths as well, most of them converging on what we thought was a military hospital, hidden deep in the trees and abandoned after the war. It had all the hallmarks of a wartime government building – geometric layout, red brick-built, metal-framed windows, concrete floors – and, to two small boys, a distinctly sinister air. It always took courage to step inside. The most frightening room of all had a concrete slab at its centre, four feet or so off the ground. We decided that this must have been the operating theatre and were sure that the dark stains we could detect were traces of blood.

It turns out that the building was, in fact, a rest and recuperation base for naval personnel, which subsequently played host to a lot of American troops in the run-up to D-Day. And the room with the concrete slab was not an operating theatre but a morgue! Given that I dream about that building, and indeed that room, to this day, it is probably just as well that we didn't know its true purpose at the time.

Beechwood House, on the other side of the road from what we called Beechwood, was one of Sparkwell's two grand houses, the home of the

Colborne Mackrells (pronounced coburn macral, although Chippy and I always insisted on rendering it as cockburn mackerel) whom we never really had much contact with. The other, just across the Baccamore Lane from Fursdon, was Blacklands, supposedly built by Brunel and certainly of that era, commanding fine views southwards towards the main Plymouth-to-Exeter railway line.

In 1954 the Hamlyn family moved to Blacklands. I remember my mother taking Chippy and me to meet them for the first time, and how impressed we were by the size of the house and the sweep of its lawns. Ted Hamlyn was a doctor and a very good one. It was he who diagnosed what turned out to be my mother's double pneumonia which nearly killed her in the mid-1950s. But besides his general practice, based at Stoke in Plymouth, he had ambitions to be a farmer, and Blacklands presented the perfect challenge. The gardens, farmland and farm buildings had fallen into a sad state of disrepair under the previous owners, and Ted set about putting things right, enlisting all the available help he could in the process.

The two older Hamlyn children, Julia and Duncan, were respectively a year older and a year younger than I was, and we soon became firm friends, romping around in the hay barns shouting "Danny Kaye", for some reason now lost in the mists of time, as we jumped off stacks of bales. But it wasn't all fun and games, by any means. Ted soon had us out in the fields, picking up stones after the plough and harrows had been through. It was a tough introduction to farming, and there could be no slacking. "If you children don't work harder, I'll beat you with an iron bar," Ted would roar. I assumed he was exaggerating but was never quite sure.

But no blame could be attached to Ted for the accident which so nearly claimed the life of my brother. It must have been in the spring, for my mother, who was also enlisted among the Blacklands farming irregulars, was rolling the pastures with an old granite roller on the back of a little grey Fergie tractor. Chippy and I were on board as well, one on each rear mudguard. As we passed under each of the trees in this particular field, we reached up to try and grab a twig. You can guess what happened. Chippy over-stretched, lost his balance and fell off the back of the tractor. There was nothing my mother could do, and the roller went straight over him, pressing him into the ground. He was carried back to the house and laid on the big kitchen table, his body a mass of yellow and purple bruising. Luckily he had landed on a soft patch of ground, otherwise it could have been the end of him. It was a salutary lesson in farm safety which has stayed with me ever since.

It was while we were living at Sparkwell that I first became conscious of sport. My father was by then contributing to and co-presenting a programme called 'Sport in the West', which was broadcast on the BBC West of England Home Service every Saturday evening, and was beginning to make a name for himself as a cricket commentator covering mainly, though not exclusively, Somerset's home matches at Taunton and elsewhere.

I am not sure which was the first Somerset game I saw, as I may have been taken to one or more as a baby, but the first one I can remember was when Lancashire played Somerset at Taunton in May 1957. My very first cricketing hero, the Australian leg-spinner Colin McCool, who was a friend of my father and had stayed with us at Fursdon, was in the Somerset side, who were captained by another early hero, Maurice Tremlett.

I only saw the first day, a Saturday, when I see from the scorecard that Cyril Washbrook made 64 out of Lancashire's first innings of 329, and I can remember being disappointed not to have seen more of Lancashire's two England bowlers, the off-spinner Roy Tattersall and the great Brian Statham, then at the height of his fast-bowling powers. Between them they bowled Somerset out twice cheaply for a comfortable seven-wicket win, but I was much less interested in the result than in the excitement of having been at Taunton to watch proper cricket, with my father in the commentary box.

If I am being honest, though, cricket took second place to rugby at that stage in my sport-following career. Quite often, when my father was covering either Plymouth Albion at Beacon Park or Devonport Services at the Rectory Field on a Saturday afternoon, he would take me with him. West Country rugby was strong at the time, and both Albion and Services were among the best clubs in region. Gordon Waddell, a Scottish international, turned out regularly at fly-half for Services, his socks crumpling further and further towards his ankles as the game went on, while some of the great Albion names from that era were Ray Ellis and the Southern brothers, Ed in the centre and Nick in the second row.

I would be put in the care of rugby luminaries like Erb Stanbury at Beacon Park or Jock Dunbar at the Rectory, usually in the committee box, while father went off to do his commentary or write his reports. Afterwards there would be orange squash in the bar for me, several pints for father, before we headed back to Broadcasting House in Seymour Road, where I would sometimes watch Ross Salmon limbering up to do his stuff as the 'Dartmoor Cowboy' after 'Sport in the West' was finished.

It must have been after one of the earliest of these expeditions that my father took me home to find fire engines outside the house and my mother in a dreadful state. At some stage during the afternoon Chippy as a toddler had somehow got hold of a glass of sherry, downed it in one, to my mother's horror and dismay, and, in the ensuing panic, a paraffin stove had been knocked over, setting light to the wood-panelled dining room. Fortunately Captain Crowley had come to the rescue with buckets of water and, by the time the fire brigade had got there, the flames were out. But it must have been a near thing.

Club rugby in those days very definitely took second place to the county game, and nowhere more so than in the south-west where Gloucestershire, Cornwall and Devon were the main contenders. Devon were particularly strong in the mid-1950s and lost narrowly to Middlesex in the 1956 final at Twickenham. The following year they had their revenge, beating Middlesex in the semi-final and earning themselves a home game in the final against Yorkshire. The County Championship was the only national domestic competition. The clubs just played 'friendlies' (even if some of them, especially where Welsh clubs were involved, were anything but).

Excitement around the county was intense. None of the available rugby grounds could possibly accommodate the thousands who wanted to cheer their county to victory so it was decided to stage the game at Devon's biggest sports ground, Home Park, the home of Plymouth Argyle FC.

I remember more of the occasion than the game. It was a filthy wet Saturday in early March and Home Park was filled to its 40,000 (at the time) capacity. My father was by now something of a local celebrity and would be doing the commentary alongside, I think, Peter West. Chippy and I were treated like princes, sitting in the Argyle directors' box, surrounded by all the great men of Devon and Yorkshire rugby. Yorkshire were the hot favourites, with a big pack and two England internationals, Jeff Butterfield and Phil Horrocks-Taylor (whom I always hated because he was for ever keeping another of my heroes, the incomparable Richard Sharp, out of the England side) in the backs.

The first half was tense and tight as the two packs slugged it out in the mud, Devon in their green-and-white strip gradually gaining the upper hand. The one moment which is etched indelibly on my memory came just before half-time when, on the far side of the ground at the Devonport end, Barnstaple's Mike Blackmore collected a well-judged kick ahead from Albion's WJ Glastonbury and went diving over in the corner, to make it

6-3 at the break (three points for a try then). I don't think I've ever been quite so excited by a single sporting moment in my entire life! Two more tries in the second half sealed the win, 12-3. It was the first time that Devon had won the County Championship in 45 years. We had beaten the mighty Tykes. Chippy and I were in heaven. I was conscious even then that I had witnessed sporting history.

3

To Plymouth

My father had left the staff of the BBC to take his chances as a freelance back in 1953 and was doing well, with an office in Plymouth and a succession of glamorous secretaries. When Chippy had reached school age, my mother had gone back to teaching, taking a part-time job at a private girls' school called Moorfields, just along the road from the BBC. Fursdon had been rented. We could now afford to become, for the first time, home owners. I remember we visited a number of properties, including a romantic ruin of a place somewhere near Liskeard, before we settled on 2 Delganey Villas, at Derriford, on the Tavistock Road on the northern outskirts of Plymouth, just across the road from the airfield. There were fields behind the house, and the Plymouth College rugby ground, where I could practise my place-kicking, was only a few hundred yards away, at the end of a private road.

Our new house was a four-bedroomed, semi-detached Edwardian villa with lawns front and back. It was renamed Harford House, in honour of our favourite Dartmoor destination. In the garden was an older building which was a cross between a barn and a cottage. It had been used as a base for the air-raid wardens during the war and something – presumably a bomb – had gone through the roof, presumably without exploding but leaving a jagged hole and making most of the building uninhabitable. A more practical man than my father (and without his perpetual overdraft) might have had the damage repaired and the cottage restored (as did happen, after we'd moved on). As it was, it made for a rather exciting adventure playground for two small boys.

The purchase price was £2,800 (£68,000 in 2020 values) so, given that the house was in reasonably good order, in a fashionable area, not far from the city centre, my parents had done well. Schools were much less of a concern then than they are now, so I was sent initially to the nearest primary school, at Crownhill, which I didn't like at all. Happily a new primary school was due to open that autumn, slightly closer to the city centre, at Manadon Vale, just below the Royal Naval Engineering College. It was, as you might expect, light, bright, spacious and, by the standards of the late 1950s, very modern. I enjoyed my time there and passed the 11+ without any bother, thanks not least to a pretty blonde teacher who took me under her wing. I wish I could remember her name.

Some of my happiest memories of Manadon Vale are of our weekly summer term trips to swim in the Tinside swimming pool on Plymouth Hoe. I had been able to swim for as far back as I was able to remember, and I liked nothing better than plunging into the clear, cool waters of a Dartmoor river, at Cadover or Grenofen bridges probably, or launching myself into the salty depths of Tinside. Our session at the pool lasted an hour. I would dive in at the start and swim virtually non-stop for the 60 minutes, up and down, up and down, using a mixture of breast stroke and front crawl. My record, for which I once had a certificate, was to swim half a mile in a session.

Swimming was always on a Monday afternoon, and I can clearly remember climbing onto the bus to take me home two days after my tenth birthday in that glorious summer of 1959 and thinking to myself that life could have nothing better to offer than being ten, living at Harford House, going to school at Manadon Vale and being able to swim up and down Tinside pool for an hour in the sunshine. And I'm not sure I was that far wrong.

Slightly less happy memories are of Manadon Vale football, at least at the outset. Sport didn't feature on the curriculum when I first went there, mainly because the school did not then have playing fields of its own. But in my second year someone decided that we should have a go at football. I would have preferred rugby (not least because I was school champion at 'British bulldog'), but football it was.

We played our first game on the recreation ground, down below the school, against one of the local schools, with me in goal. What a disaster that was! The other team were battle-hardened veterans from one of the rougher parts of the city. None of us had ever played a competitive game before and didn't have a clue, least of all the goalkeeper. By half-time I had let in six and was struggling to hold back the tears.

I have forgotten now what the final tally was, but it was without question one of the most hurtful, humiliating experiences of my entire sporting life. After that baptism of fire we gradually improved. By the following winter we were playing every Saturday morning, smartly turned out in our blue-and-white hooped jerseys with white shorts and blue-and-white socks. I played right-half and captained the side in my last year. I don't think that we won very much, but we held our own.

My other footballing memory of Manadon Vale is of February 7, 1958. That was the morning after the Munich air disaster, in which seven Manchester United players were killed, as well as the brilliant young international half-back Duncan Edwards, who died later in hospital. Manchester United were MY team. We were one of the few families to own a television set when we had lived at Sparkwell, and I had watched, agonised, the previous May as Busby's Babes were beaten by Aston Villa in the FA Cup Final, having suffered the cruel misfortune of losing their goalkeeper to an injury in the first ten minutes – this, of course, in the days before substitutes were allowed. What is more, Duncan Edwards, left fighting for his life, was my favourite player.

My pretty blonde-haired teacher turned the radio on so that we could listen to the news when school started at nine o'clock. I can recall my feelings of shock and dismay to this day, and I only stopped being a United supporter when Denis Law left the club!

My father was by now a regional celebrity, thanks mainly to 'Good Morning', the record-request programme that he and Derek Jones broadcast at 8.15 every Saturday morning. It was the successor to 'What's Your Fancy' and broke new ground, in that it was broadcast live from two locations – my father in Plymouth, Derek in Bristol. Its hallmark was cheesy humour: running jokes, featuring Blandford Forum or the Highbridge Town clock or the foibles of the producer, who was always referred to as 'Sir'.

The idea was that it should be something of an old pals act – hence calling each other 'mate' – drawing in the listeners so as to create the feeling that they were in on the jokes. This opening burst, remembered by my father in 'A Mingled Yarn', will convey the flavour:

DJ: Good morning, mate.
AG: Good morning, mate.
DJ: Lovely morning, mate.
AG: It is a lovely morning, mate.
DJ: I say, mate.
AG: Yes, mate.
DJ: I've got a letter here from someone who – well, mate –
AG: Go on, mate.
DJ: She objects to us calling one other mate, mate.
AG: Ah well, it only goes to show – one man's mate is another man's poison.
(Signature tune)

It ran for only 11 years or so, from 1955 to 1966, but in that time became a regional institution, still fondly remembered by the older generation.

But if 'Good Morning' was my father's most regular commitment, it was very far from being his only one. He had become, thanks to his erudition, his lightness of touch and his always beautifully judged delivery, very much in demand for all sorts of radio programmes, on the BBC national networks as well as the West of England Home Service. They included, for example, 'Any Questions', 'Housewives' Choice', 'Sunday Half Hour' and 'Round Britain Quiz', as well as all the cricket and rugby commentary. There cannot have been many people, the length and breadth of the South-West, who didn't know who Alan Gibson was and not many who didn't warm to him, either.

Whilst all this prominence was obviously very gratifying to his immediate family, it didn't make him any easier to live with. He was always a highly strung man, with a touch of schizophrenia about him, and he expended vast amounts of nervous energy in producing his seemingly effortless performances. As a response to the pressures, he turned increasingly to drink and sleeping pills, the volcanic outbursts of temper becoming ever more frequent. He had a habit of roaming about the house stark naked in the mornings, much to the dismay of our cleaning lady, and would wretch loudly in the bathroom every morning, as if being violently sick. In the evenings he would return often late, drunk and spoiling for a fight with my mother, something which frequently ended with him hurling his supper out of the window. On one famous occasion he put a tinned steak-and-kidney pudding into a saucepan to boil for his supper, without bothering to pierce the lid, and then forgot all about it. Fragments of steak and kidney could still be seen embedded in the kitchen ceiling from the subsequent explosion when the house came to be sold years later.

Chippy and I were usually in bed and asleep by the time this sort of thing was going on but, if he was home a bit earlier and in a better mood, he would come and sit on one of the beds in the room we two boys shared and talk about his ambitions for us. He would talk about his days at Oxford and sometimes bring in photographs of himself, at Queen's or in the Union, and talk about how much he had enjoyed it all, concluding with something like "Ants, that will be you one day, old chap." I knew from an early age what was expected of me!

I must not give the impression that he was a bad father. A distant father, yes, and a slightly frightening one as well. But I learned a lot from him. He taught me to take a deep interest in the region in which we lived, Devon and Cornwall particularly. By the age of ten I could tell you the populations of Plymouth and Exeter, that Devon was the second largest county after Yorkshire*, that the river Teign is pronounced 'tin' not 'teen' and could sing from memory 'Glorious Devon', 'Trelawney' and, of course, the Blackbird song. He also encouraged us to read, which we did, voraciously, everything from Billy Bunter and the Just William books to CS Lewis and Lord Peter Wimsey. He had an impressive library of cricket books, into which I delved happily. Particular favourites were an account of the 'bodyline' series of 1932/33 or anything to do with Len Hutton, who was my father's cricketing hero and whose world-record 364 in the Oval test of 1938 was still fresh in the memory.

It is hard to overstate the influence which my father had on how I turned out. All my life I have been trying to live up to him and his expectations of me, measuring my achievements against his. I realised early on that I lacked his intellectual capacity – that could give anyone an inferiority complex – and his prodigious memory. But I resolved, at least half-consciously, to make the best of what I'd got, not because I thought that it would necessarily please him or make him proud of me but for my own personal satisfaction.

Whether by accident or design, in a curious sort of way he made me self-motivated. There was a distinctly competitive edge to it all, certainly on my part, sometimes I used to think on his as well in the way that he would somehow belittle my progression in the NFU. He would refer to me in one of his articles in terms such as 'my son Anthony, who is something to do with the farmers'. It brought to mind FE Smith's famous remark to CB Fry, after being shown round the training ship Mercury, to which the great man had devoted his career: "This is a fine show, CB, but for you, surely, a bit of a backwater."

> *Fame is the spur that the clear spirit doth raise*
> *(That last infirmity of noble mind)*
> *To scorn delights and live laborious days*

wrote John Milton in 'Paradise Lost', and there is no doubt that my father's success gave me a taste for fame and what it meant, and it would indeed in time become a powerful motivation as I 'scorned delights and lived laborious days' at school, university and in the course of my NFU career. But at the time all it really meant was that if you had offered me a choice of career,

At that time Lindsey, Holland and Kesteven were not counted as part of Lincolnshire.

it would unquestionably have been to follow in my father's footsteps as a commentator on cricket and rugby.

Even at that age I was practising my skills. When Chippy and I were playing each other at rugby or cricket on the front lawn, I would provide a running commentary: "Sparks to Waddell, he cuts inside, kicks ahead, oh what a brilliant pick up and what a try for Services!" Or maybe "It's McCool then, the Australian leg-spinner." (I was often McCool, as leg-breaks were what I tried to bowl.) "Somerset need just one wicket for their first ever county championship. He bowls. The batsman pushes forward. He's beaten. BOWLED!!! And Somerset have won!!" It was invariably me who scored the winning try, drop goal, run or wicket. My poor brother was always cast as the hapless opposition, even if he was, even at that age, a better bowler than me and a much better rugby player.

My mother's influence was less profound but provided important balance. Her academic record was on a par with my father's; she had won a scholarship to Clifton High School, passed her school certificate exams at the age of just 14 with distinctions in virtually every subject and my bookcases are full of the prizes she was presented with at each Clifton High School prize-giving. But she made much less of it than father, being more concerned with making sure that Chippy and I were well-fed, well-behaved, well-balanced and, as far as possible, well-shielded from the marital strife. It is thanks to my father that I am driven; to my mother that I have been able to cope with the consequences.

Politics, that is to say Liberal politics, played a big part in our family life. Despite all of his broadcasting commitments, my father stood for the Liberals in the Falmouth-Camborne constituency in 1959, coming a respectable third in what was then still very much an industrial, and therefore Labour, area.

My mother also threw her hat in the ring, standing for the Peverell ward in the 1958 Plymouth City Council elections, and coming second, and doing even better in Tamerton Foliot in 1962, very nearly winning. Chippy and I were both enlisted to deliver election addresses through the letter-boxes of the recently built Southway and Whitleigh estates where the bulk of the electorate lived. By this time she had risen through the ranks of the Plymouth Sutton constituency Liberal party, eventually becoming chairman, just as my father, having switched his attentions from Falmouth-Camborne to be closer to home, was adopted as the candidate.

Quite what happened thereafter I have never been sure, but it was nothing good. After one scene too many, my father was asked to resign, and my mother went with him, "not so much from love, perhaps, as from loyalty", he would subsequently claim. I suspect it was neither. She probably felt something like: "As I was foolish enough to marry that dreadful man, I suppose I'd better go as well." By this stage in the marriage, there was no love lost on either side.

1957, the year we moved to Plymouth, was also the year of our first holiday at St Ives. My father had holidayed there with his parents as a boy, in a humble guest house at the top of the town, where Chippy and I had also spent a few days back in July 1954 in weather so foul that a German coaster was wrecked just up the coast. We watched the St Ives lifeboat bringing the survivors back to the harbour. But there was to be no guest house for the well-known broadcaster Alan Gibson and his family. Instead, we were booked into the Porthminster Hotel, above Porthminster beach, one of St Ives' grandest hotels.

I had never stayed in a hotel before, and what an eye-opener it was: silver service in the dining room, where the waiters were all English and mostly local, huge breakfasts, packed lunches fairly bursting with sandwiches, cakes and fruit and, in the evening (as Chippy and I were too young to go into dinner, other than for a special treat on our last night) a high tea of baked beans on toast or sausages and chips, served in our room. And two minutes down the hill was beautiful Porthminster beach, where I could swim in the sea or build dams in the forlorn hope of holding back the incoming tide (something I still do, given half a chance) to my heart's content.

I think it was probably the following year that we encountered Mr White. He must have been 60-ish, I suppose, presumably a widower, certainly well off, and he took a great shine to my mother, who had lost none of her good looks. It was very early in September, in the narrow gap between the end of the cricket season and the beginning of serious rugby, that we went, and my father would defray some of the considerable cost by covering Penzance and St Ives early season games.

It was whilst he was away at the rugby that Mr White joined my mother for dinner, treating her to a bottle of Chateau d'Yquem (something she never forgot). He was kind to us boys as well and a believer in encouraging children to show initiative and independence. So he offered to fund a trip for us to the Isles of Scilly, provided we went by ourselves.

So, a few days later, Chippy and I found ourselves on the quayside at Penzance, boarding the Scillonian and waving goodbye to our mother. I think we had probably eaten our packed lunches long before we even reached St Mary's so, when we got there, we set off to walk right round the island, with warnings ringing in our ears not to miss the boat back. It would be leaving at 4 pm sharp, and the ship's hooter would sound half an hour beforehand as a warning.

The trip around the island was longer than we thought, and we were still at least a mile away from Hugh Town and the harbour, when we heard the hooter sound. Panic! We're going to be stranded on the Scillies! Oh God, what will Father say?! Come on, quickly, RUN!! So we did, poor little Chippy, who was only seven, remember, struggling to keep up as I urged him along. We got there in time, but it was a close-run thing. We were greeted like returning heroes when we got back to Penzance, and I have loved the Scillies ever since, as indeed I have St Ives.

I suppose it would have been in about 1960 that Chippy and I were given our first 'railway runabout' tickets during the summer holidays from school. For, I think, 10/6 each, which my mother was happy to pay to get us off her hands, we could travel for a week anywhere within a given segment of the Plymouth-based railway network. There were three options: west into Cornwall, as far as Newquay and taking in places like Liskeard and Looe; north to Okehampton and then onwards to either Bude or Launceston; or east to Newton Abbot where we changed for the Torbay line.

Our first, and probably favourite, jaunt was to catch the 10.02 to Waterloo from Plymouth North Road (invariably hauled by a 'N' Class locomotive) to Bridestowe and then walk up the beech-shaded lane to the Fox and Hounds and so through Nodden Gate out onto the moor. If it was a fine day, we would head for the waterfall and pool on the river Lyd above which is placed the plaque commemorating Captain Nigel Hunter, and the poem he wrote here whilst home on leave, not long before he was killed in the First World War. His 'dark, still pool' is where we would swim and try to catch small fish with our fishing net, before eating our picnic lunch. Sometimes, if the red warning flags weren't flying on the Wilsworthy range, we would walk out past the ruins of Doetor Farm to the spectacular ravine which is Tavy Cleave and catch the train back to Plymouth from Lydford rather than Bridestowe.

Another favourite adventure was to take the 10.02 as far as Okehampton, change there for Bude and the sea, changing on the way back at Halwill junction for Launceston, where we would walk from the Southern Region station to the Western Region one and come home on the branch line via Lydford, Tavistock and Yelverton, to be picked up by my mother at Plym Bridge, only a couple of miles from home.

But we enjoyed going to Cornwall almost as much, and especially to Newquay, where we would surf on our body-boards from the moment we arrived in late morning to the moment we had to leave at tea-time. Goodrington Sands and the sea pool at Brixham were our favourite destinations in the Torbay area, although Dawlish and Teignmouth were fine, and there were always plenty of steam engines to be spotted and ticked off in our ABC book of Western and Southern British Railways Steam Locomotives. The former Great Western Castles and Kings were probably my favourites, but the ex-London and South-Western Railway Merchant Navy and West Country engines ran them close. At Bridestowe, on the way back, a Plymouth-bound express would come through about ten minutes before our stopping train. What a thrill it was to stand on the bridge over the line by the station as a Battle of Britain class with ten carriages behind came thundering through in a crescendo of smoke, steam and speed.

You couldn't do it now, of course, mainly because most of the tracks on which we used to travel, particularly to the north of Plymouth, have been short-sightedly ripped up, but also because I cannot imagine too many parents being prepared to let two boys make the sort of journeys that we did, aged nine and eleven, on our own. It didn't seem a big deal at the time (although I did sometimes get butterflies in my tummy the night before a long walk on Dartmoor), and we never came to any harm or had to be rescued.

There was just one occasion, when we were coming back I think from Wadebridge, when a man came into our compartment, sat down next to me and put his hand on my knee, but we were adept at being objectionable to fellow travellers who got too close and we soon saw him off. And the older I have got, the more grateful I have become that I was able to travel almost the full pre-Beeching railway network in Devon and Cornwall. It has left me with memories to last a lifetime, a fondness for trains in general and deep nostalgia for steam locomotives in particular.

I left Manadon Vale in 1961, after passing the 11+, and started at Plymouth College that September. I can't remember why I was sent there, as opposed to, say, Devonport High School, which certainly had a better academic reputation. Probably it was because my father was matey with

Ted Mercer who was in charge of rugby at the school, by which much store was set. Ted was a bluff Yorkshireman, who wrote a rugby column for Plymouth's Sunday Independent for many years which was always worth reading for its no-nonsense, north-country commentary on the game. "Stick it lads," he would say to us, "Stick it," as us forwards plodded wearily from one scrum to the next.

Chippy was a much better rugby player than I was, scrum half for the Plymouth College Prep first XV. He used to tell the story of how my father and Ted Mercer had met up at the pub one Saturday lunchtime, got stuck into the beer and then decided to go and watch the prep school team in action, and cheer on Gibson junior. On the touchline they were vocal in their praise and encouragement.

"Go on, Chips. Oh well played," cheered my father as the scrum half dispatched a defensive clearance safely into touch. This went on for some time until Chippy appeared from the other side of the pitch. He had been taken off, injured, before his cheer-leaders had arrived!

I can't say I enjoyed Plymouth College very much. It was an old-fashioned school with an old-fashioned headmaster, Martin Meade-King, which was good for rugby but not much else. One saving grace was the friends I made there, red-headed Phil Shepherd foremost among them, who now runs Somerset Film at Bridgwater. He introduced me to the delights of modern jazz so that, by the age of 13, I was much more into the likes of John Coltrane, Charlie Parker and Cannonball Adderley than Elvis Presley or Cliff Richard and the Shadows.

On a Saturday morning Phil, Andrew (Able) Lawrence and I would go round the Plymouth cinemas, asking for posters left over from whatever had been showing the previous week. These I would take home to decorate my den, which was the one weather-proof room in the semi-ruined cottage in the garden. The 'Dr No' poster featuring Ursula Andress had pride of place!

Hanging over most of my childhood, and the childhoods of countless others, there was, however, a dark cloud: the very real threat of a nuclear holocaust. Memories of both world wars were still fresh in the 1950s. When we moved to Plymouth in 1957, much of the city centre was still a bomb site. The evidence of war was all around us, every day. When the Cuban missile crisis blew up in 1962, a nuclear war and annihilation was anything but unthinkable. I remember standing outside the Plymouth College Tuck Shop that October and looking up to the sky, wondering fearfully how long it might be before it was filled with Russian bombers.

4

Monkton Combe

I was sent off to boarding school in the winter of 1962/63. This was not in itself surprising. My dislike of Plymouth College had manifested itself in my academic performance. I was in the B stream for most subjects. The only thing I was any good at was geography, despised by my father as "not a proper subject". My end-of-term reports ranged from the merely disappointing to the downright execrable.

What was surprising was the choice of school: Monkton Combe, a small, unheralded institution tucked into a steep-sided valley to the south-east of Bath, known mainly for its evangelical Anglicanism which had seen it send missionaries to every corner of the globe. My father, of course, was neither Anglican nor evangelical. He remained, at least nominally, a committed "dissenter", as he liked to term it; a Nonconformist, in other words. The explanation was that, earlier that year, he had broadcast a 'Sunday Half Hour' from the school chapel. The programme had gone well, and afterwards he and the headmaster, Derek Wigram, had enjoyed a few drinks together. The upshot was that Wigram managed to convince my father that Monkton Combe was just the school to get his under-performing elder son firing on all cylinders, and the fees were pretty reasonable as well.

So Monkton Combe it was. I had absolutely no say in the matter. I didn't fancy the idea of boarding school one bit, but I was sufficiently self-aware to know that being a day boy at Plymouth College was doing me no good and that imprisonment in a boarding school, with no alternative but to buckle down and work, might in the end be good for me.

It was a bitterly cold, dark, snowy afternoon in early January 1963 – in the midst of the worst winter since 1947 – when my mother put me on a train at Plymouth Station and I waved her a tearful goodbye. There followed the most miserable journey of my life. I was met at Bath by Noel Calvin, the Congregational Minister for Trowbridge, a great friend of my father, as Irish as you like, and a kindly, sympathetic presence. I shall always be grateful for the way he understood my misery and anxiety. He dropped me off at the school, where I was met by the master who was my designated 'tutor', Mr Whitehouse, and told that I would be joining Hill House, which, as its name suggests, was half a mile up the Combe Down side of the valley.

My trunk and tuck-box had already arrived, so all I had with me was a small suitcase of essentials. To reach my house, and thus my dormitory, meant making my way up a steep, narrow, walled path, known in those parts as a 'drung'. This, it turned out, had been entirely filled with snow, blown off the fields on either side. With every step I sank thigh-deep into the snow. Even Dickens would have been hard-pressed to describe a more pitiful sight than me battling my way up the hill on that dark, freezing January evening.

When eventually I reached the House and met the housemaster, Victor Baker, and his wife, I discovered that there was no heating, and that only one lavatory was working. The Bakers were kindly enough, as was my dorm supervisor, an American called JP Ovendon, but it was a very, very cold and unhappy thirteen-year-old boy who cried himself to sleep that night, still wearing his duffle-coat.

The first few weeks were truly grim. Most of the classrooms didn't have heating, there were only a handful of working toilets in the entire school, the food – served up by an assortment of lugubrious Eastern European refugees – was dreadful, and there was no sport of any kind to enliven the afternoons, with all the playing fields frozen solid and the river Avon, on which the school rowed, ice-bound.

The fact that I had arrived in January, whilst all my classmates had had a term to get to know the ropes, and each other, wasn't helpful either. However, I did have one fellow new boy, a lad from Pinner in Middlesex called Dave Godby. We quickly became allies and firm friends. One of the first things we had to learn was the dress code. Fourth-formers, such as Dave and myself, had to keep their grey tweed jackets – the standard Monkton Combe school uniform – buttoned up at all times and were not allowed to put their hands in their trouser pockets. Fifth-formers could leave their jackets undone, but not until you reached the lower sixth were hands permitted in trouser pockets. Fourth-formers also had to act as fags, which mainly involved cleaning out the study of whichever prefect one was allotted to. Instances of cruelty or exploitation were mercifully rare; likewise active homosexuality.

Most minor offences were punished by a pre-breakfast run, up and down the drung and then around the playing fields at Longmead, in the bottom of the valley. Beatings, often for persistent talking after lights out, were not uncommon and could be administered by either prefects or masters. There was chapel every day, twice on Sundays, plus, as a special treat, an 8.30 service on Saturday evenings in the summer term. We were allowed no contact with the opposite sex other than a joint concert with Westonbirt Girls School once every two years. At one speech day the headmaster raised eyebrows by advising parents to make the school holidays as much like term-time as possible, so as not to give the boys too much of a taste for normal life. It may have been 1963, but there were times when it felt like 1863!

That first term seemed to go on for ever. For the first three weeks or so I wore my duffle-coat all day, every day, and all night as well. Not until March did winter's iron grip begin to ease, and the little river that ran along the bottom of the valley, next to the remains of the branch line on which 'The Titfield Thunderbolt' had been filmed, still had ice on it at the end of term. The main sporting activity was skating, on the Kennet and Avon Canal, which crossed the Avon on the Dundas Aqueduct almost directly above the school boathouses. But neither Dave nor I could skate so, in what little free time we were allowed, we just mooched around, getting to know the frozen countryside.

The summer term wasn't so bad. For a start there was cricket, enlivened more than somewhat by our part-time coach, the legendary Somerset medium-pacer, Bill Andrews. Bill was tall, angular, with a nut-brown complexion, a broad smile and a stammer. He and my father had been friends since Bill had acted as his summariser during his BBC commentary audition back in 1947. I was still attempting to bowl leg-breaks at the time, and he adjusted my grip and got me more side-on. What he didn't manage to do, however, was to stop the decline in my ability to turn my leg-break. I could bowl top-spinners to my heart's content and even manage the occasional googly, but a non-spinning leg-spinner is not much use to man or beast, and, much to Bill's disappointment, I failed to make it into the school junior colts.

There were, however, cricketing consolations. The first was Longmead, the ground where we could watch the first XI if we weren't playing ourselves. Even by public school standards, it was (and still is) as pretty as a picture, set in a natural amphitheatre, surrounded by trees, with a thatched pavilion and always immaculately kept. The second was a distinct lift to what might be called my 'cricketing credibility', thanks to my father.

He had made his debut as a test match commentator the previous summer, when Pakistan had been the visitors. In 1963 the West Indies were on tour. It wasn't by any means the strongest West Indies team to visit these shores, but it had the great Frank Worrell as captain, the even greater Garry Sobers in the middle order and two fearsome fast bowlers in Wes Hall and Charlie Griffith. England were a strong side as well, captained by Ted Dexter, with Trueman and Statham to lead the attack, and a batting order which read from the top: Micky Stewart, John Edrich, Ken Barrington, Colin Cowdrey, Ted Dexter and Brian Close. Excitement was intense.

The West Indies won the first test comfortably. My father came into the TMS team for the second, at Lord's. It turned into one of the most thrilling test matches of all time. At the start of the final over, any one of four results was possible: England needed eight runs to win, West Indies two wickets, one of them that of Colin Cowdrey who had had his left arm broken by a ball from Hall earlier in the innings. And it was my father's good fortune to be on the microphone for that final over, as the country held its breath. He proved himself more than equal to the occasion, conveying superbly the almost unbearable tension as Wes Hall came charging in to unleash his final thunderbolts, Gloucestershire's David Allen impassively dead-batting him away, the stricken Cowdrey at the non-striker's end, mercifully not called upon to face a ball. My father's name was made as a test match commentator, and back at Monkton Combe I was only too happy to bask in the reflected glory.

At home things were not so rosy. My parents' marriage was disintegrating. My father was almost entirely to blame. My mother did have a long-term boyfriend – a nice man but a bit of a smoothie, his character the polar opposite of my father's – but she could hardly be blamed for that, given what she had had to put up with over the years. My mother always believed that Chippy and I had at least two half-brothers or sisters somewhere out there, and my father once came home from London with a black girl in tow, claiming she was a South African refugee whom he had 'rescued'.

The final act began when, for the second time, he drove his car into the bridge at Looe whilst heavily under the influence. On the first occasion he had somehow talked his way out of it. But this time there was no escape, and he was prosecuted by the police and banned from driving, in a blaze of regional publicity. His response was to attempt suicide. My mother came home from teaching one lunchtime to find him in bed, apparently dead, having taken an overdose. An ambulance was swiftly summoned, and he was taken to hospital, pumped out and then sectioned to the nearest mental hospital, as was the almost automatic fate of those who attempted suicide.

Chippy was at home for all this drama and trauma, and it affected him deeply. I fortunately was away at school. The mental hospital to which he was consigned was Moorhaven near Ivybridge where, as my mother has said, "He soon recovered, running rings round the psychiatrists and nurses." She took us to visit him on Christmas Day 1963. We found him, as so often, sunk in self-pity although, to read the diary that he wrote of his time there, he was by now making the best of things, his spirits lifted by the hundreds of sympathetic letters he'd received from fellow mental health sufferers. He was released not long afterwards, the first my mother knowing of it being when she got a phone call from one of his journalist friends to say that they were in the Golden Hind and could she come and collect him. When she got there, she found him gleefully brandishing his release document, announcing to anyone within earshot that "I'm the only one in here with a certificate to prove I'm officially sane."

The decree nisi came through that spring, and Harford House was sold, my mother leaving my father sitting forlornly on the back lawn, surrounded by empty milk bottles. He moved into a flat in once fashionable, now fading, Queen's Court, just up the road from the BBC in Bristol. In an estate agent's window in Plymouth I spotted a bungalow in a relatively recent development at Dousland, out beyond Yelverton on the very edge of Dartmoor, and persuaded her to buy it. She renamed it 'Larkrise', as a reference to the Flora Thompson book, although it also struck an appropriately uplifting, optimistic note. The three of us did indeed heave a collective sigh of relief. Father could get on with his career, nearer the centre of things in Bristol; we could get on with our lives, untroubled by his rages and mood swings. It was unquestionably the best outcome for all concerned.

Chippy started at Monkton Combe that autumn and settled down much faster than I had. Although small for his age, he was a better rugby player and cricketer than me and was soon featuring in the school junior colts teams. I, meanwhile, had decided to give up cricket at school and to take up rowing, which was the only sport at which the school had any sort of a reputation, having reached the final of the Princess Elizabeth Cup at the Henley Royal Regatta at least once, which was good going for such a small school. Not that I was any good at rowing. I was rather podgy for my years, reasonably well co-ordinated but neither strong nor particularly fit.

The main reason I opted for rowing was, I'm afraid, to spite my father – to show him that I wasn't going to follow unquestioningly in his footsteps but that I had a mind of my own and would make my own way in the world. It was a bad reason for what turned out to be to be a foolish decision. I was never any good at rowing and never graduated beyond the house second four. The only times I did enjoy myself on the river were when I went out sculling by myself, and even that had an unhappy ending when I capsized and had to swim back down the river to the boathouse, shamefacedly pulling my waterlogged boat behind me. I only missed one cricket season, as I abandoned rowing when I reached the sixth form, but it was a season I would dearly like to have back now.

The one aspect of life at Monkton Combe that I really did enjoy was the music. I hadn't inherited my father's piano-playing aptitude and, although I took up the French horn as an alternative, I never mastered it. But I could sing reasonably well and was in the school choir for all my time there, starting as a treble and moving on to alto and finally tenor, as my voice sank rather than broke.

We had an inspirational choir master in Jim Peschek who would arrange for us to perform in some of the great churches of Bristol and Somerset. Singing Vaughan Williams' 'Valiant for Truth' in Wells Cathedral's beautiful choir, the music seeming to soar to the heavens, was a magical experience. Then there were the biennial concerts with Westonbirt: one afternoon of rehearsal, the schools alternating as the venue, then a performance amid the rococo splendours of Westonbirt on the last Friday of the spring term, with the return fixture at Monkton on the Sunday. We sang Bach's 'St Matthew Passion' for my first joint concert and the 'Messiah' for the second, both magnificent pieces of sacred choral music which I have loved ever since.

Academically I was doing reasonably well. For some reason it was decided that I should have a first crack at Latin 'O' Level at the end of my first autumn term, when I was still only 14, and not much good at Latin either. I failed dismally but fared much better the following summer when the main bulk of 'O' Levels were taken, passing eight or nine, all with decent grades. I now had to decide what subjects to take for 'A' Level in the sixth form. Given a free hand, I would have chosen History, my best subject, English and French. But I didn't have a free hand. Monkton Combe was apparently not then equipped to offer both History and French to A Level, it had to be one or the other. So I opted for History, with Latin as the third subject. My performance in the lower sixth was undistinguished, particularly when it came to Latin, which I hated. By the end of the year, it was clear that I would fail Latin 'A' Level, so was moved to Ancient History instead, a subject which I thoroughly enjoyed.

But there was a shock in store at the beginning of my sixth form year. The head of English, Dick House – known as Mobe, as in Moby Dick – had an announcement to make at our first lesson of the new term. "Boys," he said, "I'm afraid I have a confession to make. For the past year I have been teaching 'Macbeth', on the understanding that it was one of the 'A' Level set texts. I regret to say I was mistaken. We should have been studying 'Hamlet'." There was a stunned silence. A year's hard work, completely wasted! These days there would have been uproar amongst the parents paying good money to have their sons taught the wrong Shakespeare play. Instead, we just shrugged our shoulders, and got stuck into 'Hamlet', a play I soon came to enjoy, being a lot deeper and open to more interpretations – in my humble opinion! – than 'Macbeth'.

It may have been this shock to the system which prompted a radical change in my approach to work, or it may just have been that it finally dawned on me that I wouldn't be going to Oxford if I didn't pull my finger out. So, from being one of the laziest boys in my age group, I became almost overnight one of the most hard-working. I wasn't forced into it. It was something I chose to do. Self-motivation again. Every spare moment was spent in the serenity of the upper library, reading, reading, reading and taking notes. By the end of the spring term there wasn't much that I didn't know – in my own estimation at least – about 'Hamlet', the Tudors or the Roman occupation of Britain. When it came to the mock 'A' Levels, I was top of my age group in all three subjects, on course for three straight As, with the Oxford entrance examination to follow in the autumn.

Sadly things did not go entirely to plan. For whatever reason, I did poorly in my 'A' levels – a B in history and Es in English and Ancient History. The only consolation was a Merit in history 'S' level. I've never understood why my results were so poor. I'd worked hard, I knew my subjects – or thought I did – and I wasn't frightened by the exams themselves. These days, either my parents or the school would demand a second opinion and probably get it. But then you just took that sort of thing on the chin.

The expectation was that I would have to stay on at school for an extra year and re-take the exams. There was still the Oxford entrance exam to come in the autumn, but my chances in that were not rated very high after my dismal 'A' level showing. My father wasn't best pleased, faced as he now was with the prospect of at least two more terms of school fees.

But all of that happened in mid-August, when the results came through. For the two months in between, I'd had a fine time. The weather was glorious, the West Indies were touring, captained by my hero Garry Sobers, then at his magnificent best, and my post-exam project, on the Somerset Coal Canal and its famous flight of 22 locks, meant that I could roam the beautiful North Somerset countryside, armed with my transistor radio, and listen to the commentary, whilst, of course, pursuing my researches! I think I was somewhere near Combe Hay when the West Indies lost their fifth wicket in their second innings at Lord's, only nine runs ahead of England's first innings of 355. Sobers was joined at the crease by his cousin, the young leg-spinner David Holford. I knew that I should be supporting England, but I so wanted Sobers to do well. He didn't let me down. He and Holford added 274 together, both finishing with not-out centuries as the game was saved, Sobers shepherding his young partner through what started as an ordeal and became a triumphal procession.

The other reason for looking back with particular affection on those two months was that I acquired my first girlfriend. Not just any old girlfriend, either. She was Sarah Baker, my housemaster's eldest daughter, 16 years old, stunningly attractive, a touch rebellious and a sixth-form public schoolboy's dream. The Bakers lived in a separate wing of the house to us boys, across a courtyard, and Sarah would sometimes lean out of her window not wearing much more than her nightie for a long-distance chat as we were getting ready for our 10 o'clock lights-out.

Somehow or another, I plucked up the courage to ask her if she would like to go for a walk one evening. She accepted, we went for a walk and, when we stopped and sat on a low wall to look out across the valley, bathed in the golden glow of evening sunshine, we held hands and, when we parted, I kissed her, demurely, goodnight. There were other walks, but we never got any further than that, and by the next term the magic had faded. But it is still a precious memory and, at the time, did my reputation no harm at all. I have always been lucky in love.

I enjoyed my last season of cricket at school, even if I only made it to the fringe of the first XI, being in the process of converting from a non-spinning leg-spinner to a non-swinging medium-pacer. I was accurate and consistent but, on flat pitches like the one at Longmead, that just made it easier for good batsmen to line you up.

The sporting highlights of my last two years at school both came in the end-of-summer-term swimming gala. The event at which I excelled was the 'plunge', which involves making a flat dive from one end of the pool and seeing how far you could travel in a maximum of 60 seconds without either taking a breath or making a stroke. It is not an event requiring much athletic prowess: 'the stylish-stout chaps who go in for this strenuous event merely throw themselves heavily into the water and float along like icebergs in the ship lanes' is how it was described by one critic. But it had once been an Olympic event, in 1904 at St Louis, Missouri, and, having a good pair of lungs and light bones for my girth, I was good at it. I won it twice, the second time with a distance of 65 feet, which was better than the Olympic record, and best of all was the fact that it came with a cup, presented at the prize-giving on the last evening of the summer term. I was the plunger supreme!

However, my plunging prowess did rather rub in how fat I had become. I tipped the scales at 13 st 2 lbs when I got home that July and vowed to lose weight. By the end of the holidays, thanks to a strict low carbohydrate diet and long walks on Dartmoor, I had lost two stone and was feeling altogether more comfortable in my own skin as I faced the challenge of the Oxford entrance exam. Teaching standards at Monkton Combe may not have been of the highest, but there was nothing wrong with the history department. Peter Sibley, who played rugby for Bath on the wing, had taught me for 'A' Level and, for the entrance exam, I had additional coaching from a young teacher called Robert Blake who himself was not long down from Oxford and knew what the examiners were looking for. I shall always be grateful to both of them for getting me over the line.

The exam seemed to go reasonably well, and in late November I was summoned to Queen's – my father's college, of course – for the interview. This proved to be a terrifying experience. It was held in the rooms of a distinguished historian called RAC Parker in the oldest part of the college in the back quad. Parker was a flamboyant don, with an aversion to the cold. I was summoned into a big, dark, wood-panelled room, which appeared to be lit solely by the orange glow from the electric fires which hung from the walls. I felt as if I had entered Dante's Inferno! Through a pall of tobacco smoke, I could just about make out my interlocutors, sprawled in their armchairs in the stifling heat, as the questions were fired from out of the darkness. I have no recollection of what they asked or of how I replied, but it was a truly frightening hour or so, in comparison with which every subsequent interview I have been given has seemed like a walk in the park.

My father, meanwhile, had settled down in Bristol. Chippy and I would visit him for Sunday lunch; picked up by a taxi after chapel, then a bus from Bath to Bristol. If he was feeling flush, he would give us lunch at the Royal Hotel, on College Green, followed by a generous tip to buy sweets. If not, it would be a Bird's Eye frozen roast dinner heated up in the oven at 50 Queen's Court, preceded by a visit to the Byron in the Clifton Triangle, where father and his great drinking mate Red Arkinstall would sink pint after pint of Courage Bristol Boys Bitter.

I always looked forward to these visits, not just because it was a break from school and (usually) a pleasure to see my father, but also because it meant I could collect whatever were the latest demo singles he had been sent by the various record companies. He had no use for them, as he had given up his record column in the Western Evening Herald several years before, but for a music-loving teenager they were treasure. I soon accumulated an impressive Tamla Motown library, as well as all of the early Cream and Jimi Hendrix singles. The only record label that didn't send him demo discs was, for some reason, Decca, which meant no Rolling Stones. But my record collection was the envy of my schoolmates. How I wish now I'd taken greater care of it. It would have been worth a fortune.

In the autumn of 1966 the big news on the father front was that he was engaged, to Rosemary King, strikingly attractive with big eyes, high cheek-bones and long dark hair, 15 years his junior, whom he had met whilst she was working in the BBC's Educational Broadcasting department. She later became a very distinguished social worker, and I have always thought that there must have been something of that ethic about the way she took my father on, initially giving him a new lease of life after he had been at a very low ebb and later coping so patiently with his eccentricities. Anyway, they were to be married in Rosie's home town of Croydon a couple of weeks before Christmas. Chippy and I were invited, of course, and travelled up to Bristol the day before, to meet father for the onward journey to London.

When we reached the flat we found that father had already headed off to the BBC Club, down the road, leaving a note to say that there was a letter for me, from Queen's. I opened it and discovered that I had been offered a Fitzgerald Open Exhibition to read modern history, starting the following autumn. Aside from the births of my three children, that was the single happiest moment of my life. Not only had I made it to Queen's, but I had done so with an Exhibition. Ok, so it was only worth £40 a year, but no-one could now say that I'd only got in because of the family connection. I had proved myself. My mother almost burst into tears when I rang to give her the news, before Chippy and I went skipping down St Paul's Road to the BBC to join my father, who was, for once, beaming with pride at his elder son. The wedding was not without its mishaps. My father's trousers fell down as he was seeing Rosie off to her parents at Waterloo station later that day and, when they arrived in their Bournemouth hotel for the honeymoon, he tripped over and broke his ankle. But those were two very happy days for all of us.

My final term at Monkton Combe thus became a bit of a lap of honour. I didn't have much work to do, and the combination of my Exhibition, my record collection and my father's fame had made me something of a star. The highlight came right at the end of term, with our biennial concert with Westonbirt, performing the 'Messiah'. The great challenge for us 17-year-old boys was to 'get off with' – in the sense of having a good snog – one of the girls in the three afternoons that were available.

Within the first hour, I had picked out a pretty girl, with light brown hair, who turned out to be called Anita. She returned my glances, we chatted during the breaks in rehearsal and, by Sunday, we were an item. Still with only the vaguest idea of what was expected of me, I took her back to my study after the concert on the Sunday afternoon and kissed her clumsily, my right hand frantically groping her small, soft bosoms in what I assumed was the accepted manner. She must have found it profoundly uncomfortable but, well brought up girl from Haverfordwest that she was, she didn't complain and we parted on good terms, exchanging moderately passionate letters for a few weeks before she finally faded from sight.

As I caught the train back to Plymouth for the final time, I was able to reflect that, whilst I may not have enjoyed Monkton Combe very much, the school had done its job in preparing me for Oxford, if not necessarily in preparing me for the wider world. After my father died, I found amongst his papers a letter from the Monkton Combe bursar, who recalled that first 'Sunday Half Hour' visit to the school. And that, whilst he was showing my father around the school before the broadcast, they had noticed that on the Oxford and Cambridge honours board there was only one award to Queen's, the very first, another Open Exhibition. 'You then remarked that this matter must be put right,' the letter continues. 'and it must be a great joy to you now to realise that it is your own son who has rectified the matter.'

Joy was indeed the word.

5

Hope Cove

I was still only 17 when I left school, six foot tall, with brown curly hair, chestnut eyes and reasonably trim, but horribly immature and naïve by the standards of most teenagers even then, let alone today. I remember my friend Tim Arnold, who knew far more about girls than I did, being balloon-puncturingly scornful when I related the details of my tryst with Anita. "That's a bit pathetic," he said. "Schoolboy stuff."

He was right, of course, but I knew no better. The only sex education I had had consisted of reading the dirty bits in my parents' copy of 'Lady Chatterley's Lover' and being warned against masturbating too frequently by the headmaster in the one and only sex-related talk that I remembered from school. He had begun his talk with words to the effect of "Boys, you may have noticed a strange feeling in your loins whilst sliding down one of the ropes in the gym." As I had never managed to shin up one of those wretched ropes in the first place, this did not strike a chord.

Sex did not feature highly in my list of ambitions in April 1967. In fact, I hadn't much of a clue at all as to what I might do to occupy the six months that now stretched invitingly ahead before going up to Oxford in October, except that my mother had made it abundantly clear that whatever it was had to involve earning some money. She was by now teaching English full-time at Plympton Grammar School but, with a mortgage to pay and not a penny in maintenance from my father, she certainly couldn't afford to support a teenage layabout.

I cannot recall how we came to hear about the Cottage Hotel, Hope Cove, and the fact that they often took on students as waiters or kitchen staff for the season, but the prospect appealed. I knew Hope Cove reasonably well. We had always favoured Bantham, with its sand-dunes, estuary and thatched boathouse for a Sunday on the beach when I was growing up, but we had spent a weekend at Hope Cove a few years previously, staying with our friends, the Pattens. Brian Patten had been my father's longest-serving producer on 'Good Morning', my mother and Brian's wife Joan were great friends, and they had three boys, Simon, Jonty and Nicky, with whom Chippy and I got on well. They were staying in one of the row of cottages which back onto the little headland which separates Outer Hope's two coves. There was – probably still is – an iron cannon from an ancient shipwreck in the grass on the top of the cliff.

Inner Hope, with its thatched cottages clustered around a small square, is the more picturesque of the two settlements which go to make up Hope Cove, but Outer Hope is the larger and more commercial. It has the main harbour, the Hope and Anchor pub, the shop, a kiosk selling local ice-creams at the top of the slipway and, standing proudly on the hill above the village, the Cottage Hotel.

The Cottage was, and still is even all these years later, a very traditional seaside family hotel: comfortable rooms, good if rather old-fashioned food and glorious views out over the village and harbour to the tiger's paw of Bolt Tail stretching out into the sea to the east; Burgh Island and Bigbury Bay to the west, with the Eddystone lighthouse away in the distance. The clientele was mostly older couples out of season, families with children during July and August. The staff were a mixture of locals and what you might call hotel professionals, including three Spanish waiters. At the start of the season I was the only student, although others were taken on as the hotel filled up. The hotel was owned by the Hollidays, Dudley and Carrie, well-connected in the South Devon hotel business and with a very clear idea of the sort of hotel they wanted to run and the sort of customers they wanted to attract. Standards were high. Mrs Holliday saw to that. She was not a woman to be trifled with.

Easter had come and gone by the time I started in the second week in April, so the hotel was reasonably quiet as I set about learning how to be a waiter. The head waiter was a local man, Peter Pedrick, tall, angular, slightly sardonic, hard-driving and ambitious. He had no patience with incompetence, so I had to learn quickly – how to fold a linen napkin into the shape of a sailing ship, how to carry three plates of food in one hand, how to cope when all of the diners on my 'station', as each waiter's section of the restaurant was called, arrived at once.

I also had to learn more interpersonal skills, like always being nice to the chefs (especially the head chef, another Peter and another tough nut, who ruled his kitchen with a spatula of steel), and making friends with the Spaniards. In the mornings, before lunch service started at 12, we used to play darts in the Hope and Anchor, so that I soon became fluent in subtracting from 301 in Spanish. The youngest of them, Pepe, was keen to improve his rather sketchy English, and I was happy enough to offer assistance, even to the extent of writing out for him the words to the Tremeloes' 'Silence is Golden'!

I was being paid £7 per week, plus tips or a share of the 10% service charge, if a customer opted to pay that rather than tipping direct. In the early weeks, when the hotel was quiet, I wasn't making much more than £12 in total but, come July and August, in a good week I could earn up to £25 in tips, to the extent that in ten weeks I saved £100, despite all the money I was spending on beer. The hours were 7.30 to 10.30 for breakfast, 12 to 2.30 for lunch and 6.30 to 9.30 or so for dinner, although it could be much later if the hotel was full – all of that for six days a week.

It was hard work, but I soon became pretty good at it. My technical skills were never the greatest – I left that to the Spanish – but I soon learned how to use a bit of charm to get on the right side of my customers, especially the female ones of a certain age. I also went out of my way to get on with Mrs Holliday. In the evenings she would stand at the very fulcrum of the kitchen, her magnificent bosom resting on a slightly higher section of the serving area, which could have been designed for the purpose. If there were ever any problems between impatient waiters and perfectionist chefs, it was Mrs Holliday who would adjudicate, and she was not to be gainsaid. I think she rather liked her young, curly-haired, Oxford-bound, well-meaning amateur of a waiter, and I made the most of it.

I also got on well with Peter, the head chef. If dinner service finished early, he would sometimes offer to drive me into Kingsbridge, where we would drink at the White Hart. He was always smartly turned out for these jaunts and never stinted on the Brut, of which the inside of his Ford Zephyr positively stank. I think he rather fancied me as well, although he never made a move and was equally fond of the opposite sex, without seemingly having much luck in that department.

One of the things we would discuss in the White Hart was music. We were conscious, even at the time, that we were living through one of the great eras for pop music, and 1967 was arguably its annus mirabilis. The top ten singles in the first week in June included the Kinks' 'Waterloo Sunset', the Mamas and the Papas' 'Dedicated to the One I Love', Procol Harum's 'Whiter Shade of Pale' (which would go on to be number one for six weeks), the Beach Boys' 'Then I Kissed Her', Jimi Hendrix with 'The Wind Cries Mary', the Supremes and 'The Happening' and The Who's 'Pictures of Lily'.

Two of the greatest albums of all time, the Beatles' 'Sergeant Pepper' and Jimi Hendrix's 'Are you Experienced', were released that May. I bought them both on an afternoon trip into Kingsbridge, together with a 'Four Tops Live' LP, for I was heavily into Tamla Motown, and played all three half to death on my tinny little record player in my chalet behind the hotel. Nothing evokes memories of my time at Hope Cove more vividly and poignantly than the music we were fortunate enough to be able to listen to at the time. It was a golden soundtrack to a golden summer.

1967 was also, of course, the summer of love: Haight-Ashbury, flower-power, Scott MacKenzie, 'All You Need is Love' and all that. It was a mood to which A Gibson was not immune. I liked girls, even if I didn't have much of a clue what to do once I'd found one. My first encounter was with an attractive dark-haired girl, whom a family from Surrey had brought with them as a sort of nanny to look after their two young children. I was their waiter and we had exchanged meaningful glances as I'd served her the soup but, typically for me, it wasn't until their last night that I found myself in the pub with her and we ended up back in her bedroom, for what in those days was called 'heavy petting'.

Much greater excitement was soon on the horizon. In mid-May or thereabouts, a new housekeeper arrived, tasked with supervising the chambermaids, making sure that the laundry was done properly and that the entire hotel was neat, tidy and in good order. She was tall, blonde, bosomy, 28, recently divorced and called Susan. All of at least the English male members of staff fell instantly in love with her, myself included. Not that I harboured any serious ambitions. She was ten years older than me, vastly more experienced, had her own car and was clearly completely out of my league.

Yet for some reason she seemed to take a shine to me. The breakthrough came on a golf course, of all places. She was a member at Thurlestone just along the coast, where her ex-husband also played, and she had a handicap of nine, which meant she was a serious golfer. When she discovered that I too had an interest in golf, she invited me to walk round with her one sunny afternoon.

The first hole in those days was a short par four of around 250 yards, played from alongside the clubhouse and over the road to a green perched up on a sandhill, not far from the beach, with a bunker in the face short left. She took out her driver and swung. The ball sailed away, landing on the slope running up to the green, from where she chipped up to six feet and holed the putt for a birdie three. I was lost in admiration. It was hard to believe. Here was I, barely 18 years old, fresh out of school, as wet behind the ears as you like and still very definitely a virgin, seemingly partnered with a woman who was beautiful, sexy, warm, affectionate and, to cap it all, a brilliant golfer! She didn't have time for a full round as we both had to be back at the hotel, but she played probably nine holes, with her beautiful long, lissom, athletic swing. She stopped the car a few hundred yards short of the hotel on the way back, leaned over and kissed me like I'd never been kissed before. And no, I couldn't quite believe it, either.

After that we were an item. Her hours of work didn't usually fit with mine, so opportunities to meet up during the day time were limited, and I was working every evening. We did manage to meet up for the occasional picnic or walk, but intimacy was confined to a few kisses and cuddles. To be honest, I was completely in awe of her and not at all certain of what was expected of me or of how far I ought to go. All of that changed one night towards the end of June.

A few hundred yards along the coast to the west of Outer Hope is a shallow, sandy and usually rather sea-weedy bay called Beacon Cove, accessible either by scrambling across the rocks at low tide or via a steep scramble down from the cliff-top. It was where the younger staff, not just from the Cottage but from most of the Hope Cove holiday businesses, would gather on a sunny afternoon, in between lunch and dinner. This particular evening a bonfire and barbecue on the beach was planned, starting after we'd all finished work at around 11 pm. Susan and I arrived together. It was a warm night, the drink flowed, we ate sausages and chicken and swam in the sea. Gradually the others drifted away until there was just me and Susan left on the beach, the last embers of the driftwood fire still glowing red, the first signs of dawn lighting up the sky above Bolt Tail. This surely was the moment. And it very nearly was, except that the sand on Beacon Cove has a peculiarly gritty quality, not in the least bit conducive to intimate couplings. So we just lay in the sand and kissed. It was still magical.

By this stage in the summer I had been moved from my chalet behind the hotel to what was always known as 'Captain Bell-Salter's garage'. The Captain owned the first house alongside the cliff path leading west out of Outer Hope, and at the bottom of the slope leading up to what is a most handsome property, hard by the road just opposite the car park was a double garage, with a room to one side and a toilet round the back. It had presumably once housed the chauffeur of the household. The room was a bit dark and gloomy, but comfortable enough, not more than 50 yards from pub, beach and shop, and I could play my records at full volume, without troubling the hotel guests. It was also ideal for romantic assignations.

The great moment came a few days after the barbecue on Beacon Cove. We will draw a veil over the details. Suffice it to say that I was a clueless embarrassment. It is one of the episodes in my life on which I cannot look back without a pang of embarrassment and remorse. My virginity had gone, not in the golden glow of bodies intertwined for hours of sweaty passion but in a panic-stricken spasm. Susan was kindness itself, but God knows what she must have been thinking behind the smiles.

We made love, if you can call it that, on several further occasions, marginally more successfully. I took her home to meet my mother at Dousland, who I don't think could quite believe her eyes and always insisted that Susan must have been several years older than the 28 to which she admitted. And I was taken to meet her mother, who lived in a splendid old house in Shaldon, across the river from Teignmouth. But in early August, she got a better job elsewhere and we drifted apart. There was a reunion in September, in my last week at the hotel, when she told me – in bed – that she had a new boyfriend who liked making love to her while she was wearing a plastic mac. I knew I couldn't compete with that!

So there it was. 'The cradle of your manhood,' as Chippy liked sarcastically to describe it. I wish I could say that the experience of having had a beautiful, blonde, older woman as my first lover had been the making of my relations with the opposite sex for ever afterwards. But the truth is that I was very nearly as gauche when it came to women after my relationship with Susan as I had been before it. Bobby Goldsboro may have 'seen the sun rise as a man' after his initiation in 'Summer, the First Time', but I'm afraid that Anthony Gibson remained very much a boy.

Not that that stopped me from swiftly acquiring a new girlfriend, in whom I was arguably even more fortunate than I had been with Susan. She was Jocelyne, French, from Lyons, working in the hotel as a chambermaid to improve her (already pretty good) English and earn a bit of cash in the interval between her baccalaureate and university. She was thus more or less the same age as me, slender, pretty, with dark hair; thoughtful, intelligent, quite serious, passionate – and a virgin. Which is how she remained, despite my desperate entreaties on our last night together. I am glad now that she said no. When I think of Susan, I think of what might have been, sexually. When I think of Jocelyne I simply think of what a lovely person she was and how happy we were for our few weeks together.

I enjoyed my summer at Hope Cove. I worked hard, earned good money, drank a lot of beer, lost my virginity, spent many happy sunny afternoons on Beacon Cove, swam great distances in the sea, took up smoking (a pipe, like my father) and learned quite a lot about life. Being a waiter reinforced the lessons I had had in humility as a new boy at Monkton Combe. It didn't bother me, all the 'yes, sir' and 'of course, madam', even when my diners were clearly not out of the top drawer, and I certainly wasn't too proud to suck up to the chefs, the head waiter, Mrs Holliday or whoever else could make my life easier.

By the end of the summer I had even become quite good at my job, to the extent that, when a single middle-aged man arrived as a 'chance' (a non-booked non-resident) one lunchtime and was immediately identified as the AA inspector, I was the waiter deputed to serve him. One of the hotel's two specialities (the other being lemon sole, served on the bone and filleted at the table – what a nerve-wracking business that was!) was duck à l'orange, which is what my AA inspector ordered.

Now it so happened that this was the head chef's day off and whoever was in charge decided he'd cut a few corners by taking a pre-cooked breast of duck, heat it up in the oven and pour some orange sauce over it. This I duly delivered to my guest, who took one mouthful, summoned me to the table and told me to take it back to the kitchen.

"I'm not eating this. It's been warmed up. I expect fresh duck."

So I took it back to the kitchen, where the chef had the bright idea of finding a different pre-cooked breast of duck for me to try my luck with that. Same result. Eventually a fresh duck was roasted. It didn't reach the table until about 2.30, and in the meantime I did my best to keep my grumpy hotel inspector sweet. The Cottage Hotel kept its AA Rosette.

If that was my most difficult experience as a waiter that summer, the most traumatic was when, showing off, by carrying five plates of eggs Florentine (poached eggs and spinach with hollandaise sauce), I tripped over a ridge in the carpet and the whole lot went flying across the dining room. Peter, the head waiter, was not amused, but the diners enjoyed it.

6

Oxford

Going up to Oxford in the first week of October 1967 was a bit like going back to school, after all the growing up I'd done at Hope Cove. I didn't have my tuck-box with me, I wasn't wearing school uniform and anticipation rather than apprehension was the dominant feeling, but there was still something of the atmosphere of a boys' public school about Queen's – the absence of girls, for a start! It did feel very much like the next stage on what was still the same journey.

Queen's is one of Oxford's oldest colleges, founded by Robert de Eglesfield in 1341. The 'queen' in its title, and there is only one, is Philippa, Queen to Edward III. In the early years of the eighteenth century the college was completely re-built, largely under the aegis of Nicholas Hawksmoor who produced one of the finest examples of classical, Baroque architecture in Oxford. As you come into the High from Magdalen Bridge, Queen's is on your right, the two statue-crowned wings of the front quad fronting onto the curve of the High, with the cupola, sheltering a statue of Queen Philippa, over the main entrance in between. My rooms were on the second floor of the left hand of the two wings: spacious, high-ceilinged, with big picture windows offering one of the finest views in Oxford, up the High to the University Church and Carfax.

I found myself sharing with Ian Luckraft, another freshman, son of a Plymouth vicar, reading engineering, although he would later switch to theology. He was earnest, hard-working, quite religious – none of them qualities for which I was particularly noted at the time – but we got on well, and, after dormitory life at Monkton Combe, the prospect of sharing bothered me not at all, especially as we had separate bedrooms. There were only two drawbacks: one that the big sitting room could get very cold in winter, with only a basic gas fire by way of heating; the other that we were three floors away from the showers and toilets in the basement. But I wasn't complaining. As sets of rooms go, there weren't many more handsome. I had landed on my feet.

The first term of a three-year Oxford degree course in modern history meant passing Prelims. The work required was neither particularly stimulating nor demanding, although there was a Latin paper to be passed and my abilities in that department had not improved with time. The early weeks also meant doing the rounds of the various university societies, which would organise events intended to entice and entrap their audience of freshmen. I joined the Modern Jazz Society but decided against anything to do with politics, including, stupidly, the Oxford Union. At this stage I was a nervous public speaker, and what little experience I'd had of formal debates at school had not enthused me.

I soon settled in to college life. The food was pretty good, so I ate in Hall most lunchtimes and evenings, and the college had a Beer Cellar, where Courage bitter could be purchased for 2/- a pint, using tickets from books of the things that you simply had to sign for, the bill arriving at the end of term. It was a system of which I took full advantage. When I came down, it took me five years to pay off the arrears on my 'battels', as college bills were called! In the evenings, Morrells College Ale could be purchased from the Buttery, opposite the Hall, served in antique silver tankards for drinking with dinner. And, after spending the entire summer kow-towing to my guests at the Cottage, it was my turn to be addressed as 'sir' by the college servants, including the Steward, Joe Blackadder, who may or may not have been the inspiration for the name which Rowan Atkinson (Queen's, 1975) gave to his protagonist but who was most certainly a force to be reckoned with, as was his wife, who ran the Iffley Road annexe.

My 'Scout', who tidied our rooms and made our beds every morning, was Miss Bossom, a diminutive lady known to all and sundry as 'Blossom'. She coped with a lot, mostly uncomplainingly, but drew the line if she found any evidence that a young lady might have spent the night. That would be reported to the Dean, responsible for college disciplinary matters, who was the distinguished historian of the Labour Party, Kenneth O (now Lord) Morgan. Not that there was any danger of that sort of thing happening in my first term, initial efforts to attract female companionship from the limited supply available having drawn a complete blank.

Right from the start back in the fourteenth century, Queen's had had a strong Cumbrian connection, reflecting the origins of its founder. As the centuries had gone by, its main catchment area had broadened to include most of the North-West of England and by the time I arrived, the college still had more than its fair share of 'northern chemists' who, it should be said, were mostly not nearly as dull as that description would suggest. Many of them became good friends, especially Michael Sidney from Maryport, with whom I would drink in the Eastgate (Courage) or the Chequers (Ind Coope). I was not, at this stage, a particularly discerning beer-drinker.

Much the most memorable moment of that first term came quite near the end of it, when I had a message from my father to say that I had acquired a new brother, Adam. I was genuinely very happy for him and Rosie, whom I had come to like a lot.

The Prelims hurdle safely surmounted (although my Latin mark was dreadful!), I got stuck into the meat of my degree course in the second term. My principal tutor was John Prestwich, a distinguished medievalist, who would become Senior Fellow at Queen's and who had also tutored my father, before being seconded to be a code-breaker specialising in U-boats at Bletchley Park (something that wasn't revealed until after I had come down). He was short, with a large head, a bit gnomic, highly strung, untidy but infectiously enthusiastic. You knew straightaway that this was a tutor who wanted his pupils to succeed and would do whatever he could to make that happen.

My tutorial mate was John Simkins, who had been to school at Marlborough, charming, easy-going with a deep voice and a ready smile. We were about on a par intellectually and enjoyed working together. At each Prestwich tutorial we would each read the essay we had been set the previous week, which would then be discussed, in a thick haze of cigarette smoke. Prestwich wasn't just a chain-smoker, he was a multiple chain-smoker who would have anything up to four Olivier cigarettes on the go at any one time, each burning away in a different ash-tray as he roamed around the room, sometimes taking a drag from whichever was closest to hand, often just tapping an as yet unlit cigarette on the packet.

He took us for our European medieval history, while his son Michael, who had just started as a junior fellow at Christ Church, made it a double helping of Prestwichs by endeavouring to help us learn something about the early medieval period in Britain. I don't remember him being particularly inspiring, but we evidently didn't do his career prospects too much harm, as he went on to become a most distinguished medieval historian, Professor of History at Durham University for many years.

The Assistant Steward was Nigel Lewendon, who would go on to become something of a Queen's legend, eventually retiring in 2004 after 43 years' service. His elder brother, Terry, ran the Beer Cellar. In tune with the times he started organising discos on term-time Saturday evenings but didn't have much in the way of records, and initially the experiment didn't really take off. Nigel knew about my record collection and suggested to Terry that I might be asked to run the discos. He was more than happy with the idea. I wouldn't get paid, but I would have Saturday evening free beer, which sounded pretty good to me.

And so was my career as a disc-jockey launched. The equipment was pretty basic – two decks, each with a felt pad to hold each 45 whilst I cued it up and which I'd let go of when the moment came, a 50-watt amp and a pair of ancient speakers. But it produced a big enough sound to fill the cellar's inner room, even when it was packed, as soon became the rule. I played Wilson Pickett, Eddie Floyd, Sam and Dave, the Temptations and the Four Tops, Aretha Franklin, Junior Walker and the All Stars – just about the full gamut of 1960s soul and Tamla Motown – as well as more poppy stuff like the Archies, the Spencer Davis Group, Chicago and, of course, the Rolling Stones. There was no microphone for the DJ, so I either just shouted out the name of each record or let the music speak for itself. My friends would help out, mostly by fetching me pints from the bar – four at a time! It was thirsty work, but I loved it, as did Nigel and Terry, for the discos did wonders for the Beer Cellar's takings.

I had acquired a girlfriend by this stage. She was called Judith, another attractive blonde, training to be a teacher at Lady Spencer Churchill College (now part of Oxford Brookes University) at Wheatley, a few miles out of town. I had bumped into her and her friend Anne on the morning of my 19th birthday party and invited them along. It was actually Anne who initially received the benefit of my attentions, but she went back to her home at Reading, so I took up with Judith in a term-long relationship which I think we both enjoyed, without becoming over-committed.

That summer I discovered punting on the Cherwell and would happily pole away for miles, sometimes into the most distant and weediest of backwaters, with Judith in the boat if she was free, or a couple of mates and a few bottles of beer if she wasn't. And no, I never fell in!

Cricket was my main summer-term preoccupation, either playing on the college ground or watching in The Parks. The Queen's ground is one of Oxford's prettier ones, just across the Isis opposite Christ Church Meadow, with a handsome pavilion in which beer and other refreshments were served when the college had a match. We weren't particularly strong, and I remember a terrible thrashing by the toffs of Christ Church in 'Cuppers', the college knock-out tournament.

But we did have two cricketers of genuine class in Dave Williams, a bean-pole of a slow left-arm bowler, who'd played a game for Yorkshire seconds before coming up and who would go on to play 29 games for the University, and Stuart Westley, a batsman/wicket-keeper from Preston, also a Blue, who would go on to play a few games for Gloucestershire. Much our best cricketer in this era was the Hon Tim Lamb, a more than useful all-rounder, who made a considerable mark in county cricket with Middlesex and Northamptonshire before going on to become the first Chief Executive of the ECB. He was a good friend of my brother and played with him in the college team but was just after my time. There is still, however, a Gibson-Lamb family connection, in that I share Somerset commentary duties for the BBC with Tim Lamb's cousin Stephen.

In fact, my three summers at Oxford (1968-70) were not exactly a vintage period for the University's cricket, full stop. We had just one top-class player, the barrel-chested Rhodesian opening bat Fred Goldstein. His opening partner, Asad Jahangir Khan, brother of Majid, cousin of Imran, was a useful off-spinning all-rounder, and Giles Ridley strengthened the side once he'd taken his exams. But that was about it in terms of even modestly talented cricketers, whereas the counties we played against usually fielded their strongest sides, in order to take full advantage of some early season practice, before the County Championship got going in earnest. Warwickshire, for example, came to the Parks in early May with a team featuring Rohan Kanhai, Billy Ibadulla, John Jameson, Tom Cartwright, David Brown, AC Smith and Lance Gibbs – all test players, with more than 200 caps between them! It made for some great cricket-watching (as long as it wasn't raining), albeit in what became a fairly familiar pattern.

If there was a match on in the Parks, I would get whatever work I had to do over with first thing, then wander up to the ground for about 12.30. By that stage Oxford would be something like 50/6, Goldstein top scorer with 30-odd, having carted the quicks all over North Oxford and then holed out in the deep as soon as the spinner came on. The game against Middlesex in mid-May 1968 may be taken as a typical example: Oxford 65 all out (Goldstein 33, Fred Titmus 6 wickets for 5 runs) and 79 all out; Middlesex 357 for 8 declared, winning by an innings and 213 runs. Even worse was to come in the next game, against Surrey. Five of the University's first six batsmen made 0, as we crumbled to 33/9, before eventually reaching what felt almost like the respectability of 50 all out. It was probably just as well that May was almost always a wet month in the late 1960s, or the Oxford record would have been even more dismal.

My father had started writing cricket reports for The Times by this stage and, if he was down to cover an Oxford game, I would make a special point of getting there to meet him – usually arriving well in advance, father having fallen foul of the change of trains at Didcot, a circumstance which he would, in time, immortalise. But we enjoyed ourselves when he did eventually get there, the arrangement being that he would pay for the pints if I would fetch them. One day he introduced me to one of his journalistic colleagues, a young man not long out of university himself, who impressed me immensely by offering me one of his hand-made, monogrammed cigarettes. It was Henry Blofeld, who would become a great friend of my father – and, yes, I'm fairly sure he did introduce himself to me with a "my dear old thing"!

It may be surmised from all these recollections of girls, discos, punting and cricket that study did not feature particularly highly on the Gibson list of priorities in that first Trinity term, as the summer term was officially known, and I'm afraid to say that that would be correct. I did what I needed to do in terms of writing essays and reading books, without ever over-stretching myself. I did go to a couple of lectures early on, and I am sorry now that I didn't take the opportunity to hear more of Oxford's star historians, such as AJP Taylor, Hugh-Trevor-Roper and Christopher Hill. But my finals were two years away, with no exams in the meantime, and Oxford always seemed to have far too much to offer for me to want to spend too much time with my head buried in a book.

Funds were running low by the time my first Long Vacation came around. I did have a full grant, plus my Exhibition, but the money I had saved at Hope Cove was long gone, my mother certainly couldn't afford to support me, so another spell of waiting at table in a hotel by the sea seemed the obvious choice. It wasn't the Cottage this time. Instead, I got a job as a waiter at the Links Hotel (as it was then – not long afterwards it was converted into holiday apartments), just along the coast at Thurlestone and, as the name would suggest, right next to the golf course.

Two of my friends came along, as well. Dave Godby, whom I'd kept in touch with since school, was taken on as a gardener and Michael Sidney, my chemistry-reading Cumbrian from Queen's, became the wine waiter. It was hard to say which of those two appointments was the more improbable.

Dave knew nothing whatever about gardening, and Michael knew nothing whatever about wine. On one famous occasion, a guest asked Michael for a dry Martini, something he had never heard of. He studied the label on the bottle for clues: 'delicious on its own with just a slice of lemon', it suggested, which is what he produced. The guest was not impressed. Dave, meanwhile, would have been spending his time hacking away at the undergrowth in the outer reaches of the hotel gardens, or "scranletting in the nettle flitch", as he called it, *pace* Stella Gibbons' 'Cold Comfort Farm'.

As a seaside hotel the Links had certainly seen better days, but there was nothing wrong with the food. The chef was a bit of a psychopath, who would threaten us waiters with a fearsome-looking kitchen knife if we got on the wrong side of him (which wasn't difficult), but he could certainly cook, and us waiters got pretty much the same food as the guests. His Tournedos Rossini – fillet steak crowned with foie gras – was one of the best things I have ever eaten.

We didn't last long at the Links. Dave got the sack, Michael was much too prickly ever to be a successful wine waiter and wanted to get back to his long-term girlfriend in Maryport, and I was happy enough to move on, this time into Cornwall, to the Ship and Castle Hotel in the yachtie Mecca of St Mawes. It sounded fine: a three-star hotel in an up-market resort at the height of the season, with reasonable pay and full board. It was only when Dave and I got there that the Ship and Castle showed its true colours. It had, in fact, just lost all three of its AA stars, and it soon became clear why. The food was dreadful, the staff mutinous, the accommodation tatty and the morale of the entire establishment at rock bottom.

The hotel staff were a mixture of Italians and Germans, with a smattering of Spanish and not a Cornishman in sight. The Head Waiter had been a German wrestling champion who looked as if he would have been completely at home in the Waffen SS. He would stand by the door into the restaurant, chest puffed out, hair slicked down and greet every group of guests with a click of the heels and a bow of the head. The housekeeper, another alarmingly fit-looking German, who looked as if she could crack walnuts between her thighs, was his girlfriend. They were rumoured to enjoy epic sessions of athletic sex, lasting long into the night. The Italian waiters were a pretty unpleasant lot as well, given to cornering the market in cutlery for laying up for the next meal, so that I was invariably the last to finish each shift.

The dining room at the Ship and Castle was on the floor above the kitchens. The food would come up in a lift into a glass-walled servery which acted as a sort of hub for the dining-room, where a Spaniard, Manuel, would match orders to waiters. Manuel had a withered arm and a temper so short and so violent that I was never sure if he was entirely sane. He hated the Italians with a passion, the feeling was mutual, and there were frequent noisy bust-ups.

One evening, with the service from the kitchen being as slow and chaotic as usual, one of the Italians lost patience with Manuel and started berating him at full volume. Manuel's response was to grab one of the aluminium trays, on which the food came up in the lift, and start beating the waiter over the head with it, all the time swearing loudly in Spanish, much to the mingled consternation and amusement of the diners who were able to witness the entire performance through the glass windows of the servery.

Relationships down in the kitchen were no better. Every so often the simmering tensions between the German chefs and the Italian ones would boil over into open warfare. My friend Dave was a kitchen porter, one of whose jobs was to load the potatoes into the big, revolving drum of the mechanised potato peeler. He had just done this one lunchtime when war broke out in the kitchen, and quite serious war at that. Saucepan lids, frying pans, ladles, even knives were flying everywhere as the battle raged. Dave, wisely, decided to take cover, leaving the potato peeler, which was in the direct firing line between the warring chefs, still churning away. Peace was eventually restored, leaving us waiters to find some plausible explanation for our lunchers as to why their potatoes were the size of marbles!

1968 will be remembered in Europe as a year of revolution and protest. Paris had been ablaze with student protests that summer, the Troubles had begun in Northern Ireland, Alexander Dubcek's brave attempt to cast off the Soviet yoke had been brutally suppressed even while I'd been working in that chaotic hotel in St Mawes, and the campaign against the Vietnam war was drawing students in their hundreds of thousands to protest outside US embassies, including the one in Grosvenor Square. More than 200 arrests were made and 117 police were injured when a mass demonstration had degenerated into a riot on March 17, and a repeat was planned for October 27.

All over Oxford, posters appeared, often just with that date emblazoned across them. The mood of protest was infectious. I didn't have any particularly strong political opinions at the time, other than having inherited my parents' Liberalism, but I did know what I was against: first on the list came racism, and particularly apartheid; and second was the US war in Vietnam which I, in common with I should imagine at least 90% of students at the time, wanted to see stopped.

What made up my mind to go was a chance encounter with a girl whom I knew by sight – indeed she was known by sight by just about every bloke at Queen's – the Bursar's Secretary, Susie Williams. She was attractive, vivacious, with a look of Cilla Black about her, and she wore skirts which were short even by the standards of 1968. It turned out that she and her friend, a mutual acquaintance, were planning to go to London for the demo. It also turned out that she had recently split up with her boyfriend. So we went to London, we marched, shouted and chanted with the best of them, without getting arrested in what turned out to be a slightly disappointing affair after the riot of the previous March and, after it was all over, I asked Susie if she'd like to come to a Modern Jazz Society evening the following Friday. She said yes, we went to the jazz and afterwards to the Gardeners Arms in Jericho, where she had a flat, and spent most of the night walking around Port Meadow in the moonlight. For the first time I was in love.

This did nothing, I am afraid, for my studies, especially as, at almost exactly the same time, I had taken on the responsibility of helping to organise the following summer's Commem Ball, at which two of the biggest names in contemporary music, Pink Floyd and Procol Harum, were due to top the bill. I was in charge of publicity. Shades of things to come. How I wish I still had one of the posters we produced. In the event Procol Harum dropped out at the last minute and we got Ten Years After, complete with my guitar hero, Alvin Lee, to replace them. The Ball was a great success, even if trying to dance to Pink Floyd did present something of a challenge.

I wouldn't say that I went off the rails in my second year, but I did get into a number of scrapes and acquired the reputation of being more interested in having a good time than in the finer points of medieval history or political philosophy. One of the things I liked to do, with one or two like-minded mates, was to climb on the college buildings, late at night. The roofs were easily accessible, and the geometric arrangement of the windows of the buildings which made up the front quad was ideal for moving laterally from one window ledge to the next, face pressed to the outer wall. But the Everest of every Queen's climber's ambitions was to scale the central clock-tower, which was horrendously difficult, because of the overhang that had to be surmounted, but not impossible, because I knew someone who had done it – Susie's ex-boyfriend, Tony Kerr. I tried several times but lacked the strength to haul myself up and over that final overhang. It was, I am sure,

Tony Kerr who hung an enormous banner from the clock tower reading 'GOODBYE SUSIE' when she left Queen's to go and work at St Antony's.

Considering the risks that we took, and the fact that we were invariably on the wrong side of at least six pints of beer, it is amazing that none of us came to any harm. But I knew that sooner or later we would get caught and, sure enough, it wasn't long before I found myself summoned to see the Dean, Kenneth O Morgan, for a severe reprimand and a hefty fine. We were not, however, to be deterred. The other obvious target for a night-time climber was the cupola over the college entrance, and a plot was carefully hatched. Even with the assistance of a rope, I knew that scaling the cupola was beyond me and, besides, if I was caught I might be sent down. So instead we recruited my former room-mate, Ian Luckraft, who was agile, wiry, strong and, as a hard-working theology student, just about the last person anyone would suspect of what was planned. It went like clockwork. Ian pulled himself to the top of the cupola and jammed the mortar board he had with him onto the lightning conductor with which it was crowned.

The next day there was uproar with strident demands for the perpetrators – A Gibson the prime suspect – to be identified and brought to justice. But A Gibson had a cast-iron alibi, and the investigations soon drew a blank. The mortar board was in place for months, and the culprit never found. Revenge was sweet!

My other brush with the authorities came the following February, when Enoch Powell came to Oxford to speak at a meeting of the University Conservative Association in the Town Hall. This was less than a year on from his 'rivers of blood' speech, and he had become a hate figure for all liberal-minded students, myself included. A bunch of Oxford Trotskyites organised a protest and I went along. I soon found myself in the thick of things as the protestors tried to break through the police cordon which had been set up outside the entrance to the building and, being six foot tall with an afro of curly hair, I was an obvious target. Sure enough, the long arm of the law reached out, grabbed me by the hair and pulled me, kicking and swearing, out of the mêlée and into custody. As I wrote subsequently to my father, "It was all very unfortunate and unspectacular. The policeman who arrested me wasn't even particularly brutal."

Those arrested were banged up in the cells underneath the magistrates court, which was in the same building. As I went in, the first person I saw was a fellow student from Monkton Combe, whom I hadn't seen since school. "Hello, Shack," I said. "Fancy bumping into you here!" I got off relatively lightly: found guilty of 'disorderly conduct liable to cause a breach of the peace', fined £15 and bound over. Mind you, £15 in 1969 would be something like £250 today, so it still hurt.

I spent most of the Trinity term of my second year playing cricket and visiting country pubs, often on the same jaunt. Besides playing for the College more or less regularly, I became a regular fixture in the Quondams, who played evening friendlies, mostly against villages within ten miles or so of Oxford. In this I was following in my father's footsteps. In fact, in his day they had been the Queen's *Imperial* Quondams, some bright spark having written to the Emperor Hirohito to seek his patronage, and the Emperor, presumably imagining that the Oxford connection made this a greater honour than in reality, had accepted. The association was quietly dropped after the Second World War, for obvious reasons.

Anyway, the Quondams were a side of mixed ability, captained by my friend John Simkins, who invariably opened the bowling, and usually featuring several strapping oarsmen, who could hit the ball a long way on the rare occasions when they made contact with it. The villages where we played all had pubs, to which we would repair once the game was over. So, for Wendlebury, it would be the Red Lion, where the bread and cheese was legendary; for Long Hanborough the Swan, and Morrells from the wood; for South Leigh, the Masons Arms and more Morrells; for Toot Baldon the Red Lion, and so on.

The cricket was competitive, but friendly, mostly against teams who were only too happy to buy into the spirit of Quondams cricket. There was, however, one exception, in a game played, unusually, on the Queen's ground, against a team called the South Oxfordshire Amateurs. I cannot remember who arranged the fixture, but whoever it was didn't know much about the side we were taking on. For, whilst the SOA do most certainly play cricket in the right spirit, they are also one of the most famous wandering clubs in the South of England, with fixtures against the likes of the Free Foresters, I Zingari and MCC.

The match was played on a hot evening, our visitors winning the toss and opting to bat first on a typical slow, flat Queen's wicket. The SOA opening bats looked ominously professional as they marched briskly to the middle. I opened the bowling with John and produced what I thought was a perfectly respectable first delivery, just short of a length on off stump, which was crashed through the covers and over the boundary rope before anyone had the chance to move. And so it continued, and from both ends. It was carnage.

We did just once get a sniff of a wicket, when one of the batsmen got a bit carried away against my non-swinging medium pace and put up a towering skier. Simkins circled underneath it at mid-off. "Mine," he shouted loudly, taking the responsibility as a good captain should. Plummeting like a falcon from the wide blue heavens, the ball burst through his hands, hit him square on the chest and knocked him flat to the ground. Everyone on the field burst out laughing, except our unfortunate skipper. They reached something like 175/0 in their 20 overs and then bowled us out for 36. It turned out that the SOA openers were both Oxfordshire county players. I rather doubt if the fixture has been repeated.

I had managed to stay on in my splendid set of rooms for my second year, but with a different room-mate: Dave Bradbury, a rather dour physicist from Yorkshire, who would go on to make a small fortune in computers. We had nothing really in common except our taste in music, although Dave was more of a Northern Soul man than me. So when I decided that I needed to start making some proper money out of my records by setting up my own mobile disco business, Dave was the obvious person to take over in the Beer Cellar. One of our friends in Dousland made me a console for the twin decks and amplifier, and I picked up a couple of loudspeakers cheaply second-hand. 'Mayor Daley's Official Discotheque' was the name I gave my new venture, after the notorious student-bashing Mayor of Chicago, and at the start of the next term Susie and I spent many hours tramping the streets of Oxford putting up posters and dishing out flyers advertising its existence.

From memory I think I charged £5 for a party that finished before midnight or £10 if it went on any longer. Susie had a car which we used to transport such equipment as we had, which soon included, as a real statement of modernity, a couple of flashing lights. Business was steady. I had gigs most Saturday nights and some Fridays as well. The money came in handy to pay for all the beer and, by this time, cigarettes. I had taken up a pipe in Hope Cove, without actually inhaling, but decided when I reached Oxford that I really ought to smoke cigarettes, like just about everybody else I knew. I was predictably sick after drawing deeply on my first Players untipped but soon got the hang of it. Mostly I smoked Players Gold Leaf, but every Friday, on my way back from drawing out my standard £5 spending money from Barclays at Carfax, I would stop off at the tobacconist's at the top of the High and buy twenty Passing Clouds, the elliptical, expensive, untipped cigarettes in a pretty pink packet, much beloved by John Arlott, who at one stage was reputedly getting through 80 of them every day.

What with the income from the disco and the beginnings, that summer of 1969, of my career as a cricket scorer for the BBC – of which more anon – I didn't feel that I needed a full-time job during the Long Vacation. Instead, in amongst the cricket commitments, and with Susie also between jobs, we went to stay with her parents at her home in Sutton Coldfield, and she then took a temporary job as nanny to a family who had a holiday home near Port Isaac in Cornwall. She was there for a month. I visited several times, camping – uncomfortably – at Lundy Bay. On one memorable Saturday evening she drove me over to the Cornish Arms at St Merryn – now owned by Rick Stein, then just a run-of-the-mill Cornish pub – where I got through ten pints of St Austell bitter from the wood at a cost of exactly £1!

My strategy, if you could call it that, for my second year at Oxford had been to enjoy the experience as much as I could, then make up for any shortfall in my academic progress by working hard in my third year and, as a confident examinee, doing well in my finals, or Schools, as they are called.

Well, as Rabbie Burns so wisely observed,

> *The best laid schemes o' mice an' men*
> *Gang aft a-gley,*
> *An' lea'e us nought but grief an' pain*
> *For promis'd joy.*

At the end of the summer term I had packed my accumulated essays and notes from my first two years into the window seats in my sitting room at college, with the intention of retrieving them by going up early for the start of the new term. But when I looked for them they were gone, and no-one knew where. Like most Oxford colleges, Queen's made a bit of extra money by hosting conferences during the long vacation. My rooms had obviously been pressed into service, and the essays and notes found and cleared out. I was utterly mortified. The best part of two years' work gone up in smoke, probably quite literally. I don't have a particularly retentive short-term memory, so most of what I'd learned about, for example, European history in the early middle ages, had almost entirely vanished from my consciousness. It wasn't quite a matter of cramming three years' work into one, but that was most certainly how it felt at the time.

I went to see the Dean, Kenneth Morgan, to plead for an extra year to make up for everything I'd lost. But he was unsympathetic, basically telling me that it was own fault, that I should have been more careful and that the college accepted no liability for my losses. I rather suspect that, in this day and age, rather more sympathy might have been shown, but in those days, the 'stand or fall by your own efforts' ethos was still very strong. In other words: tough luck, mate, you're on your own.

So there was nothing much for it, except to buckle down, give every waking hour of term-time to my Special and Further Subjects of, respectively, 'Commonwealth and Protectorate' and 'English Economic History in the Seventeenth Century'; and stay up for most of the Christmas and Easter vacations to try to make up the lost ground from my first two years. I was fortunate in one respect. The Queen's library is one of the most beautiful buildings in Oxford, and its first floor is sublime. Tucked away in one of the alcoves between the towering carved-oak book-cases, that glorious ceiling overhead, the air of scholarship so strong that you could almost taste it – it was the perfect environment for quiet, calm and, above all, deeply concentrated study.

In my time the accommodation arrangements were that you spent two years either in College, or the Iffley Road annexe, or the new Queen's Lane building, opened in 1969, and one year in digs. Susie and I had been spending a lot of time together and, when a colleague of hers said that his houseboat would be available for a year whilst he was abroad, it seemed too good a chance to miss. The boat was an ancient coal barge, moored in a backwater just off the Thames at New Hinksey, secured to the bank by two scaffolding poles, with rockers, which creaked and groaned alarmingly when the barge was being moved by a strong wind. On a fine day in spring or summer, it was heavenly. On a damp day in the depths of winter, it could be hellish, with only an ancient coal-fired stove for heating, an unreliable pump to provide water from the river for washing up, a chemical toilet and an atmosphere so damp that any clothes left hanging in the wardrobe would quickly become green with mildew. But yes, we had each other!

Chippy arrived in Oxford that autumn to read law, having somehow been given a place despite passing only two A Levels, neither with a particularly good grade. Despite my best efforts with the Dean, the Gibson name obviously still had some resonance with those in charge of admissions. Not that Chippy was unintelligent. I always felt that he was brighter than me. He certainly had a higher IQ and could polish off the Times crossword in half the time it would take me. But I think it would be fair to say that, unlike me when it came to the crunch, he lacked application and at Queen's most of his would-be lawyer contemporaries were similarly feckless. I say 'most of' advisedly, for Chippy's room-mate in his first year was Erik Salomonsen, then a rather gangly, heavily bespectacled youth from Torquay, now a most distinguished judge. Erik wasn't teetotal but, both by temperament and as a keen oarsman in training, he certainly didn't go in for the sort of alcoholic excess that the rest of that circle tended to indulge in. Which made one particular incident doubly unfortunate.

Chippy and Erik decided to hold a party in their rooms, on the first floor, looking out over the front quad. The usual boozy lot rolled up, and much drink was taken. It wasn't quite true that, as their subsequent arraignment put it, their staircase was 'carpeted in vomit', but it was a fairly typical student party of that era. Susie and I staggered home on our bicycles and thought nothing of it until the next morning, when I arrived at College to find the place in uproar. During the night Erik had fallen from his bedroom window and landed head first on the stone steps below. He was now in the Radcliffe Infirmary, with a fractured skull, having narrowly escaped death. Of course, the party got the blame. So far from being just a routine piss-up, it was now being characterised as a Bacchanalian orgy. Erik had clearly fallen out of the window in a drunken stupor.

Yet, as I swiftly pointed out to whoever would listen, the truth was that if there was one person at that party who was most certainly NOT drunk, it was Erik. He had gone to bed relatively early and as sober as, well, as the judge he would become. All we could conclude was that he must have been sleep-walking and, when the hearing before the Dean came around, that was the case for the defence, which was reluctantly accepted, albeit with another black mark put down on the Gibson ledger.

I didn't play any rugby while I was at Queen's, but I certainly watched plenty of it. Oxford had a good side, especially in my second and third years, when the brilliant All Black Chris Laidlaw was controlling things from scrum-half. In all my years of watching rugby, I have never seen such balance, judgement, elusiveness and deceptive speed as that stocky little South Islander had at his command.

We were beaten, narrowly and agonisingly, in the 1968 Varsity Match, when the guts of the Oxford forwards, with Laidlaw at their heels, couldn't quite make-up for the flair of the Cambridge three-quarters. But hopes were even higher for the 1969 season, with Laidlaw now captain, and one of the strongest back-rows either University can ever have fielded in Peter Dixon, Peter Torry and Steffan Jones.

In those days, both Oxford and Cambridge were a match for any club in the land, and Oxford started their season with a series of good wins, including against a Cardiff side packed with internationals. 1969 marked the centenary of the Oxford University Rugby Club and, to celebrate the anniversary, they were given a fixture against the touring South African Springboks.

At that time there was no hotter issue in British sport than sporting links with the apartheid regime. The England cricket team's tour of South Africa had been called off the previous autumn in what became known as the D'Oliveira affair, and the planned return tour by South Africa, scheduled for the summer of 1970, was already in jeopardy. The match against Oxford University at Iffley Road was to be the first of the Springboks tour, and the anti-apartheid movement, led by Peter Hain, threatened huge protests if it went ahead. I have to confess to mixed feelings about all this. On the one hand I loathed apartheid and firmly believed that cutting sporting links with South Africa would hasten its demise. My father had already announced that he would refuse to commentate on any of the Springboks' games. On the other hand this Oxford team were my heroes. I followed them to most of the away games, as well as going to Iffley Road whenever I could. I really believed that they could beat the Boks if they got the chance and what a blow that would strike against apartheid, I naively imagined, given that rugby almost defined the Afrikaner way of life.

The Government, under Harold Wilson, hadn't wanted the tour in the first place and made it quite clear that they were not going to interfere with people's right to peaceful protest. There was clearly no way that the game could be played at Oxford, so the Rugby Football Union – who were as keen for the game and the tour to go ahead as the Government and a lot of other people were opposed – really only had one option: to keep the location secret until the very last moment, in the hope that it could be played before the anti-apartheid movement could mobilise enough demonstrators to stop it.

Chippy felt much the same way as I did and, after much heart-searching, we decided that, if it was physically possible for us to get to the game between the announcement of venue and kick-off, we would go. The news came through at 9 pm on the night before the game – Twickenham at 3 o'clock. The ground was only half full when we got there, with a big group of flag-waving, chanting protestors in the East stand. We positioned ourselves at the south end of the West stand, level with the try line.

It was a memorable game. The usually unreliable Mike Heal kicked two nerveless penalties, the Oxford pack played out of their skins, Laidlaw marshalled and inspired his troops like never before and the decision to put Steffan Jones, a grizzled back-row forward, in the centre to mow down the Springbok backs was a masterstroke. We were still 6-3 up as the game when into injury time and the Boks launched one final assault. A giant Springbok winger was hurtling towards the line. The try seemed inevitable. But there was Peter Torry, corner-flagging like a good wing-forward should. Somehow he found the speed and strength to stop the winger in his tracks, man and ball into touch. The final whistle blew. Torry got to his feet, blood streaming from his nose, raised a single fist to the sky and then collapsed onto the turf, not five yards from where we were watching. I know I shouldn't have been there, but it was one of my greatest moments in sport.

The Varsity match itself was almost equally exciting. Cambridge had their usual stellar back line (John Spencer, Roger Shackleton, Tony Jorden, Gerald Davies – internationals all of them). Oxford had Laidlaw and that back row. This time we were in the North stand, looking down the ground. The first half an hour was evenly poised as the sides swapped penalties, but then, seemingly, disaster. Williams, the Oxford winger, had to go off with a broken jaw, and in those days there were no substitutes in the Varsity match. Worse was to come. Early in the second half Oxford were briefly down to 13 men as the prop, Rod Speed, a Millfield old-boy in his third Varsity match, had to go off to have a leg injury bandaged and played on one leg when he returned. When Peter Carroll, our Australian full-back, headed for the side-lines, Oxford were briefly down to 12 and a half men. Happily Carroll came back, and happily Oxford held on, their gallant pack of six and a half forwards somehow keeping a last-gasp Cambridge onslaught at bay. It may have been a win by three penalties to two but, for my money, that was one of the greatest Varsity matches ever played, for quality, excitement and, as a good partisan I must add, fairness of outcome!

My dilemma over the Springbok game had been given added point by a new friend I had made: Zolile Escourt Mbali, a black South African (a proud Zulu, in fact) who had won a scholarship to study theology. Escourt was a few years older than most of us but threw himself into Oxford life with the joy of someone who had known real hardship back at home and who had had to fight every inch of the way to get there, unlike us English ex-public schoolboys, many of whom seemed to regard an Oxbridge education as their birthright.

Another good friend was Andrew Godfrey, blind from birth, yet who loved cricket with a passion. We would sometimes go to the Parks, where I would provide an impromptu commentary on what was happening in the match – usually a clatter of Oxford wickets – although he was perfectly happy just following the course of a game through the murmur of spectators, the shouts from the middle, the cheers and applause for a wicket or a boundary and the sound of bat on ball. Cricket seems to have a special appeal for the visually impaired. I suppose it must be the sheer complexity of the game that provides such richness for the imagination to feed upon.

My main tutor in that final year was an Oxford legend, JP Cooper of Trinity. He specialised in the seventeenth century English history which was the subject matter for both my 'further' and 'special' subjects, and, even at a university which was notorious for the eccentricities of its dons, he was in a class of his own. He was a gruff, heavy, shambling, unkempt man, who lurked in his rooms at Trinity surrounded by tottering mountains of books and papers like a giant spider in a web. He spoke but sparingly, in a nasally drawl, although his preferred medium for communicating disagreement or approbation was a grunt.

The best-known story of JP Cooper is of the student who arrived for his tutorial to find the distinguished historian on the toilet, with the door ajar.

"Would you like me to come back later, sir?" he politely enquired.

"No, boy," came the voice from behind the door. "Read me your essay."

The student duly obliged. There was a grunt when he had finished.

"Mmmph, thank you, boy. Now hand me your essay. I have a use for it."

It was probably apocryphal, but not completely implausible. My tutorials with him were always pretty much one-way traffic. I suppose he would say that he was pointing me in the right direction, and then letting me get on with thinking for myself. Which I did, although I have to say that reading through some of my work from that third year – which has survived – it doesn't seem very impressive and I didn't do particularly well in either of my JP Cooper subjects in the Schools, despite their being my favourites.

The early summer of 1970, in the run-up to my final exams, was gloriously sunny: not a cloud in the sky for what seemed liked weeks on end. I had worked hard in both vacations and wasn't feeling particularly stressed. The evening before my first exam, Susie and I went to our favourite country pub, the Lamb and Flag at Longworth, better known as 'Dudley's', where we ate one of their famous pies (7/6), drank Morrells from the wood (2/2 pint) and enjoyed a carafe of red wine (10/6).

Then, as now, examinations had to be taken in 'sub-fusc', which for men meant a dark suit, white shirt, white bow-tie, academic gown and mortar board. I borrowed a suit from my friend Steve Bendall, who was at least five inches taller than me, so that the trousers were crumpled over my ankles and the sleeves on the jacket enveloped my hands.

The schedule was gruelling: 10 three-hour papers over six days – morning and afternoon on Thursday and Friday, then Saturday morning, then two more on each of Monday and Tuesday, with a final paper on Wednesday morning. It was one of the few weeks – the others all involving deaths in the family – which would give me pause for thought if I was asked by the Almighty if I would like to live my life all over again. I had nightmares about it for years afterwards, even though I coped reasonably well with the pressure at the time.

I have never felt quite such a profound sense of relief as I did at 12.30 pm on Wednesday June 10 1970, having signed off with my views on 'Would the political situation in 1657-8 have been very different if Cromwell had accepted the crown?' I headed up the High to the off-licence next to Shepherd and Woodwards, bought a magnum of Moet and Chandon and a bottle of Dom Perignon and proceeded to drink the magnum with Susie in the Nun's Garden at Queen's. The world suddenly seemed a rather glorious place to be.

There remained the question of what I was going to do next. What I really wanted was to stay at Oxford, which meant taking a further degree, in the shape of a D Phil. It wasn't that I was particularly academic, but Oxford was where Susie was, and I had come to love both the place and the person. So I applied and was interviewed by Hugh Trevor-Roper, the Regius Professor of History and the second most famous historian in Britain (after his great rival AJP Taylor). I cannot now remember what the object of my studies was to be, but it was enough to earn me an acceptance from the University. But it wasn't to be. I could not realistically expect to support myself for several more years of study, and nor could my mother (my father having long since abrogated all such responsibilities). And Devon County Council turned down my application for a grant, probably quite rightly, given that self-indulgence had been my prime motivation for applying.

So that was that. End of Oxford story. A letter arrived from Kenneth Morgan: "Dear Gibson, I enclose your Schools marks." They ranged from Beta/alpha to Beta minus minus. Typically for me, I did best in the subjects I knew least about (a B++ in political thought being a prime example) and vice versa. He concluded: "A sound enough Second, as you see."

Which I suppose it was. In effect, a 2:1. I wasn't disappointed not to get a First like my father, as my expectations never stretched that high, especially after the debacle of the lost two years' work. But it was mildly frustrating not to have done better in the subjects, like Commonwealth and Protectorate, on which I had worked hardest and, I felt, knew most. 'Could have done better' would have been a just verdict.

I enjoyed my three years at Oxford enormously. It was one of the best periods in my life. My only real regret is that I didn't make more of it: that I didn't get involved in the Union, for example, and didn't go to more lectures and didn't spend more of my time debating politics and philosophy with my contemporaries, as opposed to merely playing music for them to dance to. There is a lot to be said for beer, and women, and discos and punting, and cricket, but, with the arguable exception of punting, you don't need to be at Oxford to enjoy them. The truth is that I was probably too young to have got the most out of Oxford. Had I been a year or two older and a year or two more worldly wise, I might have got some of the post-school excesses out of my system.

7

A farmer's boy

I had no very clear idea of what I wanted to do when I arrived back in Devon from Oxford at the end of June 1970, except that I felt I could do with a break. All the cramming in the run-up to Schools had left me study-weary. The one concrete prospect was the Daily Mirror journalism training course, starting in September. The Sunday Independent, based in Plymouth, was part of the Mirror group and its editor, John Theobald, was a great family friend, so there was every chance I'd get accepted for the course. But it wasn't to be – that autumn the course was cancelled, on the basis that the newspaper business was going through something of a crisis and there weren't the jobs for trainees to go on to. The consequences for my subsequent career proved to be profound.

That summer I had persuaded my mother to move back to Sparkwell. The flat which was part of the main house at Blacklands had fallen vacant. From her point of view the move would mean she would have the company of one of her best friends in Enid Hamlyn, and for myself and Chippy it would give us the run of Blacklands' extensive gardens and the farm, plus the company of Julia, Duncan, Nigel and Jason. It also suited Enid, Ted having become a rabid Scientologist and gone off to live with his similarly inclined partner in their doctors' practice in Plymouth.

Living on the farm also offered the prospect of some part-time work. With rented land I suppose the farm ran to about 150 acres, which was enough to support a herd of around 90 dairy cows, plus followers. There was a hard-driving farm manager in Peter Tremain (whom Chippy and I always referred to as 'Whiskers'), a top-class herdsman in Howard Matticott, with my near-contemporary Duncan Hamlyn completing the workforce.

Three full time members of staff on a small dairy farm did not leave much scope for A Gibson, even if I'd been any good at practical farm work, which I most certainly wasn't. That autumn they found bits and bobs of jobs for me to do, like unblocking drains or replacing rotten or broken railway sleepers in the track – the race, as we called it – which the cows used to access their pastures in front of the house. When there wasn't any work on the farm I was set to demolish what had been a most beautiful Victorian greenhouse, pane by pane, so that the land it stood on could be incorporated in the farm. As a last resort I was allocated a calf house, three feet deep in strawy manure, and told that if I cleared it out I could keep, in lieu of wages, whatever money I might make from hawking bags of farmyard manure around the village.

In the summer there was silage to be forked and bales to be humped under the unrelenting supervision of Whiskers, sometimes long into the night. I learned some useful lessons about the tough physical nature of life on a small family farm which stayed with me throughout my subsequent career, and being able to speak the language of farming probably helped me as well, but I can't say it was an experience I particularly enjoyed.

One very happy memory of life on the farm has, however, stayed with me, and that is of Christmas. At Blacklands there was a set routine: on Christmas morning Enid would lay on a drinks party for families, workers and friends in the big sitting room, with a roaring log fire in the hearth. This would go on for several hours.

To sober up, us younger ones would sally forth in the afternoon to 'move the bullocks', which often involved driving them through the village, shouting "ho, ho" in the accepted manner to encourage them along and taking care not to let them trample any gardens on the way. This task chaotically completed, we would get back to the house, to bath and change into dinner jackets for Christmas dinner which both families ate together in the candle-lit dining-room. Christmas 1970 was particularly special because Susie and Escourt came to stay. It was bitterly cold, with snow showers on Christmas Day, and poor Escourt, who had been billeted in a freezing attic room above the flat, enjoyed the afternoon's exercise not at all. "It is so cold," he kept saying, his teeth chattering. "It is so co-o-o-o-ld." But he soon cheered up under the influence of roast turkey, claret and Christmas pudding.

There is nothing quite like Christmas on a farm. The great thing about it is the contrast which it provides between hard, physical work, sometimes in the worst of the weather – as in 1970 – and the warmth, comfort and happiness of sharing food, drink and companionship with family and friends. Pleasure is all the more enjoyable if it has been earned. Our Christmases on the farm were maybe not quite in the Squire Wardle category in Dickens' 'Pickwick Papers', but they have made for some of my happiest memories.

There was one brief spark of hope for a relief from the drudgery of filling empty fertiliser bags with manure. Westward Television in Plymouth were planning a series of programmes aimed at young people, with a young Angela Rippon as producer and main presenter. We did have a family connection with the station, as my father had for a time fronted the early evening news programme, 'Westward Diary', with Kenneth MacLeod, while my mother had appeared several times on a political discussion programme called 'Conflict of Opinion' and had more than held her own.

They presumably imagined that I must have inherited some of my parents' ability. I was asked to put together what we would now call a 'package' about Drake's Island, in Plymouth Sound, and the plans which were afoot to convert some of its impressive fortifications into, if memory serves, a youth centre. I did my best with the script and the interviews but, in all honesty, I was hopeless. I don't think either the programme or my film was ever broadcast. But they did pay me £5 for my efforts, and Angela Rippon could not have been kinder.

So, that debacle put down to experience, I found myself a job away from the farm, as a sales assistant in the China and Glass Department of E. Dingle and Co, Plymouth's biggest and best department store. Back to service with a smile. The money wasn't particularly good, but I quite enjoyed the work. My boss, John Furse, was a cultivated man, more like a university professor than a salesman, and I soon learned to distinguish between Royal Worcester and Spode, or Stuart Crystal and Waterford Glass. I also met Tony Oxley, the assistant buyer in the boys' wear department, who would become a good friend both to myself and Chippy, and Ricky Ennis, a flamboyant, black, kitchen-equipment demonstrator, who was as keen on cricket as I was.

But as the year went on, I became more and more unhappy and frustrated. Through force of circumstance as much as anything, Susie and I had begun to drift apart, and in November she ditched me. I walked up the hill to the moor at Smallhanger and wept bitter tears. I did acquire a new girlfriend, admittedly on only a casual sort of basis. She was Valerie Daw, the daughter of Ellis Daw, who three years earlier had converted his small farm, Goodamoor, across the Cornwood road from Fursdon, into the Dartmoor Wildlife Park.

Ellis was not a man to be trifled with, as many a petty bureaucrat would discover during his many brushes with officialdom. But in 1971 he had his sights trained very firmly on what he would probably have described as the four-legged vermin that threatened his embryonic collection of mainly small animals, such as rabbits, lambs and guinea pigs. At night he would take up position on the first-floor balcony of the house, armed with a rifle and guided by the searchlight he had installed to sweep the enclosures for any hint of movement such as might betray the presence of foxes and badgers. The set-up had the feel of an observation tower on a German prisoner-of-war camp about it, and Ellis was a good shot.

From my point of view it made walking Valerie home after an evening in the Treby Arms a distinctly perilous exercise. Many were the times we had to hit the gravel, as the searchlight beam swept round to the drive. Valerie was as keen on wildlife as her father and kept a pet badger which she would take for walks, a length of baler twine serving as a lead. Her legs were always covered in scratches from the animal's sharp claws as it pawed at her in affection. I've never much liked badgers since.

Gainful, worthwhile, career-shaping employment now became my main concern. I had already given up the Dingles job so that I could carry on with my cricket scoring for the BBC as the season reached its climax but, when that finished, I had no alternative but to go on the dole, to keep myself in beer, cigarettes and the occasional round of golf at Elfordleigh. I applied for all sorts of jobs, including one with Friends of the Earth, for I was already deeply concerned about plans for a reservoir at Swincombe in the heart of Dartmoor and what the china clay industry was doing to the moor around Shaugh Prior. I might have become an Instructor Officer, teaching naval history at the Britannia Royal Naval College, but just missed the deadline for applying. Teaching beckoned as a last resort.

Through all this period I was being sent job opportunities by the University Appointments Board, and in April 1972, after what had been a pretty miserable and wasted winter, they sent me details of a job with the National Farmers' Union, based at its Headquarters in Knightsbridge. It was for an 'Editorial Assistant in the Intelligence Division'. The work would involve researching, writing and editing material for the Union's publications and other purposes. Salary £1,500 per annum.

I had heard about the NFU. The Hamlyns were members, mainly because they did their insurance through the local NFU Group Secretary, John Finnegan, in Plympton. When I thought about what the job might be like, a vision of men in tweed caps, crowding into a big meeting in London, swam into view, presumably drawn from something I'd seen on the television. It didn't strike me as a very glamorous prospect, but I did at least know something about the practical side of farming, I would be able to use my writing skills and, besides, what else was there?

So I applied and was invited for interview to Agriculture House, Knightsbridge, an imposing building just down from Hyde Park Corner. I nearly didn't get there. Having failed my driving test twice, it was left to my mother to drive me to Plymouth station to catch the train for London. When the time came to leave, her reliably unreliable Austin 1100 refused to start. I had to get out, best suit and all, and push the wretched thing down the drive before it eventually coughed reluctantly into life. I caught the train with about two minutes to spare.

The interview was not the ordeal that my Oxford one had been. My sole interlocutor was Leslie Thomas, an intelligent, mild-mannered man who divided his time between London and Herefordshire and who would be my immediate superior. We seemed to get on pretty well; I had taken the precaution of mugging up on some of the farming issues of the day – much the most dominant being Britain's impending entry to the EEC – and that, coupled with at least some sort of farming background, proved enough to get me the job. I was as happy as I'd been for almost two years when the letter arrived from Knightsbridge. The first thing I did when I got the good news was to grow a moustache. I'd decided that I looked too young to be taken seriously in my new role in London and needed to age myself a touch. Twenty-five years later I shaved it off, for precisely the opposite reason!

There remained the question of where I was going to live in London, but that was happily answered when I got wind of the fact that three of my friends from Queen's were sharing a flat at 3, Cornwall Gardens, just off the Cromwell Road, only two stops on the Piccadilly line from Knightsbridge, and had a spare room. This turned out to be anything but palatial. It was tiny, with only enough space for a bed, bedside table and chest of drawers, and windowless. The Black Hole, we called it, as in Calcutta.

My flatmates were Andrew McDowell, then just cutting his teeth as a barrister, now a distinguished High Court judge, Iain Murray, who had dropped out of Oxford after failing his Mods and was now a coin specialist with Spinks, Tim Ling, a trainee solicitor who would go on to become a partner in Freshfields, and his girlfriend Angie, short, spiky, highly averse to washing up and who had as little as possible to do with the rest of us. It was a ground-floor flat, in which us young professionals lived in a state which came close to squalor. Beds were never made, washing up was simply piled up in the sink, every scruffy stick of furniture was coated with a thick layer of dust, and the one, poky bathroom represented a health hazard. But it was fun, and we rubbed along happily enough together.

There was a Waitrose just up the road, where I would buy myself a stuffed rolled breast of lamb for 50p for my supper and in the other direction, opposite Gloucester Road tube station, a Kentucky Fried Chicken and one of the first Pizza Expresses. As for a pub, on my very first evening in London Andrew and Iain took me to the Britannia, a good mile away from the flat but worth every step, for it was (and is) a Young's pub and a famous one at that. My three years at Oxford had taught me to appreciate the difference between what we were just beginning to call 'real ale' and the pressurised, artificially carbonated alternatives, and one of the things I was most looking forward to in London was drinking Young's beer, famous for being 100% from the wood.

Looking back at a diary which I wrote at the time, we do seem to have consumed prodigious quantities of Young's Special. We tended not to go out until about 9 pm but would then down five or six pints before closing time, when we would walk back to the flat and play bridge into the early hours. John Simkins, who was by now working for the Financial Times, would sometimes join us on these expeditions, as would my old friend from Devon Stephen Hopson, whom we would mock for being a 'software analyst' with IBM, although it was very definitely Steve – now retired after a stellar career in IT – who had the last laugh.

I also played a bit of chess, mostly against Andrew, spurred on by the epic contest for the World Chess Championship in which the American Bobby Fischer routed the Russian Boris Spassky in a result of global significance. I invariably lost, leaving me with another nickname to add to my collection, namely Boris. Andrew, I should say, was known as Poison, this being short for Poisoned Dwarf, which was a rather cruel reflection on his lack of inches and Scottish heritage. We call each other Poison and Boris to this day.

It was Poison who persuaded me to join him in playing rugby for London Scottish. It was a game I was never much good at, being both too fat and too slow. I was sick after the first training session at the ground which Scottish shared with Richmond and ended up playing loose-head prop for the Extra Bs (roughly the club 5th XV). My hooker was a short, evil Glaswegian, who was always looking to start a fight with the opposition front row, whereas all I wanted was a quiet life. It was just for the one season, and the only thing I enjoyed about it was being able to rub shoulders with some of the giants of the game, men like Alastair McHarg, Chris Ralston and Tony Bucknall, in the bar afterwards. I was, however, inordinately proud of the red Scottish lion badge sewn onto my rugby shirt, which I kept for years afterwards, passing it from one sweat-shirt to the next. "He's Hamish, the Scottish lion," I'd tell my children.

I would get back to Plymouth for weekends and holidays as often as I could, to play cricket for Cornwood and golf with Chippy and Tony Oxley, for whom I was best man when he married Vivienne in March 1973. This didn't have much in common with a 21st century wedding. All of us blokes got roaring drunk at the Treby Arms the night before, self ending up in a coal bunker, being sick. The church was cold and half-empty, and the champagne that was poured for the photographs at the Elfordleigh Hotel turned out to be stale lager. The bride's father – a policeman! – was so nervous he could barely speak (although he did manage a racist joke, with our black friend Ricky Ennis prominent among the guests). Tony's speech was memorable for his description of going for a pee between the service and the reception.

"When I unzipped my fly, a load of confetti came out," he told a stunned gathering. "I thought to myself: Vivienne will be expectin' more than that!"

As for myself, the previous night's over-indulgence was weighing heavily on my insides and at one point I thought I might have to make a run for it, but I got through my speech somehow, then headed for the loo. Happy days!

8

A Plumb job

I started with the NFU on July 17, 1972, at a time when, rather like me, British farming stood on the verge of an exciting new chapter. EEC entry was only five months away, an event that would have more profound effects on farming and food than any other sector of the economy, thanks to the existence of the Common Agricultural Policy.

I'd learned enough about the politics of farming in preparing for my NFU interview to know that there were distinctly mixed feelings among the grassroots farming community as to what lay ahead. The Union's President, Henry Plumb, was privately very much in favour of entry, partly because he was, and at the time of writing still is, a firm believer in European co-operation as a matter of principle, but also for the more pragmatic reason that hitching the British farmer's wagon to the star of the French farming lobby was likely to produce a lot more in terms of financial support and other benefits than leaving the industry to the tender mercies of British governments which had been looking to cut payments to farmers for at least the previous ten years. However, astute natural politician that he was, he had avoided the issue coming to a head through what would inevitably have been a highly divisive vote, so that the NFU's official position was one of neutrality, leaving it free to concentrate on getting the best deal out of the new situation for its farmer and grower members. Hence, I suppose, my appointment.

I was given an office on the first floor, which had previously belonged to the Timber Growers Association and still had their name over the door. The rest of my department – the Intelligence Division – was on the third floor, alongside what was effectively its parent body, the Public Relations Department. Our job in Intelligence was to provide the bullets for the PR people to fire, as well as keeping the organisation as well informed as possible as to the basis of the NFU's policies, through a fortnightly internal publication called 'NFU Insight'.

A large part of my new role would involve writing articles for the magazine. But first I had to learn the ropes. I was provided with a stack of NFU policy guides, briefing papers and guidance booklets for members and basically told to get on and read the lot. Given, as I say, that all of my immediate colleagues were two floors away, it made for a distinctly lonely existence for my first few months. In fact, I didn't meet the department's biggest chief, the Director of Public Relations, Jim Reedy, until the office Christmas party in December!

The first thing that struck me as I went through all the paperwork was how much more equitable and sensible the existing British farm support system was than the EEC model we were moving to. The 1947 Agriculture Act, introduced be it noted by a Labour Government, had inaugurated a system whereby farm output prices were fixed every year at a level – the guaranteed price – which was supposed to allow a reasonably efficient farmer to make a profit. If market prices fell below that level – because of cheaper imports, for example – then the Government would make up the difference through a 'deficiency payment'.

Farmers' incomes were thus protected, so ensuring that output would increase, leaving the country less dependent on food imports (a lesson that had been learned in both world wars), while prices to the consumer could fall to whatever level supply and demand dictated. The other great advantage of this approach was that it was socially fair. The poorer you are, the bigger the proportion of your income is spent on food, so the greater the benefit from keeping prices low. Conversely, the richer you are, the smaller the proportion of your income you spend on food, but the more you contribute to the cost of the deficiency payments in tax. It was a 'Robin Hood' model of policy, taking from the rich to help the poor and at the same time underpinning a key British industry.

But this approach was effectively turned on its head by the CAP. Instead of allowing food prices to find their own level and supporting farmers' incomes through top-up payments, all of the instruments of the CAP – including, most significantly, import levies and intervention buying – were geared to keeping food prices high so that farmers could make a profit. Consumers therefore picked up a large part of the bill for farm support, and the poorer the consumer, the more it hurt. Income support was being replaced by price support, at the expense of the poorest in society. To me it made no sense.

But that was to ignore the political dimension. Taxpayer-funded income support payments are all very well if you have a generous Government anxious to boost farm output, even at the expense of increasing the tax burden. In reality, as the years had gone by, successive Governments, of both colours, had been looking to screw down the level of support, either by raising prices at each annual Price Review by less than the amount that the NFU said was necessary to recoup higher costs or by imposing limits on the volume of output to which the guaranteed prices applied.

Joining the EEC would mean that, over time, the level of farm support would be determined not at the annual Price Review, in a horse-trade with an unsympathetic British Government to whom the farming vote was increasingly peripheral, but in the corridors of power in Brussels, where the politicians and bureaucrats were much more inclined to buckle before the might of the French farm lobby, especially as it would be the consumer who would pick up a large part of the bill. I soon discovered that the five-year 'transition period' which had been agreed, to cover the switch from income support to price support, would involve a big lift in farm output prices, cereals in particular.

However, my focus in 1972 was not so much on the broad sweep of policy, as on the all-important detail: the finer points of the 'intervention' system, for example, whereby beef or butter or corn or wine was taken off the market and put into store at the EEC's expense if supply exceeded demand, to keep prices high; or the 'sluicegate prices', which offered a much lower level of support for pig and poultry farmers; or the progressive dismantling of the tariffs which had protected the likes of the Cheddar strawberry growers or the plum orchards and glasshouses of the Vale of Evesham.

If there was one sector of British farming that suffered more than any other from EEC entry, it was horticulture, and in the process we lost so many of the links between areas and crops which had been so important economically and culturally. Who remembers now that the valley running up from the sea at Combe Martin in North Devon once produced some of the earliest strawberries in the country, or that the Tamar Valley was famous for its orchards and soft fruit? Those associations would probably have faded away eventually in any case, but EEC entry, with its staged opening of the floodgates to produce from the likes of France and Spain, unquestionably accelerated the process.

The other main theme of my work in those early years with the NFU was marketing. This was another of Henry Plumb's great enthusiasms. He had seen how, across much of the continent, the farmers had come together to make up for lack of scale as individuals by forming large and powerful co-operatives. These would be our competitors in the new world. The co-operative ethos was not strong amongst British farmers. They valued their independence and, unlike their continental cousins, were on average just about big enough to be able to afford to maintain it, given a reasonable level of efficiency and generous Government support. The nearest thing that British agriculture had to the big European co-operatives was the marketing boards – the Milk Marketing Board pre-eminent among them – and they relied on the force of law. It was already suspected that their days were numbered, and they only covered a handful of commodities in any case. British farmers would need to come together voluntarily to market their produce if they were to compete. That was the message which I was instructed to promulgate, through the organisation and beyond.

At Henry Plumb's instigation a new organisation was created to help farmers create the necessary business structures: Agricultural Co-operation and Marketing Services Ltd (ACMS). It needed office premises in Agriculture House. Ironically, so it seemed at the time, I was moved to make way. Not that I minded in the slightest. From being cut off on the first floor I was now in the thick of things on the third, sharing an office with Chantale Lyons whose job was to keep the NFU's 'Guide to Prices and Services' up to date. I felt that I was moving from a backwater into the mainstream. Even Jim Reedy started to take an interest in me.

Besides the day-to-day contributions to 'NFU Insight', I was also now writing features, again with a strong emphasis on marketing. Two of the first were on the Roscoff Ferry – 'The Cauliflower Boat that Goes Back Empty' – and Britain's first hypermarket, the Carrefour at Caerphilly. In the one instance a Breton farmers' co-operative, the SICA, had quite literally launched a ferry to carry cauliflowers and artichokes to Plymouth and the British market (and it did indeed go back empty, at least until the tourist trade took off). Wasn't that an example we ought to be following? The other was a sign of things to come in the retail trade. On either side of an atomised farming community – among their competitors and in their markets – scale was the name of the game.

Henry Plumb was the ideal President for his time. He believed in Europe, he understood what British farmers needed to do to compete in Europe, he commanded respect, so that he had the ear of whichever Government he was dealing with, he looked and sounded like a farmer, something which endeared him to his members and the public alike and, crucially, he understood his own strengths and weaknesses. Henry was not, is not, an intellectual. In 1942 the pressures of wartime had meant that he'd had to leave school, aged 15, to work on the family farm near Coleshill. Judging from his autobiography, 'The Plumb Line', he learned more from his local Young Farmers' club than he did from formal education. But he was shrewd, tough and a great judge of character. Unlike some more recent NFU Presidents, he did not regard himself as having all the answers. He was happy to be guided by the professional staff he had around him, not least because they were of the very highest calibre.

Asher Winegarten was the brains of the organisation. He reminded me a bit of Henry Kissinger: plump, Jewish, urbane, a touch pompous but brimming with intelligence and ideas. When it came to the Annual Price Review, he was more than a match for whoever was leading the MAFF team. In fact, the entire Economics team was one of the NFU's greatest strengths. Besides Asher there was Michael Strauss, another brilliant man who looked and sounded rather like a slightly mad German professor, and John Malcolm, as left-wing as you like in his own political beliefs but whose commitment to the cause was absolute. A word too for John Montgomery, whom I only got to know much later when he was one of my leading members in Somerset, who chaired the NFU's Economics Committee for many years during the days of the Price Review. His family had moved down from Ayrshire to Kent in the farming depression before the First World War, John eventually moving on to milk cows and make the famous Montgomery Cheddar at North Cadbury Court. Despite never having lived in Scotland, he spoke with a pronounced Ayrshire accent, so close-knit had the family been. And he had a Scotsman's guile and prudence when it came to negotiations.

The NFU's other great strength in those days was in public relations. The organisation had long since learned the lesson that, without the weight of electoral numbers to get results from Government, it needed to have the public on its side as farming supporters by proxy. Over the years many campaigns had been run, perhaps the most famous – which is still recalled by wistful veterans – being the 'Fair Deal' campaign of the mid-1960s, featuring 'Tug Tractor'. Posters reading 'Remember! The farmers' fight is your fight too' or 'Take the brake off British farming, says Tug Tractor' had appeared everywhere.

Jim Reedy, who had become my boss with the absorption of the Intelligence Division into Public Relations, had been the architect of that campaign. He was a big man, with big appetites, who ran his department with a broad brush, considerable style, a clear sense of direction and not much attention to detail. But if he was 1970s PR-man personified, he had more than enough sense to balance that with some hard-bitten professionalism in the shape of Stan Collins, his deputy, Ernie Milner, another veteran Northern journalist who did his best to keep the regional PR officers in line, David Anderson, the mild-mannered Shetlander who edited 'NFU Insight' and Vic Robertson who had come down from the Aberdeen Press and Journal to take over as Senior Press Officer. Jim's right-hand woman was Betty Humphreys, a lady of a certain age who looked as if she applied her make-up with a trowel but who took quite a shine to young Tony, as I was known. She and I would lunch in the NFU Club, drinking gin or beer and eating a cold collation, whilst most of the staff were in the canteen, down in the basement. Vera Beale, the NFU's Librarian – imagine that, a librarian! – was also very kind to me.

The farmer who, as Chairman of the Publicity Committee, had responsibility for the department was an interesting character, to put it mildly. Bob Saunders was a bachelor, who farmed between Dorchester and Wareham. In the 1930s he had achieved national notoriety as one of Oswald Mosley's henchmen in the British Union of Fascists and had been particularly successful in recruiting farmers to the cause in North Devon. He was interned during the war in the Isle of Man and afterwards ceased to play a particularly active role in what became known as the Union Movement, without ever recanting his fascist beliefs.

How much of this was known to the senior staff and elected office-holders around him in the late 60s and early 70s, I'm not sure. It only came to the fore when he stood for the Vice-Presidency, allegedly (for the voting was supposed to be kept a deadly secret) missing out by just a single vote. He was no fool and knew all about propaganda from his Mosleyite days. Solidly built, with a strikingly large head, there was something of the bulldog about him, and I am sure he fancied himself as a Churchillian figure, his portentous pronouncements not so much spoken as barked. I got to know him well later, and we got on surprisingly amicably.

You will note that I have made no mention thus far of my ultimate boss, the Director-General, George Cattell. That is because I hardly ever met him. He had been head-hunted from a senior post in British Leyland (!), not to have any influence on NFU policy but to try to turn the organisation from a loosely-knit federation of county branches, each of which was free to do its own thing when it came to staffing and finance, into a single, coherent national organisation, controlled from the centre. This was not an easy task. The County Secretaries, handsomely remunerated by the over-riding commission that they received on NFU Mutual insurance business in their patches, were the NFU's robber barons, not quite laws unto themselves but not far from it. As long as they kept their members behind them, they could treat directives from HQ as advice, rather than commands. Many were ex-military. Shropshire's Sam Badger was, appropriately, the most aggressive, Devon's Hugh Crowle probably the most frightening, and Lincolnshire's Newton Loynes one of the grandest. He it was who landed me with a summons to Jim Reedy's office one summer Monday morning.

"I've just had a very angry Newton Loynes on the phone," he began. "He understands that you were in the commentary box at the Oval with Brian Johnston yesterday and that, when Johnston suggested that the reason the gas-holders were full was that housewives couldn't afford to be cooking Sunday lunch because the price of meat was so high, you made no attempt to correct him. I would have expected better of you." I still don't know if he meant it tongue in cheek or was being serious.

At any event George Cattell did succeed in centralising finance, so that subscriptions were paid to HQ rather than to each county, but attempts to persuade counties to amalgamate met only very limited success. It would be another 17 years before the NFU was regionalised – fortunately for me!

Agriculture House, Knightsbridge was a very civilised place to work in the 1970s. The prevailing ethos was very professional, slightly old-fashioned and not prone to self-doubt. The staff complement was generous, with a wonderful mix of characters, ranging from the ex-graduate trainees like Ian Gardiner, then a shy, gawky, almost silent beanpole of a young man, who would go on to become a brilliant Director of Policy before his sadly early death from cancer, to gnarled old pros like Henry Haynes, the Deputy Director General, a veteran of the JK Knowles' era, or Alan Greig, who headed up the Livestock department. It was a comfortable place to work, generously staffed and with a clear sense of direction. Most but by no means all of the more senior staff were men, supported by a shifting population of secretaries, who ranged from the gloriously buxom like Jenny Mills to the superannuated. Mrs Pragnell, who worked for my friend Jimmy Graham in Seeds, was over 70 then and would carry on working for the NFU into her 90s!

The hours were 9.30 to 5.30, with a proper break for lunch, which allowed me to wander down to Harrods and its book department, or catch a bus up to Piccadilly and Lillywhites, where I would gaze longingly at the golf clubs I couldn't afford. On Friday lunchtimes there was a general exodus to the Wilton Arms, where the girls would drink gin and us blokes put away several pints of that rather thin bitter that Whitbread used to brew at Chiswell Street.

Towards the end of 1974 there was a re-shuffle in the PR department. It was occasioned by the murder of Donald Willcox, who worked on campaigns and internal briefings. Donald was gay and made no great secret of it. He was battered to death by his homosexual lover with a brass shell-case which he used as a door-stop. It was all quite shocking and unpleasant, but it did have the effect of creating a vacancy for a Deputy Press Officer, into which I was moved – just in time for what became known as the 'Beef Crisis' of 1974.

The previous year had seen a big jump in oil prices, so raising livestock farmers' cost of fertiliser and fuel, a big rise in corn prices, which pushed up the price of feed, and a big increase in cattle numbers which depressed the price of beef. On top of all that, a minority Labour Government had come to power in February in the wake of the miners' strike and the three-day week (which led to the NFU AGM being moved from Central Hall Westminster to the Hilton in Park Lane). The national mood was fractious, and the livestock farmers of Wales and the West needed little excuse for taking to the streets.

Then, as now, most farmers voted Conservative, despite the fact that, arguably, the industry had been more generously treated over the years by Labour than by the Tories. The returning Minister of Agriculture, the bibulous Fred Peart, did himself no favours when he scrapped the intervention buying of beef on grounds of cost. By May calves were being sold at market for as little as 50p and bullocks were being released to charge through the streets of Whitehall, giving London the feel of Pamplona. At Holyhead a boat load of Irish beef was tipped into the harbour.

Public interest was intense. In the Press Office we were never off the phone, either explaining to journalists why the crisis had erupted and what its impacts were on farmers, or defending the NFU from charges by its more militant members that it was sitting back and doing nothing while the industry went up in smoke. All of the national newspapers had specialist agricultural correspondents in those days, men (and they were all men) like the Daily Express's Alex Kenworthy, or the BBC's Archie McPhee, or the Daily Telegraph's Godfrey Brown, and they would ring us almost every day for information or comment. Vic Robertson and I were as different as chalk and cheese in background and political outlook – Vic being a hard-boiled Tory – but, perhaps partly because of that, we worked well together. The NFU's side of the story did not go by default.

It was a situation in which Henry Plumb's innate political skills came to the fore. He had to keep channels of communication with Government open, and the NFU had a court injunction and the threat of a massive fine hanging over it from the time it organised a boycott of livestock markets in 1970, so he could not condone militancy such as Holyhead or the bullocks in Whitehall. But quietly he kept in touch with the leading militants like Devon's Ian Pettyfer, just asking to be privately informed of what they were up to. He would then say to Fred Peart, or whoever, words to the effect of: "This is not action that the NFU supports or condones, Minister, but it is the clearest possible evidence of how serious the situation has become."

To make matters worse, the summer of 1974 was a wet one, and crops of silage and hay were poor, so piling on the agony. Soon the dairy farmers were up in arms as well, demanding an increase in the guaranteed price of milk to cover lower output and higher costs. In September the Devon NFU Chairman, Allin Bewes, himself a dairy farmer from Shebbear, led a large delegation to meet the county's MPs at Westminster to demand a price increase. Hugh Crowle, the all-powerful Devon NFU County Secretary and a man who could make Thomas Cromwell seem a touch naïve, had organised it all.

Now it so happened that Fred Peart had chosen this very day – whether by accident or design, I can't say – to announce a 6p per gallon (1.3p per litre) price rise. With milk prices at around 5p per litre, that represented an increase of over 25%, so quite a triumph for the NFU, and I drafted a press release accordingly, quoting the President. I was just putting the finishing touches to it when Hugh Crowle appeared in the Press Office, asking to see the statement. He took one look at it and exploded with rage.

"What is the meaning of this?" he demanded. "This was Devon's doing, and Devon's alone," and, with that, he tore the paper out of my typewriter and headed off with it to see the President, leaving a quivering deputy press officer in his wake. Devon's efforts did get due acknowledgement in the final version, which was important because Devon was the home to the Farmers' Action Group, the militant splinter group set up by Hugh Crowle's bête noire, the North Devon farmer Wallace Day. For me it was an object lesson in the tensions and rivalries that could exist between 'HQ', as we were known, and the counties.

One odd thing about these years in Knightsbridge was that I met hardly any farmers during the course of them. Henry Plumb was pretty much ever-present, of course, and there were other Committee Chairmen like Derek Maidment of Milk (known to the female secretaries as 'brothel creepers'), Don Avery of Poultry (who would take his favoured female members of staff out to Raymond's Revue Bar) and Ernest Richards, the shrewd Welshman who headed the NFU's highly professional parliamentary lobbying team. But apart from the meetings of Council – always conducted in a haze of tobacco smoke – that was about it when it came to contact with the people we were representing.

In recognition of that, a programme of visits was arranged, in which HQ staff and committee chairmen were taken to different parts of the country to meet the grassroots face to face. My visit was to Denbighshire, not far from my mother's ancestral home but a county I'd never set foot in before. We were well looked after, and the programme included a visit to a remote hill farm. The locals were obviously keen to make an impression, so pretended that their English was only sketchy and insisted on using an interpreter. To make matters worse, it was a cold and wet day and, living as I did in London, I'd had no Wellington boots to bring with me. So when we set off across a muddy field to view some sheep. I got so bogged down that, when I tried to pull my feet out of the mud, I left both shoes and socks behind. Oh my goodness, didn't they have a laugh at that. I'll bet they remember to this day the time when that London NFU smart Alec lost his shoes and socks in Eifion Williams' bog!

Meanwhile I had been cutting my teeth as a public speaker. The NFU received lots of requests from London-based organisations like schools, the Young Conservatives and other local groups for someone to come and talk to them, usually about farming and the EEC. Jim Reedy decided that I was just the man for the job.

I made my debut as an NFU speaker at Finchley Manorhill School, a girls' school in North London. It wasn't exactly a triumph. I recorded in my diary: 'The talk was reasonable, but it was a mistake to read what I'd so laboriously prepared. It sounded stilted, I went too fast, and the poor girls barely understood a word (not entirely surprising as six of them were Asians and couldn't speak English too well!).' However, I do seem to have enjoyed the subsequent tour of the school – 'Knickers, knickers everywhere!' was the comment. Subsequent speaking engagements, mostly to Young Conservative Groups in the London suburbs, seem to have been rather more successful, although not always well attended. At Friern Barnet YCs my audience numbered five! Still, you're got to start somewhere.

I was perhaps slightly more successful at writing speeches than at making them. I didn't get involved in the major Presidential addresses, such as the AGM speech, but I would draft sections of speeches – usually the policy nitty-gritty – for lesser occasions. Henry was always very kind about my efforts. He would make the odd change with his thick-nibbed fountain pen, in black ink, and then put his personal stamp on the words when it came to their delivery.

Richard Butler, the Deputy President, usually wrote his own stuff, but my services were once called upon by the Vice-President, John Cossins from Dorset, for a speech he was due to make about footpaths and how an out-dated network of rights of way needed to be 'rationalised' (a long-standing and still extant NFU demand). I hit upon the bright idea of taking the total length of footpaths in England and Wales and working out how much land it covered – land that would consequently not be available to play its full part in the drive to produce more food.

However, for reasons which I still don't quite understand, I multiplied the length by three yards, rather than the three feet which footpaths are supposed to occupy. No-one noticed, a press release was issued, trumpeting the fact that "Footpaths take 9,000 acres of land out of production", and the speech was duly delivered. It didn't take the Ramblers Association very long to spot the mistake, with poor John Cossins bearing the brunt of their mockery and contempt and being forced to apologise. He still remembered the incident 26 years later when, as Master of the Worshipful Company of Farmers, he asked me to speak at their Millennium dinner, although I think he had just about forgiven me by then.

The big event in farming politics in 1975 was the publication of the Government's White Paper, 'Food From Our Own Resources', which was supposed to provide a blueprint for how British farming should develop over the ensuing decade. It was a triumph for the NFU and Henry Plumb, in that it nailed the Government's colours firmly to the mast of expansion, in the name of increasing food security and reducing the balance of payments deficit, which was a much bigger concern in the 70s than it is now.

Yet, even before it had been published, the White Paper had been overtaken by events. We were now part of the EEC and thus the CAP, a policy which was already being bedevilled by structural surpluses of milk, cereals, beef and wine. In that context it made absolutely no sense at all for the UK to go all out for growth. It would simply make the surplus problem worse and inflate the cost of dealing with it. Henry Plumb and Asher Winegarten knew this perfectly well, of course. Their logic was that, recognising that the EEC would have to put a lid on price-supported production sooner or later, the more the UK was producing when that time came, the less painful any cut-back would be. I could see the logic of it as well, although it did leave a lot of dairy farmers feeling that they had been led up the garden path when their heavily invested expansion plans were cut off at the knees when milk quotas were imposed in 1984.

By this stage I was beginning to feel very comfortable in my new career and, indeed, in my personal life. I had acquired a new girlfriend in 1973, Mandy Wills, secretary to John Kerr in the Milk Division and the daughter of a prominent Cambridgeshire farmer. She was tall, slender, with legs up to here, vivacious, always immaculately turned out and seemingly fancied by half the male members of staff.

Our first date was playing tennis in Holland Park, after which we repaired to – where else – the Britannia. By 1975 we were living together, not in the squalor of 3 Cornwall Gardens, I hasten to add, but in the leafy suburb of Turnham Green, where Andrew McDowell had bought a house. Chippy had come to London, in a vain attempt to pass the accountancy section of his Part 2 legal exams, and gone back again to Plymouth, where he was working for Foot and Bowden, the firm founded by Isaac Foot, in which his son John, a great friend of my father, was a partner. I had a new local, another Youngs pub, needless to say: The Thatched House, near Ravenscourt Park, a splendid pub run by Bedford Jezzard, the old Fulham footballer.

In November that year Jim Reedy had a heart attack, a bad one, from which he never really recovered. Stan Collins moved up as a stop-gap, with Richard Maslen, the Regional Information Officer for the South-West, being summoned to London with a view to taking over as Director permanently. That left a vacancy. Out of the blue, Stan Collins summoned me to his office.

"You come from the South-West, don't you?" he began. I guessed immediately what was coming. "How would you feel about taking over from Richard as RIO? We'll supply you with an NFU car." I was so happy that, for a moment, I didn't know what to say. Mandy and I had decided to get married and were already looking for somewhere to live, out in the commuter belt. A move back to the South-West, for which I'd hankered throughout my time in London, and the prospect of an affordable house in the country, was the stuff of dreams, except ...

"But I can't drive," I blurted out. "I've twice failed my test."

Stan was a bit taken aback, but equal to the occasion. "Right then, lad. We'll give you to the end of the month to pass your test. If you can manage that, the job is yours. If not, it's all off."

That gave me two weeks, which I promptly took as leave, heading back down to Plymouth for some intensive practice and a hastily booked test. I have rarely been so nervous about anything in my entire life, but I passed safely enough, and the celebrations went on long into the night. A few days later I was staying with my father and Rosie at Henleaze in Bristol, having borrowed Mandy's yellow mini to commute to Chippenham for my induction with Richard Maslen. A new chapter had opened.

9

A drop of real ale

I suppose I inherited an appreciation of good beer. When I was small, my father would sometimes bring back to Fursdon a wooden pin of, I'm guessing, Plymouth Breweries Best Bitter and tap it in the conservatory. I loved the beery, hoppy smell. His favourite beer, though, was Worthington E – from the wood. I learned this when we were on holiday in St Ives, because he would spend long hours drinking it in the Porthminster Hotel's public bar, which was his favourite watering hole. He was a member of the Society for the Preservation of Beer from the Wood – the SPBW – which was a rather tweedy, pipe-smoking forerunner of Camra, that spent a lot of time bemoaning the rise of mass-produced, heavily-advertised, artificially carbonated keg beers and very little actually doing anything about it.

This family background did, however, mean that, by the time I started drinking beer, I did understand the difference between cask-conditioned draught beer, served either direct from the barrel or via a handpump, and the keg and top-pressure alternatives. Britain's brewing industry was undergoing a revolution at the time, and not in a good way. The 'Big Six', as they were known – that is to say Watneys, Bass-Charrington, Allied Breweries, Whitbread, Courage and Scottish and Newcastle – had been rapaciously buying up and closing down family-owned regional brewers up and down the country, mainly to get their hands on their pub estates, to the extent that by the late 1960s they owned between them over 60% of the nation's pubs.

The South-West was less affected by this than most regions, perhaps because so many of our local breweries had closed of their own accord. But Whitbread had swallowed up Starkey, Knight and Ford and its 'Tivvy' beers; Courage had bought the famous George's Brewery in Bristol in 1961 and Plymouth Breweries ten years later. In 1972 the six-county South-West region could boast just ten independent brewers: two in Cornwall (St Austell and Devenish), four in Dorset (Palmers, Eldridge Pope, Hall and Wodehouse and Devenish Weymouth), three in Wiltshire (Gibbs Mew,

Wadworths and Arkells), one in Gloucestershire (Donnington) and none at all in Devon or Somerset. The region did have an extensive free trade, but that was dominated by heavily-promoted keg beers like Double Diamond (Allied), Tankard (Whitbread), Tavern (Bass-Charrington) and the dreaded Watney's Red Barrel.

The very first of the 60,000-odd pints I've downed so far in my life was enjoyed at the Byron, a rather nondescript pub, just off the Triangle in Clifton. It was where Chippy and I would head to after getting off the bus from Bath to meet Father on our Sunday lunchtime visits from school. He would be propping up the bar alongside the enormously fat but splendidly cheerful Red Arkinstall, who had once played hooker for Bristol but had rather gone to seed, thanks not least to the 10 or 12 pints of Courage BA (still at that time brewed at George's in Bristol) which he would put away in a session.

It was only in my last term that I was allowed just a single pint, and it always left me slightly dizzy. At home in Devon the first pint I can remember drinking was Draught Bass at the ancient Royal Oak at Meavy, and that would have been between school and Hope Cove, when I was almost 18, so I wasn't by any means an early adopter.

I enjoyed my Morrells at Oxford and was always on the look-out for either Bass or Worthington E in the West Country, but it wasn't until I moved to London in 1972 that my interest in beer really took off, thanks to Youngs and the Britannia. Camra had been founded the previous year by Michael Hardman, Graham Lees, Jim Makin and Bill Mellor, and its West London branch held its meetings at the Britannia. So I decided to go along, which is where I met Ivan Burgess, a BBC engineer, working just up the road at Shepherd's Bush. The branch was just being divided into three, to strengthen the presence in areas like Acton and Twickenham. Ivan became chairman of the most central of the three new branches, with me joining him on the committee as 'publicity officer'. He had a beard and wore sandals over socks. I didn't!

The other big change was that, from now on, meetings would be held in the upstairs room of the Queen's Elm in the Fulham Road. The landlord was Sean Treacy, who wrote about his experiences there in 'A Smell of Broken Glass', and one of his regulars was Laurie Lee. I'm not sure we did much to burnish the Elm's literary credentials when we moved our meetings there, but we did get through a fair number of pints of Courage Best and their new draught beer, Directors, over the next few years.

top: My mother's grandfathers: 'Taid' Hughes *(left)* and 'Taid' Thomas
bottom: The prim and proper Thomas family: Robin, Ruth, Dan and my mother Olwen

top: My father Alan with his father Norman at the Cow and Calf above Ilkley, *bottom: (left)* Norman, Alan and Jenny, *(right)* Alan on holiday with Jenny

(above left) Nine weeks old, with my mother and the Will Soukop donkey at Dartington Hall; *(above right)* leaving Chippy in my wake in the garden at Fursdon with Nain; *(right)* Chippy and me in the studio; *(bottom)* At Blacklands with the Hamlyns: Julia, Chippy, Duncan, Nigel (in the pram) and me.

top: My mother standing for Plymouth City Council,
my father a rising star of the BBC West region;
bottom: Manadon Vale football team 1960 (me fifth from the left in the back row)

top: Two happy brothers in the garden at Larkrise, Summer 1966
bottom: (left) On my 18th birthday at Hope Cove, *(right)* A pair of swells! – Dave Godby
and I on our return to Monkton Combe to see Chippy at half-term, Summer 1967

top: (left) Susie, me, Escourt and Nain, January 1970,
(right) NFU Deputy Press Officer
bottom: Wesley Wyatt's dead sheep, Fitzhead, March 1978

(above) Cider correspondent
with Ken Pringle *(centre)* and
Alan Tringham of Bulmers

(right) The programme for
the second Great British
Beer Festival, 1978

My first wedding
(left) With Mandy
(below) Groom and best man back from the pub in good time for the wedding

One of the first things I did in my new role was to start a newsletter to tell the world about our branch activities, like pub crawls and brewery visits, and to pass on the latest news about pubs that were either taking the handpumps out, or putting them back in, or where you could find unusual real ales.

Pubs under threat of closure was another regular theme, and we did help to save several, perhaps the most notable being the Fox and Hounds in Passmore Street, which is still going strong, now owned by the Youngs successor pubco. It seems an extraordinary thing to say, but the choice of beer in London in the early 1970s was incredibly limited. There was Charrington's IPA, Whitbread bitter from Chiswell St, Courage Best and Directors, Draught Bass, some Ind Coope, plus the beers from our two local breweries, Youngs and Fullers. And that was about it. According to the 2020 edition of the Good Beer Guide, there are 77 breweries in Greater London. In 1973 there were just seven, and two of those, Watneys and Truman, produced no real ale.

Against that background, campaigning was a bit of an uphill struggle, but we gave it our best shot. Every month we would be out pounding the streets of West London, delivering the newsletter to our legion of Charrington pubs, where we were much more likely to encounter the unconverted than in Youngs pubs, all of which served real ale. Fullers was a particular focus. At that time its sphere of influence was very largely confined to the area around the brewery in Chiswick. The first edition of the Good Beer Guide describes the Fullers available at the Star in Belgravia, not far from where I worked in Knightsbridge and a regular port of call, as 'a rare brew for central London'. The company was also toying with the idea of scrapping its cask beers and going all out for keg. Persuading it otherwise was one of Camra's first and most important victories. By 1974 we had even persuaded them to reintroduce a draught dark mild, called Hock.

Going out with Mandy from 1973 onwards served to broaden my beer horizons dramatically. Her parents lived at Whittlesey, in the Cambridgeshire fens to the east of Peterborough, in an area which was then almost totally dominated by Watneys. But that 'almost' was important, because the local exception was the Boat, which served Elgoods of Wisbech by handpump, and very good it was too. It rapidly became my local on visits to the in-laws. Greene King was another new discovery. Most of their pubs had gone over to top pressure, but the Crown at Gayton, where we stopped on the way to the coast at Brancaster, was a notable exception.

However, the pick of the breweries in that neck of the woods was unquestionably Melbourns of Stamford. All of their pubs were in the town so to drink the beer meant travelling to Stamford, which was a good 20 miles away from Whittlesey. I prevailed upon Mandy to do the driving, and many was the happy evening we (or I, at any rate) spent drinking Melbourns' so-distinctive IPA in the Bull and Swan. How sad I was when, a few years later, the brewery closed and was turned into a museum. And how consoled I was when Ivan Burgess got the job as its first curator!

In 1975 Camra had the bright idea of staging a beer festival, more with the aim of generating interest and coverage than in making a profit from selling beer. It wasn't actually called a beer festival. Rather prissily, we branded it as the 'Covent Garden Beer Exhibition', but it was a genuinely national event, with every brewer in the country being invited to provide its products. By now I'd acquired something of a reputation for publicity, as West London was probably Camra's highest profile branch (something that probably had more to do with geography than any great PR skills on my part), and was appointed to the organising committee in that capacity.

There was only one problem. By the time we got around to starting to organise the event and fixing a date in September, I had already booked a holiday with Mandy to Guernsey, and the two clashed. So whilst I did indeed take charge of publicising the event, I wasn't actually there for it. Happily it was a roaring success. Some 40,000 people got through over 150,000 pints of beer over the four days, and the coverage we generated was priceless in terms of attracting new members.

Covent Garden wasn't available for a 1976 event and we couldn't find an alternative, so the next festival wasn't held until the autumn of 1977 at the new venue we had lighted upon, the Alexandra Palace. The Ally Pally might sound like a grand, glamorous home for the festival, but it was in fact rather tatty and run-down at the time, stuck out on a hill-top in the North London suburbs.

On the organising committee we were by no means confident that it would attract the same number of customers as Covent Garden had done, so advance publicity was paramount. It had to be free advance publicity, as well. We had enough money for posters and fliers and so on, but there was nothing in the budget for advertising. As with everything that Camra did in those early days, we had to rely on editorial coverage to publicise what we were up to. It helped no end that our cause always seemed to be particularly popular among the journalistic fraternity.

After a slow start the festival was another success. I can't claim the credit for calling it the Great British Beer Festival – that was a collective decision – but it did give the event a sense of scale and importance which, coupled with the fast-rising interest which there was in this 'real ale', was enough to overcome the difficulties of actually getting there. We managed to persuade 50 breweries from around the country to supply their beers, and total attendance topped 50,000. I did have one bright idea for getting us on the television, and that was to arrange a parade of horse-drawn brewers' drays. They made a magnificent sight as they snorted and stamped along the terrace outside the Palace.

The 1978 Festival, for which I again took on the PR role and edited the 'souvenir brochure', was staged on similar lines. The number of breweries was up from 50 to 70, but it struck me midway through the first day that it was all a bit samey. We needed something new and exciting to get us noticed in the national press. It was as I was walking back through the main hall towards the committee room, after having a pee, that the thought struck me. Here we've got hundreds of the best beers in the country all under one roof. Why not organise a competition to find out which are the best, or at least the most popular? And we could call it the 'Camra Beer of the Year Competition'!

The idea seemed to meet with general approval so I straightaway set to work. A press release was issued, the volunteers manning the bars were asked to nominate their best sellers in each of the various categories – mild, ordinary bitter, special bitter, strong ale and so on. I'd decided that we would do the judging on the following day, using ordinary punters recruited from around the hall. When the time came, I managed to persuade a representative cross-section of ages and sexes to take to the stage and, with me on the PA, away we went. What would eventually become the Camra 'Champion Beer of Britain' competition, one of the most prestigious events in the British brewing calendar, was off and running. I've always regarded it as one of the more notable feathers in my cap.

I never made it to the Camra National Executive, but being based in West London helped generate some top-level invites. One that I remember particularly well was to the Guinness brewery at Park Royal on the North Circular. All of the Camra top brass were there, and we were treated to a tour of the brewery and a slap-up lunch by all of the Guinness top brass, including Geoffery Stocks, the Marketing Director, whose idea this had been. It was a slightly odd piece of PR, given that the majority of the brewery's output was keg, albeit dispensed with the help of nitrogen rather than carbon dioxide so that the gas wasn't absorbed by the beer. On the other hand the brewing process prior to the kegging could hardly have been more traditional, albeit on a huge scale.

Park Royal was like a traditional brewery, to the power of ten. I'd never seen so many mash tuns and coppers in my life. There was also the fact, which I hadn't realised before our visit, that bottled Guinness did at that time qualify as 'real ale' because it was fermented in the bottle to produce the fizz, rather than being artificially carbonated. The process involved siphoning off a percentage of the fermented 'wort' into what they called 'gyle tanks' prior to pasteurisation and bottling and then adding back in just a spoonful or so to each bottle to produce the secondary fermentation.

The whole thing was superbly organised by Geoffery and, as you can tell, has left a lasting impression. I would next encounter him when he'd moved to Taunton as boss of Taunton Cider and, although he died a few years ago, his name remains on my lips every week, thanks to the 'Stocks Foursomes' which he inaugurated at Burnham and Berrow Golf Club and in which it is my great privilege and pleasure to play every Wednesday morning.

Boardroom-level encounters such as this show that Camra was taken seriously as a campaigning force by the giants of the brewing industry, although I always felt that there was a patronising note to their interest, as if to say something like: "Yes, this is all very nostalgic, and you've certainly got a gift for publicity, but it will soon fade away. The future is in convenience, reliability, big brands – and lager!"

Even as recently as five years ago, I had the former head brewer of Courage 'megakeggery' at Reading insisting to me that he and his ilk had been right about beer in the 70s and we had been wrong. The figures suggest otherwise, with well over a thousand breweries now producing real ales of every conceivable description across the country and cask-conditioned ale out-selling even lager. The Campaign for Real Ale has, quite simply, been the most successful consumer campaign in history.

It would be nice to be able to claim that the secret of our success was in the quality of the people like me who rallied to the cause in those early years, but it wouldn't be true. Yes, we have had some truly influential champions, like Richard Boston, Roger Protz, Michael Jackson, Joe Goodwin and Michael Hardman, but the success of the campaign is really just down to the product. Cask-conditioned draught beer, brewed from the finest ingredients and served without the addition of extraneous carbon dioxide is qualitatively different, and arguably better – in the sense of being more interesting and drinkable – than the keg and top-pressure alternatives. All we did in Camra was to point this out to people, as often and as imaginatively as possible. Once they'd tasted the difference the battle was – in most cases – won.

We never set out to destroy keg beers and lagers in the way some of the Big Six had with cask-conditioned ale. We just wanted beer drinkers to be in a position to make an informed choice. In that we succeeded and the results speak for themselves.

Moving out of London wasn't the end of my connection with Camra. Soon after we'd moved to Wiltshire I was given the task of surveying all of the real ale pubs of Trowbridge, for what was one of the first of the county real ale guides. It was not an exercise I would care to repeat. There was only one pub in the entire town that served anything (Wadworths) other than dismal Ushers PA. I did, however, go on to write about cider for Camra's monthly journal, 'What's Brewing', for a good many years. But that's another story.

I think it would be fair to say that I have retained a keen interest in beer. Being something of a nerd, I have kept a complete record of every real ale I have ever sampled. The tally now stands at 2,200 different beers from 930 breweries. I tend to prefer the more traditional brews, not too strong, quite bitter, but with plenty of malt in there as well, rather than the more modern style of ultra-hoppy, citrousy IPAs and golden ales. Among my favourites would be Holts, Donnington, Bathams and, closer to home, St. Austell, Exmoor and Teignworthy. And I still enjoy a pint of Draught Bass, even if it is now brewed by Marstons.

As for pubs we are fortunate in having two of the best in Somerset within a couple of miles, the Halfway House at Pitney and my local, the Rose and Crown at Huish Episcopi, known to everyone as Eli's.

10

Back to the West

I'd passed my driving test on Friday November 28. By 7.30 on the morning of December 1, I was at Sherston in North Wiltshire, to meet up with the outgoing South-West Regional Information Officer, Richard Maslen, and the Producer of the farming programme which he presented every week for BBC Radio Bristol, a certain Kate Adie.

I arrived in Mandy's yellow Mini, Kate was in her white MGB, but it was Richard who drove us to London, in his NFU Morris Marina. Our destination was the Royal Smithfield Show, at Earl's Court. Richard would identify three or four interviewees, with a West Country connection, while Kate would carry the tape recorder and hold the microphone, and I would observe, the plan being that I should inherit the programme as part of my new job.

The BBC was less particular in those days about the journalistic independence of their presenters when it came to a specialist subject like farming. The NFU connection did mean that first Richard and then I had to be careful not to use the programme as a propaganda channel for the NFU and to approach it as would any untrammelled freelance, but it did mean that we were unlikely to run stories which cast the organisation which paid our salaries in anything approaching an unfavourable light.

All went well. Richard found a company demonstrating a sheep shower, as an alternative to a sheep dip (it never caught on), and a beaming Alan Matthews, from Tormarton, having won a class in a strong entry of Aberdeen Angus, was only too happy to tell Richard all about his champion bullock. Alan would be a mainstay of the programme, at the summer as well as the winter shows, for a good many years to come.

Interviews safely in the can, we drove back to Sherston, in pouring rain. When Kate went to start her MGB, nothing happened. Not only that, but she had parked it with the nearside wheels in a ditch. There was nothing for it but for Richard and I to push the wretched thing, with the rain all the time beating down. When we did eventually shift it from the ditch, I was plastered in ordure from the spinning back wheel. It was a baptism of mud!

The following week we were on the road again, this time bound for a remote corner of South-East Dorset, where a farmer called Ron Cranton had been having trouble with bovine tuberculosis in his dairy herd. It was a disease which by the mid 1970s had been eliminated across most of the country, the only remaining pockets of infection being in the far west of Cornwall, along the Cotswold escarpment around Stroud and at Steeple Leaze Farm, which was our destination.

When we got there, we found Ron Cranton hunched in a chair in the big farmhouse kitchen. He looked and sounded a broken man. He told Richard how he had lost more than 200 of his Friesian cows and heifers to TB over the previous three years and that he was convinced that it was badgers that were to blame. The suggestion was soundly based, in that the farm was entirely surrounded by Ministry of Defence firing ranges, so there could be no possibility of the disease having spread from another farm, and no cattle had been bought in during the three years in which the outbreak had raged. But there was now some hope. The reason we were there was that the Ministry of Agriculture had finally accepted the possibility of a link with badgers and were planning a complete cull of the farm and the woodland and scrub around it, a policy that was already being trialled in the TB hotspot around Thornbury in South Gloucestershire.

Three years after that visit, I went back to see Ron Cranton. He was a happy man. The farm was now free of TB and remained so until eventually cows were replaced by corn, with badgers having long since recolonised the cull area. It was my first of a myriad of encounters with the vexed question of bovine TB and badgers. It seemed to me then, as it seems to me now, to be incontrovertible proof that badgers do pass the disease onto cattle and that, if you remove 100% of the infected badger population, at the same time obviously as removing infected cattle, you will eliminate 100% of the problem. It was a strategy ideally suited to relatively small, discrete areas like Thornbury and Steeple Leaze, and it depended for its effectiveness on gassing to achieve 100% clearance.

Had that strategy been pursued to its logical conclusion, we would never have had the TB explosion which started in the 1980s and is still with us today. As it was, gassing was banned as a method of wildlife control in 1982, to be replaced by trapping, which always carried the risk of missing an infected animal which would take the disease elsewhere. When the Dunnett report resulted in trapping being confined only to the farm on which a TB outbreak had occurred – even if the badgers causing the problem were from a sett on the other side of a boundary fence – all hope of eliminating bovine TB had gone.

Gassing was banned because evidence from a trial at Porton Down suggested that badgers in the furthest reaches of a big sett took what was regarded as an unacceptably long time to die when the gas was pumped in. Well, maybe. But in 1979 we were on the verge of ridding the countryside of TB. If gassing had been continued for another two or three years, we might have got there. As it was, for the sake of avoiding a slow death for a relatively small number of badgers over a few years, countless numbers of badgers and cattle have ended up being slaughtered, hundreds of millions of pounds have been spent on disease control and compensation and many thousands of farming families have suffered financial loss, crippling anxiety and abject misery. Never can a single, well-intentioned act of policy have been the cause of so much pain, loss and grief.

I settled into my new role with the NFU comfortably enough. There were no great farming controversies or crises in early 1976, and writing press releases announcing the incoming office-holders for the six South-West counties came easily enough. Rather appropriately, given my interest in beer, my office was in what had once been the pump-house for the Henry Collett brewery at Langley Burrell, three miles north of Chippenham. Why Chippenham, very much at one end of my enormous region, 180 miles from the Cornwall county office in Truro? Because it suited Richard Maslen, who lived just up the road. I soon got used to all the driving which this involved.

For the first time I had my own full-time secretary, a splendidly proportioned, highly efficient lady called Joan Townsend, known always as Mrs T, who looked after me as a mother hen would tend her favourite chick. There was also a part-time secretary, Richard's mother-in-law, Beryl Lindsay, who looked after the filing. The three of us shared the premises with the team who ran the Gloucestershire and Wiltshire county branches, which shared some committees and an administration but couldn't quite bring themselves to merge, as per the HQ master-plan. Gruff Peter Riddick was the top man, his office fiercely guarded by the substantial figure of his secretary Edna, supported by his deputy, Mike Ellingham, whom I'd worked with at HQ and whose NFU career would run parallel to mine almost throughout, and the Horticultural Secretary, Anne Williams. We all got on well together.

But there was one aspect of my new role that I found anything but easy, and that was the weekly BBC Radio Bristol farming programme. Kate Adie,

I should say, could not have been kinder or more patient with her tyro of a presenter. She had come to Bristol from BBC Radio Durham, not as a news reporter primarily but as a features presenter and producer. She shared an office with Frances Kitchen, another lovely lady and the station's cookery specialist, and was also very close to another formidable female broadcaster, Jenni Murray, who had the reputation of being something of a man-eater.

Every week, I would agree with Kate the stories we would cover – one of them almost invariably involving someone from the Ministry of Agriculture's regional office at Westbury-on-Trym, conveniently just up the road from the BBC – then I would go off with my tape-recorder, a Uher, to do the interviews, write a script and turn up at the BBC for Kate to edit the tapes, record my links and put the whole thing together.

It should have been straightforward enough, except that I really wasn't very good. The scripts were stilted and my delivery nervous, but Kate took it all in her stride and succeeded in turning my painful efforts into something broadcastable. She was clearly a rising star, with a great voice, a properly enquiring journalistic instinct and an incisive interviewing style. Even so, I doubt if either us would have believed that, barely four years later, she would achieve world-wide recognition for her reporting of the Iranian Embassy siege in London, going on to become a superb Chief News Correspondent for the BBC, specialising in wars worldwide. And I've dined out ever since on the fact that Kate Adie once edited my farming tapes!

That apart, I enjoyed a gentle introduction to my new role. Mandy and I had already decided to get married, so the move to Wiltshire could not have been better timed. It seemed sensible to buy Richard Maslen's bungalow, half a mile out of the village of Sherston with half an acre of vegetable garden attached, Mandy's parents very generously helping out with the finance.

Our wedding was in beautiful St Andrew's parish church in Whittlesey. Chippy was my best man, and my stag night, the evening before, took the pair of us plus Mandy's two brothers, Simon and Jono, and sundry West London Camra friends, to the Bull at Market Deeping, where we got thoroughly stuck in to the Ruddles County, then one of my favourite beers. Fortunately, the ceremony was timed for Saturday afternoon, allowing me time to recover in the morning and re-charge at the Boat with Chippy before the main business of the day.

It was a splendid, classically English middle-class occasion, in a marquee on the Wills family tennis court, featuring, if memory serves, three different real ales. The highlight of the proceedings was when, during the speeches, I was solemnly presented with a special extra present by Mandy's father Peter. It came in a large cardboard box, and I was asked to open it immediately. After rummaging through endless layers of packing material, I eventually discovered a large potato – the crop on which the Wills family fortunes had been built, as both growers and merchants, and thus very much the founder of this feast. It was a lovely moment.

A St Valentine's Day wedding meant a February honeymoon. We couldn't afford anything exotic like skiing. Instead, I had decided that we should visit Bishop's Castle in Shropshire, partly because I had never been to Shropshire and had been told that the little town was a lovely spot, but mainly because it was home to one of only five pubs in England which still brewed their own beer – the Three Tuns. What was more, to get there we could drive through the Black Country, stopping off at another home-brew pub, Ma Pardoe's Old Swan at Netherton, while 20 miles or so from Bishop's Castle, in the Ironbridge Gorge, there was a third, Mrs Lewis's All Nations, which we visited on our second day of married life. On the way back to Wiltshire we stopped at Tintern in the Wye Valley, more, I'm ashamed to say, because it meant I could have a pint or two at the Cherry Tree than for the glories of the abbey just up the road. And poor Mandy didn't even much like beer!

The big farming story of 1976 was, of course, the great drought. The summer of 1975 had been hot and sunny, and the winter that followed was one of the driest on record. Among what I liked to think of as 'my' counties it was, typically enough, Devon where the alarm bells first sounded. On April 2, after a meeting of the County Executive Committee in Exeter, I issued a press release warning that 'West Country farmers face a water shortage of frightening proportions', quoting Harold Retallick, one of the county's delegates to the HQ Council and a splendidly hard-bitten hill farmer from Haytor, where his family still farm, as saying: "Many reservoirs are little more than puddles. Anyone relying on mains water supplies for watering cattle will be in terrible difficulties."

I went on to say that the county branch had written to the South-West Water Authority, as it then was, warning that emergency measures such as standpipes would be useless for farmers with herds of livestock to water, adding, by way of information that 'a dairy cow drinks up to 50 gallons of water a day'.

Oh dear. It wasn't long before I had Hugh Crowle, the fearsome county secretary of Devon NFU and a man who never had any time for regional information officers under any circumstances, on the phone.

"Christ," he shouted down the line. "What on earth did you write that for? A cow drink 50 gallons of water a day? She'd be a bowser on four legs. You've made us a laughing stock."

I, of course, had no idea how much water a cow might drink in a day. It turned out that what I should have written was what we issued as an 'erratum' – that a cow uses up to 50 gallons of water a day, drinking maybe 15, with the rest being used in the milking parlour for washing down and so on. And there was a price beyond humble pie to pay for my mistake.

"You will never, ever, issue any form of statement on behalf of the Devon County Branch without me personally having cleared it beforehand," I was instructed. Message received and understood.

We had no rain to speak of that spring, but it didn't get really hot until towards the end of June. For 15 consecutive days from June 23, temperatures exceeded 90 degrees. July and most of August were searingly hot and almost entirely dry. A plague of aphids was swiftly followed by a plague of ladybirds. All across the region, but particularly around our home in Wiltshire, the elms were dying, symbolic, so it seemed to me, of a countryside slowly expiring from heat exhaustion. The corn harvest, which was under way in South Dorset even before the end of June, was the earliest in living memory, but yields were often pitiful. In the weekly 'harvest reports' that Mrs T and I compiled and issued, I was quoting Ken May, from the Exe Valley, bemoaning just a ton per acre from his winter barley, against an expectation of more than twice that, while up on the Cotswolds, Cyril Davidson-Smith, was describing his winter cereals as "the thinnest and poorest I have ever cut – like chaff".

But if the drought was bad for cereal growers, it was worse for the livestock men, and the South-West, more so then than now, was fundamentally a livestock region. Cuts of hay and silage had been light, pastures were turning brown, barley straw was being fed straight off the combine and milk yields only sustained thanks to expensive supplementary feed. My friend, the novelist Peter Benson, vividly captures the essence of that memorable summer in his novel 'Two Cows and a Vanful of Smoke', set in around the village of Ashbrittle in West Somerset:

Day after day the sun shone in deep blue skies and baked the land dry. It was hot before it rose, and when it rose it laughed at the country. On the moors and heaths, fires broke out and frightened animals from their holes. Trees were burnt to sticks, lakes dried, bushes exploded. In other places, tarmac melted and birds failed in their flight. Hosepipes were banned, stand-pipes were used and wells and springs dried up. Politicians told us to share bath water. Ashbrittle wheezed and sweated, and in the middle of the day, dogs collapsed in the road and refused to move. The green browned and yellowed, and flowers withered. Cows lay in the shade of trees, horses panted, fish died and floated in rivers that turned to drains. Every day people would stand in their gardens and stare at their parched vegetables and search the sky for rain. Sometimes a single cloud would appear and float slowly over the village, but it was only a single cloud, white and fluffy – and nothing. And as it disappeared over the horizon, the people would shake their heads and go back inside and do whatever they had to do.

By the middle of July the only remaining green pastures east of Exeter were on the Somerset Levels, and even there problems were appearing as the rhynes, which served as both 'wet fences' and as often the only source of drinking water for dairy and beef cattle, dried up. Further west, it wasn't quite so bad. West Cornwall got most of whatever rain was going, with a lovely man called Fred Hain, who farmed near Redruth and who would go on to become Cornwall NFU Chairman, reporting barley yields "well up to expectations" and adding that, although milk yields were down, "the cattle are holding their condition and look remarkably well."

Another of the very few areas actually to enjoy that blazing summer was the Culm Measures in mid and north Devon, that land of mud and rushes, usually some of the most difficult in the entire region. I quoted Gerald Manning, who farmed at Witheridge, as saying that "the good old sticky clay has really come into its own in the last two years", while Allin Bewes at Newton St Petrock up near Torrington reported that his corn was "looking extremely good and yields should be excellent."

Even so, for most farmers across the South-West this was a genuine crisis, and in genuine crises farmers' leaders need to be seen to be doing something about it. So in early August a programme of visits was arranged for the NFU's national office-holders. Sadly for me and for the farmers, the South-West wasn't allocated the President, Henry Plumb. Instead we had to make do with the less than charismatic Deputy President, Richard Butler, 'Rab' Butler's eldest son. As a wealthy East Anglian arable farmer with over 2,000 acres of prime land to his name, educated at Eton and Cambridge, with a father who had been a cabinet minister and a brother, Adam, on the way to becoming one, Richard Butler could be a hard sell to a West County farming audience. But if he rarely had anything much of great interest to say, he was at least a good listener and, on a tour of drought-hit farms in Devon and Somerset, that is all you really needed to be.

We started the tour to the south of Exeter, which is always the driest part of Devon. I remember being particularly struck by a youngish couple, John and Audrey Compton, who were milking 100 Jersey cows at Ashwater near Dawlish and who had seen no worthwhile rain since the end of March. They told Richard Butler that they had had to spend an extra £3,800 on supplementary feed for the cows over the previous ten weeks – over £20,000 at 2020 prices – and looking at their anxious faces and a desert of a farm, I didn't doubt it for a moment.

Peter Lethbridge, that year's Devon NFU Chairman, acted as host for the visit. He was the perfect county chairman for a high-profile occasion like this. He presented the situation honestly and eloquently, without exaggeration or special pleading, and in the process did the cause of the wider farming community a power of good. There have been few more intelligent, thoughtful and balanced leaders of farming opinion in my time with the NFU.

Even so, it was a hot, dusty, wearying and pretty depressing tour. From Dawlish, we went to Woodbury where they'd recorded just one and a half inches of rain since March, then on to Pinhoe to meet a vegetable grower who had had to fallow half of his 80 acres, before heading for Somerset. I did my best to shepherd the gentlemen, as they mostly were in those days, of the press, setting up interviews, providing further contacts and so on, whilst at the same time recording my own interviews for my farming programme and pausing at convenient phone boxes to relay my reports of proceedings, via Mrs T, whose shorthand was excellent, to the wider world.

However, this did tend to mean that I periodically fell behind the main party. At lunchtime on the first day, I found myself near Honiton, en route to the Somerset Levels. Never one to pass up the opportunity to visit a good pub, whatever the circumstances, I paused for refreshment at the Drewe Arms, in the almost impossibly chocolate-box village of Broadhembury. I'd heard good things about it and wasn't disappointed. All those thatched roofs simply shimmered in the heat as I laid the dust in my throat with a pint of Bass in the cool, dark corridor which served then as a bar.

We finished that day at Wynyard's Gap, on the Somerset-Dorset border, which is where I stayed the night, metaphorically girding my loins for another day of heat, dust and depression on the morrow. I wasn't wrong about that. There were familiar tales of scorched pastures, shrivelled corn and failed fodder crops at farms from Burton Bradstock in the west of Dorset to Wimborne in the east. Our final port of call was at perhaps the driest spot in the entire region, Worth Matravers in the Purbecks, where Peter Strange was strip-grazing his dairy cows on fat hen, a weed with roots deep enough to reach the moisture far below. It was all grist to the NFU's mill, in terms of seeking help from the Government in the shape of re-seeding grants, the averaging of taxation and – a demand with which I would become depressingly familiar over the next ten years or so – a 'devaluation of the Green Pound'.

The 'green' rates were the fixed rates of exchange at which EEC farm support prices were translated into the various national currencies. Without them, prices would have fluctuated every day (as eventually became the case) in line with foreign exchange rates. For a country like the UK, with a weak currency, this denied farmers the benefits they would otherwise have enjoyed from dearer imports, cheaper exports and higher support prices. The UK Government was quite happy with the system, as it tended to keep consumer prices down, and conceded the devaluations that the NFU was always asking for only with the utmost reluctance. But as a central message of NFU policy, it had to be said that 'Devalue the Green Pound to boost British agriculture' lacked a certain resonance with the general public.

That August, as the sun beat down, the reservoirs dried up and the standpipes appeared in village streets, seems in the memory to have consisted almost entirely of drought tours. No sooner was Richard Butler safely back in London than the Government decided it ought to get in on the act, and the Minister of Agriculture, Fred Peart, was despatched to the West Country to demonstrate an appropriate degree of concern, preferably without any spending commitments attached.

Fred Peart was good at this sort of thing. He was a gregarious man, who enjoyed company as much as he enjoyed a drink, and that included the company of farmers. Meetings were arranged at Bickenhall near Taunton, for the Somerset, Wiltshire and Gloucestershire NFU representatives, at Holditch for Dorset and finally at Pinhoe just outside Exeter for Devon and Cornwall. But, as with Richard Butler, he failed to cross the Tamar, an omission that was so much resented that I was asked to issue a special press release on Cornwall NFU's behalf, regretting the absence of a visit and emphasising that 'conditions in Cornwall are quite as bad as those in the areas the Minister had visited.'

Cornwall did have good grounds for being aggrieved at what was perceived as a snub, for the NFU in the county was still feeling bruised from the experience of the previous year's drought. Then, as in 1976, there were fears of a serious shortage of fodder, straw in particular, for feeding and winter bedding. But in East Anglia there were reports of ample supplies of straw, much of which would end up being burnt if a use wasn't found for it. So Cornwall NFU decided to organise what was called a 'Strawtrek' to bring surplus straw from the East to needy farmers in the far West. It was a fine idea and generated massive coverage on television and in the press, all of it favourable. This was co-ordinated farmer self-help. It showed the NFU at its very best.

A gang of volunteer farmers and young farmers was duly despatched to Cambridgeshire, to buy, bale and load onto lorries the straw that would be the salvation of Cornish dairy and livestock farmers during the coming winter. And they were well received, not least because they paid good money for straw which would otherwise have been almost worthless. There was, however, a flaw in the plan. It depended on farmers in Cornwall being prepared to buy the straw at the price which had been paid for it, and all too often they weren't. As usual, the severity of the crisis had been exaggerated. Straw was available more cheaply through the usual commercial channels.

Had Cornwall NFU merely been acting as an intermediary, putting willing buyers in touch with willing sellers, then all would have been well. But by buying the straw and then hoping to sell it, they left themselves horribly exposed. The result was first that many of the East Anglian farmers didn't initially get paid for their straw, my father-in-law among them, and second, that when the debts were finally cleared, Cornwall NFU was left with a deficit of something over £60,000, or over half a million pounds at today's prices. As the then Cornwall NFU County Secretary, Tony Robathan, remarked to me rather ruefully as I was writing this account, "The road to Hell is paved with good intentions."

Now this had all happened before I'd been sent to the South-West. But I was there for the painful aftermath. In June 1976 a special in-camera meeting of the County Executive Committee was called in Truro, to be attended by the Vice-President of the NFU, John Cossins, deputising for Henry Plumb. To cut a long story short, NFU HQ had agreed to write off the debt, with the NFU Mutual also chipping in, in exchange for the 'Cornwall Farmers' Union' changing its name to the Cornwall county branch of the National Farmers' Union and ending its association with the

Cornish Mutual Insurance Company, shifting its allegiance instead to the NFU Mutual. It was a tense, unhappy meeting, which ended dramatically with the previous year's county chairman, Venning Davey, accepting responsibility for what had taken place, resigning from all his NFU offices and walking out of the meeting to a deafening silence.

On the following Monday I put out a press release saying that Cornwall NFU would be ending its contract with the Cornish Mutual and would from October 1 have the NFU Mutual as its official insurer. I quoted Henry Plumb as saying that he fully expected the decision to be honoured and supported by all members in Cornwall and that the county branch would go forward with renewed unity and strength. Having been at the meeting, and knowing something of the Cornish character, I can't say I wrote those words with any conviction or belief. It seemed to me, as I knew it would seem to very many Cornish farmers, that the NFU nationally had taken advantage of an unfortunate situation both to humiliate Cornwall NFU and effectively to force it into changing its insurer.

The Cornish are proud of being different, proud of being Cornish and they have long memories. It would surely have been far preferable, in terms of long-term relationships, if HQ had simply bailed out the county branch and allowed Cornwall to decide to change its official insurer in their own good time, as I have no doubt, given the strength and success of the NFU Mutual, they would have done. But to make the one decision conditional on the other created a resentment which lingered for many years.

But back to the drought, and any relief I may have been feeling at what seemed to me to have been the successful conclusion of one drought tour was quickly snuffed out by the news that I would have to undertake another; this time in East Anglia, where they were between Regional Information Officers. I suppose I should have been pleased that they had asked me rather than one of my more experienced colleagues and, with the tour due to finish on the Friday before the Bank Holiday, it did mean that I would be in the right part of the world for a long weekend at Whittlesey with Mandy and her family.

John Cossins was the main man on this occasion, and the form was much as before, albeit with more emphasis on crops like carrots and potatoes and rather less on grazing livestock. We finished up in Suffolk, where the landscape seemed, if anything, slightly less parched than most of the South-West. Shortly before I left for East Anglia, on August 24, Dennis Howell, the genial Brummie Minister of Sport, who had once been a football referee and loved his cricket, was appointed Minister for Drought. On Sunday

August 29, the first thunderstorms broke across the country. On Bank Holiday Monday it fairly tipped down. Spalding, just up the road from Whittlesey, had 76 mm in a day. Never can a ministerial appointment have produced such instant success!

After that it just kept on raining. Mandy and I had planned what I called a 'busman's holiday' taking in Exmoor (ploughing controversy), West Penwith (bovine TB) and a final day on the Scillies, my most remote outpost of empire, to meet Penny Rogers, the NFU's part-time but supremely capable Secretary on the islands and her father-in-law, David, our Chairman. A storm broke as we made our way back to Penzance on the Scillonian. I headed for the bar, and the bar-stools on swivels which kept the drinker on an even keel no matter how alarmingly the boat pitched and plunged, while Mandy curled up in the foetal position on the bottom deck. I don't get sea-sick, so the voyage itself was fine. But when I got to Penzance, I found I'd almost entirely lost my sense of balance and almost fell over on the quayside. We made a frighteningly storm-tossed journey back to stay with my mother at Colebrook, this on the night that half of Polperro was washed away. It was several days before the world around me stopped rising and falling.

The regular points of reference around which my working life revolved in those days were the County Executive Committees. They met every month, barring a late summer break for harvest, and consisted of delegates elected by the local branches, plus representatives of more specialised interests like poultry, pigs and horticulture. The county's delegates to HQ Council would give their reports on the farming issues of the day, debate would ensue, sometimes heated, and resolutions would be passed, demanding this, deploring that or threatening the other. I couldn't go to all of them, as both Gloucestershire and Somerset met on the first Monday after HQ Council, with Wiltshire, Dorset and Cornwall on the Wednesday and Devon – first in line as always – on the Friday immediately after the London meeting. But I went to as many as I could, to take the farming temperature, record a few interviews and, usually, to issue a press release summarising whatever was the main outcome of the meeting. Each had its own particular flavour.

Devon prided itself on being the NFU's largest county branch and on being its bolshiest. Back in the 70s even more so than now, it was a county of small, family farms, roughly 50/50 owned and rented, often on difficult land, particularly in the west and north of the county and, of course, on the two moors. An important ingredient in the Devon farming mix was the post-war influx of first generation farmers, drawn to the county by relatively low land prices and very often borrowed up to the hilt against the 1947 Agriculture Act's promise of guaranteed prices. As the security of that system was gradually eroded and inflation took its toll on interest rates, so militancy grew. Wallace Day, who had been a Ministry adviser during the war before buying a dairy farm at Yelland near Barnstaple, both typified and acted as an unofficial leader for this faction of angry, not so young men. In the late 60s he had resigned from the NFU and started his own, militant, Farmers' Action Group. By my time he was back in the fold, although the animosity between him and Hugh Crowle was palpable.

Devon NFU has always suffered from what I would call a 'superiority complex'. Not content with holding day-long County Executive Committee meetings of anything up to 80 delegates in the imposing county office in Queen Street, Exeter (now the Farmers Union pub) immediately after every HQ Council, they also had a 'Council' of their own, when over 200 farmers would gather in the ballroom at the Rougemont Hotel, just down the road.

Wallace Day would stand with his foot on a chair to give his Council report, and there would invariably be vociferous contributions from the likes of Ian Pettyfer, Michael Phillipson, Geoffery Cox and big John Ley, who had the loudest voice of all. Devon produced some good chairmen – Michael Lee, Gerry Symons, Bill Salter as well as Peter Lethbridge spring to mind – and some highly capable Council delegates, like Bill Hosking, Robin Gallup, Len Hallet and Harold Retallick.

But it was Hugh Crowle who was the master of ceremonies. He was happy enough to listen to the militant tendency sounding off, but by force of personality and shrewd drafting he always made absolutely sure that what he regarded as the correct outcome was reached. At Executive Committees in the county office, I would sit almost literally at his feet, the top table on its platform, me in the front row, to listen and learn. The way he harnessed and channelled the grassroots passion seemed to me to be exactly how an NFU county should be run. When I in turn became a county secretary, Hugh was my role model, even if I did lack his Machiavellian streak!

Cornwall was, of course, different. The county office in Truro was a rather ugly, late-Victorian villa up the hill from the river, with a functional early-60s extension tacked on which housed the Cornwall Farmers Club and the meeting room. The mood at County Executive Committees tended to be rumbustious, slightly chaotic, laced with humour. Although Cornwall did have its share of first generationers, the majority of delegates were from farms that had been in their families not just for generations, but for centuries. You could tell from their accents not just that they were Cornish, but what part of Cornwall they came from, the rich burr of the far west contrasting with the rasping tones of Bodmin Moor and the north, and the softer brogue of the South-East.

In Cornwall, meetings tended to take their cue not so much from the personality of the county secretary, for Tony Robathan was happy to keep an unobtrusive profile, as from the two Council delegates, the two Johns. John Badcock, who grew early potatoes and broccoli at Lelant and was a major player at HQ and on the Potato Marketing Board, and John Bennett, a livestock and corn farmer from near Truro. Both were big men, with big personalities, who enjoyed a drink off-duty and who would deliver colourful, if not always entirely accurate accounts of what was going on in London, which were much appreciated by the assembled company.

However, Cornwall was different from the other South-West counties in one other respect: it had two women members of the county executive, Mrs Whitehouse, who championed the interests of 'marginal land' farmers, and Mrs Mash, who didn't have much time for humorous Cornish banter and whose contributions were always sharply delivered and to the point.

At one meeting Mrs Mash interrupted John Badcock's monologue to inquire crisply what precisely the NFU was going to do about low beef prices, or some such. "If the good lady would 'ave a bit more patience and allow me to finish, I was just coming to that," came the magisterial reply. Whereupon John Bennett, sitting alongside, dug his fellow delegate in the ribs and said, in a stage whisper that could be heard through the entire room, "Cor, you mashed 'er, John; you sure enough mashed 'er."

Dorset was, and as far as I know remains, the most gentlemanly and cerebral of the NFU's South-Western counties. The first chairman I worked with, in 1976, was Rear Admiral Tom Best, who grew apples and strawberries at Melplash in his retirement from a highly distinguished naval career and who could command a roomful of farmers with the lightest of touches. Commander John Streatfeild, from the other side of Bridport, was another retired naval officer who commanded huge respect. Among the indigenous farming community there was a bit of a divide between the Farmer Boldwoods of the Dorchester area and further east and the Gabriel Oaks of the West and the Blackmore Vale, but they shared a civilised, open-minded approach to whatever were the issues of the day. The County Executive Committee could boast only two real militants: Tom Horsington, a dairy farmer from Godmanstone, a small man with seemingly a big chip permanently on his shoulder, and John Lawrence, another dairy farmer, from Sherborne, who would bellow his disgust from the back of the room.

The two Council delegates were Bob Saunders, whom we have already encountered and who, whatever his political background, knew his stuff; and Simon Chick, who farmed in a big way on the downs above Maiden Newton and was a big cheese in FMC, the former meat co-operative, now just a company, which the NFU had rather messily taken over the previous year. Dorset could also boast the NFU's Vice-President, in John Cossins, and the Chairmanship of the Milk Marketing Board, in the infinitely urbane personage of Sir Richard Trehane.

Despite the occasional outburst from Messrs Horsington and Lawrence, meetings of the County Executive Committee, whether in the historic county office in High West Street (next door to the courtroom from which that vile man Jefferies sent so many honest Somerset and Dorset yeomen to their doom) or in the handsome surroundings of Kingston Maurward Agricultural College, were always civilised and considered. In this the farmers took their lead not just from the likes of Tom Best and Bob Saunders but even more so from their County Secretary, 'Mitch' Mitchell, who, with his flowing white beard and slight Dorset burr, always reminded me a lot of the great Dorset dialect poet and polymath supreme, William Barnes, whom Mitch greatly admired. He was another retired naval officer with a distinguished war record and was never anything less than kind and helpful to me. A lovely man, as indeed was Alan Roberts who succeeded him.

Wiltshire NFU reflected, inevitably, the county's characteristic combination of chalk and cheese – 'chalk' being the big arable farmers on the downs, 'cheese' the small dairy farmers in the vales – although there was also a third element: the dairy and corn farms on the mixture of clay soils and Cotswold brash of the north of the county.

Colonel John Littlewood, a legendary martinet of a county secretary who suffered fools neither gladly nor at all, had retired not long before I moved to the West Country, but his influence lingered on. Not least in the conduct of County Executive meetings, which he would never tolerate lasting for more than an hour and a half (Devon's went on all day). Wiltshire's meetings remained brief and to the point. Gillie Swanton, a big dairy farmer from the Swindon area, usually gave the Council report, which consisted of Gillie explaining why everything that HQ Council (or HQ Milk Committee) had decided was bad and wrong. John Bush, who was Chairman of Wiltshire in 1978, the same year that his brother Anthony chaired Somerset (both of them Old Monktonians), and who would go on to become Lord Lieutenant, provided some calming, intelligent balance. The cheese faction were heavily outnumbered by the chalk brigade, but a small band of County Council smallholders from the Mere area, led by the redoubtable Fred Morgan, more than kept their end up. Small in stature as well as in size of farm, they would pop up like Hobbits from the back of the meeting to have their four pennorth.

Farming in Gloucestershire also falls roughly into three parts: the Cotswolds, the Vale and that strange corner of the West Country and law unto itself, the Forest of Dean. Meetings of the County Executive Committee in the big county office in Gloucester always seemed to have a slightly aggressive edge to them, without quite the passion that you found in Devon or the humour of Cornwall. Bill Pullin, father of John, the great Bristol, England and British Lions hooker, spoke forcefully for the dairy farmers of the Vale. Another wonderful character was Fred Warner, from Tewkesbury, who was chairman in 1979. He had a Malapropian tendency to mangle his words. The meeting would do its collective best to suppress the laughter whenever the possible merger with Wiltshire was being discussed and Fred would speak out forcefully against 'the amalmagation'.

But in one respect Gloucestershire was the most enlightened of my six counties, being the first to elect a woman chairman, Janet Kirkwood, who farmed dairy and corn south of Gloucester and was more than capable of holding her own in a roomful of grumpy men.

And so to Somerset which, rather like the county itself, was an odd mixture, with a bit of everything. Somerset does, of course, have a proud history of rebellion going back to the Civil War (albeit more so in its towns than the countryside), and elements of that did surface from time to time in the 1970s (and rather more so when I took over in the 80s!). But for the most part, meetings took their cue from the impeccably polite, invariably punctilious County Secretary Charles Evison, from whom I learned almost as much as I did from Hugh Crowle. The county's two delegates to HQ, Paul Francis and Ralph Baker, were two of the South-West's brightest stars. Paul had taken over from Bob Saunders as Chairman of the Public Relations Committee at HQ as well as being the Mid-West regional member of the MMB, with Ralph on his way to chairing the HQ Animal Health Committee. Paul not so much spoke his reports as growled them, all the time filling his pipe, taking a few puffs and then emptying it again, so that by the end of the meeting his ash-tray would be piled high with unsmoked tobacco. He was a tough, shrewd operator; not a man whom it would pay to cross, although kindly enough under that gruff shell. Ralph was very much the rising star, a hard-driving, fast-expanding dairy farmer from Meare, who lacked patience with the rather sleepy ways of his fellow Somerset Levels farmers. I think it would be fair to say that he was respected, rather than particularly liked, by his fellow farmers.

Somerset was not a county which in those days tended to rock the NFU boat, although that rebellious streak was always lurking just below the surface, and before long the county would find itself at the forefront of two controversies of national importance, of which more anon.

There were some recurring themes in the 120 or so press releases that we issued in each of my five years as Regional Information Officer. There was the wretched Green Pound, of course, while pig farmers seemed to be in trouble at regular intervals, courtesy of that familiar double-whammy of cheap imports and high feed prices. A demonstration that we staged in Bristol in May 1977 featured prominently in The Times, reported by Hugh Clayton, the paper's Agricultural Correspondent:

> Farmers tried to win the hearts and minds of British families with sausages on Friday. They drove through fields replete with buttercups and cow parsley to stage a demonstration about pigs in the most apt setting, a gigantic, concrete shopping parade. The farming lobby's unerring sense of street theatre and the allure of free sausages broke through the reserve of the shopping crowds.

Two years later, we were back on the streets, this time of Taunton and Plymouth, in support of the West Country apple growers whose businesses were being undermined by what we liked to refer to as 'Golden Disgustings' from France. Our friends across the Channel also copped a lot of the blame for problems in the egg industry. A serious diplomatic incident was only narrowly avoided (by a grovelling apology) after I'd issued a tongue-in-cheek press release suggesting that the French agricultural attaché, one Jean-Batiste Danel might be facing a hard time at a meeting of Devon egg producers he was due to attend. 'West Country egg men are expected to be demanding Jean-Batiste's head on a charger after M Danel enters the chickens' den in Tavistock tomorrow,' I wrote. The French Embassy were not amused, and nor was the NFU's Director-General.

Another running sore was the periodic attempts made by French sheep farmers, or their Government, to interfere with the growing export trade in

West Country lamb. It wasn't hard to win public sympathy for farmers if the French could be shown as the bogeymen. Sometimes we would threaten retaliation against all of the imports of cauliflower – broccoli as the crop is called in Cornwall – that were arriving on the Roscoff ferry. It was all good knockabout stuff, which I don't think made any real difference to the way trade developed. It was, after all, what joining the 'Common Market' was supposed to be about. But it earned us plenty of column inches and airtime, kept the farming troops happy and played well with West Country consumers, which was what is was all about.

The weather was another constant in our output. There seem to have been a lot of climatic extremes in those years. Hard on the heels of the 1976 drought came the miserably wet summer of 1977, with some farmers still struggling to harvest their corn into December. Then in March 1978 we had a great blizzard. We were still living in North Wiltshire at the time and missed the worst of the snowfall. But further west the situation was dire.

At Fitzhead Farms, west of Taunton, the roof of a brand-new sheep shed collapsed under the weight of eight feet of snow, killing or badly injuring scores of ewes and their lambs. One of the partners in the business, Wesley Wyatt, had had to acquire a humane killer to despatch the most seriously injured. When I reached the farm on the Monday morning, the television cameras were already there. One of the reporters asked Wes if the animals were insured. "Insured?" he exploded. "Insured? Why would I be talking about insurance when I've got my livestock to think about? At the moment, they're my only concern." It was genuine and heartfelt, and it did the farming cause a power of good.

Two other things were noteworthy about that particular episode, the first being the birth (premature, as it turned out) of BBC Radio Somerset, set up in a broom cupboard in Taunton's Castle Hotel by Peter Davies and Derek Woodcock to provide information and help to the county in what was a genuine crisis. The second was two broadcasting debuts: my first live television appearance, when I featured on a Westward Television 'Blizzard Special' on the Monday evening, and my first report for BBC Radio 4's 'Farming Today', to which I would continue to contribute sporadically for several years until someone in the upper echelons of the Beeb got wind that I was not quite the freelance I appeared.

A few days later Henry Plumb arrived, to survey the damage and make the case for assistance (which did eventually materialise) from the EEC's 'Disaster Fund'. I did my best to keep up with him, battling along snowbound lanes in my NFU Morris Marina, but had to give up when he travelled by helicopter to visit the snowiest area of all, Exmoor, leaving me drift-bound just south of Wheddon Cross. It was a month before the last farm – John Pugsley's at Hawkridge – was relieved.

The following winter – the winter of discontent, as it became known – was unremittingly grim. Heavy snow over the New Year was followed by a severe frost in January, which wiped out half of the Cornish broccoli crop, and there was more snow in February. Then, at the end of May, came the deluge, almost washing away the Royal Bath and West Show and leaving 40,000 acres of the Somerset Levels under water and subsequently contaminated with silt, at the worst possible time of year. The only consolation for a beleaguered farming community was Mrs Thatcher winning the General Election that month. I was at a meeting of the Devon Executive as the final results came through on the Friday morning and, my goodness, weren't the farmers happy after two and a half years of being left to the not-so-tender mercies of the abrasive John Silkin.

All of these issues and exigencies were well and fulsomely reported in our local and regional media. In a farming region it was not hard to generate positive coverage for farming issues. Whenever a big story broke, I would be on the phone for hours at a time. I worked according to two golden rules: always to be as helpful and pleasant as I could, no matter how daft or tendentious the inquiry, and never to say 'no comment', and I've tried to live up to them ever since. The doyen of South-West farming journalism in those years was Jim Butcher, the Agricultural Correspondent of the Western Morning News, based in Plymouth. Jim was the very opposite of an imposing figure; a podgy little man in glasses, with a pronounced Barnstaple accent. But he knew his stuff, could churn it out and had a healthy suspicion of the influence of the established farming lobby, which sometimes brought him into conflict, not so much with me as with Hugh Crowle and the Devon big battalions.

Curiously the WMN's opposite number, the Western Daily Press, based in Bristol and covering a huge area from Dorset to Herefordshire, didn't have a farming correspondent as such. I tended to deal with the various district reporters, Chris Rundle based at Minehead most prominent among them. But the paper hadn't had a farming specialist since Bruce Noble – 'Man O'Mendip' as he styled himself – had retired a good many years before.

A chap called Anthony Collins, who was a lecturer at the Royal Agricultural College, had been writing a rather desultory column for the

Saturday edition, which carried a huge amount of farm-related advertising, and, when he decided he'd had enough, in autumn 1977, Peter Gibbs, the News Editor, asked me if I would like to take the column on, writing under a pseudonym so as not to betray the NFU connection. Living as I was in Sherston I opted for George Sherston, which had also been the pen name of Siegfried Sassoon, a writer whom I've always greatly enjoyed. For the first few columns I was conscientiousness personified, driving all the way to East Dorset for the first one, to write about the heat-exchangers which one of the Tory family had installed in his milking parlour to save energy.

But I have to confess that, as the years went by and my responsibilities multiplied, the George Sherston column got pushed further and further towards the fag end of the working week, last thing on a Friday. Not that I ever let the paper down. I knew perfectly well that, as a precarious freelance, if you failed to deliver the goods on time and in good order, you couldn't expect to last long and there would be no shortage of takers should the column come up for grabs.

I rarely if ever received any feedback from my editors on my efforts, but they cannot have been all bad, because a couple of years later I was summoned to Bristol to meet the new editor, Ian Beales, successor to the legendary Eric Price, who had had the bright idea of launching a mid-week farming column, rather more gossipy and opinionated than the Saturday straight piece. It would be called 'Grassroots', and he wondered if I would like to write it. He told me this over steak and chips at Horts Restaurant, just around the corner from the WDP building.

"Now, what about a name for you?" he mused. "I know, we'll call you Giles, because that's a proper farming Christian name, and Horton, after Horts restaurant. Giles Horton – that's who you'll be every Wednesday."

So that was settled. I would be George Sherston on Saturdays and Giles Horton on Wednesdays. The money wasn't great – the prospect of getting me on the cheap was no doubt one of the main attractions – but it came in handy, given that I'd got a mortgage to pay and a young family to raise.

Initially, only a very few people (including, I should say, my bosses at the NFU) knew the true identity of the WDP's two farming columnists but, as the years went by and I became better known, word gradually seeped out. I got myself into trouble a few times, particularly with the Giles Horton column. I was once visited by a delegation from Monsanto's European head office in Switzerland after I'd written something very critical of their new wonder-drug, the milk yield-boosting hormone called Bovine

Somatotrophin, or BST. But for the most part, no matter how hard I tried to provoke a response, feedback from the farming community was noticeable mainly for its absence, which I assumed meant that it was being well-received. However, my complacency was rather rudely shattered one evening when I was asked to talk to the NFU's Wells local branch about farming and the media and invited questions at the end.

A nice man called Gordon Talbot was one of my questioners. "I accept what you say about most journalists being fair and unbiased in the way they report farming issues", he began. "But there is just one of them I really can't stand: that Giles Horton, who writes in the Western Daily Press every Wednesday!"

More than somewhat taken aback, all I could think of in reply was: "I hear what you say, Gordon, but I'm sure his heart is in the right place!"

I had my rules as far as the freelance broadcasting and writing was concerned, as well. I would not slavishly trumpet NFU policy and campaigns, but then nor would I write or broadcast anything that might be seen as anti-farmer or anti-agriculture. It seemed to me reasonable that an agricultural correspondent should be broadly supportive of the industry he was writing about, and that was the position I tried to take. I did cross swords with my NFU bosses on some issues, like milk quotas, and some aspects of the BSE crisis and, most pointedly, the role that vaccination ought to play in tackling the 2001 Foot and Mouth outbreak, but they were the exception rather than the rule.

I would go on to write columns for the Somerset County Gazette and the Western Morning News, which we will come to in due course, as well as broadcasting farming programmes for BBC Radio Bristol and BBC Somerset Sound for over 20 years. But with the WDP I wrote the Grassroots column for 21 years, hardly missing a single week, even for holidays, until the 2001 Foot and Mouth crisis made it impossible for me to continue, and the Saturday Farm Press column for 25 years, before I was summarily sacked in 2002, for reasons that were never explained, without a word of thanks. Such is the world of freelance journalism.

But I am getting ahead of myself. By the middle of 1978 I felt sufficiently assured of my position to ask for a move of office, away from Chippenham at one end of my region to Taunton in the heart of it. My first child, Joanna, was born that May, and Mandy and I both wanted to be further west, so that the travelling wouldn't be quite such a burden, and we would be able to get a lot more house for our money somewhere near Taunton than in fashionable North Wilts. So in November that year we sold Southfields, as our bungalow was called, (to a lady with a lurcher so fierce that it would rush out and puncture the tyres of passing cars with its teeth as they rounded the sharp bend) and, after an entirely amicable hiatus, in which I moved in with father and Rosie at High Littleton temporarily and Mandy moved back to her parents, we bought a barn conversion at Clayhidon in the Blackdown Hills. It was only 15 minutes' drive from the office and less than that to the M5 but in beautiful countryside in the middle of nowhere. Perfect.

My new office was to be the bungalow in the grounds of Agriculture House in Taunton intended for the assistant county secretary to live in but which was now lying empty. We advertised for a secretary, and I interviewed a series of doubtless highly efficient but not particularly inspiring middle-aged ladies. Towards the end of the day Charles Evison popped his head around the door to offer some well-meant advice. "I know I shouldn't interfere, Anthony, but I have to say that I've always found the older ladies to be much more reliable than young girls, with all their boyfriend issues and so on."

That settled it. My final interviewee was a girl called Kendall Noyes, who had given her age on her application form as 19½. She was, let us say, very nicely put together and, more to the point, seemed to me to have something about her as well as good looks. So it was Kendall who got the job and who moved into the bungalow with me – the bungalow in which I had by now made my temporary home. Didn't that set the tongues wagging in the County Office! But she turned out to be one of many inspired (or possibly lucky) appointments; she coped with me brilliantly and ended up working in the Press Office in HQ before going on to greater things in the world of marketing.

One of the very first calls I took in our new premises was from Chris Kaufman, lead negotiator for the NUAAW, the Farm Workers' Union, whom I had got to know a bit when I'd been working in London.

"Sorry to bother you, Anthony," he began, "but I've got a rather strange question to ask."

"Ask away," I replied.

"Well," he explained. "We've been approached by one of our Somerset members who has been sacked by his employer after being caught buggering a sheep. He wants us to support him in a case of unfair dismissal, on the grounds that buggering the occasional sheep is one of the perks of the job. Tell me, is this sort of thing common in the West Country?"

I was happy to be able to confirm that it wasn't, or not at least as far as I was aware!

11

Countryside controversy

When I reluctantly submitted myself to management training in 1994, the psychometric testing revealed my 'career driver' to be 'vocational': in other words, a desire to make the world a better place and help my fellow men and women in the process. This was hardly surprising, given the multiplicity of Baptist ministers and teachers in my family history and, most of the time, it fitted comfortably with my role for the NFU. Working to make life a bit easier and more profitable, especially for the smaller family farms which are the backbone of the West Country's rural community, seemed a perfectly worthy cause.

Only in one area of my work was my conscience regularly troubled, and that was in what was happening to the countryside, which in the 1960s and 70s was changing at a faster rate than at any time in recorded history, and not in a good way. The biggest change was the loss of the elms. Dutch elm disease was a tragedy, but it was a natural tragedy. What pained me even more as I drove around the West Country in the late 70s was the extent of hedgerow removal. It broke my heart to see a fine old hedge-line bulldozed and burnt. I could understand that some of the smallest fields might need amalgamating, particularly if a farm was shifting from livestock to arable, but some farmers took it to extremes. On one dairy farm at Payhembury in East Devon, every single hedge appeared to have been removed, to create a vast green prairie of ryegrass monoculture. Or there was the farmer at Wellington who, soon after I had moved the office to Taunton, decided to drain an important wetland habitat which was home to a colony of great-crested newts, not, so it seemed, because he really needed to, but out of sheer bloody-mindedness. Fortunately he wasn't a member of the NFU so I wasn't called upon to defend his actions (something that applied to most of the worst environmental vandals).

In the drive to increase home food production, during and after the Second World War, nothing really mattered except output. Considerations of ecology or aesthetics had to take second place to what seemed to be regarded as the farmer's almost sacred duty to grow two blades of grass where only one grew before. Generous government grants incentivised farmers to rip out hedges, cut down woodlands, drain wetlands and plough moorland, and, for a time, no-one seriously questioned that this was in the national interest.

By the time I joined the NFU in 1972, opinion was beginning to shift. That was the year of David Cobham's film for the BBC, 'The Vanishing Hedgerows', in which Henry Williamson lamented the loss not just of the hedges but of much of the wildlife that depended on them. Williamson, who had of course farmed himself, in Norfolk, blamed 'science' – DDT in particular – rather than the farmer. Even so, the figure that he quoted from the Nature Conservancy Council (now Natural England) of 5,000 miles of hedges being grubbed up every year was a striking one which quickly became embedded in the opinion-forming consciousness. Other commentators were not so forgiving. In the NFU Press Office in 1974 and 75, I was frequently having to defend farmers in general and the NFU in particular against charges of environmental vandalism, motivated mainly by greed.

What made it worse was the fact of being part of the EEC and thus of the CAP. It was one thing to accept damage to the countryside in the name of national food security; quite another to have to endure it when the end result would be to add to the EEC's increasingly expensive food surpluses. The 1975 White Paper, 'Food from Our Own Resources', re-stated the case for agricultural productivity being seen as the primary objective of Government policy for farming and the countryside, but anyone with eyes in their head could see that it had been overtaken by events and that priorities had changed. By the time that I moved back to the West Country in 1976, it was no longer a question of whether a balance should be struck between agricultural production and the fabric of the countryside, but how that balance should be achieved. And before a balance could be struck, the conflict – between farming and conservation, as it was framed – had to be resolved.

It was an issue in which I was intensely interested at a personal level, so I was entirely comfortable with the fact that it was in my region that the conflict first came to a head, on Exmoor. In fact, I was coming rather late to the controversy. Ever since the Exmoor Society had been formed, some ten years or so before, to campaign against a plan to plant thousands of conifers on the Chains in the heart of the moor, concern had been growing at the way in which Britain's smallest National Park was under attack, not just from foresters but from farmers who, taking advantage of generous grants, were 'improving' the moorland, either by applications of lime and slag or by ploughing it up altogether.

The Society commissioned Geoffrey Sinclair to produce a land use and vegetation survey, which was then published under the intentionally provocative title of 'Can Exmoor Survive?'. It revealed that, over the previous ten years or so, the area of moorland on Exmoor had fallen by 3,800 hectares, or 16%. The NFU disputed the figure, but enough had been done to demonstrate that a genuine problem did exist, and that Exmoor's characteristic heather moorland was under threat. Eventually the controversy generated something called the 'Gentleman's Agreement', under which farmers and landowners planning to reclaim moorland would voluntarily give the Park Authority notice and the chance to negotiate an agreement to prevent the reclamation going ahead. Unfortunately, although some 19 proposals were indeed notified between 1969 and 1973, not a single agreement was reached and all went ahead.

As the controversy intensified, battle lines were drawn. On the one side, the National Park Officer, Major-General Dare Wilson, and a splendid collection of Exmoor worthies, drawn from families like the Trollope-Bellews, the Thomas-Everards and the Whaley-Cohens. On the other, the militant conservationists, led by the former editor of the Daily Worker and avowed Communist, Malcolm MacEwen, and the Chairman of the Exmoor Society, another doughty campaigner, Guy Somerset.

It was swiftly characterised by the press as 'The Reds v The Gentry' and made headlines all over the place, especially when the hapless Major-General attempted to suppress a highly critical report on his Committee's activities. The row that ensued when a prominent area of heather moorland in Doone country called Stowey Allotment was converted into lush green pasture led to the then Labour Government asking Lord Porchester, better known as the Queen's racing manager, but also a shrewd and knowledgeable landowner with an estate in Hampshire and no axe to grind, to lead an Inquiry and publish a report.

It was roughly at this stage that I became involved. The NFU had set up something called the Exmoor Working Party to make its case, and it was they who provided the ammunition for me to fire. Fortunately for all concerned, the farmers involved were realistic and far-sighted: men like John Edwards, Christopher Thomas-Everard, Dick Lloyd and John Pugsley. The first of its tasks in which I was involved was to rebut some of the more extreme allegations that were being made by MacEwen and co.

Thus, at the height of the 1976 drought, we issued a statement in response to the Sandford Report on moorland conservation issues, 'totally rejecting' comments by the Exmoor Society suggesting that there was a danger that Exmoor as we know it today will disappear.

However, what was interesting about that statement was that it stopped well short of insisting that any farmer should have an absolute right to do what he wanted with his land, or that it was, in fact, in the national interest for the 'improvement' of Exmoor to continue. Farming should be given 'a high priority relative to other countryside and National Park activities', but not a dominant one. Even before the Porchester report was published, the battleground had shifted from whether Exmoor's heather moorland should be protected to how that could best be achieved.

This accorded very well with my personal views on the subject. Ploughing up parts of a National Park to produce food that, in the European context, wasn't really needed didn't make much sense at any level. On the other hand it was surely wrong that individual farmers should find themselves penalised for a change in policy priorities, just because they happened to farm in a National Park.

So, given that the agreed aim of policy was that Exmoor should not be ploughed, how could that best be achieved? Messrs MacEwen and Somerset and their followers argued strongly for compulsion; for 'Moorland Conservation Orders', which would ban farmers and landowners from 'improving' the moorland and pay them a lump sum in compensation to reflect the loss of the land's capital value. These MCOs, as they swiftly became known, duly became the centre-piece of the Callaghan government's proposed Countryside Bill.

I could understand the argument for compulsion. After all, if an ordinary householder was prevented by planning laws from doing what he wanted with his property, and an appeal failed, that was that, with no compensation. Why should farmers be any different? But short of extending planning controls to the entire British countryside (for which there was at the time some support), such an approach could only be discriminatory, and therefore unfair and worthy of being compensated.

At a more practical level – and this was a point argued most strongly by Ben Halliday, the retired Oxfordshire teacher who had inherited the spectacular Glenthorne Estate on the Exmoor coast – a voluntary agreement with the farmer which involved much more than merely stopping him from carrying out a particular operation could provide all sorts of other benefits, such as improved access or the creation of new wildlife habitat. So new battle lines were drawn: voluntary agreements to protect the moor or compulsory orders?

The case for compulsion would be all the stronger if its proponents could show that the threat of damaging change was serious and immediate. Which is what they endeavoured to do, not least in the draft of a new National Park Plan, heavily influenced by the Countryside Commission, published for consultation in 1977. It spoke of moorland reclamation being 'the most vital issue confronting Exmoor' and of a 'basic clash between agriculture and amenity', the implication being that here was a situation so serious and so urgent that legislation was the only answer.

This is where I came in, drafting statements and giving briefings arguing that the problem was being blown out of all proportion, that farmers had willingly co-operated in notifying the National Park of intended improvements and that compulsion would prove counter-productive by souring that relationship. This was in March 1977. In the autumn of that year Porchester reported, largely confirming what the Exmoor Society had been saying about the extent of moorland loss and favouring the dreaded MCOs over management agreements. So that skirmish had been lost, and MCOs duly formed the centre-piece of the Countryside Bill when that was published in early 1979.

The battleground now became the House of Commons. The NFU's team of lobbyists got to work as the Bill made its way through its stages. Towards the end of January I wrote a lengthy press release, making the case for management agreements to be the primary instrument of moorland conservation. It concluded with a typically sweeping Gibsonian statement:

> Farmers on Exmoor resent the further erosion of individual liberty
> and interference by the State which is inherent in the Bill. However,
> given that legislation has to be introduced, there is at least a basis
> for agreement in the Bill – always provided that the emphasis is on
> co-operation, not compulsion.

But we were losing the argument, and towards the end of February, as a last throw of the dice, we issued a statement threatening to withdraw co-operation from the existing voluntary notification arrangements if the Bill was not amended. 'We must have a firm and precise statement that voluntary management agreements will take precedence over compulsion in the Bill, and that they will be based on fair and adequate compensation, taking into account loss of income.'

Even so, I doubt if we would have won had the Bill completed its stages and become an Act. As it was, other circumstances intervened, a General Election was called, the Bill was lost and Mrs Thatcher became Prime Minister. This did not mean that the issue would go away. The Tories were just as keen to introduce legislation to resolve a fast-multiplying range of conflicts between farming and conservation. But it did mean that management agreements were much more likely to be adopted as the preferred means of achieving that.

There was, however, one final hurdle to be jumped. The reason why so many proposed management agreements had been turned down by the Exmoor National Park Committee over the years was the cost, coupled with the suspicion that farmers might be exaggerating both the feasibility of what was proposed and their likely losses if they were prevented from going ahead.

Two developments served to quell these doubts. The first was the fact that in 1978 and 1979 two management agreements were finally reached. The first covered Ben Halliday's Glenthorne Estate. It did allow the conversion of some 60 hectares from moorland to pasture and the diversion of a footpath in the process but also protected a much larger area, as well as providing greater access, regular ecological monitoring and the preservation of archaeological sites. Ben Halliday called it 'Exmoor's answer to Porchester'.

I arranged a press visit to the Estate, partly to show just how much the voluntary approach could achieve, partly to present the NFU as a force for conciliation, genuinely concerned to see Exmoor's moorland conserved. I think it wold be fair to say that, on that latter point, the journalists, who included two relative veterans of the Exmoor controversy, Chris Rundle of the Western Daily Press and Peter Hesp (Martin's father) of the Somerset County Gazette, remained unconvinced.

But it was still a memorable occasion, not so much for seeing the bleak expanse of ploughed moorland (which is still, in my view, an eyesore) as for Glenthorne House, on what is said to be the only level patch of ground between Porlock and Lynmouth, hard by the sea at the bottom of a precipitous, three-mile, twisting-and-turning driveway, looking out across the Bristol Channel towards Wales. It has to be one of the most spectacularly romantic locations in the entire South-West. I found myself reflecting on how much Coleridge and Wordsworth would have loved it here, except for the fact that the house wasn't built till more than thirty years after they'd left Somerset.

However, as a backdrop for making the case for a fair deal for the hard-working, salt-of-the-earth, struggling livestock farmers of Exmoor, it wasn't perhaps entirely ideal! Nor, come to that, were the circumstances surrounding a second agreement, this one covering Haddon Hill, a moorland outlier overlooking Wimbleball reservoir which a landowner called Robin Grant had proposed to plough. Even I had some doubts as to how feasible that might have been, but the agreement was signed and another press visit duly arranged, concluding this time with a convivial lunch in the pub at Lowtrow Cross. The gentlemen of the press remained unconvinced.

The second important development in the situation was taking place, not in Somerset or Devon but in NFU HQ in London, where Richard Macdonald of the Parliamentary Division, fresh from a graduate traineeship, was given the task of devising some financial guidelines to provide a credible, objective basis for calculating how much compensation a farmer would be entitled to under a management agreement. Working with John Powell of the NFU's Economics department, and with no shortage of input from John Edwards and, especially, Christopher Thomas-Everard, Richard came up with a formula. The next task was to win acceptance from the other parties involved, notably the Country Landowners' Association, Exmoor National Park and, of course, the Thatcher Government, who were now promoting their own Wildlife and Countryside Bill.

After a great deal of hard work, for which I can take no credit whatsoever, agreement on the guidelines was reached with all of the interests who mattered, and a signing ceremony was held at Exmoor House in Dulverton in April 1981. I quoted John Edwards as saying that the guidelines were "fair and reasonable from everybody's point of view. They have cleared the way for the conservation of Exmoor by voluntary agreement and should bring the sterile controversy over land use on the moor to a long-overdue conclusion."

With the benefit of hindsight, it could perhaps be argued that the guidelines were more likely to result in farmers being over-compensated, rather than the other way around. (That was certainly the Somerset District Valuer's opinion!) But the involvement of the Agricultural Economics Unit of Exeter University in assessing each year by how much the 'profit foregone' might have risen or fallen effectively insulated the system from serious attack, and it did indeed remove the last obstacle to peace on Exmoor and became the basis for resolving similar conflicts in many other areas. With so significant an achievement to his name after so short a career in the NFU, it is not in the least bit surprising that Richard Macdonald should have risen to become, eventually, the NFU's Director General. That was the first occasion on which he and I worked together, but certainly not the last. Our NFU careers tracked each other, albeit with me always a pace or two behind, as we shall see.

There was, however, one further element in the equation for which I think I can claim some credit, and that was the change in attitude among farmers between, say, the mid 1970s and the early 1980s. From outright hostility to the National Park and any suggestion that their freedom to farm might be compromised, the mood shifted through reluctant acquiescence to, in the end, taking almost a perverse sort of pride in being 'champions of the Exmoor environment', leading the way in resolving the conservation conflict. It was a change of heart well summarised by a farmer quoted in Michael Winter and Matt Lobley's paper on 'The Legacy of the Exmoor Management Agreements' published in 2009:

> The management agreements as such ... didn't make much difference. The big difference was the attitude of mind between the Park and the farmers and perhaps the farmers as a whole realising that the environment was really quite important. This was something that happened. I don't know quite when it happened but it gradually happened.

For my money, the appointment of Len Curtis as a pragmatic, conciliatory, far-sighted National Park Officer was a big factor in the change of mood. But I like to think that we in the NFU played a part as well in, to quote a press release I wrote in 1979, 'encouraging farmers to accept and understand the public interest in Exmoor, and the farmers have responded.' It wasn't my job to make NFU policy, only to explain it. But the tone in which something is explained is often as important as the substance of the issue, and by coming across as constructive, as understanding differing points of view and all the time nudging farmers towards accepting that priorities were changing, we certainly did the cause no harm.

But if the gentlemen farmers of Exmoor could see which way the wind was blowing and were happy enough to let it fill their sails, the view from a very different but equally sensitive part of Somerset was less pragmatic. The farmers of the Somerset Levels and Moors have a long and proud history of determined resistance to outside interference, not just in their way of farming but their way of life. The Levels and Moors had always had the potential to become the West Country's answer to the East Anglian fens. All that was needed was drainage and a measure of flood prevention. There were formidable difficulties to be overcome, particularly on the central peat 'moors', but by the mid-seventeenth century Cornelius Vermuyden and others had shown what could be achieved in Lincolnshire and the Isle of Ely. King's Sedgemoor, which the Crown had appropriated from the Abbots of Glastonbury at the Dissolution, was the obvious target. First James I, then Charles I and finally a combination of Vermuyden and Cromwell sent Commissioners to sort out the details of a scheme which they were confident would render the land 'dry, warm, solide and full of fruit', replacing the 'few jaded and diseased cattle' with 'many hundreds of well-fed cattle and thousands of fat sheep'. But each and every attempt came to nothing in the face of the implacable opposition of the commoners and small free-holders.

It was a similar story 120 years or so later when a self-important agricultural improver called Richard Locke, of Burnham, came up with a plan to drain and enclose 20,000 acres of the moors, with the backing of the recently formed Bath and West of England Society. The commoners would have none of it. Locke related how he was 'stoned, bruised and beat by the mob till the blood had issue from my nose, mouth and ears', after which his effigy was burnt and much cider consumed. And this was a man who reckoned that his improvement scheme would increase the value of the land fivefold. The commoners weren't interested. They valued their rights to take turf and firewood, do a bit of fishing and wild-fowling and graze a few cattle when the land was dry enough in summer. Nor were they at all willing to stump up the costs involved. Locke's friend and ally, John Billinglsey, who was commissioned to write the Agricultural Survey of Somerset in 1793 and who did in the end make his mark on the Levels, provides a despairing pen-portrait of one of these 'keepers of geese', as they were disparagingly described: 'At length, the sale of a half-fed cow, or hog, furnishes the means of adding intemperance to idleness' – the intemperance being provided, of course, by cider!

Thanks to the efforts of Billingsley and his successors, the moors were gradually drained and improved over the next two centuries, but it was a piecemeal process because of the extreme fragmentation of so many Levels holdings. The fact that the freeholders lived in the villages on the higher ground, and often had common rights in all of the surrounding moors, added to the complications, resulting as it did in rights being commuted for land in several different moors. Efforts to improve the drainage infrastructure – the major rivers, sluices and rhynes – also came and went, so that frequent flooding remained a huge obstacle to the conversion of land from pasture to arable, as had happened in the Fens. The upfront cost of improvement was always a big issue. As late as 1977 a Ministry of Agriculture plan to under-drain West Sedgemoor, so that high-value crops such as wheat and strawberries could be produced from the rich peat soil of the area, was thrown out by the assembled farmers because (a) they regarded it as too expensive and (b) they didn't like being told what to do.

What this resistance to change and 'improvement' had unwittingly helped to create, however, was a wetland landscape and associated wildlife of national, if not international, importance. And what MAFF's plan for West Sedgemoor had highlighted was the risk to it, if the under-drainers got their way. Already dairy farmers like Ralph Baker at Meare and arable farmers like Pip Gibbons at Shapwick were showing what the inherent fertility of the Levels and Moors could achieve in terms of yields of silage and cash crops when subject to modern, intensive techniques. Farming partners Stan Chedzoy and Stuart Gothard's proposal to under-drain a sizeable chunk of West Sedgemoor showed that the threat was real and immediate. In 1981 the Nature Conservancy Council (now Natural England) published a Report of Survey for the Levels and Moors, which listed 10 'areas of exceptional wildlife interest', with West Sedgemoor at the top of the list. The Wildlife and Countryside Act of 1981 meant that areas such as these could and indeed should now be protected.

So in February 1982, as, by now, the NFU's Somerset County Secretary, I wasn't in the least bit surprised to receive a telephone call from Peter Nicholson, the NCC's Regional Manager, to tell me that the process of designating West Sedgemoor as a Site of Special Scientific Interest was about to begin. Nor, if I'm being honest, was I particularly concerned. Experience on Exmoor seemed to suggest that farmers were prepared to accept controls on how they managed their land, provided they were fairly compensated, something which the 1981 Act seemed to have guaranteed. If all went to plan, Somerset could once again be seen as leading the way in reaching a new accommodation between farming and wildlife.

How wrong can you be?! A few weeks later, we arranged a meeting at the Williams Memorial Hall at Stoke St Gregory, at which Peter Nicholson and his right-hand man Rob Williams (who came to be familiarly known by the farmers as 'the Beast of Sedgemoor'!) would explain to the West Sedgemoor farmers exactly what SSSI designation would mean and, ideally, would secure their co-operation. But in the meantime the official documentation had been sent out, including, fatefully, a list of the 'notifiable operations' which would not be allowed under SSSI status, without the NCC's consent. It covered just about everything that a farmer could conceivably want to do with his land, including most of what the West Sedgemoor farmers were doing already, and which had, of course, given the area its conservation interest in the first place. You can imagine how that went down!

When it came to the meeting, in vain did Messrs Nicholson and Williams protest that whatever farming operations had been carried out prior to designation would be allowed to continue, that they were not seeking to 'turn back the clock'. All the farmers could see was a future of bureaucratic interference in their freedom to farm, which they weren't prepared to accept, compensation or no compensation. Then there was the question of loss of capital value. "You're destroying the value of our farms," one farmer shouted from the back of the crowded, smoke-filled room. "Where's the compensation for that?"

And so it went on, with one farmer after another pitching in to the hapless NCC officials who were, after all, scientists rather than politicians and who had not been prepared in any way for this barrage of criticism and abuse. I wasn't chairing the meeting but did intervene once or twice to try to calm things down – to no avail whatsoever. The NFU was almost as bad as "these bloody conservationists" for ever allowing the situation to develop in the first place. At the end of the chaotic proceedings, a particularly irate farmer came up to Peter Nicholson, took him by the throat and pushed him up against the meeting-room wall. Fortunately, another farmer intervened and separated the two before any serious harm was done, but it was a nasty moment, of which there were plenty more to come.

That summer, as the controversy raged on, the NCC's Chairman, Sir Ralph Verney, a mild-mannered Buckinghamshire landowner and enthusiastic amateur conservationist, paid two visits to Somerset to find out for himself what all the fuss was about. The second of them involved another encounter with most of the 80 or so farmers and landowners with an interest in West Sedgemoor, this time at North Curry Village Hall on a Saturday evening in July. Fred Elliott, a lovely man who farmed at Wiveliscombe and would go on to be a popular and respected Chairman of the NFU's HQ Parliamentary Committee, chaired the meeting, with the Taunton MP Sir Edward du Cann – no friend of conservation quangos like the NCC – also on the platform. It was not a happy occasion. One farmer after another stood up, angrily to criticise not so much the fact of the designation as the timing of it, the extent of it and the lack of consultation surrounding it. Sir Ralph had little to offer in reply, beyond saying that his two visits had given him a much clearer idea of the strength of feeling on the issue and that he would bring his entire Council with him for a further visit in November.

At both a personal and a professional level, this was a much more difficult position for me than Exmoor had been. The local farmers wanted us to oppose the SSSI, root and branch. Yet there was no real doubt that large parts of West Sedgemoor – the undrained areas, which included a big chunk of land in the centre of the moor owned by the RSPB – were of genuinely special interest. There was pressure from on high, as well. This was shaping up to be the first real test of the 1981 Wildlife and Countryside Act, with its compensation procedures, which the NFU (based on the Exmoor experience) had played a big part in designing. There was no desire in the corridors of Agriculture House, Knightsbridge to see their carefully crafted machinery being brought to a grinding halt by a bunch of obdurate peasants in Somerset. Then finally, but crucially, there was public opinion to be considered. 'Butter versus butterflies' was how the controversy was characterised and, against the backdrop of the EEC's huge milk surplus and with milk quotas very much a threat, there weren't too many people on the butter side of the argument.

That August I drafted the official Somerset NFU response to the proposed SSSI designation. It was, though I say it myself, a carefully crafted piece of work, which recognised that 'parts of West Sedgemoor are of considerable scientific interest' but argued that the designation should be confined to those parts which could be isolated from the more productive under-drained areas in the north and east of the moor by a system of pumps and sluice gates. It also reiterated the farmers' concerns about the 'blighting' of their farms and was heavily critical of the way in which the designation had been conducted and the impact this had had on farmer goodwill.

'In total,' the letter concluded, 'we believe that these arguments add up to the strongest possible case for designating a very much smaller area than the 2,500 acres presently proposed.'

Well, a strong case it may have been, but it cut no ice with the NCC's ruling council. Nor were the local farmers over-impressed. Hardly a day went past that autumn without one or more of them ringing me in my Taunton office to tell me precisely what they thought of the NFU in general and A Gibson in particular. I endeavoured to take the sting out of their criticism by adopting a calculatedly belligerent tone in the many radio and television interviews I was asked to give, but that got me into trouble with my bosses in Knightsbridge. The situation got even more awkward when a group of the West Sedgemoor militants, egged on by Chris Rundle of the Western Daily Press, decided to do what Levels and Moors farmers had always done when threatened by outsiders – burn a few effigies!

The event was staged at the Black Smock, a slightly sinister pub which stood alone on the eastern edge of West Sedgemoor. It owed its name to a legend that a witch had once lived there who, finding her home besieged by witch-hunters, made her escape up the chimney, getting her white smock covered in soot in the process. She eventually gave her pursuers the slip by turning herself into a hare. Anyway, as a venue for an occasion with heavy overtones of witch-craft, it could hardly have been better chosen.

A makeshift scaffold had been set up in the car park, from which three effigies had been hung, representing Sir Ralph Verney, Peter Nicholson and Stan Davies, the regional boss of the RSPB, who had made himself particularly unpopular with the West Sedgemoor farmers for his outspoken support of the SSSI. As a final slightly bizarre twist, a Sherman tank had been drawn up alongside the scaffold, by courtesy of Chris Osborne, a plant hire contractor at Langport whose business revolved around drainage and dredging on the Levels. All the most prominent farmer militants were there, men like Peter Maltby, father and son Dick and David House, Russell Darbishire, Norman and Valerie Parker, David Perrin and a good many others, plus a good showing of pressmen and television crews. I was there, not in my official NFU capacity, for we had disowned the protest, but as a 'journalist', recording proceedings for my BBC farming programme and doing my best to keep a low profile.

After a rousing re-statement of the reasons for the protest, the effigies were duly torched and, being made of straw, quickly went up in flames. Up to that point the atmosphere had been almost festive, even though it was a Monday morning and no cider had been laid on. But as the flames climbed higher and the flaming effigies slipped from the nooses around their necks, a silence fell as the savage symbolism of what was happening was brought home to the farmers and their families standing round.

Soon people started drifting away, saying little. A sense of shame hung heavily in the air. The television reporters got their interviews, the photographers their pictures, the journalists their quotes and the farmers had the publicity they had been seeking. But did it do the cause any good? Well, yes and no. It made no difference to the West Sedgemoor designation, which was duly confirmed, covering the entire area of 2,500 acres. Most of the moor has since been bought by the RSPB and turned into a thriving nature reserve.

But it did set alarm bells ringing in the corridors of power in London. When I got back to my office in Taunton that lunchtime, the first call I took was from a furious Sir Richard Butler, demanding an explanation for "this appalling demonstration". Taking my cue from his predecessor as President, I replied that there had been nothing we could do to stop it, but that it did show the depth of feeling among the local farmers, to which the Government would be well-advised to respond.

A few weeks later, on Saturday March 5, the Secretary of State for the Environment and, by a happy coincidence, the MP for Bridgwater, Tom King, arrived at Burrowbridge Village Hall to sort things out. This was another chaotic occasion, in which the pot was given a further stir by the presence of a small group of demonstrators from Friends of the Earth, who emptied a container of white water all over the car park to symbolise the EEC's milk surplus.

In the meeting itself debate was heated. Humphrey Temperley, who farmed not far from West Sedgemoor and was the leader of the Liberals on Somerset County Council, got himself physically thrown out of the meeting when he advanced on the platform to make the case for designation. It could all have ended very nastily, but Tom King, firm, decisive, measured, was exactly the right man for the occasion. He gave no ground on the West Sedgemoor designation, or the absence of an appeal procedure. He did, though, have something to offer on the question of land 'blighted' by an SSSI designation: if blight could be shown, compensation would be paid. He also repeated the NCC's assurance that there would be no turning back of the clock. Anyone farming in an SSSI could carry on as before. Coming from Tom King, respected local MP and Secretary of State, that cut a lot more ice than it had done coming from Peter Nicholson or Sir Ralph Verney. But perhaps the most telling thing he had to say was on the broader picture.

"There are forces in our society," he declared, "who would like to see this Wildlife and Countryside Act destroyed – not because they want to help farmers but because they want to see compulsion, confiscation of your rights and planning controls. If we in Somerset fail to make this Act work, we run the risk of letting in something very much worse."

That struck home. The farmers, not just of West Sedgemoor but in all of the ten SSSIs that were eventually designated across the Levels, did make the Act work – significantly assisted, it should be said, by a man called Richard Cooke, who was essentially given the task by Tom King, not so much of pouring oil on troubled waters as pouring money on them. Scores of management agreements were reached over the ensuing few years, all of them involving handsome levels of compensation.

It was a good outcome. The most important areas of the Levels had been protected from damaging change, the farmers were being compensated and an accommodation reached which could and would form the basis for resolving similar conflicts the length and breadth of the country. Only in one respect was it less than satisfactory, in that it relied on a farmer threatening a damaging change for him to qualify for compensation. With the coming of the Somerset Levels and Moors Environmentally Sensitive Area in 1987 – something that Somerset NFU and its County Secretary enthusiastically supported – that weakness was addressed. Farmers who were content just to carry on farming the land in the ways that had created the Levels landscape and its wildlife in the first place could be modestly rewarded for so doing, without having to threaten anything.

Critics, both of SSSI management agreements and of the ESA, would argue that all of the money spent on them produced very little in the way of positive improvement. Outside the reserves operated by the RSPB and the Somerset Wildlife Trust, numbers of breeding waders have continued to decline and other measures for assessing bio-diversity have revealed, at best, the maintenance of the status quo. It was the absence of evidence for genuine 'enhancement' which led to the ESAs being dropped, to be replaced by the much less location-specific Countryside Stewardship Tier 1, supplemented by the vastly more expensive Tier 2, in which large amounts of money were piled onto very small areas in the hope – mostly unfulfilled – of creating valuable new habitat.

Both the landscape and the biodiversity of the Levels and Moors has suffered from this change in policy. To many of the farmers who had been happy enough to take their £50 or £65 per acre ESA money for restricting fertilisers and sprays and pollarding their willows every five to ten years or so, the £33 on offer from Stewardship looked much less attractive than the rent they could earn by letting the land for grass keep, with no strings attached, or, as has increasingly been the case, for maize, with operators of heavily subsidised Anaerobic Digester (AD) plants able to offer big money for land on which to grow the maize which they need to make their plants run efficiently.

The result has been that most of the good work of the 1987-2005 ESA period is being undone. Hundreds of acres of what had been typical Levels pasture, in the Brue valley especially, is now wall-to-wall maize in summer, bare ground in winter, which is polluting water sources and releasing huge amounts of CO_2 as the peat soils are ploughed. Elsewhere, the classic Levels landscape is becoming overgrown and weed-infested. I am not in the least bit optimistic that the Government's new Environmental Land Management Scheme (ELMS) will make a worthwhile difference. The clamour from the conservation lobby is for more water. A powerful lobby, which numbers the former Chief Executive of the Environment Agency, Baroness Young, among its adherents, would like to turn the Levels back into the swamp they were in King Alfred's day.

That is a subject to which we will return. For the moment, let us just say that we worked very hard in Somerset to turn countryside controversy into countryside co-operation in the 1980s, we arrived at a series of measures which halted damaging change, and it feels very much as if that legacy is being betrayed by what is happening thirty years on.

12

Somerset County Secretary

It had never been my ambition to become an NFU County Secretary. My broadcasting for BBC Radio Bristol, my columns in the Western Daily Press and increasingly frequent appearances on regional television had re-kindled my media aspirations. Bruce Hockin, the HTV news anchor, had suggested to me that I ought to apply for a job as an HTV reporter, and that was very much in my mind in early 1981. My five years as Regional information Officer had been enjoyable, challenging and, by and large, successful, but I felt it was time to move on.

We were by now happily established in Applehayes Cottage at Clayhidon, high in the Blackdown Hills. It was a barn conversion, with all the usual barn conversion issues, like damp and a log fire that smoked and an unconventional lay-out of rooms, but the neighbours were friendly and the surrounding countryside as glorious as it was unvisited. Our second daughter, Rebecca (whom we've always known as Becky), had been born in August 1980, and we had a big, black Newfoundland dog called, inevitably, Nana. Our nearest pub, the Half Moon, was the best part of a mile away, but we never saw a police car up there from the start of one year to the end of the next, and I spent many happy evenings there, drinking Whitbread Trophy (it was at least real draught) brewed at the old Starkey Knight and Ford plant in Tiverton, in the congenial company of our hosts, Jack and Edie Pike (always known as 'Mother'), and sundry fellow locals. It could be very bleak in winter in the Blackdowns, but these were happy years.

One of my drinking pals was Richard Kallaway, a local dairy farmer whom I'd originally come across at Devon NFU meetings. He and I were playing skittles in the York at Churchinford one Saturday evening in the spring of 1981 when he said to me words to the effect of: "Spose you'll be going for the Somerset job, then? Good number that."

Now I did know that Charles Evison was retiring, after 26 distinguished years as the NFU's Somerset County Secretary, but it hadn't occurred to me to apply for the job – too bureaucratic, too much at the beck and call of the county office-holders, too much management and not enough freedom.

But Richard persisted, pointing out something that I hadn't realised, that the salary (starting at £14,000 a year) was based on over-riding commission paid on NFU Mutual insurance business in the county. "It's got to go up every year by inflation at the very least," he added. "Hugh Crowle's probably on at least £50,000 by now."

That settled it. The first thing I did on the Monday morning was to get my application in. I was short-listed, with interviews at the end of May. But I was very far from being the favourite for the job. That distinction fell to Shaun Leavey, ex-Brigade of Guards, Assistant County Secretary in Kent and East Sussex, and the very model of what I imagined an NFU County Secretary ought to be. Mike Ellingham, Peter Riddick's deputy in Wiltshire and Gloucestershire, was another strong candidate. My hopes were not high, but I'm naturally competitive, and I made up my mind that I wasn't going to lose out through lack of effort.

The day of the interviews dawned hot and sunny. Kendall wore one of her shortest and flimsiest dresses to mark the occasion. My brother was due to arrive after lunch, for us to pick up Mandy and the two girls and drive to Cambridgeshire after work for a few days' holiday. The format was the standard one for NFU county positions in those days – dinner with the county office-holders the evening before, to test manners and other social skills, then a grilling by a roomful of farmers, each of them primed with at least one question to ask. It was intimidating, but then it was also the kind of situation one was likely to encounter in doing the job, so to that extent it was a fair test.

I remember only two questions. The first was from Paul Francis, who asked me how I saw the role of the NFU. I replied that the NFU was not an end in itself but a means to an end, which was to put more money in the pockets of its members. He nodded approvingly, emptying and then re-lighting his pipe. The other came right at the end, when the County Chairman, Dick Pearce, asked me what my weaknesses were. This has now become an interview standard, but it took me completely by surprise. Frantically I searched my mind for a weakness which could also be seen as a positive. "I can sometimes be just too committed," I ventured. "Rushing in when maybe it would be better to hold back." This was true but probably not so clever, for that was precisely the reputation I had acquired in some of the more conservative NFU circles.

After the interview Kendall, Chippy and I went out for lunch at the nearest pub. I was convinced that I'd not done enough and that the job was

Shaun's. Which it would have been, but for the fact that when his turn to be interviewed came along, immediately after lunch, he decided halfway through that this wasn't the sort of job he wanted, made his excuses and headed for the car park, with Dick Pearce in hot but vain pursuit. Shaun's mind was made up. The Somerset NFU worthies could be a domineering lot, and being domineered was definitely not his style.

So that left the issue between the talented but maybe unreliable Anthony Gibson and the safe pair of hands of Mike Ellingham. I got the decision but, from what I could gather, it was a close-run thing. When I was called in to be given the news, I almost burst into tears with gratitude and happiness, all misgivings about my ability to do the job for the moment set aside. That evening we didn't so much drive to the Isle of Ely to stay with Mandy's parents as fly there. The next day Chippy and I played golf at Woodhall Spa, and at lunchtime I took the chance to ring Hugh Crowle, to give him the news. "Christ!" he said. "They must have taken leave of their senses." I think he was joking!

It was quite a task I was taking on, at the age of just 31. Somerset and South Avon, as it was officially known, was one of the NFU's largest county branches, with over 4,000 farming members. The local branches were organised into nine 'Groups', each looked after by a full-time Group Secretary, usually with an assistant and always with a fully-staffed office.

The Group Secretaries were paid a nominal £150 a year by the NFU and earned all the rest of their money from what was then a 10% commission on their NFU Mutual premium income, in what was pretty much – allowing for the occasional raiders from outside – a captive market. It is an arrangement that has come under strain on many occasions over the years, but it works. The NFU work may account for only a tiny proportion of a group secretary's income, but it is what his or her reputation will be founded upon. The better he or she does the NFU work, the easier it becomes to build the insurance business. Originally only NFU members could qualify for NFU Mutual Insurance. That link had crumbled by the time I became County Secretary and was formally scrapped some years afterwards. But the essentials of the arrangement – the co-dependency of looking after your members and providing them with insurance – happily remain intact and are at the heart of the success of both organisations.

I was fortunate in my team of Group Secretaries. They offered a fine mix of experience, enterprise and eccentricity. Bridgwater's John Garland, Wells' Owen Spencer and West Somerset's Jim Conchie had nearly a century of working for the NFU between them. The slightly younger generation included Owen's equal partner at Wells, Alan Goymer, Maurice Blight at Clevedon (who became known as 'Planning Blight' on account of all the permissions he helped his members obtain), the towering figure of Nick Bennett at Weston-super-Mare and laid-back Richard Loveridge at Ilminster, who rang me shortly after I'd started to tell me that he wouldn't give me any trouble as long as I left him alone.

Nor were they all male. At Taunton Ken Trump was partnered with Anne Elder, Pauline Wilcox worked with John Garland at Bridgwater, and Beryl Palmer was assistant to Evan Wilson at Yeovil. Virtually all of them were older than me, most of them vastly more experienced, and many earned a lot more than I could aspire to. Managing them could thus never be a matter of issuing orders, especially as I was only one of three masters that they had to serve, the others being the Mutual and, of course, their membership. Other than chivvying them to recruit and retain members, I didn't see it as my role to tell them how to do their jobs. My task was to make sure they were well informed on policy and technical issues and do what I could to ensure that Somerset NFU was successful in delivering the goods for the membership and was well regarded inside and outside the farming community. Achieve that, and both membership and insurance would look after themselves.

In the County Office I had a Deputy County Secretary in the dogged persona of Bill Leach, who also looked after horticulture, a quite brilliant Secretary/PA in Kay Mayberry and three part-time ladies, Grace, Iris and Lenus, who kept the wheels turning. We even had a caretaker, Mr Hellings, who lived in a flat on the premises with his family, looked after the meeting room lettings and brought round a trolley with coffee every morning and tea every afternoon. It was all very civilised and quite old-fashioned, but none the worse for that.

I started as County Secretary on the first of October 1981, working in harness with Charles Evison for the first few weeks, as he introduced me to all the people I would need to know in the course of my job: the police, the water authority, the banks, the County Council, MAFF, and so on. In terms of how to approach the job, he offered this: "I clear my desk every day, Anthony, and I strongly advise you to do the same." It was true, although I learned subsequently that much of the desk-clearing involved asking Kay to forward memos from the Group Secretaries to the relevant staff member at HQ with a note attached reading: "Attached refers. Please deal."!

Charles was both a magistrate and a Mason and tentatively inquired if I would be interested in either. I politely declined. One other piece of advice from Charles I remember, which served me well throughout my NFU career: "Never serve chicken at a farmers' dinner!"

It didn't take long for my first real test to arrive. The weather on Sunday December 13 was foul. Normally on a Sunday morning at this stage in my career I would drive into Exeter first thing to broadcast my farming half-hour at 7.30 for the new commercial radio station, Devonair, but one look outside ruled that out. A howling gale was whipping heavy snow into huge drifts. It was so cold that the diesel fuel in farm tractors and milk tankers was waxing up, just when the vehicles were needed most. Most farms in Somerset were without electricity, some without mains water as well.

In the afternoon the weather suddenly changed. Snow turned into torrential rain as the wind switched to the west at storm force ten. The tide along the Somerset coast that night, driven in by the storm and allowed full play by exceptionally low atmospheric pressure, was the highest of the century – 7.95 metres above Ordnance Datum at Bridgwater, with a 1.45m surge. Eye-witnesses described a five-foot tidal wave sweeping across farmland up to a mile inland. By eight o'clock that evening the sea defences were over-topping or breached and being washed away.

By the next morning twelve and a half thousand acres along the coast were under water, with the waves almost reaching the M5. Over one thousand homes and commercial properties were flooded including, as I soon discovered when the phone started ringing later that evening, scores of farms. There were reports of thousands of sheep, cattle, pigs and poultry being drowned and, on top of that, this was salt water. The damage to autumn-sown crops would be huge.

First thing the next morning a call went out to the Group Secretaries to meet me at the Manor Hotel Pawlett, on the A38 just inland from some of the worst of the flooding. We decided that the first thing we needed to do was to establish the extent of the damage. A form was quickly designed, so as to provide a standard basis for assessing loss of crops and livestock. All of the affected farms were visited over the next couple of days, NFU members or not.

Meanwhile the press were on the case. We had yet to appoint a replacement Regional Information Officer, so this too fell to me. One of the farms I suggested to an ITV news team as being worth a visit was Harold Reason's pig unit near Burnham-on-Sea, as I'd heard from Nick Bennett that scores of his pigs had drowned. It proved to be a fateful suggestion.

Although the pigs weren't strictly speaking Harold's – he was rearing them on contract for someone else – he put on a command performance for the cameras, shedding copious tears alongside a grim heap of carcases. That night ITV News at Ten led with the Somerset flood disaster and Harold Reason weeping over his dead pigs. The following morning the phones in county office were red hot from people ringing up from all over the country to offer money, not just to the stricken Harold but for all of the other farmers who'd lost stock to the floods.

I had already issued a press release, headed 'Snow, floods and power cuts bring chaos to Somerset farms' and quoting the line from Hamlet: 'When sorrows come they come not single spies but in battalions.' It talked of the possibility of applying to the EEC Disaster Fund for assistance. But in the meantime what were we going to do about all of these offers of money? I rang Charles Evison to seek his advice. "What you need to remember, Anthony, is that there's only one thing worse than a flood disaster," he replied. "And that's a flood disaster fund!"

Nonetheless, with the full support of the Chairman, Dick Pearce, and the other office-holders, we decided that there was nothing for it but to set up a fund. But it would have to be at arm's length and base its awards on objective criteria, with claims verified by respected volunteer farmers, who would know better than anyone else whether one of their fellow farmers was trying it on.

The Somerset NFU Flood Disaster Fund was duly launched to the world that Wednesday. By the weekend thousands of pounds had been donated. Three independent trustees were put in charge of assessing and paying out on claims: Charles Evison, an experienced auctioneer and valuer called David Powell and Harry Beard, a respected ADAS farm advisor. We had decided that this was to be no long drawn-out process and set ourselves a deadline of the end of January to make payments towards the uninsured losses suffered by the 40 or so farmers who had lost stock or crops to the floods, from Porlock in the West to Lydney in the Forest of Dean.

In the end we raised well over £50,000 – roughly £200,000 in present-day terms – in the space of a month, and it was indeed all paid out by the end of January without, as far as I am aware, a single word of complaint from any farmer, recipient or not. According to the information we had collected from the farms, the losses had amounted to 69 cattle, 959 sheep, 1,589 pigs, 874 poultry and one hive of bees. Add in the salt damage to winter crops and the total uninsured cost was put at around £150,000, so we'd covered at least a third of the farmers' losses. It did us a power of good, with the general public as well as with the membership. One of my most lasting memories of that time was the day we presented a cheque to Gordon Parsons at Stogursey. The smile on his face as he held a lamb in one hand and the cheque in the other was worth all the effort.

It was an important episode for me as well. I'd become known as a good front man, with the gift of the gab, but perhaps lacking in Charles Evison's organisation skills. I felt now that in the way the fund had been organised – quickly, cleanly, efficiently, with all the usual disaster fund pitfalls avoided – I had proved that a way with words was no barrier to being a good administrator. As County Secretary I was an all-rounder.

Being responsible for the efficient administration of one of the NFU's largest and most prominent county branches, at the same time as being acting Information Officer, and writing two newspaper columns and presenting two radio programmes every week, meant that my life lacked nothing in the way of variety or challenge. But I was never content just to keep the wheels turning smoothly. There were always new challenges to be met, new aspirations to be realised, and for those, it seemed to me, I needed a bit of extra help.

In the summer of 1982 I'd found myself at the Dyer family's ancient and handsome Blackmore Farm, just outside Cannington near Bridgwater, to take part in a live broadcast for BBC Radio One's 'Talkabout' on young people and farming. I was on the panel; the audience were members of Somerset Young Farmers' Clubs, the presenter was (I think) Steve Wright, the listenership in the millions. I was my usual upbeat self, about farming, food and prospects for the future. Most of those who spoke from the floor took a very different line. "Idn no future in farming," they were saying. "We'd be better off out of it. Government couldn't care less. My advice to anyone from outside? Don't touch farming with a barge pole."

But there was one exception to this grim litany of misery and complaint (which the young farmers had learned from their fathers). A pretty girl with big brown eyes stood up and admonished the assembled company for their negativity, with both passion and eloquence. Blimey, I thought. We could do with someone like her on the staff at County Office. When it was all over, I introduced myself. She was, she said, the daughter of a farmer near Bath, in her last year on a BSc course at Wye College, part of the University of London. The name? Rebecca Pow, at the time of writing the MP for Taunton, a junior Minister at Defra and the widow of Charles Clark, much-loved auctioneer and former Chairman of Somerset County Cricket Club.

It took me the best part of 18 months to convince the NFU powers-that-be in Somerset and Knightsbridge that a job should be created for her but, thanks not least to her stellar performance at the Bath British Food Week in the spring of 1983, we got there in the end. She started with the NFU in January 1984 as Assistant Editor of the Somerset Farmer, assistant reporter/producer for the BBC Radio Bristol farming output, and, shortly afterwards, administrator of 'A Taste of Somerset', of which more in due course. Whenever we came across something of genuine interest to broadcast, I'd encourage her to offer a report or an interview to BBC Farming Today on Radio 4. She did, they liked her efforts and, in the spring of 1986, they offered her a full-time job. Since when, she has never looked back.

My in-tray was not easily cleared in the 1980s. Quite apart from the battles over farming and conservation, we found ourselves locked in combat with the Conservative Group who ran Somerset County Council over their plans to sell the County Smallholdings Estate in 1983. This got quite nasty, with demonstrations outside and inside County Hall, featuring young farmers dressed in stockmen's white coats and a vicious word-of-mouth campaign against me personally, spreading the lie, as it assuredly was, that my motives were party political.

This was an accusation that, because of my family background with the Liberal Party, was made at regular intervals throughout my NFU career. It was always nonsense. For the record I was approached by the Conservatives to stand as their Somerset candidate for the European Parliament, when Sir Fred Warner retired, and by the Lib Dems to follow John Burnett as MP for West Devon in 2005. I said no on both occasions.

Despite the valiant and unstinting efforts of Michael Fry, we lost the battle over the County Farms in 1983, when a decision to offer them for sale to sitting tenants was forced through, but can fairly claim to have won the war, when the Tories were voted out at the next County Council elections and the new Liberal administration reversed the decision. However, it was inevitable that the farms would go sooner or later, given that such a large chunk of the County Council's capital assets was being used to provide opportunities for such a small number of would-be farmers, with very little either in the way of financial return or wider benefit. It is remarkable that the concept, introduced to provide 'farms for heroes' in the wake of World War One, has hung on for so long.

Pig farming always seemed to be in trouble in those years, so much so that on one occasion we decided to leapfrog the UK Government and go direct to Brussels, in an expedition facilitated by Richard Cottrell, the Bristol and Bath MEP who was a fierce critic of the CAP but much in sympathy with a largely unsupported sector such as pigs. This turned out to be a real endurance test. We left Taunton at six o'clock on a Monday evening, on a minibus which took us to Dover and the ferry to Calais. Most of us then stayed up all night, drinking, under the benign gaze of our county chairman, Clifford Taylor, who was a teetotaller. We reached Brussels in time for breakfast with Richard Cottrell and the NFU's top man in Brussels, Martin Haworth, before embarking on a series of meetings with Commission officials. Proceedings concluded with a boozy lunch at a restaurant called the Corkscrew, with good old Henry Plumb in attendance, before the equally exhausting return journey, in which Rebecca was chased around the upper deck by a randy West Somerset pig farmer. Fortunately she escaped!

However, far and away the biggest issue for farming in a dairying county like Somerset was the prospect of milk quotas. It had been blindingly obvious for years that the EEC could not go on forever producing millions of litres more milk than could either be consumed within its borders, or exported without a huge subsidy attached. The cost of either storing the surplus butter and skimmed milk powder, or effectively dumping it in countries like Russia and Egypt, had been spiralling out of control, and with it public and political hostility to the CAP.

The options for the policy-makers in the EEC Commission essentially boiled down to two: drastic cuts in support prices, to deter over-production and limit its cost, or a quota on output per farm, with severe penalties for exceeding it. In the UK the Milk Marketing Board had, less than five years previously, spent some £80 million of dairy farmers' money buying a fleet of more or less clapped-out creameries from Unigate which would otherwise have been closed down. It needed throughput to justify that decision. Sir Steve Roberts, a no-nonsense, self-made Shropshire dairy farmer who was the Board's Chairman, made his position crystal clear: "Quotas will be introduced over my dead body," he declared. As per usual, given the amount of cross-over between the two organisations (eg Paul Francis, NFU Council delegate and MMB Regional Member), the NFU took the same line, as indeed did Michael Jopling, the Minister of Agriculture.

But at grassroots level the preference was far less clear cut. In the Western Daily Press, using the cover provided by my Giles Horton by-line, I argued the case for quotas. They would tend to favour smaller producers, who were happy just to plod along, with no real ambition to invest and expand. It had been the larger producers who had caused the problem in the first place, and it was only right and proper that the burden of any cut-back should fall on them. Farmer opinion was almost equally divided. When we staged an open meeting of members to decide the county NFU's policy on the issue in March 1983, the price-cutters got the verdict, but only by a handful of votes.

It soon became apparent that this was all of purely academic interest. In Brussels the decision had already been taken. In September that year Graham Meadows, formerly of Farmers Weekly, by now a senior Commission official, as good as told a meeting at Cirencester that quotas were coming, and coming soon: probably in April the following year. But no-one seemed to be listening. The NFU, the MMB and MAFF all remained in a state of denial; no contingency planning was done; no positions were taken on vital details of the new system, such as the base year against which a farmer's quota would be determined. There was no real expectation, in Somerset or anywhere else, that the Council of EEC Farm Ministers would reach a decision when they met in early March 1984. But they did. Quotas would be imposed from April 1, limiting levy-free production to the amount which each member state had produced in 1981.

Even though we had been arguing about quotas and price cuts for the best part of two years, it is hard to over-state the strength of the shock waves which the announcement sent through the Somerset farming community. It wasn't just the impact on individual businesses which provoked outrage, but the fact that the UK's Minister of Agriculture seemed to have caved in to the French, the Dutch and the Danes, by accepting the biggest cut-back in output of any EEC member state, when the UK was still less than self-sufficient in butter, whereas the Dutch, for example, were producing seven times what their home market could absorb!

It was left to Member States to decide how to relate that 1981 production baseline to individual farmers. The simplest option was to take 1981 output as the quota, minus something to be allocated to hardship cases. Or it could be 1983 production, minus a percentage to reflect by how much output had increased between the two years, or an average of 81, 82 and 83, again minus a percentage. Whatever basis was chosen, there would inevitably be thousands of dairy farmers who would say that it was unfair and apply for extra quota. An appeal process would have to be devised.

Now, throughout my NFU career in Somerset and the South-West, I was always looking for the opportunity to make NFU membership indispensable. The quota special case procedure seemed to fit the bill to perfection. No other organisation had either the coverage or the knowledge to match us. If a dairy farmer wanted more quota, far and away his or her best chance of getting it would be by tapping into the NFU's expertise. So, whilst organising ritual protests against quotas – QUOTAS KILL COWS, our ubiquitous posters declared – I was actually much more concerned to mobilise our resources, and in particular our field-force of Group Secretaries, to help our members and to help ourselves.

We were fortunate that year to have John Hughes as Somerset County Chairman. He was a Duchy of Cornwall tenant of a dairy-and-arable farm at Newton St Loe just outside Bath, and he was the perfect front man for a high-profile year: friendly, articulate, intelligent but with a passion for his calling that shone through everything he said or did. It always seemed to me that whenever he appeared on radio and television he would leave his audience feeling better disposed towards farmers and farming than they had been before. Edwin White, who chaired the Somerset Milk Committee, was another eloquent spokesman, especially as he was as much a victim of the way quotas were imposed as anyone, having recently switched to selling his milk direct, which caused all sorts of issues with the 'special case' rules (about which I am sure, to this day, we were right and MAFF was wrong).

We called the Group Secretaries together and gave them a training course in how to help their members apply for extra quota. The details need not detain us. Suffice it to say that the application form was a complex, multi-coloured affair, which you needed a training course to understand, especially as the 'explanatory notes' concealed more about how applications would be judged than they revealed.

It was a four-stage process. First, a farmer filled in that form to apply. That then went to the MAFF 'Divisional Executive Officer' who, in the case of Somerset (as distinct from South Avon) applicants, was Humphrey Abbot, a bright but unconventional civil servant on the fast-track, whose hobby was riding his 500cc motorbike at great speed around the roads of Somerset. He turned up at several key meetings still in his leathers. Farmers whose claims were rejected by Humphrey could then appeal to a 'local panel', drawn from a mixture of respected farmers and professionals from one of the neighbouring counties. Somerset cases were dealt with by the Dorset panel, chaired by a fierce retired admiral called Pritchard, which gave out more 'nil' awards than any other in the country; South Avon cases by the Gloucestershire panel, who were rather more generous. If a farmer was dissatisfied with the Local Panel decision, he or she then had a final appeal to the National Milk Quota Tribunal, albeit with the caveat (designed to deter trivial appeals) that, if the Tribunal considered the Panel's decision to have been over-generous, quota could be docked.

We made our assistance available without additional charge to any Somerset member who wanted it, at every stage of the process. The Group Secretaries helped out with the completion of nearly 1,000 application forms. I had taken on Harry Beard, by now retired from ADAS, to help cope with the demand for appeals to either the local panel or the National Tribunal, most of which were dealt with through County Office. Between us we did a few local panel hearings, but it wasn't really until the final stage of the process that we came into our own.

By now I had found myself a new Secretary, Kay Mayberry having retired, covered in honour and glory. The new girl was Angela Thomas, from a Quantock farming family, and a keen huntswoman who arrived each day in her battered Land Rover. So keen, in fact, that she said she would only take the job if I allowed her Thursdays off during the hunting season. She had the best shorthand of anyone I've ever known and could be frighteningly efficient, which was just what I needed at one of the busiest periods in my entire NFU career.

Milk quotas were finally abolished in 2015 and had been losing their relevance for several years before that, as milk production waned across Europe. So it is easy to forget just how large they loomed in every dairy farmer's consciousness back in 1984. For hundreds, if not thousands of dairy farming businesses, an adequate quota meant the difference between success and failure.

The Government chose 1983 production as the basis for initial quota allocations, minus 6.5% for the increase in national output since 1981, with a further deduction of 2.5% for reallocation to 'special cases', making 9% in all. But for many Somerset dairy farmers, the cut in what they would have expected to produce in a normal year was far greater than that. The spring and summer of 1983 had been miserably wet. Many farmers' output – especially those more traditional producers, with spring-calving herds – had been at least 10% down because of the weather, leaving them facing a cut of almost 20%. And these weren't the farmers, by and large, who had caused the over-production problem.

The other major category were those many farmers who were in the middle of an expansion plan, part-funded by the Government's Farm and Horticulture Development Scheme. All of their financial planning had been based on being able, say, to increase cow numbers by 20, 30 or even 50%. Instead of which they were being forced to cut back.

Then finally, there was the category known as 'exceptional hardship cases', by which MAFF meant (but didn't properly explain) farmers who hadn't been milking cows in 1983 and therefore didn't have any quota at all.

Harry and I did a few local panel hearings to get the feel of things, although most of the work at this stage was done – very well – by the Group Secretaries. It was when the National Tribunal hearings started in January 1985 that we really came into our own. If a farming member asked for assistance, Angela would make an appointment for them to come and see either me or Harry, to go through the case and decide whether or not to appeal.

We weren't in the business of taking on no-hopers. We needed credibility. Usually both the farmer and his wife would turn up, often so it seemed straight from the farmyard. The county office stank of slurry, iodine and Jeyes fluid for months afterwards. Some were bullish, some resigned, others utterly cast down. I would start off by asking the farmer for his production records over the previous three years. He would usually turn straight to his wife. "Missus do look after the paperwork, see. I jus' milks the cows."

I suppose that in about two-thirds of cases we could find some arguable grounds for going ahead with an appeal. I would then write up the notes, Angela would type them and send them off to the member, and we would turn up at the appointed hour, usually at the MAFF regional office at Westbury-on-Trym for the case to be heard. We were put under oath, me as well as the farmer – a dubious procedure at best, given the cobbled-together nature of the process. I would then make the case, and the three members of the Tribunal – usually a farmer from outside Somerset, a retired professional such as a bank manager or consultant, and someone with a legal background – would ask questions. Each hearing could take anything from ten minutes to an hour and a half. We soon discovered that decisions were made immediately afterwards, but not communicated to the unfortunate farmer for weeks, sometimes months, later.

It was an appalling process – and I said this at the time – not least because, so far from following the published guidelines, the Tribunals were instead operating to their own set of rules, put together by the national Chairman, Lord Grantchester, and his MAFF side-kick, Jim Reed. As time went by, we gradually cottoned on to what these unwritten rules were and adjusted our arguments accordingly. I had always rather fancied myself as a barrister – I might even have pursued a career as one, had the business of qualifying not been so protracted and expensive – and I became quite an accomplished performer.

Towards the end of one particularly long and tiring day in March, I found myself in the waiting room in the MAFF offices at Taunton, representing a woman farmer from the Taunton area who had been particularly badly treated, by her husband as well as by MAFF. Sitting there was a large and doleful-looking farmer with, as I soon discovered, a strong West Midlands accent. I asked him about his case. It turned out that he had sold up his business in Walsall in early 1984 and moved to Cheddar to milk Jersey cows with a view to selling the milk direct. So no quota. A classic 'exceptional hardship' case, thought I. Would he like me to speak for him, always provided he joined up as an NFU member the following day? He would.

When I appeared at the door of the Tribunal, there was an audible groan. I could see them thinking: "Oh no, not that bloody man Gibson again, just when we're due to knock off for the day." Five minutes later, the farmer and I walked out of the building, he with an award of 600,000 litres of quota to his name, as I'd pleaded with the Tribunal to give the decision on the spot, so as to put the poor man out of his misery. It was enough for the 200 Jersey cows he'd said he was planning to acquire, and I'm pleased to be able to say that, if he didn't buy quite that many, he did at least produce and sell some milk.

The same could not be said for another exceptional hardship case, which I presented at Bristol. This was, I think, the third time this particular farmer had been before the Tribunal, trying to convince them that he was genuinely committed to going into milk and was therefore entitled to quota. This was on a Saturday morning, and again I could sense that the members of the Tribunal had had enough. At the end of the hearing, I said something to the effect of: "Sir, this poor man has been waiting to know if he has a future in farming for weeks. It must have been agonising for him and his family. Can you please seek head office's approval to give him your decision straight away?"

After some hurried mumbling to the Clerk, this was agreed, and the phone call made. Ten minutes later, we were called back in. "We can give you the decision," said the chairman. "We've accepted your case and decided to award you 500,000 litres, enough for the 100 cows you're committed to buying." I could have punched the air with delight, but not for long. No sooner had we left the hearing than the farmer turned to me and said, "Thanks ever so much for doing that. Now, can you give me some advice as to how I can sell all this quota?" At that, I could have punched the farmer. He'd never had the slightest intention of going into dairying.

But he, I'm glad to say, was the exception rather than the rule. Most of the cases that we took on and won were entirely genuine, including the very last I was involved in. This was at the MAFF offices at Starcross, on the first day of the Devon County Show, towards the end of May, which shows how long this business went on for. It was another exceptional hardship case which had been to Tribunal at least twice before: a young couple who had quit the family partnership to start out on their own. They'd brought their child, a babe in arms, with them to the hearing.

"I'll just sit here while you two go in and do your best," the farmer's wife had said.

"I've got a better idea," I replied. "Why don't you come in with us and bring the baby with you? If he cries a bit, then so much the better."

You can imagine the rest for yourselves. We got the quota!

It was an exhausting few months, especially as I got pleurisy in the middle of it and had to soldier on regardless, but not unsuccessful. In all, I went before the Tribunal on 74 occasions, winning roughly two-thirds of them, and bear in mind that these were all cases that had already been turned down at least once. Harry Beard's success rate was just as good. All told, Somerset NFU staff won some 11 million litres of quota for our members at appeal. Even at 1984 prices, that was worth some £1.5 million; when quota prices reached their peak in the mid-1990s, more like £8 million. These days professional indemnity lawyers would have a fit if I, as an unqualified, uninsured amateur, attempted anything similar. But we took all those cases without generating a single complaint from a member, and that included the ones that we lost (although I never had quota deducted). It was an episode that I like to think showed the NFU at its very best.

The end of the special case hearings did not mean the end of milk quota-related work, by any means. We tried, and eventually failed, to persuade HQ Legal Department to take up some of what I regarded as miscarriages of justice from the Tribunal process, while the division of quota between landlord and tenant was a running sore, which saw us sending delegations first to Westminster and then to Brussels (another exhausting trip).

Nor was milk the only sector bedevilled by surplus problems. In 1985 and 86 a great debate developed over whether NFU policy should be based on further price cuts, quotas for everything or – an option championed in Somerset by Bridgwater's Brian Rowe and at NFU HQ by Sean Rickard – a quota on nitrogen fertiliser. Somerset often seemed to find itself at loggerheads with head office!

David House, from Dykes Farm, Stoke St Gregory, was County Chairman in 1985. One of his first statements, which I duly reported in the Somerset Farmer, was to warn Somerset County Council that the county was in danger of being seen as a soft touch by the convoys of 'hippies', as we called them, who were increasingly taking to the roads in the summer months. Sure enough, in May 1986, a ramshackle collection of some 70 buses, lorries, caravans and trailers encamped themselves in a field at John Case's farm at West Camel, alongside the A303, about two miles east of Podimore roundabout.

My group secretary for the area, Evan Wilson, who fancied himself as a bit of a law-enforcer, was swiftly on the scene, as were the police. There had been other similar incursions over the previous year or so, and the police were wary of wading in and sparking off what could develop into a riot, as had happened at Stonehenge. This was in the days before the Public Order Act (which was effectively a response to events in Somerset), so that it was down to the landowner, not the authorities, to take legal action to remove trespassers, something that John Case was pursuing with our support, even though previous experience had shown that, a day or two before an Order became effective, the travellers would up sticks and move on, leaving the farmer to pick up the bill.

A stand-off soon developed. I turned up with Claire Faun, who had taken over from Kendall as secretary to Peter Forde, the Regional Information Officer, and from Rebecca as Assistant Editor of the Somerset Farmer, and there were plenty of farmers hanging around outside the entrance to the field as well. The policeman in charge came up to me with a suggestion.

"If you ask your farmers to go in with their tractors and start shifting those vehicles, there's bound to be a punch up, and a breach of the peace will mean my officers can intervene," he offered.

"OK, so will you give me an undertaking that, in that event, none of my members will get arrested?" I replied.

"Oh no," he said. "They'll just have to take their chances."

"In that case," I said, "no deal."

There was eventually some movement. A splinter group called 'Rainbow Village', who were more hippy-ish than the crusty majority, pulled out of the field and onto the main road.

"Follow that convoy," I said to Claire. "And ring me whenever they look like stopping so that we can warn the farmers in the vicinity."

So off she set, no mobile phone of course (my first car-phone didn't arrive until 1988), eventually reporting back after all sorts of twists and turns, that the Rainbow Village was now happily encamped at Westonzoyland airfield.

Eventually, on the day before the Court order was due to come through, the main bulk of the convoy did indeed move out, escorted by the police. They drove two miles down the road to the other side of the Podimore roundabout – and into a field owned by a farmer called Les Attwell, the police making no attempt to stop them!

This second incursion coincided with the Royal Bath and West Show, at which the guest of honour was the recently appointed Minister of State for Agriculture, John Gummer. My 'County Secretary's Diary' in the Somerset Farmer takes up the story:

> Those wretched hippies! Not only did they invade, scandalise and terrorise poor John Case and Les Attwell, but they also interrupted my usual exhausting Show routine of cocktail parties, receptions and lunches.
>
> I'd arrived on the Wednesday to find John Gummer in a flap. He'd heard on the radio about our unwelcome visitors and decided he ought to give himself a share of the limelight. As a result, our half hour with him on milk quotas, swine fever, cereals problems and beef premiums became only ten minutes, during which Mr Gummer managed to say a great deal, whilst signifying very little.
>
> The Gummer-hippy confrontation when it came was amusing, but little else. The verbose little man found himself hemmed in by the great unwashed, nose to nose with one particular black gentleman, sporting an abandoned coal sack on his head, no shirt and, as the holes in his jeans made painfully obvious, no underwear either. The unspeakable had finally come face to face with the ineffable.

As we shall find, it was not the last occasion on which John Gummer and I would cross swords. As for the hippy problem, it did gradually fade away, despite the Public Order Act making little or no difference, especially when the Glastonbury Festival tightened up on gate-crashers. But the police response remained as cynical as before. A few years later, a big hippy convoy was spotted heading towards Taunton. The Somerset and Avon force quickly mobilised, escorting the convoy over the Devon county boundary and onto the old airfield at Smeatharpe, not far from where we lived at Clayhidon, and then melting away. They had not, of course, bothered to tell their Devon colleagues!

I enjoyed my eight-and-a-half years as Somerset County Secretary. I was fortunate in both my staff and my elected farmer office-holders, men like John Hughes, Fred Elliott, Geoff Hewett and Maurice Adams. We may have been regarded by NFU HQ as 'wild men of the West' but, by pioneering management agreements on Exmoor and the Somerset Levels, we made an important and entirely positive contribution to the way in which the relationship between farming and conservation developed, while I like to think that the Somerset voice came across loud and clear on every farming issue that affected the county. We were never backward in coming forward.

I worked hard, perhaps too hard. I had umpteen county committees to service and soon learned that the best way of coping was to write the minutes as the meeting went along, so that all I had to do afterwards was to dictate what I'd written for Angela to type up – and action the various decisions, of course.

Fortunately, with the exception of the joint Pigs Committee with Dorset, my committees met in the daytime rather than the evenings. Even so, from October through to April, I would be out two or three evenings every week, speaking at branch meetings or Young Farmers' clubs or goodness knows what else.

Then there were the dinners. Every NFU group had one in those days, usually on a Friday evening, and the County Secretary and his wife were expected to attend, and most likely to speak. The menu was always the same – vegetable soup, over-cooked roast beef with slushy vegetables and a dried up Yorkshire pudding, followed by either apple pie or sherry trifle, washed down by, if you were lucky, two small glasses of cheap red wine. And poor Mandy always seemed to find herself sitting next to the dullest farmer on the top table.

Fatstock Show dinners were another regular fixture, although this time only for me, as these were strictly men-only affairs, and distinctly boozy at that. My very first was at Highbridge, where Maurice Wall held sway. Naively I'd assumed that the fact that there would be no women present would mean that I could get away with telling blue jokes, forgetting that, in that part of Somerset especially, the farming community numbered more than a few teetotal Methodists in its ranks. For my *piece de resistance* I gave them the golfing gorilla joke, which concludes with the words, complete with graphic accompanying actions "Big ... deal ... five ... fucking ... feet." Two farmers walked out on the spot, resigning their NFU memberships the next day. It taught me a lesson I have never forgotten: if you have even the slightest suspicion that a story or a joke might offend someone, then don't use it.

Then there was the Somerset Farmer to be edited. Thanks to our idiosyncratic but extraordinarily successful advertising manager, John Benjafield (persistence wasn't in it; I always thought that the advertisers took space just to get rid of him), it was – alongside the Dorset version which he also looked after – far and away the most profitable county journal in the country.

My 'County Secretary's Diary' was not the sort of contribution one would usually have expected from a senior NFU official in those days, but the members seemed to enjoy it, although I did get myself into hot water over the issues of the levies which farmers who retailed their own milk had to pay to the MMB for the privilege. I took the side of the producer-processors, as they were called, whose main spokesman was John Taylor of Cricket St Thomas. Our two MMB members, Paul Francis and Denley Brown, warned me that this was an issue which had the potential to bring the Board crashing down, and they were right.

It was in this context that I first encountered the only man with whom I ever seriously fell out in the course of my NFU career (and even then, it was more a case of him falling out with me, than the other way around). This was Derek Mead, who would go on to become one of the most successful and wealthy property developers in Somerset and a thorn in the flesh of the NFU establishment for many years. I was in my office one afternoon when Angela rang through to say that there was a Mr Mead on the phone for me. 'Says he's a member at West-super-Mare,' she added.

I picked up the phone but barely had time to say hello before Derek pitched in. "'Ere," he said, in his deliberately exaggerated Somerset accent. "Thic Steve Roberts ..."

"The Chairman of the Milk Marketing Board, you mean?" I interjected.

"Yeah. 'E's a fucking wanker."

It was only the first of many similar conversations over the years.

I did my bit for the Young Farmers' movement, first as President of the Taunton club. In 1985 we won the national drama competition at that year's

YFC annual gathering in the Isle of Man, with a production of Roald Dahl's 'James and the Giant Peach', starring Rebecca Pow and Charles Clark.

For some reason I was asked to give the address at the annual Somerset YFC Harvest Thanksgiving service in Wells Cathedral in 1988. Never one to duck a challenge, I accepted, taking as my theme the thought that we jolly well ought to be grateful for having more than enough food to eat and stop beating farmers over the head for producing surpluses. I took my father, and wore his old preaching gown for the occasion, and I have never felt more daunted in my life than when I mounted the steps to the pulpit and looked out across the sea of expectant faces that filled the nave. I got through it, and I think father was reasonably proud of me, but it wasn't, in all honesty, my finest hour. I performed much more confidently and eloquently on two subsequent occasions, the second of which was the service to mark the retirement of Bishop Jim Thompson, who was such a lovely man and who did so much for the farming community in his time in Somerset.

As for my broadcasting and journalism, the Devonair programme went soon after I got the Somerset job – Hugh Crowle saw to that! But the weekly BBC Radio Bristol farming programme was augmented with daily pre-recorded reports which were broadcast in the early morning, which I shared with Rebecca, our task made much easier by the launch of BBC Somerset Sound from its studio in Paul Street, Taunton in 1983. Giles Horton and George Sherston continued with their weekly contributions to the Western Daily Press, and in 1986 I started a new column, fortnightly this time, for the Somerset County Gazette.

What with all of this, my BBC cricket commitments in the summer, and at least one round of golf a week, I didn't have nearly as much time for my wife and family as I should have. In 1984, we moved house, to Burcombe, which had been Richard Kallaway's brother Dave's farm, and my son George was born soon afterwards. It was in the very heart of the Blackdowns, only a couple of miles from Applehayes, but it had four bedrooms, a big kitchen and an even bigger sitting room, which was the Devil's own job to keep warm in the winter.

The farm buildings were still in full use, so there was always plenty going on – George's first word was 'tractor'! The surroundings were even more blissfully pastoral than at Applehayes, looking out across green fields and big trees to the junction of two valleys. It was the sort of house I might have dreamed of living in when I was growing up, and with the sort of family I might have dreamed of as well.

As the 1980s wore on, so my father became a real concern. He was still writing lucidly and amusingly for The Times, but his mood was ever-darkening and, as his drinking increased, so his health deteriorated. For Rosie and my half-brother and sister, Adam and Felicity, life at the Old Market Tavern in High Littleton had become a nightmare. In the autumn of 1985, Rosie gave him an ultimatum – either mend your ways, cut down on your drinking and stop making our lives a misery, or you're out.

It made no difference. In November, when she asked me to see if I could say anything that might make a difference, I arrived at the house to find him in his bed, apparently dead. As on several occasions in the past, he had taken an overdose of sleeping pills; not enough, as it turned out, to kill him, but enough, so he must have thought, to deter Rosie from throwing him out.

Things didn't work out as he had doubtless planned. Initially he was sent to a rehabilitation centre near Weston-super-Mare, to dry out. He'd only been there a few days before he escaped, hiring a taxi to take himself back to High Littleton and then expecting poor Rosie to pay the fare when he got there. But she was having none of it.

My next trip to the Old Market Tavern was to collect him and take him to the flat which had been rented for him in Queen's Court in Clifton, where he and Rosie had lived back in the early 1970s. It seemed as if nothing had been done to the building in the interim. The flat was cold, damp and shabby. I left him there, surrounded by piles of books, his typewriter, tins of baked beans and a bottle of whisky. He was sunk in self-pity, made no attempt to look after himself and might have died of neglect had not some kind soul realised what was happening and had him taken to hospital.

From the BRI, he was transferred to Ham Green, a unit which specialised in alcoholics on their last legs, which is where he spent Christmas. I took Mandy and the children to visit him through driving rain on Christmas Day afternoon. Shades of Moorhaven in 1963. We all thought he was on his way out, yet the damage to his liver was not nearly as bad as might be expected from his bottle of whisky a day (at least) habit and he staged a remarkable recovery. Mandy very gallantly agreed that he could come and stay with us at Burcombe while he continued his convalescence, and from there he moved into a flat in Taunton which I'd found for him, just up the road from my office, so that I could keep an eye on him. The deal was that he could drink beer, as long as he stayed off the whisky and, for a couple of months, he stuck to it.

In the meantime, I'd convinced his sceptical bosses at The Times that he would be fit enough and sober enough to resume his cricket reports. He was asked to cover the game between the Combined Universities and the Indian touring team starting on June 12. That morning I collected him from his flat and drove him to the station. "Now remember," I said to him as I helped him onto the train. "No whisky." He said nothing until he was on board with the door safely shut. Then he called to the guard, who was passing. "Which way's the buffet car? I need a scotch."

"That'll show my bastard of a son who's the boss," he must have thought, and it was indeed a cruel blow after all the effort that Mandy and I had put into his rehabilitation. He did cover a few games that season, but his writing had lost its zest and his drinking was soon as bad as ever. His last game was Somerset against Sussex at the County Ground. It was curtailed by rain and finished prematurely, much as my supremely talented father's career had done.

After that, he went to live first in sheltered housing and then in a succession of nursing homes, from each of which he would get himself ejected on account of his drinking and the associated outbursts. For the last ten years or so of his life, I saw him regularly, taking him to either the Cottage in Kingston Road, the Pen and Quill or, latterly, the Half Moon in Stoke St Mary, often in the company of Richard Walsh, a teacher and fanatical Somerset follower, who could not have been kinder. It was a sad final descent.

This all added to the pressures on my life, which were considerable. I was working too hard, drinking too much, not spending enough time with my family, taking too much for granted and, at the NFU, unsettling change was in the air. The NFU was being 'regionalised'. My job was disappearing.

On April 1 1989, the NFU South-West Regional Office opened for business in Exeter, with Richard Macdonald as Director, and Anthony Gibson as Senior Policy Adviser. In my mind at least, it was not much of a cause for celebration.

13

Cricket for the BBC

Cricket has been a big part of my life for as long as I can remember, as, indeed, has cricket commentary. When Chippy and I played against each other on the front lawn at Harford House, I would provide a running commentary, invariably more effusive about my efforts than my brother's, and, being two years older, I invariably won, even if he did grow up to be the better cricketer. Coming from Devon, which was, and is still, only a 'Minor' county (not a designation which any Devonian enjoys!), I shared my loyalties between the two nearest first-class counties, Somerset and Gloucestershire. In each team I had a hero: Colin McCool, the Australian test leg-spinner who played five seasons for Somerset; and the great Tom Graveney, surely one of the most elegant batsmen who has ever played the game, for Gloucestershire. Both men were friends of my father and stayed with us when they came down to Plymouth to take part in one of his broadcasts. Tom gave us a cricket ball, which we promptly lost.

At school in Plymouth and later at Monkton Combe, I was happy enough to bask in the reflected glory of my father's test match commentator status. I suppose I must have day-dreamed about becoming a sports commentator myself, but I never had any serious aspirations and it was not an ambition that my father encouraged. He was, however, instrumental in gaining me my BBC debut. This was in 1969, when I was at Oxford and the West Indies were on tour. They were due to play Gloucestershire in a three-day game at Bristol, staring on Saturday May 17, with my father and the West Indian commentator Roy Lawrence – a lovely man who knew his West Indies cricket inside out and back to front – as the two commentators.

Bill Frindall had taken over from Arthur Wrigley as the BBC's lead scorer, but for some reason he wasn't available to come to Bristol, so the producer, Anthony Smith, asked my father if he knew anyone who could stand in and I was volunteered. My fee would be £5. I did, of course, know how to score, but that was in a conventional score-book. Father knew, from working with Bill Frindall on Test Match Special, that broadcast scorers used a very different set of score-sheets: a linear one, over by over, with columns for each batsman,

162

so that you could see exactly how each over was played and tot up how many balls each batsman had faced, an increasingly important statistic given the rise of one-day cricket; a sheet showing the cumulative bowling figures, which would be handed to the commentator whenever the bowlers were his focus; and what might be termed the 'master score-sheet', which was a rather more elaborate version of a standard scorecard, which the commentator would use when he was summarising what had been going on. At this early stage I didn't have any of these 'Frindall scoresheets', as they were known, so had to design my own, based on my father's slightly sketchy recollections.

Thus armed, I travelled down by train from Oxford on the Friday evening, looking forward to the morrow. But Saturday dawned wet. In fact, it poured down all morning. There was never even the remotest prospect of any cricket, and by lunchtime play had been abandoned for the day. So, in time-honoured fashion, the commentary team headed for the pub, in this case the County Ground Hotel, just outside the main entrance, which had a licence allowing it to remain open all afternoon on match-day Saturdays. I cannot remember exactly how many pints of Courage BA we got through that afternoon, but it was a fair few, and by the time I staggered onto my train back to Oxford at Temple Meads, my disappointment at the absence of cricket had been suitably assuaged.

Fortunately, the fact that I had not been able to show what I could do as a scorer meant that, out of fairness, I ought to be given another go. This didn't come around until August, in the long vacation, when Tony Smith asked me to go to the Cheltenham Festival, for three days working with Brian Johnston. He and my father were friendly enough, but never soul-mates in the way that father was with John Arlott.

I don't think I had ever met Brian before, but he turned out to be exactly as I had expected, genial, jokey and garrulous – with one important exception, and that was his sheer professionalism. He made cricket commentary sound like the easiest thing in the world, but that was based on a deep and shrewd understanding of the game, plus great concentration and attention to detail. I soon discovered that if a batsman reached 50 while we were on air, I had to have the vital statistics – minutes, balls, boundaries – in front of him virtually as the run was scored, and that the bowling figures had to be bang up to date for the fall of every wicket. I always felt under greater pressure with BJ, as he was known then, than with any other commentator, but in the process I became a much better scorer, faster and more accurate, than I would have been without his tutelage.

I first worked with John Arlott the following summer. It was a game at Bournemouth in early August, and he was sucking on an empty pipe, having just given up his sixty Passing Clouds a day habit. This meant that he wasn't at his most relaxed or communicative – 'grumpy' would be a fair description – although friendly enough to me and not as demanding as Brian. That evening he drove me to my father and Rosie's flat in Queen's Court, where he was staying the night before going on further north. He had got through a fair quantity of claret during the day, without showing any outward signs of it, and our first stops were at two of his favourite second-hand bookshops, in Bournemouth and then Wimborne, to see if they had any of the first editions that he collected. He wasn't a particularly fast driver but, in his tank-like Austin Princess, he showed a fine disregard for other road-users and the niceties of the highway code. We just ploughed steadily on, relying on other drivers to stay out of our way. At one point he drove straight across the middle of a big roundabout, offering "Aargh, that didn't used to be there" by way of explanation. We got there safely in the end, but it was a memorable journey.

My other favourite memory of Arlott came later that month, at Taunton where Yorkshire – challenging for the County Championship as usual – were the visitors. In those days, as the Championship moved towards its climax, the BBC offered running commentary on Radio 4 at intervals during the day. It was a warm day, and John had with him his 'Man Friday', Bill Shepheard, Hampshire's public address announcer, his unique style featuring frequently in my father's reports on Hampshire cricket for The Times.

At that time Bill was a large man (he later slimmed down), with a big smile, who enjoyed life to the full and was devoted to Arlott. The pair of them in the Taunton commentary box didn't leave much room for the scorer, but they were such good company that it mattered not at all. At around 12 noon, John decided it was time for Bill to procure the ingredients for what I gathered was their standard Taunton lunch – four bottles of the County Stores house claret and one of their famous turkey pies. Half an hour or so later, Bill returned complete with wine and food and, once the final broadcast of the morning session had been delivered, they tucked in, John producing a corkscrew and two glasses from one of his two enormous briefcases.

Play resumed on schedule at ten past two (11.30 starts in those days) when, with little or no warning, we heard the Radio 4 announcer say "And now, for the latest on Yorkshire's crucial game in the County Championship against Somerset, it's over to our commentator John Arlott at Taunton."

Whereupon a slightly flustered John lifted his wine glass and spoke into it: "And here at Taunton Yorkshire, put in, are 90 for three ..." before expostulating "Oh my goodness me!" as he realised his mistake.

But if Brian Johnston and his successor as the BBC's Cricket Correspondent, Christopher Martin-Jenkins, were the two most professional commentators I worked with, John Arlott was certainly the hardest working. He would almost always reach the box before I did in the mornings, and I would find him there, hammering away at his little portable typewriter for his latest article or book, something he would often return to in the intervals between commentary or reports. I feel privileged to have been able to work with him. As my father said of him in a tribute in the Cricketer magazine after John's death: "His most endearing qualities were his kindness and his generosity in word and deed. He would never speak badly of anyone."

My first professional encounter with Henry Blofeld was at Northampton in July 1973. I was suffering from a dreadful hangover, having spent the previous day with my father at the Oval for the second day of the West Indies test match, where we celebrated the Liberals' two by-election wins at the Isle of Ely and Ripon; and the previous evening in the Horse and Groom in Belgravia, marking Mandy's departure from the NFU to go to work at FMC next door. I'm not sure Henry was exactly at his sparkling best, either. This was my diary entry:

> *It was another cold and cheerless day and the cricket was equally unexciting. Henry Blofeld, a nervous but entertaining man, was the commentator and Norman Preston and Christopher Wordsworth* came into the box in the afternoon. Two pints at lunchtime in the amazingly grotty pavilion revived my spirits and I was able to listen to the Test for most of the afternoon as a distraction from Northants' boring batting.*

And Henry *was* nervous, to the extent of his knees knocking under the rickety table which served as the commentary desk. He had only broken into the magic circle of Test Match Special the previous year and was desperately keen to cement his position. I'm not sure our day together helped him much in that regard. It was genuinely one of the dullest day's play I have watched (David Steele batted almost all day for 77), at one of English cricket's most unlovely grounds, but we got the job done. It was the first of many days spent in Henry's engaging company, and I never knew him nervous again!

---

* *Norman Preston was editor of the Wisden Cricketers' Almanack (1952-80); Christopher Wordsworth reported on cricket for The Observer.*

By this stage in my scoring career I was equipped with the official Frindall score-sheets and was probably getting 20 or so days cricket a season, mostly in the south of England and London but sometimes further afield. At Bournemouth one summer I had the privilege of working with Robert Hudson, a rather stuffy man who was the BBC's Head of Outside Broadcasts. We were perched on the roof of a BBC Land Rover and made an inviting target for the small boys, who took to lobbing oranges and paper cups of water at us, much to Hudson's chagrin.

However, the incident that perhaps gave me the most pleasure was at Portsmouth, where I was working with Neil Durden-Smith, who was often my father's rival for the final spot in a TMS team, and, ex-Royal Navy, suave, immaculately turned out, married to Judith Chalmers, was his polar opposite in outlook and demeanour. On this occasion he was wearing a smart navy blazer, club tie and pristine, perfectly creased, white chinos. We were commentating from the rugby stand, which was uncomfortable and cramped. Midway through the afternoon, Neil opened a bottle of red wine and poured a large measure into a big plastic cup.

Not long afterwards, the Sport on Two presenter came over unexpectedly. Neil hastily grabbed for his lip mike, in the process knocking over his wine, which went all over those beautiful white trousers. What's more, because we were live on air, there was nothing immediately he could do about it, except give his report and feel the wine spreading down his trouser legs. As with Bob Hudson at Bournemouth, we were surrounded by small boys, who thought this the best joke in the world, especially when a furious Neil came off the air and stood up to reveal a huge red stain, from crotch to knees. I decided that sympathy would be rather better received than laughter. These days, of course, we would share the experience with listeners and have a great laugh about it. But Neil Durden-Smith didn't think it funny at all.

I must have been quite a good scorer because by the time the first cricket World Cup came round, in 1975, I seem to have been second in the pecking order, after Bill Frindall. I scored several of the early games, working with a variety of commentators, overseas as well as home, and was highly delighted to be asked to do the final at Lord's, between West Indies and Australia, scoring for the BBC's World Service commentators.

We were broadcasting from a makeshift box, on the top floor of the Lord's pavilion, outside the main BBC commentary box. I can't remember exactly how many commentators were crammed into what looked and felt like a garden shed, but it must have been at least eight. Not all at once, you understand; they would take it in turns to give an Indian, or a Pakistani or maybe Kenyan perspective on events. But, my goodness, it was crowded, and it was a baking hot day.

The consolation was the cricket. With all due respect to England's last gasp win against New Zealand in the 2019 World Cup final, this for me was the greatest day of international one-day cricket that has so far been played. We had Jeff Thomson bowling faster than anyone I have ever seen, a majestic Clive Lloyd century, three quite brilliant Viv Richards run outs and, just when it seemed that the West Indies had the match won, a defiant last-wicket partnership between Lillee and Thomson which almost carried Australia home. All of this at a Lord's packed to the rafters, with the thousands of West Indies supporters bringing colour, noise and vibrancy to the game in a way that only they could. It was a great day.

I didn't see the final of the 1979 World Cup, but I did make my mark on the tournament. This was at Old Trafford, where India were playing Sri Lanka, still only an ICC Associate Member and a bit of an unknown quantity, especially as the touring party had not included an official scorer. Play started late on the Saturday because of rain, Sri Lanka making 238/5.

As a scorer in those pre-computer days, you were continually adding up batsmen's scores, bowling figures and extras to make sure that all the figures tallied, so that any mistakes could be spotted and corrected. I have always been reasonably numerate, so this wasn't usually a problem, except that towards the end of the Sri Lankan innings something seemed to have gone wrong which I couldn't fathom. I eventually decided that the scorers must have mis-identified one of the Sri Lankan batsmen and, to make their figures add up, had got two of the batsmen's scores and the total wrong.

I got to the ground early on the Monday morning, when India were due to reply, and sought out my opposite number in the BBC television box, Irving Rosenwater, to see if he agreed with me that the score was wrong. He did, so we asked to see the two umpires, Kenny Palmer and Alan Whitehead. We explained what we thought had happened, they agreed with us, and the innings total, plus the scores of two batsmen were changed. And then, to put the icing on the cake, Sri Lanka bowled out India, Gavaskar and all, for 191 for their first World Cup win.

This was the high water mark of my career as a cricket scorer for the BBC. By now I was, of course, living in the West Country, where an unassuming young man called Keith Downer had already established himself as the BBC's go-to scorer. I was still used from time to time, at Worcester, maybe, or Edgbaston, but my 20 days a season had come down to no more than six by the early 1980s. I did score the 1983 Benson & Hedges Cup final at Lord's, when Joel Garner blew away the Northants batting to give Brian Rose his fifth trophy as Somerset captain, but that was for BBC Radio Bristol, for whom the regular commentary team, headed by Phil Tottle, were pushed aside in favour of the station's bosses, Peter Davies and David Solomons, with me as 'special guest' scorer. The very last cricket I scored for the BBC was in September of the following season, on both occasions with Henry Blofeld.

Nottinghamshire, with a narrow lead over Essex in the County Championship, had come to Taunton for their final game of the season. I was hired for all three days, working with Don Mosey on Saturday and Henry on Monday and Tuesday. After a damp start the game grew in excitement as it went on. On the second evening news came through that Essex had beaten Lancashire, meaning that Notts needed to win to secure the Championship.

An Ian Botham declaration set Notts 297 to win in what became 60 overs. It was a fair target on a pitch by now taking spin, which suited Vic Marks, who picked up wickets at regular intervals. At the start of the final over 14 were still needed, with Mike Bore, a red-headed left-arm seamer who wouldn't win many 'best-looking cricketer' contests, on strike against Stephen Booth's slow left-arm. Bore carted the first three balls for 4, 4, 2, and seemed to have the game and the championship won. But off the fifth ball, going down the ground to take advantage of Taunton's short straight boundaries, he just slightly miscued. The ball was coming in the air, just to our left in the commentary box.

Henry was beside himself with excitement, but we knew that the ball would disappear from view under the stand below us. I leaned out of the window as far as I could. There was a fielder there. He caught it, and I knew immediately who it was: "Ollis," I shouted to Henry, and Richard Ollis indeed it was, on as a substitute. Keith Fletcher's Essex had won the Championship. It was an occasion, a catch and indeed a name still ruefully recalled by the Nottinghamshire faithful.

My swansong as a scorer came later that month, when the inaugural 'Silk Cut Challenge' was played at Taunton. This was billed as a contest between the world's best all-rounders – Ian Botham, Kapil Dev, Imran Khan, Clive Rice, Richard Hadlee and Malcolm Marshall – and they were indeed an outstanding bunch, in an unparalleled era for all-rounders. The formula devised for deciding the winner was complicated, to say the least, which is presumably why ITV, who were televising the event live, hired Bill Frindall as their scorer, leaving a vacancy for a BBC scorer which I was happy to fill.

I will not bore you with the details. Clive Rice won it by a mile, simply by playing the system more effectively than his rivals. Despite that, it should have been a wonderful day's cricket. Instead of which, I recorded in my diary:

> *The cricket turned out to be pretty inconsequential, and that, plus the fact that the outside broadcast equipment broke down, produced a rather light-headed mood in the commentary box. Henry B and I made the most of the two bottles of wine donated by Silk Cut, and by 6.00 when it had to end, I was well away.*

By that stage, however, I had already moved on to the next stage of my BBC cricket career, as a reporter on Sunday League games for BBC sports output. My first game was at Bath, in June 1983, Glamorgan the visitors. By the standards of those days it was a high-scoring game, Glamorgan making 235, an innings built around 130* from the under-rated John Hopkins, and Somerset getting home with an over to spare, thanks largely to 84 from Nigel Popplewell.

My father had always boasted of how he delivered his post-match reports off the cuff, exactly to time. "They're not bothered with what you say, just how long you take to say it," he explained. It was good advice – for a confident and experienced reporter – which I often followed later in my career. But on this, my debut, I took fright and scripted my 40 seconds. Inevitably, it overran. Black mark, I thought.

I reported a few more games that season, and the next, and was encouraged by a comment from Caroline Woodard, who had been our producer for the Silk Cut Challenge that "Peter Baxter (TMS Producer and head of cricket OBs) feels he's been very wrong in not giving you any commentary this season."

'Commentary?' I noted. 'Now, that would be something.'

My chance came the following year, when Peter rang up to ask if I would be available to provide reports and commentary for a mixture of Sport on Two and the BBC World Service on the first day of Somerset's county championship match against Warwickshire at Taunton on June 1. Of course, I said yes, albeit possibly with a note of hesitation in my voice, for June 1 was the fourth day of the Royal Bath and West Show, when I would normally be expected to be on the NFU stand and was already committed to helping the Chief Livestock Steward, Edwin White, in presenting a special display of champion livestock for the benefit of the general public, the main livestock classes having finished the previous day. In the event I got to the Bath and West first thing, did my stuff with Edwin and then headed back to Taunton as fast as I could, arriving just before the start, Keith Downer already in residence as my scorer.

I was hoping for an interesting but uneventful day, to provide a gentle, undemanding start to my career as a BBC cricket commentator. But from the moment that Vivian Richards strode menacingly to the crease at 28/1, I could sense that this day was going to be anything but. Richards was quite magnificent. He treated all the Warwickshire bowlers, who included Gladstone Small, with utter disdain, batting with power, precision and – especially when Norman Gifford came into the attack – real venom. I don't know what Gifford can have said to upset him, but his bowling figures speak eloquently of the revenge which Richards exacted: 18 overs, one for 135!

He hit 42 fours and eight sixes in his 322, including one which sailed over the commentary box and into St James' graveyard, allowing me to make a feeble joke about the Warwickshire wicket-keeper, Gordon Tedstone. His first 100 came up in 105 balls, his second in 76 and his third from 63. For sheer quality of stroke-play, it was the greatest innings I have ever witnessed. His cover-driving in particular was sublime, or maybe 'sumptuous', which was the adjective I chose for one of my reports (and was subsequently mocked for by my brother). By mid-afternoon we were broadcasting all round the world. I didn't know whether to laugh or cry. Anton Ferreira, an angular medium-pacer, was the bowler as Richards stood on the verge of his 300.

I was so nervous, I could barely think, resorting to cliché at this moment of truth. "And here comes Ferreira, his arms pumping," I said. "And Richards whips him through the on-side for four and his 300. What an innings! What a cricketer! Quite magnificent!" (or words to that effect). I have actually heard the commentary several times, usually as a question in a cricket quiz: who was the batsman going to 300? I have always felt that 'Who was the commentator?' would be much more of a challenge!

Still, as debuts go, it had certainly been a memorable one and, as I downed a post-match pint in the Masons Arms, I didn't feel as if I had let the side down. Other games followed that season, as I gradually grew in confidence, but I never felt remotely that my position was secure. I had been offered no training or advice, nor was there ever any feed-back. The only indication as to whether my performance had passed muster was a phone call to ask me to do another game. I had, of course, picked up a lot from sitting alongside Brian Johnston and John Arlott, but they and the other test match commentators always made it seem so easy, and for me it was anything but.

Ian Botham resigned the Somerset captaincy at the end of that 1985 season, and Peter Roebuck was appointed in his place. I wasn't in any sense privy to what was going on in the Somerset dressing room, but I did know that Roebuck was unhappy with the attitude of Somerset's three superstars and that he and Botham in particular did not get on. It seemed to me a deliberately provocative move on the part of the Chairman, Michael Hill, and the Director of Cricket, Brian Langford, and I was sure Vic Marks, who had a foot in both camps, would have been the better choice.

As the 1986 season went on, it became clear that a storm was brewing. It broke when I was at Old Trafford on August 23, for the first day of Lancashire's game with David Graveney's Gloucestershire, who were challenging for the Championship. It was Andy Peebles, the Radio 1 DJ, cricket nut and mate of Ian Botham, who broke the news, as he came bursting into the commentary box to report that Somerset were sacking Richards and Garner and that Botham was sure to go in sympathy. I was dumbfounded. It just seemed so unnecessary. If Somerset were unhappy with Richards' and Garner's performance, why hadn't they been called in, told as much and effectively been put on notice? Instead of which, as I knew, earlier in the season, Brian Langford had taken Richards to one side and told him that there was a place for him at Somerset for as long as he wanted.

Being the BBC's nearest cricket reporter to Taunton, I soon found myself in the thick of things. As luck would have it, Somerset's next home game was against Essex, Gloucestershire's main rivals, and I was sent along to cover that, and also to pick up what I could about the Richards/Garner/ Botham situation. The BBC's Sports Editor spoke to me down the line. "Take your tape-recorder and see if you can get an interview with Botham. You're a local bloke. He'll surely talk to you."

Hmm. Knowing a bit about Botham and his feelings on the subject, I wasn't so sure, but I had to try. So I sought out the Somerset Secretary, Tony Brown, and asked him, as per standard etiquette, if it would be OK if I spoke to Ian Botham.

"It's no good asking me," he replied. "I don't control who he speaks to. You'd better ask him yourself."

So I went on into the dressing room, where the great man was stretched out on a bench, smoking one of his favourite Hamlet cigars.

"Er, Ian," I ventured. "I'm Anthony Gibson, from the BBC. The Sports Room have asked if you could possibly give me a short interview about, you know, everything that's been going on?"

"Fuck off," he replied, without moving. "Go on, just fuck off." So I did.

I didn't meet Botham again until the summer of 2019 on the pier at Weston-super-Mare, where we were launching the autobiography which I'd ghosted for Brian Rose. Beefy was the guest of honour. I introduced myself again. "We have met before, back in the 1980s, when I was working for the BBC," I said.

"Working for the BBC, were you?" was his response. "In that case, I probably told you to fuck off!"

But he did at least say it with a smile.

My other great day as a BBC network cricket reporter came in May 1988. Somerset were playing Worcestershire but, as it was an unexceptional midweek match, starting on a Thursday, I hadn't been asked to cover it. I did go down after tea on the first day, to watch some cricket and collect my father from the Stragglers Bar and take him back to the nursing home in which he was now living. When I got there, Worcestershire were something like 200/5, Hick 110 not out and batting like a god against an uninspired attack on a pitch as flat as the M5.

I didn't think too much more about it until mid-way through the following afternoon when, out of the blue, I had a call from the BBC Sports Room in London. "Have you got a Uher (tape recorder) with you?" they asked. I said I had, the one that I used for my farming programmes. "In that case, can you get yourself down to the County Ground? Hick's coming up to 350 not out. If he gets close to 400, start commentating and record it."

In less than ten minutes I was in the commentary box, armed with my Uher. Which was just as well, because Hick wasn't hanging around. On a hot day he seemed to be toying with a tiring attack. There was something almost contemptuous about his strokes. As with the Richards' 322, I was conscious that I was witnessing genuine cricketing greatness.

I recorded my commentary on the 400, as requested, and shortly afterwards, the players went in for tea, Hick 405 not out, only 20 runs short of beating Archie MacLaren's first-class record score in England of 424.

"Get over to the pavilion and see if you can get an interview," the Sports Room decreed. By the time I got there, Charles Emery, on the PA, had announced that Phil Neale, the Worcestershire captain, had declared. There would be no record. I could scarcely believe it.

Still, it was one of only seven 400s scored in the entire history of first-class cricket, and I was just about the only non-local reporter in the ground, so an interview was an imperative. As I reached the pavilion, I spotted the BBC Points West cameraman, Clive North, whom I knew from dozens of farming interviews. He was there with a camera, but no reporter.

"Come on," he said. "You do the interview and I'll film it."

We waylaid Hick and his captain as they emerged from the dressing room, and I got my interview. Later that evening, it featured on the BBC television nine o'clock news.

But the Sports Room hadn't finished with me. "We want a voice-piece of a minute, and can you put together a feature for Cliff Morgan's Sport on Four for tomorrow morning?"

It all went well. At close of play, Phil Neale confessed he didn't even know about the MacLaren record, and Peter Roebuck, dressed only in a towelling dressing gown, gave me a quite brilliant interview. I sent the package up to London from the BBC's Paul Street studio and then almost burst into tears with a sense of achievement and relief that the challenge had been laid down and I'd risen to it.

What it was not, however, was career changing. I carried on working for Sport on Two and Sunday Sport for a few more seasons, but I was going through a difficult time, both at home and in the NFU, and I didn't make the progress, either as a reporter or as a commentator, that Peter Baxter must have been hoping for.

My final ball-by-ball commentary was at Old Trafford in 1990 when, in the quarter-final of the NatWest Trophy, Gloucestershire were swept away by Wasim Akram and Lancashire. At the halfway stage I felt that my commentary had gone pretty well, especially when I was asked to provide a three-minute summary before the start of the Gloucestershire innings. For commentaries, unlike Saturday and Sunday afternoon reports, we had summarisers, in this case Lancashire's Paul Allott. He waited patiently as I burbled my way through the three minutes and, when I eventually brought him in, said dryly. "Well, there's nothing more for me to add, Anthony. You seem to have said it all." It makes me squirm to think of it, to this day.

My last Sport on Two outing was in 1995, when I made a mess of reporting a dull game at Edgbaston between Warwickshire and Notts. When the phone didn't ring at the start of the following season, I decided to cut my losses and offer myself to BBC Radio Bristol. Phil Tottle, Mark Davis (former Somerset fast left-armer) and I worked well together over the next couple of seasons. An opening partnership between Mark Lathwell and Marcus Trescothick in a big game at Canterbury lingers in the memory. But then the BSE crisis blew up, and cricket had to take a back seat. I carried on working sporadically for Radio Bristol till 2005, but it wasn't until after my retirement from the NFU that my commentary career resumed.

One of my few regrets about my career is that I didn't do more rugby commentary. I did enjoy one glorious season, in 1989/90, when the Somerset commercial station, Orchard FM, came on the air. They had made much in their franchise bid to the Independent Broadcasting Authority (IBA) of covering local sports, so I persuaded the programming boss that what they needed was someone to cover Bath Rugby and that I was their man.

Happily he agreed, and I was armed with a brick of a mobile phone and sent off to provide a mixture of commentary and reports on every Bath game, home and away, for the entire season. Despite the shortcomings of the equipment, I loved it! Rugby is much easier to commentate on than cricket, because there is always something happening. You don't have to fill with eulogies to the beauties of the Quantocks, or speculation as to the destination of a passing train, during long periods of relative inactivity. What is more, this was a truly great Bath side, featuring Stuart Barnes, Jeremy Guscott, Richard Hill, Jon Hall, Gareth Chilcott, Andy Robinson, Victor Obogu, Dave Egerton, Simon Halliday, Graham Dawe and, my own personal favourite because he farmed not far away from us in the Blackdown Hills, Richard Lee.

We were edged out in the Courage League by Wasps and Gloucester, but in the Pilkington Cup final, in front of a near-capacity crowd on a gloriously sunny day at Twickenham, Bath were at their very best. A powerful Gloucester side was not so much beaten as crushed, 48-6, as we ran in eight tries in the best club rugby performance I have ever seen. It was, however, a case of saving the best till last, for me as well as for Bath, because that was the last rugby match I commentated on. By the time the next season came around, Orchard FM had abandoned its sporting pretensions and defaulted to the standard commercial local radio format of pop music and phone-ins.

I did also enjoy, if that is the word, a brief and inglorious career as a football reporter. It came about like this: one afternoon in early October 1986, I took a call in my NFU office from the BBC Sports Room in London.

"Hello Anthony, do you know anything about football?" the conversation began. Now, the truthful answer would have been 'not much'. But I knew enough to be aware that Plymouth Argyle were close to the top of the old second division, and guessed straightaway that this was the occasion for the call. "Oh yes," I lied. "I've followed Plymouth Argyle all my life."

That was true up to a point, in that I did always look for their result on a Saturday afternoon, taking a perverse pleasure if they'd lost, Argyle always having seemed to me to be a rival to my beloved Albion and Services. And I did know the rules of the game, or most of them, and had I not played right half for Manadon Vale Primary School back in 1960?

"Oh, that's good," said the sports producer. "We had you down as more of a rugby man. How do you fancy a trip to Plymouth next weekend, to cover their match against Sunderland for us? It's a big game for both teams."

So that was settled. I duly drove down to Plymouth on Saturday October 16, armed with my big box of a COOBE (Commentator Operated Outside Broadcast Equipment) and Uher, heading first for the Lounge, a pub in Stoke, to meet my friend Tony Oxley, who really had followed Argyle all his life. Two pints of Bass and some useful background later, I headed for the ground.

Arriving at the main gate, I announced myself as "Anthony Gibson, BBC Sport on Two" and asked to be directed to the commentary box. The gateman looked at me blankly, as only gatemen can.

"Don't know nothing about any BBC", he said, blankly. Someone who did know something was eventually summoned. "Oh, you're the bloke down from London, are you? Well you can't use the commentary box. BBC haven't bothered to come here for years, so we've allocated it to the hospital broadcasters. We've got you a seat in the stand."

Now, had I been Alan Green or Mike Ingham, I would doubtless have kicked up an almighty fuss and the hospital broadcasters would have been evicted from what was, technically, BBC property. But I wasn't, so I took what I was given, and there was at least a plug to connect the COOBE, which was perched weightily on my knees. There was, however, a fatal flaw to this arrangement, which I discovered about halfway through the first half, when Sport on Two came over for a 40-second up-date.

Argyle were already one up and, at the very moment they came over to me, it looked as if they might score again. Whereupon all the pasty-munching Plymothians around me stood up, something I was unable to do because of the COOBE. I could see nothing. I'd just got going when there was the most tremendous roar. A goal had obviously been scored, but who was the goal scorer? As the chap next door to me sat down, I put the lip mike to my chest and hissed at him desperately: "Who scored?"

"Argyle, mate," he replied.

They went on to win 4-2, and I think I got at least one of the scorers correct!

Despite such disasters, I was asked again, several times, the most memorable of which was the following February, when Blackburn Rovers were the visitors, complete with Ossie Ardiles, on loan from Spurs. Argyle won 3-0 after Ardiles was forced to limp off early in the second half, the victim of a hideous challenge by Argyle's resident clogger, Nicky Marker.

"See if you can get an interview with Ossie afterwards, and ask him what he thought of that tackle," I was instructed.

I duly made my way down to the changing rooms, waiting for the Argentinian to emerge. When he did, eventually, I thrust my microphone at him in best football reporter fashion. "What about that tackle, Ossie?" was my opening salvo.

"Ah, sorry, me no speaka the Inglese," he replied, which I knew was a complete lie. But it was all I could get out of him.

I bowed out as a football reporter at a Torquay United cup-tie against West Ham in January 1990. I don't think anyone but me either noticed or cared when my reports were heard no more. But I can, I'm sure, lay claim to one football broadcasting record that will never be beaten. I am the only person ever to have reported the first professional game he had been to *in his life* for a national broadcaster.

14

Cider then

Growing up in South Devon, one couldn't help but be aware of cider and the culture surrounding it. However, it was not a drink which featured at home in Sparkwell or Plymouth. My father was a beer man. His only recorded encounter with cider was on a cricket tour of South Devon whilst captaining the Oxford Crocodiles, a side more notable for their sociability than their cricket ability. In an evening match against Buckfastleigh they unwisely visited the local pub before the game and, even more unwisely, got stuck into the local scrumpy. The Crocodiles were bowled out for 26, the local paper headline reading 'Oxford cracks shattered'.

Early and disastrous encounters with rough cider are the stuff of which Devonshire childhoods are made, but I am afraid that, in my case, there were no such rites of passage. The first pint of cider I can remember drinking was in the Hope and Anchor in Hope Cove, when I was working as a waiter at the Cottage Hotel. It was priced at two shillings a pint for visitors, one shilling a pint for locals, a category in which I was included. It was typical Devon scrumpy – cloudy, sharp, strong. After that, I stuck to the beer.

I did discover one very important quality of cider when I was working on the farm at Blacklands. As we young lads sweated long into the night in the top of the hay barn, stacking the bales which were being remorselessly piled onto the elevator by Whiskers, the farm manager, regular draughts of the local cider kept us going most wonderfully. It was strong, but we soon sweated it out. A similar quantity of beer would have sent us to sleep.

My first professional encounter with cider, as it were, came shortly after I was moved down to the South-West as Regional Information Officer in 1976. That spring the Chancellor, Denis Healey, announced in his Budget that cider was to be brought into the net of excise duty, something from which it had been exempt since the 1920s. The NFU, representing farmhouse cider-makers, didn't like this one bit but, by the time the announcement was made, it was too late. The die was cast. The only argument was over an exemption for very small producers to spare them all of the paperwork and inspections which paying the duty of 22p per gallon (half the rate on beer) implied. We wanted 10,000 gallons, if memory serves. The Government, with the support of the larger producers, proposed 1,000. It was fixed in the end at 1,500 gallons, this being the amount that a farming family and its workforce might be expected to consume themselves over the course of the year. Mind you, they would need to be thirsty. For a household and workforce of, say, five adults, that works out at 300 gallons per head, or not far short of a gallon a day!

The situation stirred my campaigning instincts, especially given the involvement of the big brewers, who were lobbying for no exemption at all for even the smallest commercial producers, for fear that it might set a precedent for smaller brewers. So, that summer, I circulated the NFU's South-West county branches, asking for details of members who were cider-makers, so that I could compile a list and send them a questionnaire, the results of which could be used in the Excise Duty battle.

The response was a bit muted, but I did get a letter from Vincent Yorke of Bushley Cider near Tewkesbury, which seemed to put the case eloquently. He was selling cider at 70p per gallon (!). Excise duty would take that to 92p, and that in turn would push the business through the £5,000 VAT threshold, meaning his selling price would need to rise by a third to £1 per gallon.

> Not a penny in our pockets and a pittance for the Chancellor, but a mountain of idiotic forms and red tape for a part-time cider-maker, who is just continuing a local tradition, seeing no reason to stop it.

Another to return his form was Horace Lancaster, who farmed and made cider near Milton Abbot, on the Devon and Cornwall border north of Tavistock, and this really got me interested.

> Still cider only. The apple juice only is fermented. NO sugar or yeast is added. I therefore make a natural farm cider and its proof spirit is between 9.8% and 14.3%. If I have to pay the higher rate of tax on my cider it will be about £3.11/gallon which will mean the end of my Devon farm cider being sold as no-one will buy it.

He suggested that I came and saw him, which I did. It turned out that he was producing about 26,000 gallons a year and had been visited by Customs and Excise to verify capacity and take samples of his cider. Not long afterwards, he had been sent a bill for many thousands of pounds, with a letter explaining that, on being tested, his ciders had been found to be above the 8.7% abv (alcohol by volume) limit for cider and would therefore be treated – and taxed, retrospectively – as wine.

He gave me some of his cider: 'Felldown Head' was his brand, which was both the name of the farm and a none too subtle indication of the effect it could have on the unwary, to which was added the old tag: 'Bread may be the staff of life but cyder is life itself.' It was wonderful stuff, which I can remember to this day. It was deep gold in colour, rich and appley in flavour, not sharp, but with a wonderfully vinous quality. It was most definitely not a cider to be trifled with. I just wish now that I'd asked him for the names of the apple varieties that went into it.

Fortunately Horace had Devon NFU on his side, and they in turn involved his local MP, Peter Mills, who took up the case with enthusiasm. That, plus the attendant publicity which I was able to generate, eventually persuaded Customs and Excise to back down. But only as far as the retrospective tax bill was concerned. For the future, 8.7% abv was the limit. Horace was disgusted and not long afterwards put the business on the market. But there was a happy ending, in that the man who bought it, Nigel Lawrence, remained true to Horace's traditions and became in time a valuable ally in cider campaigning.

If I had been halfway towards becoming a cider campaigner before that visit, a combination of Horace's troubles and Horace's cider completed the job. I was still quite active in CAMRA, so I wrote to the national Chairman, Joe Goodwin – a splendid man, who sadly died much too young – outlining the threat to smaller cider-makers and asking that its West Country branches be circulated with a request that they get in touch with their local producers, suggesting that they lobby their MPs as well as generating as much local publicity as possible. At this stage CAMRA as an organisation was broadly supportive of 'real cider' and the people who made it, without having any very clear idea of how to define it, or what best to do by way of promoting it. Given my NFU role on the one hand, and my involvement with the Great British Beer Festival on the other, it wasn't long before I became CAMRA's unofficial 'cider person'.

That summer Mandy gave me a two-gallon Whiteways Cider stone jar, with a tap at the base for dispense. I would take it with me on my travels around the region, stopping off at cider-making farms to get it filled, usually at a price of about £1 a gallon. I tended to favour those who were relatively near the main roads, like Gordon Rich just off the M5 near Highbridge, or Tom Gray and Eric Bromells, both at Tedburn St Mary on the A30 west of Exeter, or, further north, Tony Cullimore, off the A38 south of Gloucester.

The few remaining 'cider houses' were another fascination. The Olde Cider Bar in Newton Abbot had long been a favourite. Chippy, Tony Oxley and I would head there on Boxing Day morning, prior to a visit to Newton Abbot races in the afternoon. In those days it sold Inchs, from Winkleigh, as a medium, and a strangely greenish brew produced by Hunts as the dry. And when I say dry, I mean it. It could take the enamel off your teeth.

Living in north Wiltshire as we were then, our nearest cider house was at Purton, not far from Berkeley, in the Severn Vale. There was no bar as such. We sat in the front parlour and were brought typically sharp Gloucestershire cider in blue-and-white-striped china mugs. It wasn't until 1983 that I visited the cider house at Woodmancote, known familiarly as the Monkey, to write about it for CAMRA's 'What's Brewing' newspaper. You couldn't drink inside the pretty thatched cottage, but this was a summer visit and to sit in the garden was a joy. A glorified garden shed provided shelter when the weather wasn't so good and, as far as I know, it is still open, albeit with (now as then) restricted opening hours, but you will have to find it for yourselves. When I wrote about it in 1983 I promised the proprietor Graham Durbin that I wouldn't reveal its exact whereabouts for fear of its limited facilities being overwhelmed, and that still holds good today.

In my cider-related researches, it had struck me how little was generally known about the West Country's farmhouse cider-makers. Here, surely, was a gap in the market which I would be well placed to exploit. Perhaps, I thought, I could produce the equivalent of Frank Baillie's ground-breaking 'Beer Drinker's Companion', but for cider. So I wrote to the publishers whom I thought would be most likely to be interested in the concept, given that they were based just a few hundred yards from the Olde Cider Bar in Newton Abbot and specialised in books about the West Country (and railways!), David and Charles. They turned me down flat. My father later explained why: the firm's founder and managing director, David St John Thomas, was a life-long teetotaller, to whom anything to do with cider, given its associations, was anathema.

But I did eventually compile my list of cider-makers, in the West Country and beyond, and indeed still have it. It contains plenty of familiar names: Perry's, Gray's, Julian Temperley's 'Burrow Hill', Hunts, Sheppey's, Hecks, Rich's, Bromells, Hancocks, Roger Wilkins and, slightly further afield, Symonds and Aspall House. Some famous names have gone: Philip White, whose brightly painted farm wagons used to draw the tourists to his farm at Ashill on the A358 between Taunton and Ilminster, Churchwards of

Yalberton, Williams Bros of Nailsea and Vernon Bland of Oldbury-on-Severn. One thing which hasn't changed was the domination of the cider market by three big producers. In the late 70s they were Bulmers, who had maybe 55% of the market, Taunton Cider (owned by a consortium of big brewers), with 20 to 25% and Coates Gaymers with around 20%. Between them, they accounted for over 90% of the total market and most of the rest was shared by the larger regional producers like Westons, Inch's and Merrydown.

The dominance of cider's 'Big Three' was even greater than that of beer's 'Big Six', and the potential for a campaign to do for real cider what CAMRA had done for real ale was obvious – on the face of it. But then how do you define 'real cider'? Purists, like Julian Temperley or John 'Dixie' Dix, would say that it should be made from 100% pressed apple juice, either wholly or mainly from recognised cider apple varieties, allowed to ferment using the natural yeasts and then dispensed without the use of extraneous CO_2. 'Keeved cider', using a method similar to that for champagne to produce a naturally sweet product, would also count as 'real'.

But techniques commonly used by cider-makers from the smallest to the largest, such as sulphiting and adding a standard yeast to give consistency, or adding artificial sweeteners to produce medium and sweet ciders, or even watering down to keep the strength below the 7.5% abv at which the recently fixed higher duty rate kicks in, would be outlawed. As for using concentrates as opposed to pressing your own, what detectable difference could it make to the end product, assuming that the concentrated juice comes from cider varieties?

In 1978, I wrote to Fred Beech, the Deputy Director of the Long Ashton Research Institute, who were the fount of all cider-making knowledge, seeking his views on the use of concentrates. He replied that, years previously, Long Ashton had conducted trials on using apple concentrates to make cider and had then subjected the results to a sampling session by experts alongside ciders made from pressed apples.

Provided we had used genuine cider apples and the best methods of processing to avoid loss of quality, the audience could find no difference in the flavour of the ciders. The Swiss, and some of our own makers, prefer to make cider from concentrate throughout the year since it gives them a fresh, fruity product when sold shortly after fermentation.

And, as he went on to point out, the use of concentrate was a useful buffer against the inconsistency of apple supplies, given the tendency, particularly of older orchards and varieties, to crop every other year.

As a consequence of all this, CAMRA decided to draw its definition widely. In one of my earlier 'Inside Cider' columns for What's Brewing, I imagined how this might play out:

Picture the scene: you walk into a strange pub, probably in the West Country. "Got any real cider?" you ask the landlord.

"What do you mean by 'real', squire?" he replies.

Now is your chance. Take a deep breath, and away you go:

"Traditional draught cider, my good man, is made from a primary fermentation of cider and dessert apples with a dominant yeast derived from a natural cider apple yeast; sugar may be added; natural conditioning may be induced by the addition of further amounts of yeast and sugar prior to casking and there must not be total filtration or pasteurisation; the cider must be dispensed without the use of extraneous carbon dioxide." (Make sure you get this bit right – in an early real ale guide to Devon it appeared as 'extravenous'!)

If that doesn't satisfy him, nothing will!

The definition has since been simplified. It still excludes the use of concentrates but, to the cider cognoscenti, it also still covers a multitude of what they would regard as sins and, unless you are a genuine expert, sorting the sheep from the goats is well-nigh impossible.

Cider first featured in CAMRA's Good Beer Guide in 1979, and I helped organise a modest representation of the cider-maker's art at the 1980 Great British Beer Festival. At the time I produced a list of cider-makers, excluding the Big Three. It had 50 businesses on it, most of them just farm-scale operations with no particular wish for additional publicity or custom, lest it leave them without enough cider to keep their regulars happy (or maybe put them on the radar of Customs and Excise!). Although excise duty was the last straw for several medium-sized cider businesses (like Horrells of Exeter, who produced for Devenish, amongst other regional brewers), there was something of a revival in the early 1980s with, as I reported for What's Brewing, 'at least a dozen small cider-makers setting up in business in the past year'. Most were genuine enthusiasts; others 'simply cowboys', as I described them.

One such, whom I wrote about, was a bloke from Cheddar who got the chance to buy for next to nothing several tons of Granny Smiths, which had been rejected or were otherwise surplus to requirements. Aha, he thought. I'll make cider from them and flog it to the tourists as 'genuine' Somerset Scrumpy. However, when he took delivery of the apples, he discovered there was a problem: they were all still wrapped individually in blue tissue paper, as was the way in those days. Oh, to Hell with it, he must have thought. The paper won't do anyone any harm. I'll just put them through the mill as they are. Which was fine, except that the cider came out bright blue and not even the most gullible tourist could be persuaded that this was the traditional Somerset way.

Whether that was apocryphal, I know not, but it has certainly passed into modern cider folklore. There were also rumours at the time (probably emanating from Dixie, one of the great cider characters, who had migrated from his Derbyshire home and a job with the BBC to make cider with Julian Temperley in Somerset and who eventually set up his own business in the Marchioness Shed in Bristol's dockland) that another enterprising entrepreneur had made cider from a load of rejected grapefruit. And it is certainly true that at least three purveyors of 'Traditional Cornish Scrumpy' were buying in cider in bulk from one or other of the Big Three and simply re-branding it.

However, to my campaigning mind, this sort of thing was all very small beer indeed when set alongside the vastly greater fraud being perpetrated against the cider-drinking public by the Big Three cider-makers. Their crime, as far as I was concerned, was to trade on images of the country traditions of cider-making, giving the impression that the apples used were from Somerset or Devon or Herefordshire or wherever, when the vast majority of their raw material came from overseas, as concentrate. In 1984 my friend Dixie did the sums for me:

> Taking the total tonnage of cider apples grown in 1983 (MAFF figures): 34,944 tonnes x 170 gallons of juice per tonne = 5,940,480 gallons. Declared sales of cider were around 60 millions gallon. So we are left with a figure of 54,059,520 million gallons of 'Genuine Traditional West Country Cider' produced from eastern European, French and Italian concentrate.

This was a situation in which my CAMRA interests coincided exactly with my NFU ones. For not only were consumers being deceived, my apple growers were being denied what ought to have been a very profitable and much-needed market for their fruit. In both my What's Brewing columns and articles for the Western Daily Press, I endeavoured to lift the lid on what was going on. The Big Three were unimpressed.

The first of them I crossed swords with was Coates Gaymers, who had swallowed up Coates at Nailsea and Whiteways of Whimple and who now owned Showerings of Shepton Mallet, but whose main cider brand was

Coates Olde English. They swore blind to me that none of their cider was made using imported apple concentrate, but what they were certainly doing was using at least 50% of non-cider apple varieties, mainly cooking apples from the Eastern counties. They had got on the wrong side of their many Somerset apple suppliers by refusing to take up to 70% of the bumper crop of 1980, with the result that thousands of tonnes of apples, in Devon as well as Somerset, had gone to waste. I concluded an article, which was perhaps more notable for its campaigning zeal than its strict accuracy, by suggesting that the company change its advertising jingle from 'Coates comes up from Somerset where the cider apples grow' to 'Coates comes down from Norfolk, where the cooking apples grow'.

They were not amused! My editor, Brian Glover, was sent a stinging letter from Coates Gaymers' Marketing Director, the aptly named Mr Frost, pointing out the error of my ways and demanding corrections. But the episode did have a rather more positive outcome, in that I established a constructive dialogue with a company which was important to apple growers in Somerset. I was taken out to lunch by Gerald Frost and endeavoured to persuade him and his head cider-maker Phil Owens of the merits of producing a "top quality, traditional draught cider, aimed at the premium market". At the time, they demurred: "Maybe one day the time will be right for tapping into the 'traditional' market, but not yet."

But the time did eventually arrive. In May 1986, I was invited to the Shepton Mallet mill to be given an exclusive pre-tasting of a new cider which was being launched, called 'Addlestones'. It was billed as 'serious cider', and the first paragraph of the press release issued by the company to mark its launch spoke of the product as being 'in every way like a real ale and is a real breakthrough for the serious cider drinker'.

It was also a bit of a breakthrough for Somerset's apple growers, as 50% of the fruit which went into it was bittersweet cider apples, and the sugar and juice that were added at casking meant that fermentation continued in the keg, creating the cloudiness and variability which were its main features. Bob Chaplin, who was much involved in the development of Addlestones tells me that there was a genuine sense of pride at Shepton Mallet at having developed a cider which combined tradition and technology (particularly in the method of dispense) to such good effect. It was a commercial success as well and is still available on draught and in bottle.

Bulmer's took most of their apples from Herefordshire and so were less significant to me in my NFU role. They also were the least guilty in terms of the proportion of their ciders which were made from concentrate. They claimed – and I've no reason to doubt this – that a third of their raw material was home-grown cider apples and, when you've got 60% of the market, that's a lot of apples. Their PR in those days was second to none. Rather than wait for me to have a go at them in What's Brewing, they launched a pre-emptive strike. I was invited on a two-day visit to their vast cider mill in Hereford, put up at the splendid Bulmer-owned Red Lion at Weobley, and treated to a slap-up lunch on board the Royal Train, which stood in Bulmer's own siding, headed by the gleaming No 6000 King George V.

Unlike some other big beasts in brewing and cider-making, Bulmers had decided that there might be something in this 'real ale thing'. "We are hoping to launch something of a traditional draught campaign, but we'll be relying on word of mouth and chaps like yourself," is how it was explained to me by the company's Product Manager for draught ciders, Ken Pringle. I did my best for them, praising their 100% bittersweet apple bottled cider, Bulmer's Number 7, to the skies, and concluding that, of all of the draught ciders produced by the Big Three, Bulmer's 'West Country Extra Dry' was the pick of the bunch: 'It is a genuinely dry cider, not unlike a high-class farmhouse cider, and it is the sort of distinctive product which Bulmers will need if they are serious about winning a slice of the real ale trade.' That was written with feeling. Westcountry Extra Dry (which Bulmers had inherited when they'd bought the West Country Cider business in Gloucestershire) was the cider which old George served in my Sherston local, the wonderful Carpenters Arms, so I'd sunk many pints of it. The locals liked to top it up with a drop of gin!

How sad it is – and how telling – that neither Number 7 nor West Country Extra Dry features among the Bulmer's brands that have survived the Heineken takeover.

If Coates-Gaymers and Bulmer's did not exactly change their ways in response to my strictures on the one hand, encouragement on the other, they did at least acknowledge that there might be a parallel for cider in what had happened with real ale, and act upon it. Taunton Cider, by contrast, shifted not an inch. I had first crossed swords with them in my NFU role in the 1970s, over apple prices. The 1976 Dorset NFU Chairman, Rear Admiral Tom Best, had returned to the family farm and orchards at Melplash in West Dorset after a distinguished career in the Royal Navy, supplying Taunton Cider with cider apples. Dissatisfied with the £30 or so a tonne he was being paid for his fruit by Taunton Cider, and with the backing of the NFU, he was instrumental in getting some like-minded growers together to form the Norton (as in Norton Fitzwarren, where Taunton Cider was based) Cider Growers Association to negotiate prices with the company. They did a great job. Over the next ten years or so, the price more than quadrupled to £122.50 per tonne (which is £4 a tonne more than the 2020 price!). It might have looked like a victory for a bunch of small growers over an over-mighty buyer, but Taunton Cider knew what they were doing. Being seen to play fair by their apple suppliers was a stroke of public relations genius, which both diverted attention away from what else was going on at Norton Fitzwarren as well as silencing the most likely source of criticism.

I had always got on well with Taunton Cider's enthusiastic PR person, Jeanette Keech, and knew the incoming Chief Executive, Geoff Stocks, from his time as Marketing Director at Guinness. I would be invited to the company's Wassail at Monty's Court every January where we ate, drank, frightened the evil spirits away and were each presented with a handsome reproduction vintage cider mug, all of which I still have. But when the cider grapevine revealed to me that roughly 90% of Taunton cider was being made from imported apple concentrate, whilst the company was all the time trading on its Somerset heritage, the relationship rapidly cooled.

This was more an NFU concern than a CAMRA one. In the early 1980s a surplus of apples in the 'on' years was causing hundreds of acres of orchards to be grubbed up, just at the time when farmers most needed alternatives to the mainstream markets – milk, grain and beef – all of which were over-supplied. 'Diversification' was just becoming a buzz-word, and cider apples – an unsubsidised crop for a genuine, profitable and growing market, in which Somerset could boast unrivalled expertise – seemed an ideal option. John Hughes, who had been my County Chairman in 1984, agreed. But first we needed some publicity.

In those days, large chunks of the NFU's AGM in London were taken up in approving the reports of the Union's umpteen committees, of which the Cider Fruit Sub-Committee, chaired by diminutive, apple-cheeked Charlie Pullin from Tintinhull (and how much more Somerset can you get than that?!), was one of the smallest and least regarded. In most years Charlie's moment in the spotlight consisted of mounting the dais and saying: "Mr President, I beg to present the report of the Cider Fruit Sub-Committee for 1985 (or whatever). One, two, three (referring to the numbered paragraphs). Mr President, I beg to move." And, to the cheers of his Somerset colleagues, that would be that.

But this time was different. John Hughes had something to say:

"Mr President, we come up from Somerset, where the cider apples grow; or at least where they used to grow. Sadly, we now have a situation in which orchards are being grubbed up and thousands of tonnes of apples are being left to rot, while almost 90% of the 60 million gallons of cider drunk in this country last year was made from apple concentrate imported from France, Switzerland, Yugoslavia, Hungary and all points East. Mr President, Adge Cutler must be turning in his grave."

He went on to suggest three measures: clear labelling to indicate whether the product was made from home-grown apples or something else; orchard re-planting grants; and a fair price for cider apples. His speech was received with acclamation and made the national press the next day.

For the next few years we campaigned our socks off. An interview I gave to the Daily Telegraph, in which I repeated the 90:10 ratio of imported concentrate to home-grown apples, got me into trouble with Bulmer's, who promptly leant on Herefordshire NFU. This earned me a rebuke from the recently appointed Director of Public Relations at HQ, Warren Newman, a cold fish with whom I never got on, in which he defended Bulmer's ("who are NFU members") pointed out (fairly) that Somerset cider-makers were among those with the worst record when it came to sourcing raw material and added that "we have to rely on county secretaries using their judgement in public statements and seeking facts from HQ."

Happily, however, the apple growers of Herefordshire seemed to agree with me and by 1987 were making common cause with Somerset in calling for an industry-wide agreement, under which growers and cider-makers would work towards a situation whereby at least 50% of home-produced cider should be made from home-produced cider varieties of apples by the turn of the century. If that sounds a modest target, then there was a reason for it. At the time, the entire UK acreage of cider varieties was sufficient to supply barely 10% of the annual production of cider and, with the cost of planting new orchards running at around £2,000 per acre, that wasn't going to change in a hurry.

But that was really as far as the campaign got. The National Association of Cider Makers, dominated then, as now, by the big boys, would have none of it, while the smaller cider-makers lacked both the organisation and the political will to fight for real change. Conscious of the need for smaller cider-makers to speak with one voice on issues such as raw materials and excise duty, Julian Temperley had a few years earlier formed a Farmhouse Cider

Makers Association, with the immediate priority of agreeing a definition of 'traditional farmhouse cider' which could then be used as a basis for protection under consumer legislation. But could Julian's members agree on a definition? Could they, be blowed. As I wrote at the time:

> *Cider-makers are a fiercely independent bunch, turning out a product*
> *for a particular market in the best and most economical way possible.*
> *They do not want anyone playing God Almighty when it comes to*
> *telling them how to make their cider. They want to do their own thing.*

And, believe me, that still applies.

Looking back on those years, I think it is fair to say that we did make some progress, without achieving anything like the breakthrough that has so transformed the market for draught beer. What we did do was to put the issue of 'real cider', or 'traditional cider' or whatever you want to call it, on the map. The drinking public did come to understand that there was a qualitative difference between the mass-market brands and the more traditional alternatives, even if the latter couldn't be accurately defined.

What we failed to do – not least because we never really tried to – was to address the other issue which has bedevilled the development of a quality market for cider throughout the last 50 years and more, and that is the sheer alcoholic strength of the natural product. Time and again, I was told by executives of the Big Three that they wanted nothing to do with 'traditional' or 'farmhouse' cider, because of its connotations of roughness and drunkenness. At Hereford, Shepton Mallet and Norton Fitzwarren, 'scrumpy' was a dirty word. The situation was further complicated by the rise of the super-strength 'white ciders' which was just beginning in the 1980s, with the launch of products like Taunton's 'Diamond White', which was widely blamed for fuelling the cricket hooligans who periodically gave Somerset cricket a bad name. Campaigning against the watering down of cider was hard work when the strength of the product was the source of so much trouble.

What we did do, I believe, was to sow some seeds: seeds of distinctiveness, quality, innovation and authenticity, from which has grown much more recently the craft cider movement and a thousand new small cider businesses. We stopped the rot and prepared the ground for a renaissance, the fruits of which we are now enjoying, as we will discuss in due course.

15

A taste for local food

It was in the autumn of 1983 that I took a phone call from Chris Rundle of the Western Daily Press, in which he told me of a conversation he had had with Derek Hector, the television cameraman and a scion of the Hector withy-growing dynasty at North Curry. They had been struck, he said, by the number of new small, farm-based food and drink businesses that were being set up around Somerset and wondered if the NFU would be interested in doing something to help them grow and prosper – setting up some sort of organisation to help them get their products to market, for example.

I'm sure the NFU would be interested, was my response. I knew that my colleague in Cumbria, David Hellard, had done something similar, bringing together a group of his local producers as a one-off for an event in London, which he'd called 'A Taste of Cumbria'. Perhaps we could call our group or organisation 'A Taste of Somerset'? Why don't we bring a few people together to see what they think of the idea?

One thing led to another, and by December we had the official blessing of Somerset NFU behind us, an enthusiastic County Council and, most importantly, a group of producers prepared to serve on a board if, as we were planning, it was set up as a company limited by guarantee. They included June and Robin Small of Charlton Orchards, William Theed, who had a business selling quails and quails' eggs from his Combe Sydenham estate in West Somerset, Charles Clive-Ponsonby-Fane, who was making wine at Brympton D'Evercy near Yeovil and Richard Sheppy, who was looking to expand his farmhouse cider business on the A38 between Taunton and Wellington. John Hughes, the incoming Chairman of Somerset NFU had been persuaded to act as the initial chairman of the new organisation, so placing it firmly under the NFU's wing. A meeting of existing and would-be farm-based food businesses was arranged in Taunton, and the forty or so people who turned up gave the concept their enthusiastic support. 'A Taste of Somerset' had been born, the first such food group in Britain.

Farming in Somerset in the early 1980s was still very much a business of family-based, small-scale, commodity production. Farm cider-makers

189

were, of course, selling direct, as were the milk 'producer-retailers', as they were known, although the unpasteurised 'Green Top' milk that they sold was under constant attack from health campaigners and their regulatory supporters.

The only sector in which any significant value was added before products left the farm was Farmhouse Cheddar, in which a relatively small number of substantial dairy farmers were making serious money. But because of the scale required, and the capital costs, that was pretty much a closed shop and it was strictly regulated (and protected) by the Milk Marketing Board. Attempting to break into the Farmhouse Cheddar magic circle was simply not an option for a small, struggling milk producer looking for a way to boost his family income. Under the pre-CAP regime of guaranteed prices and deficiency payments, even a smallish farmer could make a decent living given a reasonable standard of technical efficiency. But in the face of Europe-wide over-production, commodity prices were falling further and further behind inflation, and quotas and set-aside were looming on the horizon.

At the same time, consumer interest in food as something more than just fuel was just beginning to awaken. The industrialisation of the British food supply chain was a process that had started with the industrial revolution, in which the vast majority of the population had been physically separated from the processes, values and culture of food production, leaving scale and price as the only real concerns. The British diet had effectively been homogenised. People ate more or less the same things, cooked in the same way in Southampton as in Newcastle and all points in between. Beyond traditional associations between places and products, like Devonshire cream or Wensleydale cheese or Welsh lamb, the market for foods specific to or characteristic of a particular locality had ceased to exist. A consumer survey a few years later revealed that the only 'regional' products valued for their origins by the average shopper were Scotch beef and Jersey Royal new potatoes.

But by the early 1980s consumer sentiment, influenced by foreign travel on the one hand and the rise of the supermarkets and their burgeoning product ranges on the other, was becoming more discerning, as it could well afford to, given that the proportion of average income spent on food was falling rapidly. The market for organic food was tiny, but it was growing. Likewise demand for free-range eggs. In short, we had the happy correlation of a farming sector looking to add value through on-farm processing and local branding, and a growing section of the consumer market looking for something special or different.

At national level, the quango Food From Britain had been set up by the Thatcher government, but its main role was to build the market for British food exports. At that stage, it wasn't really interested in developing the domestic market for local foods, so we had to look elsewhere for the financial backing that we needed if we were to make an impact. I had already identified Rebecca Pow as just the person we needed to run the organisation, and eventually persuaded NFU HQ to cover half her salary – for her work in helping me with the BBC farming reports and the Somerset Farmer – with Somerset County Council picking up the other half, for her work with Taste of Somerset.

By the time the Bath and West came round at the end of May, we had everything in place for the official launch, in the Taste of Somerset marquee, next to the British Farming and Food Pavilion. We had 12 exhibitors and claimed 40,000 visitors over the four days of the show. As a debut it could be counted a modest success, if not quite a roaring one.

Rebecca and her enthusiastic volunteers on the Taste of Somerset Board did everything you would expect of a nascent food-marketing group – leaflets, car-stickers, in-store promotions, local shows and so on – but our life-blood was publicity. The opportunity to generate plenty of that priceless commodity came round later that summer, when an exchange visit was organised between a group of farmers from Somerset NFU and their counterparts from the county's twin district of the Orme in Normandy. It coincided with the three-day Alençon Agricultural Fair, at which a free stand was offered to Taste of Somerset to sell a selection of Somerset products.

So far, so cordiale. But then the French customs authorities at Le Havre got involved. They demanded special import licences for marmalade, cheese and boned and stuffed ducks, as well as health certificates for the Somerset vineyards which were exporting their white wines. It was more cock-up than conspiracy, but official outrage was clearly required, so John Hughes and I decided that we would boycott the expedition in protest, in a blaze of local publicity.

Thanks in part to the intervention of the Bristol MEP, Richard Cottrell, a former HTV reporter who knew all about generating publicity, the muddle was eventually sorted, and most of the products made it to France. Tony Uloth, the Bath and West's Chief Executive, and a fluent French speaker, stepped in to lead the ToS party, something which he did with great charm and diplomacy, assisted by Rebecca and Claire Faun.

To avoid any further difficulties with French Customs, the produce was stored in the luggage compartment of the minibus in which the party travelled. Not all of the produce survived the trip, but enough wine, goat's cheese and – a particular favourite with the French show-goers – Exmoor farmhouse fudge was sold for John Hughes to be able to claim that "food and drink producers in Somerset have notched up a spectacular success with their first overseas sales trip" in a subsequent press release. 'Spectacular' might be pushing it a bit, but the episode had done our profile no harm at all.

That Christmas, Rebecca had the bright idea of selling Taste of Somerset hampers. For £34 you got two bottles of wine (one from Moorlynch Vineyard, the other a fruit wine from C&M Country Wines), some Sheppy's vintage cider, goat's cheese, a Christmas pudding, chutney, preserves, cheese straws, honey, tea (from Miles of Minehead), rum truffles and Exmoor fudge, plus the hamper itself, made from finest Somerset withies, of course. Despite what was a daunting price tag (£110 at present day values), they sold well, so well that Rebecca had to enlist some of her fellow Taunton YFC members to help pack the hampers, long into the night. One of them was Charles Clark. A few years later, she and Charles were married. That's something else we've got a Taste of Somerset to thank for.

The next big ToS event was the 1985 Royal Bath and West Show, which was due to be attended by the Queen, no less. The Taste of Somerset exhibition was duly put on her itinerary, and she spent several minutes there, chatting happily to Rebecca and Claire about Cheddar strawberries, cider and cheese and showing a genuine interest in what we were up to. The following year Somerset County Council came up with the money which allowed us to take a stand in the British Food pavilion at the Royal Show at Stoneleigh. As I reported in the Somerset Farmer:

We took almost £5,500; we attracted a great deal of publicity for Taste of Somerset and its individual members; we entertained Frans Andriessen, the EC Farm Commissioner, Sir Henry Plumb, junior Farm Minister Peggy Fenner and Angus Ogilvy and, above all, we flew the flag for Somerset food and farming at British agriculture's most prestigious shop window.

It was hard work though ... Every day's work was at least 12 hours of cider-pumping, sausage frying, pie selling and money counting, with the temperature hovering around the 90 mark.

Rebecca had left for the BBC by then, and it became hard to sustain the momentum. But Taste of Somerset didn't so much run out of steam as run out of money. Our members did pay a modest subscription, but it didn't amount to nearly enough to pay for even a part-time administrator, and the County Council's three-year funding package was coming to an end. We did obtain sufficient sponsorship from Taunton Cider to produce a 'Taste of Somerset Guide to Good Food and Drink', put together for us by the cookery writer Janet Lawrence, but it was the core costs that were the problem.

By this time our Somerset example had been followed in the other South-West counties. Across the region we had Devon Fare, Dorset Harvest, Wiltshire Larder and, in Cornwall – typically – two rival groups, called Cornucopia and Food from Cornwall. They all had in common support from their county councils, but in every case it was essentially pump-priming support, the expectation being that the food groups would eventually become self-sustaining. Realistically that was never going to happen. There simply weren't enough farm-based food and drink businesses in any county, even Devon, to cover the costs involved in running a worthwhile marketing operation. By the end of the decade every food group in the West Country seemed to be facing the same stark choice: to operate on a purely voluntary basis or to give up.

There was, however, a third way, which had already been signalled by the NFU, with its move to what was called 'regionalisation' in 1989. If the South-West's NFU county branches could be brought together and run from a single regional office, why not the South-West's food groups? It wouldn't mean the counties losing their individual identities any more than had the NFU's version of regionalisation, but it would provide sufficient critical mass to support a full-time administrator and office.

This seemed to me straightaway to be the obvious way forward and, happily, I was not alone. We were hugely fortunate in having people within each of the county groups who were prepared to sink their narrow county loyalties for the sake of a regional set-up which would be not just the least bad alternative to the status quo but could actually have the capacity to be far better.

In Somerset, we had Ansell Egerton, a recently retired main-board director of News International, who had been recruited to the cause by his near neighbours at Creech St Michael, June and Robin Small; Dorset gave us George Streatfeild, who was building his Denhay Farms Cheddar cheese and bacon business into one of the most successful in the region; from Cornwall, there was Michael Horrell, originator of Yarg cheese and highly influential in the county's farming community; Devon came up with Roger Curnock, proprietor of the Edgemoor Hotel at Bovey Tracey, who also represented another set of very interested parties – the restaurants, pubs and hotels for whom serving good local food was a very potent point of difference; while the Wiltshire chairman, Tristram Sykes who, although not a producer himself, was a highly respected gentleman farmer who knew how to open doors.

We were fortunate in one other respect, and that was in the support which we got from Food From Britain, and in particular from Mary Curnock-Cook, who has since gone on to greater things as Chief Executive (2010-17) of UCAS, the universities admission service. She shared our vision of a single regional food group, covering the six South-Western counties, run from a single office, linked to the regional NFU in Exeter. Not only that, but she managed to persuade her FFB colleagues to come up with some significant financial support, to get the new organisation off the ground so that it could stand as a role model for other regions. Finding a name for it wasn't difficult. A Taste of the South-West sounded a bit clunky, so Taste of the West we became.

Diane Lethbridge was appointed as Administrator (later Chief Executive) and proved to be an outstanding choice, steering the organisation through 14 years of growth and achievement, to the point where it was far and away the largest and most successful regional food group in the country. I was company secretary for all of those years, and we were fortunate in having an outstanding board of directors, led initially by Ansell Egerton and subsequently Tristram Sykes, with Michael Horrell, George Streatfeild, plus Mary James from Somerset and Brian Jennings from Devon, ever-present and ever-committed.

Since 2005, when the loss of regional financial support once again threatened the organisation's existence, provoking a major and distinctly traumatic upheaval, a new and arguably even more successful model has emerged, master-minded initially by Carol Trewin and, after her sadly early death, by John Sheaves as Chief Executive. The organisation is now completely independent financially, funded by its 1,100 members – split roughly equally between producers and suppliers/caterers – and 100 affiliates. Its annual Taste of the West Awards attracts almost 1,500 entries from producers and catering outlets. My only involvement now is with the occasional – and always very welcome! – judging commitment, but the Taste of the West story, and the part I was able to play in getting it off the ground in the first place, is one in which I will always take great pride.

Back in the 1990s Taste of the West was very much a producers' organisation geared mainly to building markets in the retail trade. Our targets did include pubs, restaurants and hotels, but they were by no means central to our focus. And despite our best efforts, the food on offer through the vast majority of the region's catering outlets was pretty much indistinguishable from what you might expect in any other region of the country.

This came home to me most forcefully when I was on holiday with the family in Northern Spain in 1994. We travelled on Brittany Ferries' Val de Loire to Santander and stayed in a converted farmhouse about fifty miles further west in Asturias. I had never been anywhere near this part of the world before and had no real idea what to expect, except that it often rained in the afternoons (which turned out to be true).

Two things struck me almost immediately. The first was the Asturian cider-drinking tradition. As I discovered in the very first bar that Chippy and I visited, it is a ritual conducted with an almost religious solemnity and attention to detail. First is the 'escanciar': in your right hand, you hold the uncorked bottle of cider (which is quite sharp, more like Devon cider than Somerset's), stretching your arm as high as it will go; in your left, the broad-brimmed glass beaker, which you hold as low as you can, slightly tilted so as to maximise the distance between bottle and glass. Then you pour and, if you're any good at all, you pour with the utmost nonchalance, confident that years of practice will direct the golden stream unerringly, not merely into the glass but onto the inner side of the glass, just below the brim. The idea is that the long drop will maximise oxygenation of the cider, producing a gentle, almost creamy effervescence.

But that's only the half of it. Only about an inch is poured at any one go. The escanciador is required (and I use the word advisedly) to drink most of it and then hurl the last few drops against the side of the bar, off which it will drain into a gutter. This is called the 'culin', and the logic this time is that, cider-drinking being a group activity, by swilling out the glass with cider, you have disinfected it for the next recipient of the escanciar. There are echoes of this – the sterilising effect of the cider and the sociability of a single drinking vessel – in the big, two-handled cider mugs which were traditionally handed round in cider-houses in the West Country, but we never had anything like this degree of ceremony attached. And it isn't just something quaint, laid on for the tourists. Wherever you go in Asturias, from the roughest roadside cafes to the smartest restaurants in Gijon or Oviedo, cider is being poured from a great height and then hurled into gutters. Chippy, I should say, was far more adept at it than I was, and we both put in plenty of practice!

The cider-drinking ceremony soon proved to be a prime example of how seriously Asturians take their regional traditions of food and drink. If cider was everywhere to drink, then so – and this was the second thing that struck me – were Asturian dishes like Fabada – a pork-and-bean stew, not unlike cassoulet – or beans with clams. There was really nothing on any restaurant menu which did not have an exclusively Asturian provenance: no pizzas, no burgers, no pasta. What we were being offered was the local produce prepared to best advantage in the local way. For the first time it dawned on me what a regional 'cuisine' amounted to. It was integral to what might be termed the 'Asturian experience', and how much pride the locals took in it, as well! I decided there and then that, if Asturias could boast of such a distinctive, authentic cuisine, based on the products which it grows best, then so should the South-West of England, a 'West Country cuisine' no less.

It took some time to turn the vision into a campaign but, by the beginning of 1997, we had got there, ably assisted by the likes of Tom Jaine, a former editor of the Good Food Guide, who lived in Totnes, Joyce Molyneux of the famous Carved Angel restaurant in Dartmouth, Michael Raffael, food writer for the Daily Telegraph, and Kit Chapman, proprietor of Taunton's Castle Hotel, who numbers Gary Rhodes, Chris Oakes and Phil Vickery among his many chef proteges.

The first thing we had to do was to convince ourselves that there was such a thing as a West Country cuisine, in the sense of a style of cooking and a range of dishes based on the things we grow best, extending beyond the likes of Cornish pasties and Devonshire cream. It was Tom Jaine, a food historian if ever there was one, who convinced us. In the introduction which he wrote to the 1998 Guide to Good Food in the West Country, which we prevailed upon him to edit, he based it on three groups of ingredients: dairy farming and pasturage, giving us beef, milk, butter, cheese and cream; orchards and cider production; and the whole range of fish.

The three groups of ingredients I have listed permeate more than just a few dishes. They contribute to a lifestyle, a daily reality. That other parts of the country have also adopted them does not disguise their regional origin – which should be celebrated.

All of that said, it was actually quite hard to point to more than a handful of genuinely West Country dishes, as opposed to products. Pasties we have mentioned, and you could extend that to almost the entire breed of pies. But beyond that, we were struggling and, besides, why should cooks be constrained by tradition when it comes to making best use of regional produce?

So our definition of what we eventually decided to call 'West Country cooking' became what we called 'a fusion of locality and materials', with a strong added dash of seasonality: the sort of food that Kit Chapman had been serving at the Castle and Joyce Molyneux at the Carved Angel for many years and on which another of our most enthusiastic supporters, Michael Caines, would build his reputation over the years that followed.

We launched the campaign with a magnificent West Country lunch at the Castle, and the first 'Guide to Good Food in the West Country', edited by Tom Jaine, was published later that year. There were recipe books as well, on 'Cream', 'Baking' and 'Vegetables', put together by Michael Raffael, as well as a Westcountry Cooking Suppliers Guide to help pubs and restaurants source the sort of products they needed. We even had an administrator, Portia Spooner as she is now, who ran things with great charm and efficiency and went on to work with Rick Stein on his television programmes.

But we were maybe just a bit ahead of our time. What you might call the 'local food culture' was not so deeply embedded twenty or so years ago as it has since become. We were funded by the EU's rural development programme, Objective 5 (b) as it was called, but once that money ran out, there was no way we could sell enough guides and recipe books to keep the thing afloat, and it was re-absorbed back into Taste of the West, which is perhaps where it might have been best placed, all the way through.

Even so, we were trail-blazers. One of the last West Country Cooking initiatives I was involved in, with Michael Caines and Kit Chapman, was the launch of the Exeter Festival of South-West Food and Drink in 2004. Thanks to people like Derek Phillips and Michael Caines, it has since gone on from strength to strength and its example followed the length and breadth of the country.

However, small-scale businesses producing and specialising in West Country foods, whilst very important to the wider economy of the region, was by no means the full story. The vast majority of the South-West farm output went not to the artisan market but to the mainstream food markets: supermarkets and catering suppliers for fresh produce; creameries, feed mills, meat companies and their associated manufacturers for everything else.

In 1999 the first Tony Blair government had created nine Regional Development Agencies (RDAs) charged with growing the economies of their respective regions, that for the South-West being the six counties from Gloucestershire to Cornwall. Agriculture and the food industry was obviously a major sector and, at the time, which was one of great economic difficulty for farming, badly in need of the sort of shot in the arm that the RDA ought to be able to provide.

I knew from my experience chairing the St Merryn Meat Producer Club – essentially a bit of PR gloss for Tesco's meat-procurement programme – how weak not just the primary producer's voice was but even that of some of our larger processors in the face of the genuinely big battalions of the food industry.

Nonetheless, it seemed to me that something could and should be done to make sure that more of the value that was added to South-West food stayed in the region, including on the region's farms. Again I looked overseas for a model and found it in Ireland, where the Government had created something called 'Bord Bia' to mobilise and develop its food industry at home and build export markets overseas. What we needed, I decided, was a 'Bord Bia for the South-West', a development agency, funded by the RDA, to do for mainstream food manufacturers and their farmer and grower suppliers what Taste of the West had done for the speciality sector.

And so, in 2002, the organisation 'South-West Food and Drink' (SWFD) was born, with high hopes and the best of intentions. But this was not, I am afraid, a story of success. It came under the wing of the South-West RDA and the post-mortem that was produced on that organisation's performance sums up succinctly what went wrong with SWFD:

In 2002, we identified the activities we thought were important. However the expected role of SWFD and outcomes and outputs were unclear and this created significant tensions with other organisations in the region.

The 'other organisations' were mainly Taste of the West. The bloke who we appointed to run SWFD never really grasped what it was all about, which was the mainstream food-manufacturing businesses. Instead, he kept trespassing onto Taste of the West territory, in search of the easy pickings that were available in the speciality sector at a time when consumer interest in local food was increasing by leaps and bounds. In 2005, the RDA 're-defined' SWFD's role as a delivery vehicle for RDA funding, something that seems to have worked well up until the organisation was wound up in 2010, with the RDA following it to the scrapyard – in a foolish and doctrinaire decision driven by Tory party politics – in 2012.

16

The mad cow years

As far as I was concerned, BSE first reared its ugly head at a meeting of the Somerset NFU Executive Committee at the Wessex Hotel, Street in October 1987. Ralph Baker, by now Chairman of the HQ Animal Health Committee, was giving his report and referred to what he called "this mystery disease", which had been given the name 'Bovine Spongiform Encephalopathy'. It had first been identified a year or so previously and there had now been around 40 cases, most of them on dairy farms in the South-West, including herds in Cornwall, Devon and Somerset. As Giles Horton, in the Western Daily Press that week, I suggested that:

> The chances are that, like leptospirosis, BSE is much more widespread than we imagine, and that cattle suffering from it have been either sent down the road as impossible to milk or their deaths have been attributed to Staggers.

We'll just leave that hanging there, for the time being.

It wasn't long before the Ministry of Agriculture's top epidemiologist, John Wilesmith, was linking the new condition with the brain disease of sheep, called Scrapie. The effects on the brain looked similar at post-mortem, and the possibility that it had crossed species to cattle provided a plausible explanation, through the practice of including the rendered-down remains of ruminant animals, including sheep, as a high-protein ingredient in cattle feed. The fact that some renderers had reduced the temperature at which the material was processed in the late 1970s provided an obvious explanation of why now and not earlier. The obvious extension of this link – that if scrapie had crossed from sheep to cattle, it might very well cross from cattle to humans – was already causing concern within the NFU, even if not, apparently, in MAFF or the Department of Health.

Events moved swiftly through 1988. In April the Southwood Committee was set up to explore the origins of the disease and recommend what action the Government should take. In May the Government announced that the carcases of BSE victims would be excluded from the food chain, prompting a reluctant Treasury to agree to compensation for the farmers who lost cattle to the disease, but only at 50% of market value (on the basis that the animal was diseased) and, even then, not until August. In July the use of meat and bone meal in ruminant feed was 'suspended' – not banned, be it noted, until the following January.

However, even at this relatively early stage in the saga, we in Somerset were anything but happy with the way the Government was handling things. Slow, short-sighted and grudging would be a fair summary of their approach. That July I wrote a column for the Somerset County Gazette, headlined 'Penny-pinchers posing peril'. In it I pointed out that scientists had known since the turn of the year that infected meat and bone meal was the likely cause of BSE. I continued:

> Yet it was not until June 2 that the Ministry introduced a temporary ban on the inclusion of blood and bone meal in ruminant feeds, or publicly admitted the link between scrapie and BSE. How many more cattle were infected with BSE during the months when the Ministry suspected the link, on the basis of strong circumstantial evidence, but failed to do anything about it?

My other main criticism concerned the risk to human health. A ban on BSE cattle entering the food chain had been announced, but it hadn't been implemented, and nor would it be until the following month.

> In the meantime BSE victims are being slaughtered in the usual way, and the meat going for human consumption. Why was compulsory slaughter and incineration not introduced immediately if it was justifiable at all? If a Foot and Mouth outbreak is suspected, controls are imposed on the spot. Why should BSE be any different, especially given the human health risk which, however slight, is still among the terms of reference of a top level inquiry which has been set up to investigate the disease?
>
> The answer to these questions boils down (if you forgive the expression) to Government penny-pinching. Publicly-funded disease eradication goes against the grain with this particular administration.

That is an assessment, I should say, that has subsequently been endorsed by the MAFF Permanent Secretary from 1993 to 2000, Richard Packer, in his book 'The Politics of BSE' (which is basically an extended defence of MAFF's role in the entire saga). In it he describes the six-month delay between recommending slaughter and compensation and acting on it as 'unfortunate', conceding that 'in the absence of a compensation scheme more animals may have gone for human consumption than would otherwise have been the case.' Others would probably use stronger language, but the message is the same: as I said, slow, short-sighted and grudging.

Whilst the number of cattle succumbing to BSE continued to increase exponentially, there was some better news around the corner. In the spring of 1989 Professor Southwood published his report. It endorsed the scrapie-BSE link and concluded – on the basis that there was no evidence that humans had ever caught scrapie from eating sheep – that: 'the risk of transmission of BSE to humans appears to be remote' and that 'it is most unlikely that BSE will have any implications for human health.'

Both conclusions were immensely reassuring, both in human terms – thousands of us weren't going to die – and in the context of the market for beef. They enabled us to say, as we did over and over again, that BSE was a serious animal health problem, not a human health problem. British beef and milk was therefore safe. It was a mantra that kept us going for the next seven years.

For those of us working for the NFU, publication of the Southwood report took some of the BSE pressure off and allowed us to focus on other issues, of which there was certainly no shortage! Reform of the Common Agricultural Policy was top of the agenda. The CAP budget was £750 million overspent. Either support prices would have to be cut, or further controls placed on the volume of output to which the support prices applied, as per milk quotas. The debate boiled down to price cuts versus supply management, with the NFU very much in the latter camp. A voluntary set-aside scheme for cereals was on the cards, and measures like 'extensification grants' and quotas on nitrogen fertiliser were much discussed.

Help for small farmers was another burning issue, especially in Somerset, where the county NFU was rediscovering its radical outlook. The NFU President, Simon Gourlay, had no time for this sort of social engineering, but we persuaded him to come down at least to listen to what our small farmer champions, like Peter Parker from Wiveliscombe, Michael Fry from Over Stowey and Geoff Gill from Huish Champflower (all of them comfortably under 5'9"!), had to say.

This was not a success. On the very first farm we visited, Gourlay spotted a brand new tractor and baler in the farmer's shed. "Well, you can't be doing that badly, with all that new kit," he commented, snootily. It turned out that the machinery belonged to the farmer's son, who was running a contracting business as there was no room for him on the family farm.

We weren't very popular in the corridors of NFU power in Knightsbridge. They called us 'the wild men of the West'. I reminded our troops that precisely the same pejorative label had been attached by NFU HQ to the Somerset campaigners for the creation of the Milk Marketing Board, back in 1931, and look how that had worked out!

Younger readers may be surprised to learn that another of our concerns was climate change. Yes, in the late 1980s, more than 30 years ago. We didn't actually call it 'climate change'; the preferred term in those days was 'the greenhouse effect', but the concern was just as genuine as it is now. I wrote about in my County Gazette column in February 1990, in a train on my way to London, after a relentless succession of storms had left half of Somerset and Devon under water. It was only the latest of a whole series of unusual climatic events which had been making farmers' lives even more difficult than usual.

'Is this all something to do with the greenhouse effect?' I wondered, before going on to write about a report that had been produced the previous year of a conference at the Centre for Agricultural Strategy at Reading University. The messages from the conference were that global warming was real, and it was a threat, bringing with it 40% more rain in the winter, 40% less in the summer, with a greater tendency towards climatic extremes. Global temperatures were forecast to rise by 0.5°C up to 2010.

It wasn't all bad news. Warmer summers would mean that crops like grain maize, sunflowers, soya beans and even tobacco could be grown successfully in southern England and the higher concentration of CO_2 in the atmosphere would boost crop yields, by up to 40% in the case of winter wheat. And yes, the amount of methane being pumped out of the back ends of cattle and sheep was a real worry.

It hasn't worked out quite how that report predicted. The rise in global temperature is pretty much spot on, and winters are certainly warmer. But we haven't really seen the new crops that were being forecast back then, and my impression is that winter and summer rainfall amounts are much the same. I offer you my final two paragraphs by way of conclusion:

> The experts at Reading seemed to conclude, on balance, and with a great many ifs and buts, that a gradual warming of the climate would be beneficial to British agriculture, especially as the timescale of the effect would be sufficiently extended to allow farmers, plant breeders and so on to adjust.

But that is to disregard those 'climatic extremes'. I remember thinking, at a cricket match at the height of last summer, "if this is the greenhouse effect then let's have more of it". I felt very differently about it when my train sped past an old orchard, in which almost every tree had been uprooted. If that is the greenhouse effect, then the sooner we do something about it, the better for everyone.

I think that has stood the test of time pretty well!

Then there was the noble failure that was Liscombe Research. As part of the post-war agricultural settlement, the Government had provided a free advisory service to farmers – initially the National Agricultural Advisory Service (NAAS), later the Agricultural Development and Advisory Service (ADAS) – and had funded a fleet of experimental farms, to provide the research results on which NAAS/ADAS advice was based. This had under-pinned the rapid post-war growth in productivity.

However, it fitted not at all with Mrs Thatcher's philosophy that the Government should only get involved in funding things where the market couldn't deliver and, if research and advice was so important to farmers' livelihoods, why shouldn't they pay for it themselves? So a report was commissioned – the Barnes report – which recommended that the Government should withdraw from funding farm research work of immediate benefit to the industry – 'near-market research', as it was known. That should be funded by the farmer and grower beneficiaries, leaving the Government to concentrate on long-term, blue-sky research.

On the back of that report, in March 1988, the Minister of Agriculture, John MacGregor, announced that the Liscombe Experimental Husbandry Farm on Exmoor would be closed unless industry funding could be found to keep it afloat. Why Liscombe, rather than any of the other EHFs? Partly because much of its work – particularly on silage additives – was unquestionably 'near-market' and partly because (precisely as a result of that near-market bias) it was highly regarded by the farming community which it served. Liscombe open days would regularly attract over 5,000 farmers.

My first response was defeatist. On the morning that the news came through, Clinton Rogers of BBC Points West turned up at my office in Taunton with his film crew for an interview. I was indignant, of course, but downbeat at the prospects of saving Liscombe: "You cannot expect to run an Experimental Husbandry Farm on the basis of voluntary donations," I said – something which proved eventually to be all too true.

However, it soon became apparent, as outrage spread through the grassland farming community, not just in Somerset but across the whole South-West, that the effort to 'Save Liscombe' would have to be made. Wesley Wyatt, first-class farmer and forceful character, was the Chairman of the Liscombe advisory committee. When he joined forces with John James, the irascible driving force behind the South-West's most successful agricultural co-operative, Mole Valley Farmers, they were not to be gainsaid.

There followed a frantic two months of meetings, negotiations, press releases, radio and television interviews and leaflet-writing. When it came to the costs that our farmer-funded initiative – which we had already decided to call Liscombe Research – would have to shoulder, MAFF were less than helpful. For December 1989 to March 31 1991, we would need to find £140,000; but beyond that, the 'full economic cost' would be charged, taking the total cost for the initial three years to just over £400,000, or not far shy of a million quid at present-day values. This, at a time when the average lowland livestock farmer in the South-West was enjoying, if that is the word, an income of just £1,700 a year!

To raise the money, we decided to leaflet every farmer in the four South-West counties, asking them to commit to paying £50 a year for three years, in return for free, exclusive access to Liscombe research results. Somewhat to my surprise, the response was positive. By the middle of June we had 1,300 standing-order mandates under our belts, plus promises of around £30,000 in sponsorship, and were able to write to the Minister responsible, the redoubtable Baroness Trumpington, to tell her that we were in a position to proceed.

Wesley Wyatt was elected Chairman of the new company, as it became, supported by a Committee whose names I will list in full, given the tremendous amount of hard work and commitment which they all gave to the venture, all of it entirely at their own expense. The Liscombe Research ' Roll of Honour' therefore reads:

Wesley Wyatt, Wiveliscombe (first Chairman)
Geoff Hewett, Trull (who succeeded Wes as Chairman in 1991)
David Cray, Camelford
Brian Peace, Rackenford
John Kingman, Dartmoor Prison Farm
David Moore, Torrington
Eric Norman, Brendon Hills,

Hector Delbridge, North Molton
Robin Slade, Exton
John James, Mole Valley Farmers,
Malcolm Appleton, loyal and hard-working Liscombe farm director.

A special word of thanks as well to Helen Robinson, my supremely calm, competent and numerate PA who also worked so hard to make Liscombe Research a success.

The new organisation was officially launched that November, on a horribly bleak Exmoor day. But it was an occasion that was lit up by the Baroness Trumpington, resplendent in scarlet, who had cut the State Opening of Parliament to be with us. "Lead kindly light amidst the encircling gloom," she boomed at Wes, in the words of Cardinal Newman. I suggested in the County Gazette that:

> It was an appropriate quotation (even if Wesley probably wouldn't have appreciated its source) because the cold grey fog lay thick across the slopes of Winsford Hill. And more than that, because of all the political and economic gloom that presently encircles farming. We needed a boost. The success of Liscombe Research has provided it.

Sadly, this story does not have a happy ending. Much good work was done by Liscombe Research, producing valuable, cost-saving results. But when it came to the crunch of trying to raise another three years of funding from our farmer subscribers and sponsors in 1992, the response was dismal. By the end of August, only 519 members had renewed at the new rate of £75 a year. Shortly afterwards, with little or no prospect of any more cash coming in, our contract was terminated.

Not long afterwards, Liscombe was sold, to a local farmer, who ploughed most of it up to grow flax, purely for the subsidy attached. It proved to be largely unharvestable in the Exmoor autumn climate and ended up being burnt, all of this at the taxpayers' expense. It was a sad and ironic postscript to what had been a brave and far-sighted venture. But I was at least able to offer this consolatory thought to the Committee, and indeed to everyone else – self included – who had worked so hard to make Liscombe Research a success: it is better to have tried and failed, than never to have tried at all.

Food health scares were a feature of the late 1980s and on into the 90s. Besides BSE, we had listeria in soft cheeses, and then the salmonella in eggs crisis, triggered when Edwina Currie, then a junior Health Minister, had said in a television interview in December 1988 that "most of the egg production in this country, sadly, is now affected with salmonella". She later claimed that, instead of 'most', she had meant to say 'some' and had been referring to flocks, not individual hens. But the damage had been done.

The media balloon went up, egg consumption fell by 60%, two million hens were slaughtered, and millions of pounds were wiped off the value of eggs and their producers' incomes. To be fair to Mrs Currie, there undoubtedly was a serious salmonella problem in egg production at the time, and the action that was taken by the industry in the wake of her remarks has left us with one of the lowest levels of salmonella in the world. I normally didn't have much to do with poultry. That was the preserve of the Regional Poultry Secretary, the indefatigable, irrepressible Paul Cooper. But on this occasion it was all hands on deck, and I lost count of the number of radio and television interviews I gave over that Christmas period, defending the healthiness of West Country eggs.

Roughly a year later, we were up to our eyeballs in television crews and radio reporters again, when the 'lead in feed' crisis broke. It was Monday November 6, and I was in my office in Exeter, the NFU having been 'regionalised' earlier in the year. My first call of the morning was from John Russell in our Launceston office.

"I've just had one of my members on the phone. Something to do with lead poisoning. Know anything about it?"

No, I replied truthfully. I rang the Ministry of Agriculture. It sounded as if all Hell was breaking loose. Something must be badly wrong. And so it proved. Bit by bit, the grisly saga began to unfold: lead had got into a cargo of rice bran en route from India to Rotterdam. There it had been processed into maize gluten replacer pellets and three boat-loads sent on their way to Teignmouth. Six feed compounders had bought the stuff from the importer and sold it on to around 300 farmers, some of whose calves were now dying of lead poisoning. How serious was the contamination, I enquired?

"Very serious indeed," came back the reply.

"Oh shit," said an NFU regional spokesman.

As the day went by, we did our best to piece together what had happened but, without the statements that had been promised from the Minister of Agriculture and the Milk Marketing Board (who were testing milk from the unlucky farms), it was impossible to give any sort of clear indication as to what the implications might be, for both animal and human health, beyond that this was serious. With the media almost literally beating at our doors for a comment, I gave an interview that evening to BBC Radio Devon. Would entire herds of cattle have to be slaughtered, the reporter inquired.

"Well possibly," I replied – which, as I ought to have known perfectly well, is as good as saying "Yes, definitely" in circumstances like these.

The next day was an important one. I was due to collect my father and drive him first to Plymouth and then on to Taunton to launch 'West Country Treasury', a collection of his radio scripts and articles from the 50s and 60s, which he had re-edited for publication as a paperback book. It wasn't going to set the world on fire (most of his editing having consisted of substituting 'we' for 'I', as it was supposed to be a joint effort by the pair of us), but it had given him something worthwhile to do in his sheltered accommodation in Taunton in between visits to the pub.

But before that there was a media firestorm to be survived. It turned out that my Radio Devon interview had made it to the national news and that I was in the firing line from both NFU HQ and MAFF for being 'alarmist', especially as the MMB then issued some initial results, which seemed (misleadingly, as it turned out) to be reassuring.

As for the book launch, we had several television crews in attendance. But they weren't in the least bit interested in the feats of William Dampier or the strange experiences of Edith Pegler. All they wanted to talk about was bloody lead poisoning.

Still, the book was a modest success, and the response to the lead-in-feed crisis again showed the NFU at its best. It turned out that there was no real risk to health, and Richard Macdonald and our NFU legal advisers put together a class action to claim damages against the feed companies, which resulted in every claimant being compensated in full, with no complaints from anyone. At the time I wrote that 'on the Richter scale of farming disasters, the lead in feed scare measures somewhere around 6 – serious, but not cataclysmic.' That still seems about right.

While all this was going on, the NFU itself was going through a major upheaval. For almost twenty years, successive directors-general had been trying to convert the organisation from what was essentially a federation of 39 semi-autonomous county branches into a single, centralised, national organisation. You can't really blame them. Quite apart from the difficulty of speaking with one voice from such a disparate set-up, standards of finance and administration varied enormously. The largest, most efficient county branches, like Somerset and Devon, were run at a net cost per member of less than a third of that of some of the more profligate. But attempts at change had repeatedly foundered on the rock of the membership. The 'gentlemen', as we staff liked to refer to the members, liked things as they were. There had, as we have seen, been a few mergers, and finance at least had been centralised. But beyond that, the structure was little changed.

So the recently appointed Director General, David Evans, an economist, who had joined the NFU from a senior position in MAFF, decided on a cunning plan. Rather than recommend changes himself, and risk being voted down by the membership, he would commission an independent agency to look at the NFU's structure and recommend changes. As the proposals of an expert third party, they would be much more difficult to reject. He chose McKinseys, the management consultants. They set to work in 1988 and, to no-one's surprise, recommended a structure based on eight regions plus Wales.

The proposals that finally went to the NFU's ruling Council stopped short of counties being amalgamated. The democratic structure of county executive committees and so on would remain more or less unchanged. It was the staff out in the counties who would be regionalised, thus meaning fewer of them but in more specialised roles. All of this was announced on the day of the 1988 South-West Dairy Show, at the Bath and West, where the mood among staff was grim. I wasn't particularly worried about my own position; in fact, I had some hopes of becoming the new South-West Regional Director. But I guessed that my deputy, Bill Leach, might be in the firing line, and so would my faithful, hard-working office staff in Taunton.

David Dent, a bluff, ruddy-faced Yorkshireman who looked as though he might have been hit in the face with a frying pan in his youth, was given the task of going around the country to interview staff and decide who should go, who should stay and in what role. It earned him the nickname of the 'Grim Reaper', although he undertook his unpleasant task as fairly and as sympathetically as anyone could. I didn't get the Regional Director job. That went to Richard Macdonald, who had beaten me to the Devon county secretaryship three years previously and was, rightly, regarded as a much safer pair of hands. My profile was high, and Somerset had been well run, always hitting our subscription targets. But against the considered, capable, diplomatic Richard Mac, I never stood a chance. Instead, I was made 'Senior Policy Adviser' for the South-West. "Playing to your strengths," said David Dent, and he was probably right.

The new set-up provided anything but a comfortable ride over the first year or so. We were based in the Devon NFU offices in Queen Street, Exeter, which was a creaky, dusty rabbit-warren of a building. June Harry survived from the old Devon secretariat, but otherwise we had to recruit a completely new team of support staff, who inevitably took a time to settle in. Instead of the three other county offices being closed and sold off, as would have made obvious sense, the members insisted that they remained open, which added to costs and complicated staffing issues. The Cornish were particularly resentful at 'being ruled from Exeter' as they saw it, and Dorset weren't much happier.

That we got through these distinctly choppy waters, with crises like lead in feed erupting all around us was thanks not least to John Glanvill, our first Regional Chairman, a tough and shrewd Jack Russell terrier of a man who farmed at Woodbury and would go on to be Chairman of Devon County Council. No-one could have stuck up for his staff more loyally and to such good effect.

Even so, it was a good few years before the 'NFU South-West Region', now in its smart new office at Pynes Hill, out near the motorway, generated any real loyalty among the membership, and even that probably wouldn't have happened without the two big farming crises of BSE and Foot and Mouth. County identity is very strong in the South-West. It means a lot to be a Cornishman, a Devonian or whatever the demonym is for those born in Dorset or Somerset, whereas even after thirty years and more, the South-West region is still seen as an artificial construct, created for bureaucratic convenience. I may regard myself first and foremost as a 'Westcountryman', but I am very much the exception.

The difficulties of operating as a region were strikingly demonstrated that summer, in Hyde Park of all places. 1989 was the centenary of the establishment of MAFF's predecessor, the Board of Agriculture, so it was decided to designate it 'The Year of British Food and Farming', the centrepiece being a four-day exhibition in Hyde Park.

For up to two years before the event, county committees set up for the purpose, supposedly with support from their County Councils, had been beavering away on their contributions – with varying degrees of commitment. But Avon County Council would have nothing to do with it, Devon and Cornwall were lukewarm and Wiltshire pulled out altogether. The response from farmers and the food industry across the region to fund-raising appeals ranged from the hostile to the apathetic, and what had been intended as the region's theatrical centrepiece – the 'Farm Show', written by Graham Harvey of The Archers fame – had to be cancelled for lack of sponsorship. It was left to a jewel of a farmer from West Dorset to pull the whole thing together. Ray Bere, who farmed at Rampisham, was as genuine a yeoman farmer as you could find; he might have stepped straight out of a Thomas Hardy novel. Through all the county bickering, he sweated and smiled, fending off the brickbats with either "Something will turn up" or "It'll be alright on the day."

And so it was! The best part of a million people visited the Festival over the four days; the South-West stand was adjudged one of the two best in the Park and won deserved plaudits from the national press, Ray himself being described as 'authentically rustic', which he may or may not have taken as a compliment. At the end of it all, I praised the event in the Western Daily Press as 'simply marvellous, the best possible advertisement for the farming and food industry'.

Various attempts to repeat the exercise have been made over the years. The supermarket Asda sponsored a repeat performance in Hyde Park in 1992, but it didn't really work and, much more recently, an initiative led by NFU Vice-President (as he then was) Guy Smith got as far as a launch reception in St James's Palace. But both genuine commitment and worthwhile sponsorship have always proved as elusive as they were in the earlier stages of that 1989 event. Which is a shame.

So what, meanwhile, of BSE? By the spring of 1989, it was spreading like wildfire through dairy herds in the South-West and beyond. It was also dawning on MAFF and SEAC, the special committee which had been set up to guide the Government's response, that, given the lengthy incubation period of the condition, tens of thousands of tonnes of the organs of cattle which could be carrying the 'prions' that caused the disease had almost certainly been going into the food chain over the previous ten years or so.

The Southwood Committee had concluded that there was no risk to human health, but plenty of other experts disagreed, and the media were only too happy to report their misgivings. I was far from convinced as to the safety, not so much of beef joints or steak as of the manufactured products into which the relevant offals were most likely to have found their way.

In May 1989, channelling Evelyn Waugh, I wrote of the 'batsqueak of apprehension' I had experienced on biting into a propriety steak-and-kidney pie. A month or so later, a ban on the 'Specified Bovine Offals' (SBO) entering the human food chain was announced. But, almost unbelievably, it didn't become effective until that November.

In the Somerset County Gazette, in May 1990, I was not impressed:

> *It was precisely that sort of delay and muddle which has given some*
> *people all the excuse they needed for alarming the public with their*
> *wild claims. The howl of revulsion has broken upon us.*

The immediate pretext for the outcry was the death of Max, a Siamese cat, in Bristol. Its symptoms had been suggestive and, at post-mortem, the tell-tale signs of a spongy brain were found. BSE had apparently jumped species again. Would humans be next, especially given the vast amounts of potentially infective material which had been allowed to enter the food chain since BSE was identified?

The Government's response was typically chaotic. On the one hand we had John Gummer, by now Minister of Agriculture, making a fool of himself by feeding his daughter Cordelia with a hamburger in front of the television cameras to demonstrate that "British beef is safe". That was on May 10 1990. Yet, less than a month later, he was acceding to French demands to ban exports of bone-in beef from Britain unless it could be proved that the animal had come from a farm which had not had a case of BSE in the previous two years, which suggested that British beef was anything but safe. Meanwhile, prices were tumbling, the press were having a field day and beef farmers especially were at their wits' end.

There was, however, just one chink of light. In my Giles Horton column of May 16 that year I wrote about a theory being propounded by Roger Eddy, an experienced and respected vet at Shepton Mallet who would go on to become President of the Royal College of Veterinary Surgeons, whom I knew well. His theory, to which I subscribed almost as soon as he'd explained it to me, was that BSE was not scrapie in bovine form but a specifically bovine type of spongiform encephalopathy which had previously gone unrecognised:

> *I have been in practice for 25 years and as far as I am concerned, cattle*
> *with the typical symptoms of BSE are nothing new. We always used to*
> *get the odd one, but nobody thought too much about it.*

From that it followed that what was most likely to have happened was that infected offal from one or more of these unrecognised BSE victims had found its way into cattle feed, so starting a chain reaction of infection.

Two things added to the weight of this theory. The first was that rendering temperatures had not been altered at the time which would have fitted with the 'scrapie origin' hypothesis. The second was the fact that spongiform encephalopathies were known to be highly infectious within species but were rarely, if ever, known to have crossed the species barrier. Trials involving feeding infected brain tissue to mice and guinea pigs had borne this out.

The important thing about all of this from my point of view, in arguing the case for the safety of British beef, was that, if BSE hadn't crossed species from sheep but was a specifically bovine condition, then the chances of it crossing into humans were vastly reduced. As for Max the cat, what he had died of was not BSE, but FSE – feline spongiform encephalopathy.

By November 1990 all of the measures necessary to halt the spread of BSE in cattle and to protect against any theoretical risk of spread to the human population were in place and farmers were now (as of February 1990) receiving 100% compensation for BSE casualties. It had only taken the Government three years!

17

Regional Director – in the eye of the BSE storm

In the spring of 1992 a new post was created at NFU HQ: Director of Regions. The intention was ostensibly to make sure that the regions did not follow their predecessor counties down the diverging performance/semi-autonomy route, although it did also provide a convenient stepping-stone for Richard Macdonald on his journey to becoming Director General. That created a vacancy, of course, and I was the favourite to fill it.

Not that I was a shoo-in, by any means. David Evans had his misgivings, and I don't doubt that there were several prominent members in the South-West who felt that I'd got too big for my boots over the previous three years as Senior Policy Adviser. I was fortunate in that there appeared to be no particularly strong contender from outside the organisation, leaving Mike Ellingham, our Senior Technical Adviser, as my main rival. Again, as with the Somerset job, it must have been very close, for Mike was nothing if not competent, level-headed and knowledgeable, but I got the nod.

There followed a rather chequered couple of years. At almost exactly the same time as I took up my new post, I was required – and I use the word advisedly – to sign a new contract of employment, on pain of dismissal. Not that I was alone. All of us former county secretaries, on over-riding commission contracts, were issued with an ultimatum, albeit with sweeteners attached. We felt pretty sore about it, but the commission had served us well and, at least, provided an elevated platform to which future increases could be applied.

The next ruckus, not unusually for me, was with the Minister of Agriculture, John Gummer. The following January, after a difficult year for livestock farmers everywhere, he announced a 27% cut in the headage payments that hill farmers were paid on their cattle and sheep, something which I'd worked out, on the basis of Exeter University figures, would reduce their incomes by at least 10%. We put out a press release saying as much, which was picked up by the BBC 'Today' programme. They ran a piece on the morning of January 12, which just happened to be the same day on which John Gummer was due to address the Devon NFU Annual Meeting. It included an interview with a Welsh hill farmer, and a clip from me:

He's sold the hill farmers short. He has said, as a Minister, that he wants to see the hills protected, that he wants to protect the environment, the economy and the social structure of the hill areas – that's why these subsidies are paid. And by cutting them, he's not only damaging the farmers in the hills, he will be damaging the very many other businesses who depend on farmers in the hills, damaging the hill economy and the environment as well.

Succinctly put, I thought, but the sort of thing you might expect from an NFU spokesman responding to a cut in subsidies. It was put to Mr Gummer live on air, who replied, with a typical degree of sophistry, that he was actually increasing the sheep subsidy and continued, "What Mr Gibson says, as so often, is entirely untrue." There followed further self-justification, before he signed off with: "And that spokesman for the Devon NFU *(i.e. me)* is wrong, as he's been on every occasion you've interviewed him, I think."

It was an extraordinary outburst, the 'as so often' – implying that I was a serial liar – amounting, I thought, to defamation. My lawyers thought so, too. But, for understandable reasons, the NFU chose not to pursue it, and I couldn't afford to, so I let the matter drop, comforting myself with the thought that I'd well and truly got under Gummer's skin. But it was a rather tense Devon NFU Annual Meeting that afternoon!

However, it wasn't long before I was in trouble with my bosses at the NFU – again! This was at the time when the policy agenda was dominated by reform of the CAP and the various options available. In common with people like Oliver Walston, Anthony Rosen, Wesley Wyatt and the Federated Farmers of New Zealand, I felt that the CAP regime of subsidies, quotas and heavy governmental interference was doing British farming no good at all and that we'd be better off taking our chances in a free market, and I said as much at a Lib Dem conference that I was invited to speak at in Torquay in September 1993.

My remarks were reported in the now, sadly, defunct magazine 'Farming News' under the headline 'NFU Director speaks out against subsidies'. Within a week I found myself in Richard Macdonald's office in London, being lectured on the error of my ways and given a final warning (which seemed rather over the top to me). He told me that I had "ignored the counselling given to you at your appointment and subsequently." Counselling! Anyone would think I was slightly unhinged.

A year later, and it was David Evans who was threatening me with the sack, this time over my reluctance to go on the management training course which the NFU had booked for me at Sundridge Park, to address my 'inexperience in management'. I decided that I had better things to do than waste four weeks of my time being reminded of the bleeding obvious by a bunch of jargon-spouting suits and declined the opportunity.

"You'll go on the course, or you're on your way," shouted a furious DG down the phone at me. So I went, and it wasn't, in fact, unproductive. I've referred already to the 'vocational driver' which I turned out to have, and another psychometric test suggested that the occupation to which I was best suited was Field Marshal, on account of my combination of strategic thinking, man management and attention to detail (ha ha). But by that stage, I'd got the hang of how to fill in all the questionnaires!

While all this was going on, I was doing my best to help the NFU South-West region tackle the two big political talking points of the early 1990s: reform of the CAP, and the abolition of the Milk Marketing Board. On both issues farming opinion was split, between the supply managers and the price cutters in the case of the CAP, and between the managed transitioners and the over-our-dead-bodies brigade with the MMB.

After what seemed like years of Euro-wrangling the EU Farm Commissioner, Ray MacSharry, produced – guess what! – a compromise. Prices for the main commodities would be cut, but farmers would be given either area payments on crops or headage payments on beef and sheep by way of compensation, which would in turn be subject to quotas. Thus was IACS – the Integrated Administration and Control System – born.

Every farmer had to fill in an IACS form every year to claim his or her payments. It was another Brussels-sent opportunity for the NFU to make itself indispensable to its members, and we grabbed it with both hands. Huge meetings of farmers were staged across the region at which we explained the new system. One of the last I did was at Churchill School, south of Bristol. There must have been 700 farmers there, no PA system and just an old-fashioned overhead projector to show my slides. I have to admit that I loved it, because I knew my stuff, as did Mike Ellingham and my two top-notch policy advisers Alison Best and Robert Deane. The open meetings were followed by 'surgeries' in every group office, to which members could come along and have their forms filled in by either the Group Secretary or one of us regional staff. Yet again, the lawyers strongly advised against it, and yet again it cemented thousands of memberships.

The demise of the MMB had been inevitable from the moment we joined the EEC. As, effectively, a statutory monopoly it didn't fit at all with the EEC's competition regime. It was only a matter of time before it would be subject to some form of legal challenge and, when that reached the European Court, the Board would lose. Against that background it was a miracle that the MMB clung on for so long.

Loyalty to the MMB still ran deep. It had been pressure from the South-West – Somerset and Wiltshire, in particular – which was the deciding factor in the Board's creation, back in the dark days of the 1931 agricultural depression. So it was distinctly ironic that one of the earliest legal challenges to the Board's powers was brought by two of my Somerset members, John Taylor of Cricket St Thomas fame and John Gunningham from Weston-super-Mare, who objected to paying a levy on the milk they pasteurised, bottled and sold direct.

The Board survived that challenge but, when it lost a case brought by the Dairy Trades Federation (representing the big dairies) over its 'end-use pricing regime' (charging a different price, depending on what the milk was going to be used for), the writing was on the wall, especially as neither John Gummer nor his boss in Number 10 were fans of statutory monopolies and made it quite clear that the Government would not intervene. By the beginning of 1993 it was obvious that the Board would have to turn itself into some form of co-operative and lose its monopoly power as the first buyer of all milk produced in England and Wales.

That being the case, the big question was: what sort of co-operative? Opinion in the South-West was unanimous on that. We wanted a single, national co-operative, incorporating all of the processing capacity which the Board had acquired when it bought the Unigate creameries back in 1979.

But Gummer and co said no. They weren't going to replace a statutory monopoly with a supposedly voluntary one. They gave the Board two options: either create a series of regional co-operatives, each of them with processing capacity, or hive off the processing capacity and create a single co-operative which would buy milk from farmers and then sell it on for processing.

With the minimum of discussion with milk producers out on the ground, the Board went for the single procurement co-operative. The regional members were despatched, not to consult with the NFU county milk committees but to inform them. It was a fait accompli. The new organisation would be called Milk Marque, while the processing plants would be floated off as a separate company, Dairy Crest, in which all pre-existing producers would be given shares.

I didn't think it was the right decision at the time and would argue that the subsequent, distinctly chaotic history of milk marketing in England and Wales bears that out. But most dairy farmers seemed happy enough, even if the choice of Andrew Dare, ex-Dairy Trade Federation, as the boss of Milk Marque did raise a few eyebrows.

Around 80% of milk producers in the four South-Western counties signed up for Milk Marque and, when the new milk pricing mechanism was tried for the first time, it produced a near 10% increase. I, meanwhile, was anxious to make sure that the 20% who had opted to join one of the independent groups did not feel alienated by the mainstream-orientated NFU. So we set up something called the South-West Producer Group Forum to give them a voice.

Meanwhile, although the blame-game for declining numbers of breeding waders was still rumbling along on the Somerset Levels, the Environmentally Sensitive Areas were working well. In the West Penwith ESA, in the far west of Cornwall, take-up was over 90%, while on Exmoor it was close to 70%. In 1993 two more ESAs were designated in my region, covering Dartmoor and the Blackdown Hills. This latter was a bit of a personal triumph.

Three years earlier the Countryside Commission had proposed making the Blackdowns an Area of Outstanding Natural Beauty. This was no big deal, from a farming point of view, as I knew perfectly well from experience with the dozens of other AONBs across the region. But I soon discovered that the Blackdowns farmers didn't see it that way.

They were dead against the ANOB, as they tended to call it, fearing that it would mean all sorts of extra restrictions on their land and buildings. On the other hand, what really would make a difference to the mostly small, often struggling family farms of the area was ESA status, which would reward them for essentially carrying on as before. But, although the Blackdowns was on the long list of potential ESAs, it didn't seem likely to make the next batch.

So I hatched a cunning plan. The NFU, on behalf of the farmers, would not stand in the way of AONB status, if the Blackdowns was made an ESA, something which would, after all, serve precisely the same purpose as the AONB and probably much more effectively. We didn't make a public song and dance about it, but I made sure that those who needed to know were aware of the trade-off, and, to (almost) everyone's surprise, the Blackdowns duly got its ESA status.

If that was a minor triumph, then the live export of calves was a running sore through the early 1990s. I can't say I much liked the idea of three-week-old Friesian bull calves being packed onto lorries and shipped across the channel from Plymouth or Poole to veal units in France, but we had to defend it. Not only was the trade worth big money, but it also provided a market for animals, many of which would otherwise have been shot at birth (as was sadly demonstrated when the trade was eventually ended by BSE).

There were some distinctly dodgy characters involved in the calf dealing fraternity. It was a popular issue with press and broadcasters, and I frequently found myself crossing swords with the likes of Compassion in World Farming's Joyce D'Silva or someone from the RSPCA. Our argument was that whether an animal's journey involved a short sea crossing or not was largely irrelevant. What mattered was whether it was well treated on the journey; welfare standards in the live export trade were closely monitored.

But public opinion was pretty solidly against us, or so I thought until I took part in a live television debate with the RSPCA's Richard Ryder, late one Friday evening at the HTV studios in Bristol. Ryder, I think, was guilty of over-confidence and came across as smug. I played the 'struggling West Country dairy farmers desperately need this trade and wouldn't be party to anything that involved cruelty to their livestock' card for all it was worth. Even so, I was amazed when the result of the phone-in vote came through, and I discovered that I'd won! Only later, when I bumped into my old comrade in arms, John Hughes, did I discover a large part of the reason for this unexpected triumph.

"Oh yes," he said. "Good, wasn't it? Once I knew it was on, I got hold of a few mates and we all rang in to vote. And if you keep pressing the last number redial key, it's surprising how many votes you can cast in five minutes!"

Good old John. 'Fighting Farmer Hughes', I called him. He died, suddenly, of a heart attack, in November 1995. I gave the address at his funeral. I have known many fine men and women in my time with the NFU, but he was one of the very best.

Generally speaking, these were good years for farming. Norman Lamont's 'Black Wednesday' in September 1992, when the pound had fallen out of the Exchange Rate Mechanism, had triggered a slump in the value of sterling and a consequent boom in farm output prices. In 1995 farm incomes adjusted for inflation were back to levels not seen since the mid-1970s. With cases of BSE falling steadily and the new CAP regime bedding in reasonably comfortably, all seemed set fair.

So I was in reasonably good spirits when, on March 20 1996, I set off from my office on the outskirts of Exeter to drive to Dorchester for a meeting of the Dorset County Executive Committee. I stopped at Tesco to fill up with diesel and noticed the headline in that day's Daily Mirror, on the news-stand. 'OFFICIAL: MAD COW CAN KILL YOU,' it read, in great black letters. Hmm, I thought, a storm is brewing.

Not that the claim came as a complete surprise. There had been rumours of a series of cases of CJD among younger people which might be different from so called 'classical' CJD, and the Guardian had run a story on this basis back in February. But the latest official word from SEAC, given by its Deputy Chairman, Robert Will, to The Times the previous December, and referring specifically to the cases of CJD in younger people, was that 'no link between BSE and CJD has been established.'

Maybe half an hour later, as I was pulling off the A30 dual carriageway to take the A35 towards Bridport and Dorchester, I tuned into the BBC One O'Clock News. The BSE-CJD link was the top story, and it was abundantly clear that this was not based on rumour or supposition. The Health Secretary, Stephen Dorrell, was due to make a statement in the House of Commons that afternoon, confirming that a new strain of CJD had been identified which was almost certainly linked to BSE in cattle. I pulled into a layby and just sat there for five minutes, aghast.

My first thoughts were for my family. My son George, now 12, had a fondness for pub sausages, which tended in those days to be made from the cheapest ingredients possible including no doubt, back in the 80s, the Specified Bovine Offals that were now banned from the human food chain. I had always insisted to Mandy and the children that eating beef – even eating cheap pub sausages – was perfectly safe. Had I now condemned some or all of us to die from a truly horrible disease?

Then there were the implications for my livestock farming members in the South-West. The beef market would surely collapse and might never recover. I had lost count of the number of times I had publicly rubbished the predictions of Dr Richard Lacey and others that hundreds of thousands of people could die from BSE in human form. If those predictions were now to come true – which was entirely possible, given the huge volume of potentially infective material that I knew had gone into the food chain back in the 1980s – then there could be no way back. I was staring catastrophe in the face, both personally and professionally.

However, the farmers of Dorset are a phlegmatic lot, and we didn't get around to discussing the afternoon's events until the eighth item on the agenda, after debates on hot-air balloons, badgers (inevitably) and a presentation from Richard Macdonald, as Director of Regions, on his plans for shaking up the NFU's staffing. The relevant minute reads:

> *The Regional Director summarised statements which had been made that afternoon by the Secretary of State for Health and the Minister of Agriculture. It appeared that a new strain of CJD had been identified, and that there was a possibility that ten cases of disease in people under the age of 42 might be linked to exposure to BSE prior to safety measures being introduced. MAFF had introduced a range of safety measures to eliminate whatever small risk remained.*

That last sentence pointed to the only leg we had to stand on in defending the good name of British beef: if BSE had spread to humans, it had done so before SBO was banned from the human food chain in 1989; as of now, the route of spread had been closed off. British beef was safe!

I left the meeting early, to drive to Bristol to appear live on BBC Points West. When I got home to my barn conversion just outside Ilminster, I wrote a feature for the Western Daily Press. After that, in a state of something approaching shock, I sat down in front of the fire with a bottle of red wine and wept, not for myself, or even so much for my family, but for all the beef farmers across my region and beyond who were now, through absolutely no fault of their own, facing disaster. For all the drama of the foot-and-mouth outbreak five years later, March 20 1996 was the single most traumatic day in my NFU career.

I was still feeling pretty shattered the following morning but pulled myself together in time for a live 'BSE Special' on BBC Spotlight from Plymouth that evening, followed by a gruelling 90-minute phone-in. The following day the Devon NFU Executive was due to meet in Exeter. With Peter Crozier, the Devon Chairman, it was decided to tack on a big public meeting at Exeter University, open to any farmer from the South-West region.

We asked the President of the NFU, David Naish, to speak and the Minister of Agriculture, Douglas Hogg. In the event, we got neither, Richard Macdonald deputising for Naish, and Angela Browning, a junior MAFF minister and MP for Honiton, for Hogg. What we did get was a huge turnout of anxious and angry farmers from across the region and a full complement of press and broadcasters, national as well as regional, as this was the first chance to sample farmer reaction since Dorrell's fateful announcement.

I wrote in my diary afterwards:

> *We had blanket coverage. I was interviewed live for BBC Radio Five, the World at One and the BBC television news. Richard (standing in for the President) performed adequately. Angela Browning was feeble, hiding behind her scientists. I ate beef at the Somerset Group Secretaries' dinner that evening (washed down by at least three bottles of red wine), steak for lunch yesterday and beef casserole last evening.*

There, that's defiance for you! And we were defiant. Determined to reassure an anxious public that all of the necessary safeguards were in place and had been for the last six years.

One of the first things we did was to set up a BSE Emergency Committee, chaired by the Somerset NFU Chairman, Alan Bartlett, a dairy farmer from North Cadbury and a calm, measured, thoughtful but decisive presence amidst the mayhem. The next few weeks were chaotic, as measures to save the British beef industry were argued over, repeatedly changed and, usually belatedly, put in place.

Chief amongst them was the so-called Over Thirty Month Scheme (OTMS). This was based on the premise that only a handful of cattle aged less than 30 months had ever succumbed to BSE. The Government's scientific advisers, on SEAC, had recommended the de-boning of the carcases of older animals. But that was impractical and hideously expensive. So the NFU's Chief Policy Adviser, Ian Gardiner, came up with a simpler alternative: that cull cows (a category later extended to any bovine aged over 30 months) be excluded from the human food chain altogether and either incinerated or rendered down. That way, the consumer could be 100% certain that British beef posed no risk to health, even if, as some had suggested, BSE might find its way into the food chain through poor practice at abattoirs or on parts of the carcase not counted as SBO.

I had my doubts. "Panic is about to be succeeded by panic measures," I noted. But I was in a minority. Douglas Hogg was keen on the idea (unlike the Treasury, who were horrified at the potential cost), as was the NFU's President, David Naish, and by March 30, when I caught the train to London for a regional directors' meeting, it was NFU policy. When I got back to Taunton that evening, I stopped off at Sainsbury's to buy something for my supper. The supermarket had that day cut beef prices by 50%. There wasn't a steak, a roasting joint or even a packet of mince left on the shelves. That lifted the spirits. Not for nothing do the French call us 'Les Rosbifs'.

In the meantime there were members to be informed, consulted and reassured. We embarked on an exhausting series of open meetings across the region, the biggest of which turned out to be at Kingston Maurward in Dorset on the day before Good Friday, April 4. Richard Macdonald was the main man for this one, but it soon became apparent that there were far too many farmers there to be accommodated in just the college lecture hall where he was due to speak. So I conducted an overflow meeting, standing precariously on the mantelpiece in the main entrance hall, which was packed with over 100 farmers, standing room only. Richard did the BBC 2 Newsnight interview that night, but I wasn't too bothered at being upstaged after umpteen interviews earlier in the day. But my goodness, was I glad to get home that night! I can still remember the feeling of relief.

It didn't last long. On Easter Saturday, Angela Browning came along to our BSE Emergency Committee in the Regional Office. By this stage the EC Commission had banned British beef exports, not just to the rest of Europe but to the entire world. We put to her our list of demands:

> Compensation for the destruction of the thousands of tonnes of
> unsaleable beef in store;
> A cull cow disposal scheme, plus emergency aid for the slaughter
> of over-age 'clean' cattle;
> Rejection of the concept of 'BSE-free' status for some farms;
> Beef premium top-up on all cattle slaughtered for as long as the
> export ban remained in place.

In the end, we got most of what we asked for, although the situation remained chaotic for months. Capacity at both abattoirs and renderers was hopelessly insufficient to cope with the number of cull cows and over-age beef cattle that were coming forward, particularly as the compensation for the clean cattle was set too high, so that it paid farmers to wait until animals reached 30 months and then put them through the scheme, rather than marketing them in the normal way.

The backlog of cattle waiting to go into the scheme was growing by between 10,000 and 20,000 a week, so that by mid-June it was over 200,000. 'Farcical' was the word I used to describe the way the scheme was being operated. The Prince of Wales could not have been more sympathetic when we met him at the Royal Cornwall Show.

But if MAFF was incompetent at home, it was inept abroad. The export ban was the main bone of contention. Brussels wanted a UK 'framework' for its progressive easing, starting with what it called a 'selective cull' of animals most at risk of developing BSE. There was no logic for this demand whatsoever. BSE cases were already falling rapidly and all of the scientific projections suggested that, with the measures in place to keep meat and bone meal out of all animal feed, it would die out completely by around 2001. A Selective Cull would make no difference to that. But neither Douglas Hogg nor the Prime Minister, John Major, could shift opinion amongst their fellow EC Ministers, and a Selective Cull did indeed feature in the so-called 'Florence Agreement' which set out the terms for lifting the ban.

That was in June. On July 19 John Major visited Cornwall, and we were invited to meet him in a hotel near Falmouth. Lifting the export ban was his absolute priority, and by this stage he had come up with a timetable for that to be achieved. The first stage of this would be when the OTMS backlog had been cleared and the Selective Cull was under way. That, according to Major, would happen "by October". I hadn't met him before and found him a surprisingly impressive personage, bigger and more imposing than I'd been expecting, with a natural air of command.

Philip Stephens, the Cornwall NFU Chairman, and Brian Peace, representing the Country Landowners' Association, were there as well, and we had a perfectly civilised conversation, in which all the expected questions were asked and all the expected answers were given – until I asked him about that timetable. "How realistic is it, Prime Minister, if you're being honest?"

"It's pretty speculative", he replied. "If we could meet the timetable I'd be very pleased, but I think it will take longer."

He also said, as a sort of parting shot: "This problem with beef is the worst problem I can remember in 17 years in Parliament."

I knew how he felt.

Over the weekend, a journalist on the Financial Times rang to ask how we'd got on. I relayed the PM's comments on the deliverability of his timetable. They made headlines on the Monday morning. My reward for obtaining this really rather important insight into the Government's thinking was a telephone call from Richard's successor as Director of Regions, Roger Ward, followed up by a letter inviting me to attend a meeting in his office 'within the framework of the NFU's disciplinary procedures for Regional Directors'. "In the meantime, I ask you to refrain from briefing journalists from the national media and, when briefing the local and regional media, to do so only with authorised NFU position statements."

Ye Gods and little fishes! I had been working my balls off for months on the BSE crisis, to be rewarded with a disciplinary interview!

top: Serious stuff on West Sedgemoor: Stan Chedzoy explaining
to Sir Richard Butler why the NCC have got it all wrong

bottom: Exmoor battle-line: the improved grassland of Stowey Allotment meets the
surrounding moorland from which it was controversially converted in the 1970s.

NFU Somerset County Secretary, hard at work

Taste of Somerset
Claire and Rebecca meet the Queen at the Bath and West Show, 1985

top: Father with Joanna
right: On Branscombe beach
with Becky, George and Joanna

top: A distinguished panel and me at the Bath and West, 1995: *(from left)* Michael Eavis, Auberon Waugh, Clive Aslet (editor of Country Life) and Tracy Worcester, the animal welfare campaigner; *bottom:* The newly appointed NFU South-West Regional Director, with *(from left)* Devon's Brian Jennings, Dorset's John Hosford, Somerset's Peter Wyatt, Director of Regions Richard Macdonald and Cornwall's Robin Bailey

Two styles of campaigning
top: On the air at the Bournemouth BSE demonstration, Autumn 1996
bottom: A rallying cry at an anti-hunting ban meeting at Westpoint, December 1997

top: Launching the Westcountry Cooking campaign at the Castle Hotel, Taunton, with Diane Lethbridge and TV chef Phil Vickery

bottom: Mentors and friends: Wesley Wyatt *(left)* and Dick Pearce

left: My brother Chippy with a bottle of cider, demonstrating the escanciar

below: Brothers in arms

To be fair to Roger, this was the work of "the other end of the corridor", as he liked to put it: that is to say the President, David Naish, and his fellow office-holders. Even so, it left me feeling distinctly pissed off.

We drew breath while the farmers harvested their corn over August and planned our 'Autumn Beef Campaign'. This would involve leaflets, posters, burger giveaways and demonstrations, all on the theme 'Why British Beef is Best'. There was no shortage of volunteers to take part. The BSE crisis had thrown up a new clutch of militant campaigners, led by one Richard Haddock.

I had first encountered Richard at the Royal Cornwall Show in 1994. He was having a celebratory drink on the NFU stand with his wife Caroline, having just won the Aberdeen Angus breed championship, and started sounding off to me about what a useless organisation the NFU was. As usual in these situations, I suggested to him that, if he felt like that, the best thing he could do was to get involved and change things for the better. He took me at my word!

At any rate, when it came to the BSE crisis, he could hardly have been more helpful to the cause. He donated one of his bullocks to provide the burgers for the giveaways and was ever present, whether at open meetings for farmers or town centre happenings for consumers. He was, however, rivalled for both prominence and outrageousness by the self-styled (as I hasten to make clear) 'Four Witches'.

The women in question were Mary Down, a dairy farmer's wife from South Somerset, and her daughter Jane, a good friend of Claire's; Sandy Loud, who milked cows with her husband to the west of Okehampton, and Pat Bird, another dairy farmer's wife from near Bude. When it came to what they got up to at demos, they very much did their own thing, and I was only too happy to let them get on with it. They had their own brightly coloured sweatshirts made, with 'This cow's not mad' on the front of them and 'She's bloody furious' on the back, and there was indeed a sort of divine fury about what they got up to. Goodness knows how many hundreds of miles they travelled in the cause, all at their own expense. The media loved them, of course.

Anthony Jeanes, a distinctly angry young dairy farmer from South Somerset, was another loose but highly effective cannon, while the imposing figure of George Baker, who had earned himself lasting fame in the West Country farming community years earlier by turning his muck spreader onto a group of anti-hunting demonstrators, was not only ever present, but a vital source of information on the sometimes murky world of slaughtering and rendering. If I wanted to know what was *really* going on in the meat trade, I would ask George.

And all of the 'British Beef is Best' campaigning did have its effect. By September consumption was on the increase, particularly in the South-West, and producer prices were, at last, on the rise.

As summer turned to autumn, all the focus was on the backlog, which the NFU was putting at over 300,000 animals by mid-September. Against that backdrop it was scarcely believable that the UK Government, in the person of Douglas Hogg, making a complete ass of himself by insisting on wearing his silly fedora hat, should prompt the EC Beef Management Committee into cutting the compensation for over-30-month steers and heifers by 10%, from 83p per kg to 75p per kg liveweight, which worked out at £40 to £50 per head. The response from farmers was furious. 'The unkindest cut of all' is how I described it in a press release. The logic of it might have made sense – to make the scheme worth less than the market – but the timing could hardly have been more insensitive.

The Minister who had been put in charge of the OTMS, Roger Freeman, Chancellor of the Duchy of Lancaster, was despatched to the West Country to quell the unrest. He met us at the Deer Park Hotel, near Honiton, on October 1 – private meeting with NFU and CLA first, then a press conference. The 'Four Witches' were in attendance, of course, plus all of our most prominent militants.

Freeman actually gave a pretty good account of himself. But when John Hoskin from Dorchester (with whom I'd been at village school in Sparkwell back in the 50s) told him that he'd had 102 cattle booked in for the scheme since May and that the cut was going to cost him £4,000 to £5,000, he was forced to admit that "it does seem unfair". He said he would take that back with him to London, together with a demand that, to clear the backlog faster, cattle should be incinerated in the open air, on pyres, as would happen with a foot-and-mouth outbreak. But essentially, he gave no ground.

Feelings were still running high two days later, when the Bath and West managed to persuade Douglas Hogg to face the music at their South-West Dairy Show. This time it was the turn of one of the oldest and most grizzled of our militants to come to the fore. My old friend Ian Pettyfer had once tried to kidnap Harold Wilson, as Prime Minister, on the Isles of Scilly. D. Hogg was small beer by comparison.

By now ostensibly part of the establishment as Deputy Chairman of Devon NFU, Ian had lost none of the fire in his belly and was determined to show this pipsqueak of a Minister of Agriculture exactly what he thought of him. He told me what he proposed to do. I said something to the effect of "I'm not sure that's entirely a good idea" and left it at that. Ian was one of the most intelligent, thoughtful men I worked with but, once he was set on something, there was no turning him aside.

In what was supposed to be a private meeting in the St Ivel lecture theatre, Hogg gave a burbling performance, defending the Government's position on the export ban (the selective cull had recently been abandoned) and the cut in compensation. For an intelligent man, he was hopeless in front of a crowd of farmers. Then he invited questions. Ian Pettyfer stood up:

"Minister, will you give an assurance that the cut in compensation will not apply to cattle in the backlog?"

Hogg: "No, I will not."

Pettyfer: "In that case, I have to tell you that you're a fucking disaster."

There was a stunned silence. Outside the building a huge crowd of farmers had gathered. A cheer went up when news of the exchange reached them. Shortly afterwards, Hogg decided that he'd had enough and headed for a side door, not daring to face the multitude out front. He was spotted as he tried to scuttle away and almost engulfed, only saved by the presence of a BBC television crew. Of all the humiliations that he suffered during the BSE crisis, this must have been one of the worst. Yet it was all so unnecessary. If he'd had any sense, or guts, he would have gone out onto the balcony of the building and addressed the crowd. They would have been polite enough. They weren't out to lynch him. They just wanted their voices to be heard.

Our Autumn Beef Campaign reached a climax a week later, in Bournemouth where the Conservative Party Annual Conference was being held. Thousands of farmers converged on the town from all parts of the country. It turned out to be the biggest farmer demonstration in Britain since the beef crisis of 1973-4. We gathered in Meyrick Park. David Naish made a speech. There were cheers, jeers, chants and catcalls. I had a headset on for the entire morning, providing what was virtually a running commentary on the occasion for what seemed like every radio station between Land's End and Tewkesbury.

The Government did respond. John Major invited the NFU hierarchy – Gibson not included – to his hotel for a 90-minute private meeting. Rather more usefully, Douglas Hogg announced a top-up to the beef premium, to be paid on finished cattle sold since July 1 and worth, he said, £29 million. Enough cold storage had been found to double OTMS throughput without having to resort to open-air incineration. There was no movement on the cut in OTMS compensation but, that apart, we could justifiably claim a success, especially as the Bournemouth demo – on our patch, don't forget – had been very much a South-West initiative.

After that things calmed down. Somewhat to my surprise, MAFF did indeed succeed in boosting OTMS throughput to 60,000 animals a week, and by the end of November the backlog had gone. Cases of BSE continued to decline; a selective cull based on groups of cattle likely to be at most risk, rather than entire herds or age-groups, was introduced in early 1997, at an eventual cost of £120 million, despite the fact that even the MAFF Permanent Secretary, Richard Packer, had concluded that it would not advance the elimination of BSE by a single day or indeed serve any other useful purpose apart from keeping our EC partners happy. The beef market continued slowly to recover.

BSE was far and away the worst thing to happen to British agriculture in my working lifetime, but it could have been so much worse. Two things saved the beef industry from meltdown. The first was the Over Thirty Month Scheme. The assurance that it provided came at a huge cost, to be sure. Over its ten-year life span, over eight million animals went through the scheme. That was the equivalent of two-and-a-half million tonnes of beef, worth something like £3.75 billion at farm-gate prices. Add in the cost of compensating the farmers, renderers and abattoirs, and you are left with a bill of around £8 billion – £1,000 per animal – and all for a measure that, in scientific terms, was never justified. Was that money really well spent? Who knows? The alternative might have been worse.

The second factor in the beef industry's salvation was that the epidemic in cases of new variant CJD, predicted by the likes of Professor Richard Lacey, never materialised. At one point, Lacey suggested that up to four million people might die of vCJD. In the event, the death toll to date has been 178. Some of the more insistent doom-mongers are saying that the worst may yet to be to come. I think that unlikely, given that thirty years has now passed since the risk of infection was at its highest in the late 1980s and that the pattern of vCJD cases, with only two since 2011, does not support the contention of an incubation period longer than that.

It seems to me that two possibilities flow from that. The first is that BSE only crosses the species barrier with the utmost difficulty, which suggests that the unfortunate victims were either particularly susceptible or consumed unusually large quantities of infected offal, something for which there is no evidence. The second possibility is that, just as BSE was a disease of cattle which had previously gone unrecognised because of the very small number of cases, so vCJD may be a previously unrecognised form of human spongiform encephalopathy, which only came to light when scientists started looking for it. Again we may never know.

Some good did come from the BSE crisis. It produced the Food Standards Agency which, whatever one thinks of some of its edicts, does have a credibility with the consuming public which no set of politicians could ever have, especially after the way BSE was handled. Standards of hygiene and safety improved at every stage of the beef supply chain. And, whilst 'farm assurance' – the concept of a set of standards intended to guarantee good practice on farms, such as those which underpin the Red Tractor logo – would surely have become established under any circumstances, BSE undoubtedly hastened its development.

As for the NFU in the South-West, we came out of BSE with our membership augmented and our reputation enhanced. Credit for that belongs equally to membership and staff. We had worked as a team to fight for the beef industry and the livelihoods of our members and to restore the confidence of our consumers in the safety of British beef. "British Beef is Safe," we shouted from the rooftops; "Back British Farming," we urged the public. It was, and they did.

18

Golfing memories

I didn't have much of a family background in golf. My mother's father, Dan Thomas, played a bit at Stinchcombe Hill when he was teaching at Dursley, and I have an ancient photograph of his parents essaying practice shots on the beach at Llandudno, his flamboyant mother Ellen, wielding a cleek, seeming to have a particularly fine swing. But other than being an admirer of Bernard Darwin's prose style, my father took no interest in the game and probably, with typical inverted snobbery, rather despised it.

For all my best playing years, golf was a brotherly activity. Chippy and I discovered it at St Ives, on the putting green (still there) behind Porthminster Beach, with gun metal putters and battered Dunlop Warwick balls. In those years we watched just about whatever sport we could on television, but it wasn't until Arnold Palmer came on the scene that we took even a passing interest in golf. We certainly had no intention of acquiring any golf clubs when we caught the bus into Plymouth soon after the start of the 1964 school summer holiday with a £5 note to spend, the money being a typically generous birthday present for my brother from my mother's gentleman-friend.

We headed for the second-hand shop at the bottom of Cornwall Street in the city centre which had always been a bit of a magnet. Peering through the window, we spotted some ancient golf clubs, priced at five shillings each. They had wooden shafts and rusted heads: a spade niblick, for extracting the ball from bunkers and ruts, a more conventional wedge-style niblick, a mashie niblick, a mid-iron and some sort of cleek. Not that we knew the names of the various clubs then, but that was what they turned out to be after we'd bought them. But we did know enough about the game to realise that there was one obvious omission – a wooden club of some sort, to give the ball a good whack off the tee. Fortunately the shop had one of those as well, a rather less ancient steel-shafted weapon, priced at thirty shillings. The balance of our money we invested in a selection of second-hand golf balls and, when we got to WH Smith, a copy of Tommy Armour's 'How to Play Your Best Golf All the Time' – arguably the best golf instruction book ever written, which I still have and still consult. I suppose there may have been a putter as well but, if so, I have no recollection of it. I suspect that we decided that, on the 'greens' on which we would be playing, the cleek would suffice.

Thus equipped, we caught the bus home and headed straight for Yennadon Down, the nearest stretch of moorland to where we lived at Dousland. Just the other side of the moor gate was a grassy platform, as obvious a first tee as you ever saw. The surrounding moorland consisted of a great deal of gorse, cut through with just the occasional avenue of green grass, with some puddled-down grassy areas by the boundary hedges where the ponies had been fed the previous winter.

As the elder brother I assumed the honour, teed my ball on a tuft of grass and swung. I can clearly remember the shot. It wasn't perfect, by any means. Like most beginners I sliced it, but there was a resounding, satisfying crack and the ball sailed away against the wide blue heaven. Like millions of golfers before and since, in that instant I was hooked. Chippy's opening drive wasn't quite so impressive. He topped it, but it still scuttled an encouragingly long way across the ruts and through the bracken. And it was easily found, unlike my more grandiose effort, which took at least ten minutes of searching to retrieve from a gorse bush.

So we had clubs, balls, guidance and, after those two opening blows, boundless enthusiasm. All we needed now was a course. Not having been born to golfing parents, lacking any golfing connections (golf was frowned upon at school as an individual rather than a team sport) and without any money for green fees, there was only one thing for it – create our own!

The terrain was maybe not ideal, on account of all that gorse. But then St Andrews itself was once a mass of whins, as they call gorse in those parts, with just narrow ribbons of fairway winding their way through the undergrowth. So whilst ours was moorland, rather than links-land, and our fairways were rougher and narrower even than the Old Course at its most ancient, we did start our golfing careers in much the same way as the original Scottish (or possibly Dutch!) pioneers had started theirs.

The greens were small, rough and almost incidental. Keeping one's ball out of the gorse was paramount, not just in terms of winning the hole but in being able to come back to play again on the following day. The golf ball attrition rate was frightening. Our saving grace in this regard was the fish man, who called with his van every Wednesday tea-time. Learning of our enthusiasm for golf, and living next to a course (Staddon Heights, we guessed), he became our regular supplier – at no charge, as long as our mother kept buying his fish!

So, as the railway runabout tickets were discontinued on the back of the Beeching vandalisation, golf on Yennadon Down took their place. We would play for hours, until it got dark or, more likely, until we ran out of balls. We taught ourselves all manner of shots, with one notable exception: the aforementioned putting, which simply wasn't possible in any recognisable form on the rough patches of grass we called 'greens'. It has been the cardinal weakness of my game ever since.

Years later I learned that Henry Longhurst had similarly played his first golf shots on a stretch of moorland, in his case just down the road at Yelverton. I never met him but, belying his later gin-soaked, crotchety reputation, he had once been a very fine golfer – something which, unlike our Dartmoor debuts, he and I most certainly did not have in common!

I didn't play any golf at Oxford. The thought never even occurred. I didn't move in those sorts of circles. I was, however, following the professional game by then, and I spent a memorable four days watching the South African, Harold Henning, win the Dunlop Masters at Little Aston, just down the road from where Susie's parents lived near Sutton Coldfield. The course was a picture of almost dream-like perfection.

The move to Blacklands in 1970 provided the opportunity to dig out our ancient clubs again. I could practice to my heart's content in the fields, and there were games of 'long-distance golf', where the ultimate goal might be a telegraph pole a mile and half away across six fields and two streams. But beyond that, my mother's friend Enid Hamlyn was a golfer, a member of a club, no less, at the Elfordleigh Hotel, a few miles away, and she it was who gave me my first chance to play on a proper course.

The Elfordleigh was a nine-hole course (now 18) on rolling parkland, with some handsome trees. Enid lent me an old golf bag and a few clubs to supplement my own, and off we set. I don't remember much of the round, except that I was rather overcome by nerves and didn't play nearly as well as I'd hoped – a state of affairs with which I would become all too familiar over the years ahead! But it was an introduction to real golf and, when I discovered that my friend at Dingle's, Tony Oxley, was not only a golfer but also owned a car, trips to the Elfordleigh became a regular occurrence, with Chippy joining us during the Oxford vacations. The green fee was 60p, and you could go round the nine holes as often as you liked. Chippy and I once set ourselves the target of playing 100 holes in a day and were going strong at 72 when the course filled up with a ladies fourball match and we had to give it best.

After I moved to London, I would make a point of playing some golf with Tony and Chippy whenever I returned home for the weekend or a longer break. By this stage I had begun acquiring some rather more modern clubs to supplement the old hickories. The first of them was a Ben Sayers seven iron, procured by virtue of the coupons from the Gold Leaf cigarettes that I smoked. A Dunlop nine iron was similarly acquired, thanks to Players Number 6, and I bought one or two relatively cheaply in the 'odd clubs' section at Lillywhite's in Piccadilly, although my pride and joy was a Ben Sayers driver.

My first experience of serious golf came by virtue of the NFU Club Golfing Society. One of my colleagues in the Intelligence Division (he later went on to run the Seeds department) was Jimmy Graham, a mild-mannered Scot with that slightly querulous Ayrshire accent, who was a good golfer and a member at Sandy Lodge. The NFU Club, which I frequented at lunchtimes, had a golfing society and Jimmy put me down to play in its meeting in 1974 at Wentworth, then as now one of the grandest clubs in the country. I performed respectably in a morning single around the less famous East Course and was due to play with Stanley Blow, a wealthy Kent fruit farmer who had driven me to the course in his Rolls Royce, around the West course in the afternoon fourballs. It would surely be a round to remember, on one of the most famous courses in Britain.

Oh dear. It turned out to be one of the most hateful and humiliating experiences of my golfing life. Everyone else seemed to have a caddy or, at the very least, the very latest in golf trollies. I had my random selection of ancient clubs in Enid's heavy black leather bag circa 1955, which I lugged around by its single narrow strap. I picked up at the first, when heading for double figures. At the short second I did actually hit the green with my seven iron, only to take three nervous putts. As for the rest, my memory is a blur of dark trees, clinging rough, water-filled ditches and lost balls. Stanley could not have been kinder, which only made it worse. God, was I glad to get back to the clubhouse for a drink and the presentations – which turned out to be memorable in themselves.

The President of the Society was the NFU's Honorary Treasurer, Colonel Jock Wilson, a splendidly choleric figure who no longer played himself but who was decidedly fond of a gin and tonic, of which he gave every appearance of having consumed more than a few during the course of the afternoon. When he came to present what was a large and very splendid silver trophy to the winners, he dropped the cup, which landed on the edge of the platform and bounced away across the floor. It was hastily retrieved by one of us onlookers and handed back to the Colonel, who this time managed to hand it over without mishap, before posing with the winners and their trophy for photographs.

"Ahem, sir," ventured the photographer, for Jock Wilson was not in the best of humours, "but would you mind turning the cup the other way round, only this side is rather badly dented?"!

You will be relieved to learn that I do not intend to treat readers to a round-by-round history of my life in golf – although, believe me, I could do, as I have kept a record of virtually every round I've played since about 1979! But I must give a mention to 'The Cat's Whiskers', a competition inaugurated in 1977, the CAT in question being the initials of the three founders, Chippy, Anthony and Tony (as in Oxley). In its initial format, which stretched over several months, we each chose a course on which we would play 36 holes of stroke-play, with the fourth and final day at a course which none of us had ever played before.

In that first year, Chippy chose Yelverton, Tony Whitsand Bay, while I went for Royal North Devon, with the last day at Saunton in early November. I did eventually win, despite taking over 100 to go round my chosen venue but not until a month later than planned. At Saunton, after playing pretty well in the morning, I was walking to the first tee after a distinctly bibulous lunch when I turned my ankle, nastily and painfully. I managed to complete the 470-yard first hole – making a par four, thanks to a long putt – but after that the pain became too great and I hobbled back to put my foot up in the clubhouse while Chippy and Tony completed their round.

After the obligatory post-round beers, my discomfort was such that there was nothing for it but to stop off at the North Devon Infirmary in Barnstaple, where a badly-torn ligament was diagnosed and plaster applied. We then stopped on the way back to Plymouth (using the old road) at the Duke of York at Iddesleigh – ancient, thatched, flag-floored, inglenooked, nicotine-stained, welcoming, essence of Devon. We were so taken with the place that we vowed to return on the way back from the re-run of the final day, so beginning an association that lasted for over twenty years.

We changed the format of the competition in 1979 to three consecutive days on three different courses and invited other like-minded spirits to join us. Every other year we would stay, drink and dine (splendidly) at the Duke of York, driving to Saunton, Westward Ho! and either Bude or

Okehampton. Tony Bull was the landlord in those days. "Help yourselves to whatever you like from behind the bar, boys. Just keep a note of what you have and we'll settle up in the morning," he would say, before heading off to bed at closing time. One night the police arrived at around 1 am (for the Duke of York's reputation for drinking after hours was not entirely undeserved) , our beer and darts in full swing.

"You're all under arrest," said one of the two police constables.

"I don't think so," replied Miles Elder, a Cat's Whiskers stalwart. "For a start, we're residents, and secondly I'm Sergeant Miles Elder of the Avon and Somerset Police, so clear off." Which they did.

Besides our biennial Iddesleigh/North Devon visitations, we had some splendid CW trips over the years: to West Cornwall, St Enodoc and Trevose; to Parkstone, Broadstone and the Isle of Purbeck in Dorset; to Royal Porthcawl, Southerndown and Ashburnham in South Wales; and to Borth, Aberdovey and Royal St David's further north. One year we even made it to France. Wherever we played, it was an exhausting experience – 36 holes around a long and challenging seaside links, usually in early April, on each of three days, interspersed with three evenings of serious beer drinking.

Perhaps I could be allowed just two Cat's Whiskers anecdotes, which will give the flavour of what it was all about. The first was in 1982, when we headed to Cornwall for the first time, with Mandy's brother Jono (a county hockey player, which rather showed in his golf swing) and his great mate John Poustie, both prep-school teachers. Now Poustie, as he was always known, was a very considerable sportsman, who had played cricket for St Luke's and fly half for Exeter, with a very considerable thirst. But his golfing experience was rather more limited. When he signed in to pay his green fee, he would announce himself as 'Poustie from Carnoustie', because he claimed once to have played there. On that first morning he was in the match in front of me and regained the clubhouse maybe 20 minutes before I did.

"How's it going Poustie?", I enquired on walking into the bar.

"Not so bad, Gibbo", he replied. "I've slammed back four pints of Bass already." And he had, too.

That evening he and Jono perpetrated the perfect sting, in a beer drinking contest at the St Mabyn Inn, which Chippy and I were nailed on to win, having both won the drinking cup at Queen's, with best times of around four seconds for a pint. We backed ourselves heavily. Jono was a long-odds outsider. But his glass had been emptied, with ours still almost half full. He was a pourer. We were gulpers.

Then there was the time when we were in Wales in 1994. Our first day was at Aberdovey, a magnificent, atmospheric links which will forever be associated with Bernard Darwin, having been laid out by his wife's family, the Rucks. We had all had a few pints at lunchtime, as usual, but only another couple at close of play as we had to drive 30 miles or so up the coast to stay at a pub in Llanbedr. Chippy went on ahead in his big maroon Rover with Jason Hamlyn for company, and I was expecting to find him in the bar, playing darts, when I reached the Victoria. But no sign. What had happened? As the minutes ticked by, with still no sign or news of Chippy and Jason, so concern mounted. Happily, at around ten, they appeared.

"Where on earth have you been?" we asked, with one voice.

"Get me a pint and I'll tell you," said Chippy. "It's a long story."

It turned out that they'd been stopped by a policeman in a Panda car for speeding, and Chippy had been breathalysed, giving his name as Owen Glendower. Unsurprisingly, given the number of pints of Strongbow he'd consumed during the day, he'd failed. But the policeman was on his own and some way from his home station of Dolgellau.

"You, Owen Glendower, had better come with me," said the policeman. "Your mate can drive your car, assuming he's not under the influence as well." (He wasn't, but then nor was he insured.)

So off they set in convoy. But after a few miles, they came up behind a Volvo, veering wildly from one side of the road to the other. "He's obviously drunk, look you, but what am I to do?", the policeman complained, liltingly. " I can't arrest him when I'm on my own and already got you as a prisoner."

"I'll tell you what," said Chippy, thinking quickly. "Why don't you ring up the station and set up a road block." Which is what the copper did, explaining on his radio that the suggestion had come from "the prisoner".

The upshot was that the Volvo was duly stopped. It turned out to be being driven by one of the local vets, who was grappling with a sick sheep (as tends to happen in those parts). He was duly breathalysed, cleared and sent on his way. Now all this had taken some considerable time, and it wasn't until about two hours after his arrest that Chippy was breathalysed at the police station to confirm the roadside result. And, of course, he had passed. Pints of Robinson's Best all round! What a night that was!

The era of three day Cat's Whiskers golf and drinking marathons is sadly long departed, I'm afraid. Nowadays we play just 36 holes on a single day – a round on each of Saunton West and Saunton East, with only a modicum of beer consumed. Our most recent winner was Wesley Wyatt, at the age of 87!

I am the only survivor of the three originals. Chippy died in December 2000, Tony Oxley followed him, from the same cause, in 2009 and of the other Cat's Whiskers stalwarts, Donald Harmer, John Poustie and Miles Elder are also now playing their golf in the Elysian Fields, while John Knight is no longer fit enough to take part. I am counting upon my two sons-in-law, Phil and Nick, to keep the flame alive; possibly, eventually, with some assistance from my golf-averse son George.

The first club I was a member of was Chippenham, no more than two miles from the office at Langley Burrell, to which I was introduced by Richard Maslen, whose father-in-law, Tom Lindsay, had overseen the extension of the course to 18 holes. I remember thinking, when the letter from the Secretary arrived, that I had broken into the 'magic circle' of golf club membership (for being a member of a club and having a handicap mattered much more when you wanted to play at one of the smarter clubs than it does now).

It was at about this time that I met John Knight in the back room of the Carpenters Arms in Sherston, where the irascible George held sway. He, John, was a civil engineer who had moved to the village from the Vale of Evesham with his wife Gwen and was as keen a golfer as me (Gwen was even keener) and much more experienced. They had been members at Broadway and were now at Stinchcombe Hill. We played there, at Chippenham and, on winter Saturdays, at Royal Porthcawl, and eventually as members at Burnham, for many years, our families holidaying together at Saunton, and remaining close ever since.

Links golf was my thing. When we moved to Devon in early 1979, I vowed to join Saunton, securing an introduction thanks to a farmer I'd met during NFU golf. It was, to be sure, some 55 miles distant from where we lived at Clayhidon, but that meant I qualified for 'country membership', at £60 or so per year, and I could usually get there in less than an hour and a quarter. Two years later I joined Burnham and Berrow, 25 miles up the M5. So I have been a member of the two clubs with the finest courses in the West of England for some 40 years – and my Saunton membership entitles me to a half green fee at magnificent Royal North Devon!

Sunday morning was my favoured time for Saunton in the early years. I would drive to Exeter first thing, to broadcast my farming half-hour on Devonair at 7.30 and then drive rapidly up the old A377 for a 9.15 (ish) tee-off with the lovely Hubert Peters, as kindly a Devonian as ever walked the banks of Taw and Torridge. Hubert had been an engineer with the Royal

Navy in the Second World War and was by now the Chief Engineer at the Yelland Power Station across the estuary, whose chimney marked the line for the drive at the sixth tee on the East Course. He kept the machinery in perfect working order for 364 days a year, in readiness for its one moment of glory – on Christmas morning, when it was the last station on the grid to be brought on line! We would play an 18-hole medal or Stableford, before I headed back to Clayhidon for lunch with the family and an afternoon kip!

Apart from the quality of the golf and the glory of the surroundings (this was before they built that hideous monument to stupidity and greed, the Fullabrook wind farm), the great thing about Saunton was Open Week. This was always the first full week of August, and every year from 1983 to 1996 I would take the family up to North Devon, usually with Chippy and my mother in tow, to stay in a holiday cottage for the week. The ideal day involved Chippy and I playing in one of the competitions first thing in the morning, then beach with the family in the afternoon. The weather was not exactly reliable, and one or two of the cottages were a bit damp, but these were happy holidays.

I never actually won anything in Saunton Week. I did make the quarter-final of the knock-out competition, the Saunton Plate, one year, only to be beaten by the legendary Pay Huyshe, a retired schoolmaster from East Devon, who must have been pushing 80 at the time. Every August he would drive up to Saunton on his ancient moped, play in every competition in Saunton Week and camp at Lobb Fields in his equally ancient one-man tent. One year we feared for his life when, in stepping back to pick the line off the first tee on the East course, he fell backwards into the brambly undergrowth which covered the precipitous slope behind him. He was eventually rescued, scratched and bruised but otherwise unscathed, and went on to play his round. And he was much too steady for me!

Chippy did record a win, although I wasn't there to witness it. I was commentating at Old Trafford when – typically – he took his putter from fully 80 yards out at the last on the East and knocked it to three feet to win the Open Monthly Medal. My only appearance on the Saunton honours boards is for the Committee Cup in 1981, when I went round the East Course off the back tees in 77, net 65. My final full shot was a 2-iron from 200 yards out at the last which found the centre of the green. It provides a warm glow to this day.

But perhaps my best competitive round was played on the other side of Barnstaple Bay, at RND, in their Open Week (always a fortnight later than

Saunton's) in 1983. I played in the distinguished company of Jack Scott, son of Michael, nephew of Denys and nephew as well of the incomparable (according to Bernard Darwin) Lady Margaret Scott, of that great golfing dynasty. Knowing that I had to beat a nett 68 to have any chance, I came to the last needing a five. This is my contemporary account:

Anxious, shortish drive, down the right. Left me 197 yards away, with the burn in front of the green to carry. 5 wood, blocked right. It finished in a thick clump of weeds, the only one for yards around, and the ball was barely visible. Hack with a sand wedge – off the socket to back left of green. Putter to 12 feet. The last putt never looked like going in but somehow ducked in on the right-hand side.

Of such moments does competitive amateur golf consist.

Mandy and I went to the prize-giving on the following Saturday, where the highlight was David Stirk winning the 36-hole scratch competition, the Kashmir Cup. On what was a dark, drizzly, typically windy Westward Ho! afternoon he had gone round in 68 – the same as his age! That put my efforts in perspective!

John Goodban was the king of Saunton in those days. He had been playing there since 1926 and had won everything in sight, on both sides of the bay. A photograph of him wearing the red coat of the President of the EGU dominated the lounge bar. He set high standards, for himself and for his club, and suffered fools or vulgarity not at all. I was always rather in awe of him, but he seemed to take to me, perhaps because of my role with the NFU, as his family were farmers in Kent. I played with him one year in the 36-hole Easter Challenge Cup, on a typically filthy April day, and was round in the morning in nett 73. "That was very well played, Anthony," he said, as we walked off the last green. Never was a compliment more treasured.

Saunton has been my home club since I joined in 1979, but Burnham and Berrow is where I have played most of my golf over the years. My first visit was for an NFU event in the midst of the 1976 drought which, in the absence then of any fairway watering system, had reduced parts of the course to a sandy desert. But I took to the place immediately – the rolling fairways, towering sandhills, fast greens, magnificent views across Bridgwater Bay and a proud history that included JH Taylor as the club's first professional – and when the chance to join came in 1981 I seized it.

Initially, just as at Saunton, most of the golf I played was in competitions, with no particularly regular partners. But after Chippy moved to Bristol in the early 1990s, he joined as well, and we would play on Saturday afternoons, after a preliminary visit to the Royal Clarence Hotel for darts, pool and some of its excellent home-brewed beer. I would win the occasional medal, Stableford or cup competition, of which Burnham has plenty. By the mid-1980s my handicap was in single figures and stayed that way for a decade, albeit never lower than eight.

"I'm nine handicap at golf, as in most things in life," I liked to say. "I just wish that there was something at which I was scratch."

I had discovered quite early in my golfing career that one of the most cost-effective ways of getting to play courses other than one's own was to enter their open competitions. The entrance fee was always much less than the weekend green fee, you got to play the course at its best and there was always the possibility – remote in my case – that one might win a prize.

My very first was at Chipping Sodbury, a long slog of a course next to a huge quarry, and I would have won it, with a nett 68, but for the fact that my handicap of 17 was not yet official, as I had ruefully to admit. I never came close to winning again, but Chippy and I enjoyed plenty of tough, competitive golf in 36-hole opens at courses like Teignmouth, East Devon, Okehampton, Launceston and RND.

What with all of that, and the ever-present rivalry between the pair of us, we both became useful players off our handicaps. However, only once were we both presented with cups at a prize-giving, and that was at Burnham in 1999. I have a photograph of us with our trophies, captioned '1999, the first year in which we both won trophies'. How sadly misplaced the implication was to prove.

After Chippy died in 2000 my enthusiasm for golf rather waned. I organised a 'Chippy Memorial Cat's Whiskers' at Saunton in October 2001, after which we spread his ashes on the sandhill to the left of the 16th tee on the West course. There is no better view anywhere on the links. Both courses are spread out below in the most wonderful, rippling panorama of greensward and sand, whilst away to the West there is the sea and Hartland Point. To hit a soaring iron shot from this tee, on a fine summer's evening, with the sun dipping toward the sea in a blaze of golden glory is as close to golfing heaven as one is ever likely to experience. Chippy loved nowhere better.

My handicap has crept gradually up since then, and I no longer bother to enter competitions. Most of my golf these days is played in the Stocks group at Burnham, inaugurated by and named after that same Geoffrey Stocks with whom I had so often crossed swords when he was the boss of Taunton Cider. We're an amiable body of senior golfers, most of whom have been distinguished either in life or in golf or in both. Our members come from as far afield as Tewkesbury, Dorchester, Appledore and Dartmoor and number in their ranks two former Presidents of the EGU, in Paul Fisher and Tony Hill, two winners of the Oxford and Cambridge Golf Society's President's Putter, in Michael Anderson and John Midgley, as well as past or present Presidents of Burnham (Nick Brown and David Lloyd Jenkins) and RND (Charles Churchill). I am one of the younger members, having been introduced in 2009 by Wesley Wyatt who, at the time of writing, is still going strong at 88. We play 'friendly' foursomes (which sometimes have a distinctly competitive edge), come rain or shine, and enjoy a good lunch afterwards. Harry Vardon had this to say of foursomes golf (where you and your partner take alternate shots):

A really good foursome when the partners play harmoniously and the holes are well fought-out, is a splendid change from the ordinary form of golf. The interest and excitement of each member of the party often seems to affect the others, and to lead up to an intense mutual keenness which is often superior even to that experienced in single play. There is a wholesome satisfaction in the community of interests. The winning of a hole is coveted as it was never coveted before.

With all of which I would whole-heartedly concur, adding just this caveat: foursomes golf may be the best form of the game when you are playing well, but it is assuredly the most hateful if you are playing badly!

My favourite courses? They are all links, I'm afraid. Not entirely out of golfing snobbery (although there is no doubt a smidgeon of that) but because links golf is simply the best. To be by the sea, often with glorious views, on crisp turf, fast greens, not a speck of mud and as good in the depths of winter as at the height of summer, with almost always a breeze (at the very least) to add interest and challenge is golf as it should be. The scent of wild thyme at Saunton on a hot day in August; the view from the fourth tee at Burnham across Bridgwater Bay to the Quantocks, Grabbist, Dunkery and, away in the distance, Foreland Point; the crunching of the waves on Westward Ho!'s pebble ridge and the salt-sea smell of the incoming tide: these, far more than the holing of putts or the winning of cups, are the golfing memories I most cherish.

From that you will gather that my four favourite courses are Saunton East and West, Burnham and Berrow and Royal North Devon. I find it impossible to separate them. Of those I know less well, I think of the links of the Royal West Norfolk Club at Brancaster in Norfolk, with the tide creeping in to the salt marsh at the eighth and ninth, or the incomparable (as they were in 1981) greens at Hunstanton, or the magnificent closing stretch at Deal, played into the breeze and the setting sun, that wonderful homecoming along the Camel estuary at St Enodoc, Betjeman poems running through my head, and maybe the finest of all golfing views, the panorama of St Ives Bay from the West Cornwall links at Lelant, with Godrevy – Virginia Woolf's 'Lighthouse' – as its focal point.

As for favourite golfers, the triumvirate of Taylor, Vardon and Braid are my heroes, just as much as they were Bernard Darwin's. Thinking of whom, no-one can surely ever have been such a devil on the golf course and such an angel with pen in hand as the irascible Darwin. I have read his books over and over again. His prose has a rhythm, a rectitude and a descriptive power unequalled by almost any English essayist (Darwin himself would cite Hazlitt), let alone English sports-writer.

Among the moderns, I was an Arnold Palmer man. I have always preferred, in any context, the swash-buckling over the mechanical. Tom Watson I warmed to, not least because of his love of links golf. And then there is Tiger, the black man who beat the whites at what has always been very much their own game. I admire most of all his mental toughness on the course – a quality I have always lacked – and I have always revelled in the discomfiture of the lounge-bar closet racists (of which there are still more than there should be) when Tiger triumphs yet again.

But perhaps my greatest golfing hero is a man who very few golfers even will have heard of. He was Ernie Foord, brought up as one of five in a cottage in Berrow in the 1880s to poor but hard-working parents. When the Burnham Golf Club opened in 1891, his father Walter became green-keeper (having first helped to create the course, with spade, horse and barrow) while his mother, Sarah, ran the bar. Ernie and his brothers Fred and Bill earned pennies for caddying as they taught themselves the game – no doubt with some assistance from JH Taylor who himself had only recently graduated from caddy-hood at Westward Ho! – on the Burnham links.

In 1900, at the age of 16, Ernie became the professional at what was already recognised as a championship links. In 1903 he went round in 63, against a 'bogey' (roughly the equivalent of today's 'standard scratch score') of 79 – a round described by the magazine Golf Illustrated as 'probably a world record score'. In 1913, he beat the by then five times Open Champion JH Taylor in a 36-hole match. In 1912 he went round Burnham's championship course in 73 – using just his putter! For my money, knowing what Burnham was like in those early years, with its drives over mountainous sandhills and sand everywhere, that has to be the most remarkable round of golf ever played.

Ernie went on to emigrate to the USA with his brother Fred, when his job disappeared during World War One, and to succeed the great Walter Hagan as professional at Oakland Hills in 1924. I'm two-thirds of the way through a book about him, which I will finish when I've been able to find out a bit more about the career in the States of a man who must surely qualify for the title of 'golf's forgotten hero'.

19

Troubled times

The late 1990s was a difficult, sometimes very unhappy period for me, both professionally and personally. Quite apart from the BSE crisis, these were tough years for West Country beef and dairy farmers, as the pound strengthened and prices slumped. By 2000 farm incomes, adjusted for inflation, were back to levels not seen since the depression of the 1930s.

We also had a change of political masters. I might have thought of that sunny Friday morning of May 2, a landslide for Tony Blair's New Labour having been confirmed, as a golden moment, but very few of my members did. There would surely be ructions ahead, especially when we discovered the identity of the new Minister of Agriculture: Jack Cunningham, a political bruiser who had been given the clearest of mandates to cut the farming lobby down to size.

My own life was in some turmoil. My marriage was breaking down – through no fault of anyone but myself – and I had left Burcombe to go to live on my own in a barn conversion at Horton Cross near Ilminster in 1994. By 1997 divorce proceedings were in train, involving more sadness than acrimony, but even so it must have been a hugely unsettling time for the children.

My father, meanwhile, had suffered a series of small strokes, which had progressively reduced his mobility and power of speech. By early 1997, having got himself thrown out of just about every nursing home in Taunton, he was a mumbling, wheelchair-bound wreck who had even given up his books. I would take him out to one of the local pubs about once a week, where we would sometimes be joined by Richard Walsh, a Taunton schoolmaster and unquenchably enthusiastic follower of Somerset cricket, who was kindness itself.

Towards the end, conversation with my father became impossible. I would embark on a monologue, telling him what I'd been up to or what was happening in the wider world. He would just sit there, open-mouthed, staring into space, occasionally slurping at his pint of beer (I wouldn't allow him whisky, something he resented to his dying day), completely uncommunicative. For a man who had been so erudite and eloquent, it was the crowning irony.

It was on April 5 1997 that I got a phone message from his nursing home, to say that he had a chest infection, which was not responding to antibiotics and that he was "very poorly". All four of us his children managed to visit him before the end, but I'm not sure he recognised any of us. He died on the morning of April 10. I got the news in a call on my mobile phone as I was coming back from buying a lunchtime sandwich at Tesco's. The emotional floodgates burst only when I rang Mandy.

I wondered at the time why his death should have hit me so hard. He honestly wasn't much of a father to any of us. In his younger, healthier days, he had always seemed too bound up in his own career to take much interest in his children (sounds familiar!), while towards the end he had mostly been sunk in incoherent self-pity. When I visited his nursing home a day or so before he died, the matron had said to me, "You know, he didn't like you very much", and that was true. I was the one who bundled him from wheel-chair to car, from car to wheel-chair to pub, and back again, who denied him whisky and who evinced precious little sympathy for what I considered to be his largely self-inflicted woes. If that sounds harsh and unsympathetic, it was really only Mandy and me who did anything to give him a worthwhile life in his closing years and, if I never really loved him, I certainly admired and respected him.

The funeral was held at the Silver Street Baptist Church, which he had occasionally attended as a boy at Taunton School. Adam and I read lessons, and David Foot, the Guardian cricket writer and theatre critic, gave the address. Considering how rude my father had sometimes been both to him and about him, he was generous enough, without entirely pulling his punches.

Johnny Woodcock, my father's friend and colleague on The Times, would have been a better, more sympathetic choice. But he was there, as indeed were Peter Baxter, the Test Match Special producer, representing the BBC, Frank Gillard, who had given father his first job with the BBC West of England region back in 1949, Dickie Dodds, the old Essex cricketer and Moral Rearmament campaigner, and a chap who said that he was an old flame of my mother from her Oxford days – he told me that he had 'loaned' her to my father for a function and had never got her back.

The wake was held in the Old Pavilion at the County Ground, where we drank to my father's memory and reflected on the pleasure which he had brought to so many people down the years, through his writing and broadcasting. I'll conclude with an assessment of him that I wrote for 'Of Didcot and the Demon', the collection of his cricketing writings which was published in 2009:

It would probably be fair to describe Alan Gibson as a mild schizophrenic, and he was undoubtedly manic depressive. Almost every aspect of his character had its exact opposite somewhere else in his psyche. He could be perfectly charming – and an utter bastard. He was an intensely sociable man – much given to condemning people whom he hardly knew as "bloody fools" on the flimsiest of evidence. He could moralise about the sins of the flesh with all the fervour of a dissenting preacher – and then go out drinking and womanising. He could be generous to a fault – and vicious to a degree. He was highly self-motivated – yet his problems were always someone else's fault. He was devoted to his wives and children – and frequently made their lives a misery.

What was not in doubt was the depth or strength of his intellect or his complete command of the English language. He was a true polymath, blessed with a remarkable memory. Not only was he a voracious reader, with tastes ranging from Billy Bunter, through science fiction, to the romantic poets, but he could remember details and plots, sometimes from even minor books, read decades previously. He claimed to have memorised the entirety of Milton's Lycidas whilst in the sixth form at school, and I don't doubt it for a moment. When he used quotations in his Times cricket reports he did so entirely from memory.

I suppose it could be argued that he was almost too blessed with intellectual gifts. By the age of 40, he was a multi-faceted broadcaster, a cricket and rugby reporter for the national press, a prominent Liberal politician, who had come second at Falmouth-Camborne in the 1959 general election, a scriptwriter, playwright, radio panellist, occasional television performer and a most impressive preacher. He could turn his hand to so many different subjects – be so many different people – dominate the conversation in so many different areas – that he never quite fixed on what his central purpose in life was and never really derived much satisfaction from his achievements, perhaps because he knew that they were only a small part of what he was capable of.

After the committal I put the urn containing his ashes in the boot of my car to await a suitable occasion for their spreading, and there they stayed, for the rest of that summer. The poor old boy travelled more miles in those four months than he had done in the previous 15 years. We had decided that the ashes should be spread at Knill's Monument, on a hill above St Ives, which was one of his favourite spots, and a visit to West Penwith in August for NFU business happily coincided with Adam camping nearby. But a communication breakdown spoiled our plans, and I ended up spreading half the ashes on my own, keeping the remainder for a later date, which turned out to be in October, with Rosie and Felicity there as well as Adam and myself (no Chippy, be it noted). I like to think that father would rather have enjoyed the familial chaos.

The last three years or so of the twentieth century was a fractious time in farming politics. The fall-out from the BSE crisis and plunging prices had created a new militancy, fomented by the likes of Richard Haddock and David Handley, who would go on to form the Farmers for Action splinter group. The fact that the Government seemed determined to act on its manifesto commitment to ban hunting further poisoned the atmosphere. The countryside may not have been in uproar, but it was seething with resentment at what seemed to be a concerted attack on its primary industry, its most cherished form of winter recreation and almost its entire way of life.

Sir David Naish felt the full force of West Country angst when he spoke at a meeting of livestock farmers in Launceston Town Hall, towards the end of May 1997. Beef exports remained banned, while the strong pound had made competing imports significantly cheaper. The fact that some of the beef was coming from countries which had had BSE cases of their own, without any accompanying restrictions, only added salt to the wound. The farmers started arriving at 6 pm for a start at 7. By the time I got there, with about 15 minutes to spare, the big Council Chamber was packed to the rafters, stern-faced Cornwall and Devon farmers standing in the aisles and spilling out into the street. Up on the platform Naish confessed to me that he was anxious and nervous. "I don't have a cheque-book and I don't have a magic wand," he said. "I can't say I'm looking forward to this at all."

In the event he did pretty well, facing down demands for militancy ("counter-productive") and declining to attack the supermarkets ("You don't go to war with your customers"). The militants had their say: "It's all the fault of the Europeans and the NFU," bellowed Hugh Whitley, Dartmoor farmer and heir to a brewing fortune, from the back of the hall. "You all deserve a bloody good kick up the backside." But, in exchanges and arguments which would be repeated at countless similar occasions over the next three years or so, the majority accepted that a Government with a 170-seat majority in the House of Commons, based squarely on urban Britain, was unlikely to respond positively to a bunch of Tory-voting property-owners taking to the streets.

There were demonstrations, like the one when Chris Smallwood's South Devon cow, Mayflower, made many a front page pictured being led through Downing Street, and there were some unofficial port blockades aimed at imported beef. I remember one in particular, at Millbay Docks in Plymouth, in which a refrigerated lorry had its doors forced open by Richard Haddock and his not so merry men. Its cargo proved to be lettuce!

Hill farmers were particularly angry and, in the autumn of 1998, Lord Donoughue, the urbane junior Agriculture Minister in the House of Lords (who famously almost didn't get the job, as Tony Blair had initially rung up a quite different Donohue) was despatched to Exmoor to placate the angry natives. It was arranged that we should meet him at Warren Farm, in the heart of the moor, farmed by Andrew Hawkins. It was at the end of a two-mile driveway. Whilst he was there, being briefed on the ruination of the hills and the need for copious amounts of dosh, a small but determined contingent of militants, led by Peter Delbridge (whose farm at Twitchen had been cut out of the waste by a Delbridge back in the late sixteenth century and had been handed down from father to son ever since), closed off the gateway with tractors and Land Rovers and announced that the Minister would be held to ransom until he agreed to their demands. It was all sorted out in the end, but it left its mark on the amiable Bernard Donoughue, who made his escape from MAFF soon afterwards.

For the NFU's South-West Regional Director, all of this meant treading a fine line between the HQ line of 'militancy will get us nowhere', and sounding angry enough to keep the rebels on side. For the most part I managed it.

Much the same applied to the hunting ban. Hunting with hounds was one of three, unofficially, taboo subjects at NFU meetings, the others being religion and party politics; the reason being, of course, that these were matters of conscience or conviction, unlikely to be susceptible to reasoned debate. I always told my chairmen to move 'next business' if anyone tried it on. But in this instance there was a way around the embargo. Hunting, it was argued, was an important weapon in the farmer's armoury of pest-control measures. Opposing a ban could therefore be justified on those grounds, without any position being taken on the rights and wrongs of hunting per se. It was just sophistry, of course, but it suited me well enough, knowing how strongly probably 80% of my NFU South-West members opposed the ban (the other 20% were mostly tenants, fed up with having their winter cereals churned up by a field of what could sometimes, in the Beaufort Hunt especially, amount to several hundred riders, at their landlords' behest).

So I dutifully attended the two Countryside Marches in London and spoke powerfully at a big anti-ban rally on the Devon County Showground at Westpoint, concluding with Kipling's oft-quoted lines about the people of England having not spoken yet. It was all in vain, of course. Tony Blair needed to chuck his left wing a toff or two to keep them happy.

For myself I have barely ever ridden a horse, let alone gone hunting, and, although I've spoken at a fair few hunt dinners, I have always felt, given my coal-mining, school-teaching, Baptist-ministering antecedents, a bit of an outsider. On the other hand I do cherish the culture and, especially, the literature of hunting. Siegfried Sassoon's 'Memoirs of a Fox-Hunting Man', Somerville and Ross's 'Adventures of an Irish RM', the Rev WS Thornton's 'Reminiscences of an Old West Country Clergyman' and, of course, Surtees' Jorrocks stories are among my very favourite books. I am also an old-fashioned liberal, in the sense of being against any unnecessary or prejudice-driven (in this case, class prejudice) restrictions on how people live their lives. So when I spoke so passionately against the ban, I meant it.

Ben Gill, a red-haired, short-fused Yorkshireman with a high opinion of his own abilities, took over from Naish as NFU President in February 1998. We did not get on. I regarded him as a show-off, who would do well to listen more and pontificate less; he regarded me as a trouble-maker, who would do well to spend more time in the office, managing my region, and rather less in television studios. There was probably more than a grain of truth in both assessments. There was, however, one thing that we could agree upon, and that was the absolute necessity of restoring public faith in the safety of British food, in the wake of a whole series of food health scares, from salmonella through to BSE. It was against that background that the Red Tractor, and the standards of 'farm assurance' which underpinned it, was born, championed by Ben Gill. It was probably his greatest achievement.

Another theme of those troubled times was 'partnership in the food chain' – the idea that farmers should work together with processors and retailers, the big supermarkets especially – as allies rather than enemies. I played my part in that by accepting an invitation to chair the 'St Merryn Meat Producer Club' committee.

From nowhere St Merryn had been built by a formidable pair of bruisers, ex-boxer from the East End Terry Johnson and a rugged, gravel-voiced Cornish meat trader called Bart Stacey, into the biggest meat processor in the western part of my region. Terry and Bart took no prisoners, but it was their biggest customer, Tesco, who really called the shots, and Tesco, ever-conscious of its public image, wanted to be seen to be doing the right thing by its embattled farming suppliers in the West Country. Hence the 'Producer Club', as an indication that we were all part of one big happy beef and lamb supplying family.

It wasn't like that in practice, of course. Steve Murrells and the other Tesco bosses listened politely enough to what my committee said about what they could do to create a genuine partnership – like paying a better price, for a start – but very little changed in practice. On the other hand I did learn a lot about the meat trade and the network of farmers and dealers which underpins it, something which would come in very useful when the Foot and Mouth crisis erupted a couple of years later.

Richard Macdonald had by now succeeded David Evans as the NFU's Director General and was intent on internal reform, which gave the activists something else to fall out about. In August 1999, after facing down our militant tendency at a bad-tempered meeting in a barn at Sparkford, I noted in my diary that 'the farmers are fighting like ferrets in a sack.' We managed to channel some of the anger and frustration constructively, through a 'Keep Britain Farming' rally at the Labour Party conference in Blackpool that autumn and a mass lobby of Parliament, which helped produce a 'Summit' at Ten Downing Street, at which Ben Gill put the case for a whole range of measures to Tony Blair, who by now did seem to be taking a genuine interest in the undoubted problems of British farming. The fact that the Prime Minister took the trouble to meet up with some of my grassroots farmers when he visited Cornwall to speak at the Eden Project that March did the cause no harm, either.

The result was a 'package of measures', announced in early 2000, which did indeed seem to address most of the worst problems. Unlike a previous effort, announced the previous autumn, which I had (much to Ben Gill's fury) condemned as 'a smoke and mirrors job', this lot did genuinely appear to be worth the £200 million which the Government's spin-doctors were claiming. There was compensation, paid by the EU but set off against the UK rebate, for the impact of the strong pound on farm prices, and a long-standing West Country demand for a lifting of the weight limit for cattle going into the Over Thirty Month Scheme was granted.

As I was happy to acknowledge in my Western Morning News column for that week:

> That the package bore the Prime Minister's personal stamp is a tribute, first, to Ben Gill, on winning the intellectual arguments, and, second, to the South-West farmers who Mr Blair met during his visit in February for illustrating the human side.
>
> Let us treat the package for what it is: overdue recognition of the quite unprecedented economic problems in agriculture, and confirmation that this government is not engaged in a cynical exercise in re-structuring farming out of existence. If that had been the agenda, Tony Blair could simply have told Ben Gill to get lost, and it would probably not have cost him a single vote.

'Regionalism', in the shape of the devolution of responsibility for economic development to the various English regions, was something else we had Mr Blair to thank for. In 1999 Regional Assemblies and Regional Development Agencies were established, that for the South-West encompassing the full six counties, from Gloucestershire to Cornwall.

The Regional Assemblies were supposed to provide democratic accountability but were largely just glorified talking shops. The RDAs, on the other hand, commanded real clout, armed as they were with multi-million pound budgets to be invested in growing the economy. It was a concept which I was eager to embrace, partly because I had always been keen on the 'South-West Region' as an entity, partly because it offered the possibility, if we played our cards right, of some serious money being invested in growing the region's food and farming sector, and partly for the selfish reason that it provided the perfect justification for expanding my empire.

It would be fair to say that my enthusiasm was not widely shared, either in the farming community or more broadly. Having been born in Devon, living in Somerset, with a daughter born in Wiltshire and a mother born in Gloucestershire, not forgetting a grandfather who had been a Baptist Minister in Falmouth, I had family connections with all of the South-West counties bar Dorset and, even there, I had always felt myself at home. I regarded myself, then as now, as a Westcountryman.

When I was growing up, in the 50s and 60s, the sense of belonging to a region as well as to a county had been much stronger, right throughout the community, thanks to the existence of the BBC's West of England Home Service. The listenership for my father and Derek Jones' 'Good Morning' stretched from Tewkesbury to Blandford Forum (especially Blandford Forum, which became one of many standing jokes) to the Isles of Scilly and all points in between. Broadcasters such as AG Street, Ralph Wightman, Johnny Morris and Frank Gillard were the voices not of counties, cities or towns but of the West Country, and the programmes were all the better for having that broad, well-funded, regional base. The advent of BBC and, later, independent local radio changed all of that, arguably not for the better. Regionalism had been usurped by parochialism. Perhaps the advent of the RDAs would revive the sense of regional identity.

So I lost no time in getting ready to take advantage of the new arrangements. My regional board took little persuading that farming and food was likely to be given a higher priority by a regional agency conscious of the sector's importance to the South-West economy, than by a central Government dominated by politicians from urban and industrial constituencies.

In 1998 we set up something called the 'South-West Agricultural Liaison Group', bringing the rural organisations like the Country Landowners Association, the Tenant Farmers Association and Taste of the West together so that we could speak with one voice to the RDA. My strategic vision (and I tended to have a lot of those!) was to create something like the Chambers of Agriculture, which seemed to wield so much power in regional France. As a title it fell foul of the RDA for having too narrow a focus, so it became instead the South-West Chamber of Rural Enterprise – CORE being the perfect acronym – and it did an effective job, under Chairmen such as Sir Harry Studholme and David Fursdon, for as long as the RDAs existed.

The Cornish were all in favour of regional devolution – as long as their region stretched no further east than the banks of the river Tamar! "The only thing that unites Devon and Cornwall is a shared hatred of Bristol," observed the Minister responsible for setting-up the regional arrangements, Richard Caborn, after one particularly fractious meeting.

In the NFU context the idea of extending the South-West region to include Wiltshire and Gloucestershire was not well received in Agriculture House, Truro. Partly, this was down to the innate conservatism of the

Cornish in the smaller things in life (which sits alongside an equally strong liberal approach to the broader issues). More practically the Cornish farmers were worried that our focus on the small, family, mainly livestock and dairy farms of the four most Westerly counties might be diluted by the advent of the barley barons of the Cotswolds and the Wiltshire Downs.

I can't say that this ever bothered me. I'd spent enough time at NFU meetings in Wiltshire and Gloucestershire back in the 70s and early 80s to know that the concerns of most farmers there were no different from those of their counterparts further west. Besides, with six counties behind any particular policy or demand rather than four, we were 50% more likely to succeed!

In the event the Cornish did effectively get their very own 'region', thanks to the EU Objective One programme. Between 2000 and 2014, under the initial programme and subsequent 'convergence', the EU pumped over £700 million into the Cornish economy, in an attempt to lift its GDP from just 68% of the EU average, as it was calculated to have been, to a more respectable level. The figure included some £120 million – £60 million from Europe, matched by £60 million from the UK Government – aimed specifically at Cornish farming and food.

Taken as a whole, the money did make a difference. You only have to consider the Eden Project or Newquay airport or the dualling of the A30 to appreciate that. But I would struggle to point to any improvement in Cornwall's agricultural fortunes which can be credited to Objective One. Maybe the expansion of the creamery at Davidstow (now under its Japanese owners), and arguably the very welcome proliferation of artisan food businesses, which have helped make Cornwall somewhere that you would want to visit because of the food, rather than despite it. But although the programme director, the late and much-lamented Bill Bawden, did his level best to see that the money was productively used, too much was wasted on projects that only lasted for as long as the EU funding did, or were 'capacity-building', in the jargon. Agencies created to guide and direct the spending of the EU's largesse often ended up using a lot of it themselves. As for Cornwall's GDP, it is now claimed to be at 83% of the EU average but only because the original calculation was apparently wrong, so the county should probably not have received the money in the first place!

And were the Cornish grateful to Brussels for all of that funding, which they would certainly never have got from the UK Government? No, they were not. In 2016 the county voted solidly (56.5%) to leave the EU!

Devon didn't much like the idea of a six-county South-West region, either, but were bought off shrewdly by whoever it was who decided to base the RDA in Exeter, which promptly started styling itself as 'the South-West's regional capital'! It had always seemed to me – given the hostility to Bristol – that the sensible place on which to centre the region was Taunton, which is as close to its geographical heart as anywhere. With that in mind, I had been encouraging Somerset NFU in its plans to sell its Headquarters in Trull Road and invest the proceeds (with a top-up from HQ) in a new office building out by junction 25 of the M5. It would, I added, make the perfect regional office if the South-West was to be extended to take in Wiltshire and Gloucestershire.

I made no secret of this ambition, and my staff, most of whom lived in or near Exeter, made no secret of their objections to it. In the event Richard Haddock struck some sort of a deal with Gloucestershire to defeat my plan when it came to the vote on the regional board. I was furious at the time and even considered resigning, although on this occasion (as doubtless on many others!) I was wrong and my team were right.

All this, and yet another reform of the Common Agricultural Policy – 'Agenda 2000', as it was known – to be debated and explained. These years were nothing if not busy, as can be gathered from an entry in my diary for November 1999:

> *An exhausting week at work. Two AGMs (Dorset on Wednesday, Cornwall on Friday) and lots of other Agenda 2000, livestock crisis, you name it meetings. On Tuesday, I wrote my Western Daily Press column, attended a Taste of the West meeting about training courses for chefs with Michael Caines, gave three television interviews (one on planning, two on the French), drove to Plymouth for an Objective One meeting at Sutton Harbour, then to Roche for a St Merryn meeting and then Two Bridges for a Dartmoor Hill Farming Committee meeting. Home to Langport by 11.*

Not every day was like that, of course, but I did work hard.

You will note the 'Home to Langport' reference. I had quit my barn conversion near Ilminster in the autumn of 1998 to move into Hill Cottage, next door to my long-term girlfriend Claire Faun's cottage looking out from the southern slope of Langport's 'Hill' across the river Parrett to Huish Level, Muchelney and the distant hills on the Dorset border.

The house was owned by the Smallwood family and was much larger than I really needed, but I had always liked Langport – ancient, a bit scruffy, a real melting pot of eccentric locals and slightly Bohemian toffs; "the second best fighting town in Somerset after Bridgwater", as I once heard it described. Two of my all-time favourite pubs – Eli's at Huish Episcopi and the Halfway House at Pitney – were just up the road. Plus, of course, there was Claire.

Hill Cottage was the largest of the three cottages overlooking the river, with Claire's Underwall in the middle and Buchan Cottage, which Claire had rented for several years back in the early 90s, on the other side. The expectation was that Buchan Cottage would be sold by the Hallett family who owned it, once the existing tenants moved out, and the plan was that I would then buy it.

This duly came to pass the following summer, when my offer was accepted within an hour of the cottage going on the market, leaving at least six other would-be buyers disappointed. Having been let out for over ten years, it wasn't in the greatest shape, but it was just the right size for me, it had a garden running down to the Long Sutton Catchwater, south-facing with glorious views over the Levels and beyond, and Claire was next door. Perfect.

I also, out of the blue, received an honorary degree, an MSc, from Plymouth University. I suspect this was the doing of Martyn Warren, one of the principal lecturers at Seale-Hayne, the much-loved agricultural college which had become part of the University and with which the NFU had close ties, not least because so many of its leading members had finished their educations there. Not long afterwards the University proposed closing the college and selling the property, moving the agricultural and land use faculty to Plymouth. We fought the proposal long and hard, but ultimately to no avail, and in 2005 Seale-Hayne closed for ever. It was a sad loss which, despite the excellence of the University of Exeter's Rural Research Centre, has never really been made good.

20

Me and my brother

My earliest memories of my brother are of bath-time together. I suppose I must have been about five and Chippy three. I didn't know quite what to make of him, except that I didn't much enjoy attention being diverted from myself! I rather suspect that, even as early as that, we had already started to fight. I also suspect that this was mainly my fault. As both my wives and my children will attest, I have always been rather too inclined to tease, or to mock, usually just for the fun of it, although with Chippy it was designed to provoke. Temperamentally we were not dissimilar. I was the more spiteful, he had the fiercer temper. All through childhood, we would fight at the slightest pretext. It drove our mother to distraction. Being bigger and heavier, I usually won, leaving Chippy tearfully complaining to his mother, who would wearily comfort him and scold me. "You big bully," she would say. "You should be ashamed of yourself." Well, I was, and I am.

Right up until his late teens, my brother was small for his years. He was a cherubic child, with dark brown curls, big brown eyes behind long lashes and apple cheeks. His father liked to describe him as "beautiful but dim". It was meant as a joke, I suppose, but it stayed with Chippy and it hurt. For he was anything but dim. I'm not sure if our IQs were ever measured but, if they had been, I'm sure that his would have been higher than mine, even if it did turn out that I was rather better at applying what brains I'd been given.

But if we were deadly rivals at home, fighting like cat and dog, we were brothers in arms when out in the world together. Being the elder brother taught me to take responsibility and Chippy was usually happy enough to go along with whatever I suggested. Whenever challenged about what we were doing or where we were going, I would take the lead. "Me and my brother ..." I would begin.

I have written already about our adventures on the railways of Devon and Cornwall. We liked to have a compartment to ourselves and had developed all sorts of techniques – farting, putting our feet up on the seats, manufactured coughing fits and so on – for making interlopers feel uncomfortable in the hope that they would move on. Coming back to Plymouth late one afternoon, we tried every trick in our book to dislodge a middle-aged lady who had entered what we regarded as 'our' space, to no avail. When we reached North Road, she turned to us and said "I am really very sorry to have been such a nuisance to you, boys, but it's a very crowded train and there was really nowhere else for me to sit." My goodness, didn't we feel small!

We went, of course, to the same schools – Sparkwell, Manadon Vale, Plymouth College, Monkton Combe – but didn't see so much of each other because of the two year gap – gulf, as it seemed – between us. Academically I had the edge, but Chippy was much the better sportsman, whether that was as a scrum half at Plymouth College or as a fearless hockey goalkeeper and slow left-arm bowler at Monkton Combe. He was in the first team at every age group, while I languished on the fringes, at best. Somehow or other, he only managed to pass two A levels, neither with a good grade and, like me, had to rely on the Oxford entrance exam and maybe a touch of the old pals act to secure his place at Queen's, to read law. In the interval between school and university he, like me, worked as a waiter at the Cottage Hotel until that is, he got on the wrong side of Mrs Holliday and was sacked!

By this time he had acquired the name by which I addressed him for the rest of his life (and beyond): the Arab. I'd first heard it used by John, the Cottage Hotel's porter, whose Devon accent was as thick as clotted cream. It was a term of affectionate disapproval, originating in Victorian London as a term for street urchins and lingering on in the South Hams. "You Arab, you," John would say to me, whenever I did or said anything that warranted comment. Chippy had something of the urchin about him at this time in his life, and there was something about the name that suited him. To the family, he was Chippy. To his friends, girlfriends and colleagues, he was Andrew. To me, he will always be The Arab.

It was between school and university that he all of a sudden filled out and shot up. When he arrived at Hope Cove, he was a slim, five foot eight inches or so. By the time he reached Oxford, he was six feet tall and 14 stone, and he certainly didn't lose any weight during the three years of enthusiastic beer-drinking that ensued. His first year and my third overlapped, and we did see a lot of each other, usually in the company of his fellow Queen's lawyers, Nigel Tranah and Geoff Wakelin, who were as disinclined to over-work themselves as was my brother. I probably should have done more to keep him on the straight and narrow, but I was too taken up with cramming for my finals, and just let him get on with it. He did as little work as he could possibly get away with, and finished with a Third – something that he never confessed to his father!

One thing which we did not have in common was our attitude to women. Chippy didn't really have even any casual girlfriends at Hope Cove or Oxford, let alone any serious ones. It wasn't that he couldn't attract girls but more that he couldn't be bothered to make the effort. He seemed to be quite content being vicariously in love with whoever my other half may have been, or the girlfriends of his mates – Geoff Wakelin's admittedly very sexy Jeannie being an obvious case in point.

Throughout our adult lives together, the twists and turns of my sometimes chaotic love-life were an open book to Chippy, his a much more private affair. His first real girlfriend was Sallie. They met at Foot and Bowden, he an articled clerk, she a legal executive. She was blonde, pretty and diminutive – think Charlene Tilton with a slight lisp – and she was as devoted to Chippy as he was to her. She was also married but seemingly in a distinctly loveless relationship.

It was a long time before I met her, but that was partly to do with the fact that their time together was precious and they wouldn't have wanted to waste any of it on family niceties. But I suspect he might also have been worried as to how I might respond to her, be that chatting her up, mocking her lisp or merely being flippant about the woman who was, unquestionably, the love of his life.

Sallie was good for Chippy. She broadened his range of interests – in music and the arts especially – and she bolstered his self-respect, without ever getting in the way of his golf, his cricket or his pub-going. He was in love, but the commitment was for the moment, not for life. It wasn't a case of my mother's long-standing affair with a married man with the genders reversed. Unlike Eric, Sallie did eventually get divorced, leaving herself free to marry Chippy and spend the rest of her life with him, happily raising the family that I am sure – despite his bachelor lifestyle – was what he really wanted.

But it wasn't to be. No sooner were they free than they split up. Chippy may have confided in Mandy as to what had happened and why, but he certainly never did to me. We neither of us shared our deeper emotions with the other. It was easier to swim in the shallows of cricket, or golf, or politics, or the latest farming crisis, or his legal cases, than to venture into the deep, dark waters of relationships. There was unspoken mutual support when either of us was going through a rough time, but it never went beyond that. Chippy was always much more inclined to share his problems with Mandy or, later, with Claire, than he was with me. And with his mother his emotional life was even more of a closed book.

As for his relationship with his father, post-school, there wasn't one. The inner resentment that had been created by being treated as a second-class son always simmered just below the surface. He, like I, enjoyed basking in the reflected acclamation of father's cricket-writing in The Times, but he never had the occasion, or the proximity, as I had, just to bump into his father at the cricket or go to stay for a few weeks between houses or jobs. For my father and Chippy to meet required a special effort, and that was beyond both of them.

With his mother, living just up the road at Plympton and later Sparkwell, he remained close. She was, I think, more motherly to Chippy than to me, perhaps, consciously or not, making up for the way he'd been treated by his father. He lived under her roof until his mid-20s, when he somehow put enough money together – he'd inherited a tendency to extravagance from his father – to buy a tiny cottage at Horrabridge, just across the river from the Leaping Salmon. Not that he was a mummy's boy, by any means. Both of them were acutely conscious of what had happened to my mother's younger brother, Uncle Robin, who sacrificed his life to that of his demanding widowed mother.

His legal career got off to a slow start, owing to his repeated and, given his obvious intelligence, almost inexplicable failures at his Part Two exams. In 1973, after he had come down from Oxford, he came up to London for six months to sleep on the sofa at 3 Cornwall Gardens and take the exam. We had a fine time together as I took him to my favourite pubs, one of which was the Carpenters Arms in Pakenham Street, where on Saturday evenings we would drink Bass and play bar billiards with half of the London Welsh rugby team.

On our return from one of these expeditions, he fell the full length of the escalator at Warren Street tube station, fortunately too drunk to sustain any serious damage, just as had been the case when falling down a steep flight of stone steps at Salcombe when he was working there as a waiter. (I was washing glasses at the Ferry Inn). Undaunted, he turned up for service next morning at the Salcombe Hotel with the skin scraped off most of one side of his face and was promptly sent back to his lodgings, so as not to put the guests off their breakfast.

When he did eventually pass Part Two, he became a good lawyer with a ruthless streak, his judgement never clouded by sentiment. He took his clients as he found them, be they angels or rogues. He soon came to specialise in personal injury claims, on the side of the defence. If a hotel owner had left a swimming pool half empty and a drunken guest had made the mistake of diving in, paralysing himself in the process, Chippy was the man to limit the liability. The insurance companies loved him. He was an early adopter of video technology, wielded by private detectives. Many was the lead-swinger, claiming thousands of pounds for whiplash or some other debilitating injury, who was caught on camera playing an athletic game of tennis or giving his children piggy-back rides.

It must have been in the early 1990s that he left Foot and Bowden and went to work for their near neighbours, Wolferstans, who were planning to open an office in Bristol and had decided that Chippy was just the man to get it off the ground. He found himself a secretary, a pleasant and efficient woman called Tricia Howard, who not long afterwards achieved unwanted notoriety as Paddy Ashdown's girlfriend, a relationship of which Chippy was blissfully unaware until the news broke.

He found himself an absurdly large and expensive flat in Clifton and graduated from a flashy but unreliable Triumph TR7 to a petrol-guzzling Rover SDI. We saw a lot of each other from then on, playing golf virtually every weekend, either at Burnham or Saunton, drinking beforehand at either the Royal Clarence in Burnham-on-Sea or the Check Inn in Barnstaple. In a period of considerable turmoil in my life, meeting up with my brother every week provided a pillar of stability that I could cling to.

Neither Foot and Bowden nor Wolferstans had any particular relationship with the NFU, so that, professionally, our paths only really crossed once, and that was on the vexed question of organo-phosphorus sheep dips and the illnesses that they were said to cause. I had first come across the issue in around 1985, when I had rung Richard Webber, a well known sheep farmer on Exmoor for a quote on how the lambing season was going for one of my Western Daily Press columns. He sounded terribly croaky, so I asked him what was wrong. "Dippers 'flu," he said. "If I go anywhere near sheep dip, it gets me like this."

Now, coming from Richard Webber, not only a hard-bitten Exmoor farmer but the originator of a highly successful sheep contracting and equipment company called Shearwell, this had to be taken seriously. It soon turned out that he was very far from being the only sufferer. It also turned out that, unhelpfully, one of the side-effects of the syndrome was an obsessive preoccupation with the symptoms and a burning sense of injustice at the inability to hold anyone to account for them.

Richard Webber didn't fall into this category but some of the other more prominent victims soon got themselves the reputation, especially with the farmers who didn't seem to suffer any ill-effects and for whom o/ps (organophosphorus dips) were the best defence against the dreaded sheep scab, of being serial whingers, not to be taken seriously. Elizabeth Sigmund, a friend and confidante of Ted Hughes, the Poet Laureate, became involved. I used to dread her phone calls, knowing that I could be in for at least half an hour's worth. Her commitment to the cause was total, and admirable, but injustices are righted by logic based on a cold hard facts, not emotion based on fellow feeling.

The controversy dragged on for years; in fact, vestiges of it linger to this day. I was convinced that the sufferers had a case. In the early 1990s we carried out a survey of NFU members which showed that an alarming proportion of sheep farmers had experienced more or less serious side effects from dipping sheep. Various attempts were made to put a group of claimants together, so that a legal action could be mounted, with the NFU's support. Wolferstans became involved, and Chippy was moved back to Plymouth to take charge of the case, or 'class action' as it was called. Between us we did everything we could to make the case stand up. The dip manufacturers were adamant that o/ps were perfectly safe when properly used, and they had plenty of science on their side.

Essentially, what we had to do was to pin the illness of one or more of our group of sufferers on sheep having been dipped, with a particular o/p product on a particular day, with all of the standard safety precautions in place. Given that most if not all of the allegedly damaging exposures had happened ten or more years previously, this proved to be impossible. So what we tried to argue instead was that the illnesses were caused by prolonged, low-level exposure, but the science behind that was uncertain. In the end there was nothing for it but to give up. We had succeeded in getting legal aid, but there was really no point in taking a case with no realistic prospect of success.

My own theory, for what it is worth, is that o/p sheep dips were the cause of serious illness in many hundreds, if not thousands of sheep farmers and their workers, but that it was not the o/p chemicals per se which were the problem, so much as impurities introduced in the manufacturing process.

This was first suggested to me by Ifor Davies, the Ministry of Agriculture's Regional Veterinary Officer, at a meeting in the late 1980s. It accounted for the apparently random occurrence of the problem, and also for some of the other more bizarre episodes for which o/p dips had been blamed, like sheep having their feet drop off after dipping.

There are historical precedents for this sort of thing, as well. With the notorious Agent Orange defoliation campaign during the Vietnam war, it was the dioxin impurities in the herbicides that caused huge amounts of human illness and suffering, not the herbicides themselves.

I doubt we will ever know, for certain. Manufacturing techniques no doubt improved as the years went by, as the dip companies sought to protect themselves against the claims. But, to my dying day, I shall continue to believe that a lot of farmers were made very ill by o/p sheep dips and have been denied justice.

But we digress. Throughout our adult lives Chippy and I remained close. With no family of his own, 'Uncle Chippy' became part of ours. We spent every Christmas together, and every Saunton holiday, as well as trips abroad to Brittany and Asturias. Mother would come too, to help Mandy out with the children while Chippy and I were off playing golf or darts. Close, to be sure, but also competitive. I was the better golfer, he was much more skilful on the pool table and there wasn't much in it at darts.

At one activity – non-competitive, it should be said – he was unquestionably my superior, and that was crosswords. If it took him longer than 15 minutes to complete the Times crossword, he would be disappointed. For several years in the 1990s he reached the finals of the Times Crossword Competition at Cheltenham, never winning but always doing well. I still do the Times crossword most days, but it takes me twice as long to finish as it would Chippy, and many is the time that I've been bamboozled by a clue and thought to myself: "The Arab would get this, no problem."

None of this should be taken as implying that he didn't have a life away from me and my family. He had many more friends than I had. He was my best friend. We shared the same enthusiasms, held much the same political opinions, and were completely at ease in each other's company. We each hated losing to the other but would be each other's most fervent supporter if we were matched against anyone else. Rivalry didn't descend into fighting, as it had so often when we were growing up, but there was still an underlying tension in the relationship.

Chippy had inherited his father's temper, especially on the golf course. I remember an incident at Wrangaton, on the edge of Dartmoor. A member inquired snootily whether we had paid our green fees, as he passed us, on his way out, as we were coming home.

"Of course we have," I replied, meaning to leave it at that.

"C***," said Chippy, under his breath, before proceeding to hack his ball into the nearest gorse bush. There was a moment's ominous pause, then he set off back down the course at full speed, waving his driver in the air like a battle-axe, to tell the "f***ing, stuck-up, stupid wanker" exactly what he thought of him.

With a few drinks inside him and things not going well, he could be an unexploded bomb, primed to go off at the slightest pretext. His lip would curl, and the yellowing eyes narrow. During one Saunton holiday he erupted midway through a fairly drunken game of Trivial Pursuit, having first insisted that every answer had to be word perfect and then being hoist by his own petard over 'automobile' as opposed to 'autocar'. "That's it," he exploded. "I've had enough of this bloody holiday and your bloody family. I'm off." Whereupon he got into his car and drove himself back to Horrabridge at high speed, three sheets to the wind. The next day he was back, as if nothing had happened.

Chippy smoked roll-ups, which he would roll himself, very skilfully, without the aid of a machine, and would often do so as he was driving along. I had moved from cigarettes at Oxford, through a period with a pipe (my father's influence) to Hamlet cigars. Make of the contrast what you will. He liked a drink, cider especially, but then so did I, and we both steered well clear of the spirit habit which became my father's downfall.

He was good for me because he always kept my feet on the ground, treating my prominence on regional television and so on with a sort of amused disdain, if he even bothered to mention it at all. Three days after the BSE crisis broke in March 1996, on a Saturday morning, we held the first meeting of our NFU South-West 'BSE Emergency Committee' at the Regional Office in Exeter. It was a tense, anxious, sometimes angry affair. Meeting over, I drove to Burnham to meet Chippy at the Royal Clarence. Three pints and a few games of darts and pool later, we were on the first tee, BSE forgotten. There were many occasions when he kept me sane.

Chippy was not blessed with the best of health. As a child he had been hospitalised twice, once with acute appendicitis and then with pneumonia. As an adult, he suffered from gout, and those yellowing eyes suggested liver trouble, which his doctor confirmed. The fact that, apart from the golf, a bit of cricket and an occasional game of tennis, he took no exercise and so carried a lot of weight, didn't help either.

Given that history, I was neither particularly surprised nor concerned when, in the summer of 2000, he started to complain of what he called "a pain in my guts". It seemed to come and go, and he dealt with it by taking ibuprofen. Had it been me, I would instantly have feared the worst and been off to the doctor for a cancer check-up. But for some reason, that never occurred to me. Claire told him he ought to see a doctor, but he took no notice and, if he had his suspicions, they were never voiced.

In September we flew out to Algarve for a holiday in Claire's cousin Timothy's apartment in Carvoeiro, as we had the previous three summers. Chippy came with us for the first week and seemed to enjoy himself, despite the stomach pains and frequent visits to the loo. I had no sense of foreboding as I dropped him off at Faro airport and watched him head for departures, golf clubs over his shoulder, his ancient wooden surfboard strapped to his tatty maroon hold-all.

But when we got back a week later, there was worrying news. On getting back to Plymouth, Chippy had virtually collapsed and been unable to go back to work. He would be going into hospital for tests. The initial results were inconclusive. It might be irritable bowel syndrome, Crohn's Disease was a distinct possibility and, the sting in the tail, there was just a chance it might be bowel cancer. He would need a scan. This was carried out on Wednesday October 18.

Claire broke the news to me when I got home that evening. It was indeed cancer. I wept brief but bitter tears. I collected him from his recently acquired house on a redeveloped naval base in Plymouth that Friday and drove him up to Langport in the expectation of playing golf at Burnham on the morrow. Naively we both imagined that surgery would sort him out. Mother rang when we got home to ask how he was. "As well as could be expected," I replied.

On the following day we did indeed drive to Burnham, stopping on the way at the Rosewood Inn, for our usual game of darts, at which – much to my concealed delight – he beat me fair and square. But golf was beyond him. We gave up after he topped his drive into the rubbish in front of the third tee and walked sadly back to the clubhouse. I wondered briefly to myself whether this would be the last golf we ever played together, but then dismissed the thought. We were both still pinning our hopes on the surgery.

This was a difficult time at work. I was in the middle of trying to negotiate complicated ESA agreements for several Dartmoor commons, my staff were unhappy and unsettled at the prospect of having to re-apply for their jobs as a result of a Gibson-inspired re-organisation of the NFU's regions, and on October 24 the Phillips report into BSE was published, which was anything but encouraging. The balance of medical opinion seemed to suggest that the worst, in terms of cases of new variant CJD in humans, was yet to come.

During the course of the day, I drove 400 miles to give a series of television interviews, all of them defensive. Much the most uncomfortable was when I found myself in the HTV studios in Bristol with Jerry Wiggin, the MP for Weston-super-Mare and a junior MAFF Minister, and Dr Churchill, from Devizes, whose son Stephen had been the first victim of vCJD. They played me a clip from an interview I'd given ten years previously in which I'd said that "British beef is completely safe" and asked me if I regretted it.

Looking back now, I suppose that was fair enough, but I was very angry about it at the time and had a furious row with the presenter, Richard Lyddon, after the recording was finished, pointing out that if I'd said anything else back in 1990 it would have been pounced upon as a clear indication that British beef was not safe, with consequent huge damage to the beef market. But, even to myself, I was forced to admit for the first time that vCJD probably was BSE in human form. 'Very depressing and guilt-inducing,' I noted in my diary.

As I was writing that, Chippy was under the surgeon's knife. Shortly after I'd finished, my mother rang with news of the operation, which was anything but good. The tumour was much larger than they'd expected and had spread to his liver. It was the worst moment of my life. After I'd put the phone down, I burst into tears, swore viciously against heaven and earth and gave myself up to utter desolation. What had my poor brother done to deserve such a cruel twist of fate? If only he'd gone to the doctor back in the summer. But then perhaps he might pull through. Cancer treatment had advanced enormously in recent years, and at least the filthy tumour was out.

Except that it wasn't, as I discovered when I spoke to Chippy the following day. The cancer in his liver had proved impossible to remove.

"Just about as bad as it could be" was his description of his condition. "Still, I'll survive," he continued, before adding, "Except I might not."

There followed a nightmare of a week. On the Wednesday evening after work I visited Chippy in the Nuffield Hospital in Plymouth. His oncologist arrived whilst I was there, a calm, matter-of-fact man, accustomed by his profession to dishing out the worst news. I sat in a chair at the end of the bed, the doctor by Chippy's side.

"Tell me as calmly as you can what you believe has happened to you," the doctor asked.

Chippy provided a word-perfect, clinically impeccable account of his personal tragedy, almost as if he was describing the misfortunes of one of his clients. "And I gather," he concluded, "that the tumour has made friends with my liver."

We both asked the doctor what the prospects were. With chemotherapy, he suggested, he might expect an 'extension' of up to nine months. An extension on what, we asked? How long would someone in this condition expect to survive without treatment? He hedged, but eventually we got it out of him: "I suppose, on average, it would be about six months."

So that was it. Fifteen months more to live, 'on average', provided that chemotherapy reduced the size of the tumour, which it might well not.

After the doctor had gone, we both tried to put a brave face on things.

"Well at least you're not going to die in the next few months," I offered.

He agreed, but I could tell by the way the colour had drained from his sweaty, mortifyingly sagging face that this was scant comfort. I suggested that he should concentrate on getting fit, so as to be able to go to the pub, play golf, maybe go away on holiday. After all, the doctor had been talking averages, and Chippy had an above-average constitution, or so we thought, and a big heart.

But the poignancy of the situation bore in on both of us. I could barely force the "Cheers, Arab" out of my mouth as I went to leave, tears already rolling down my cheeks. God knows what he must have been feeling, or how much he cried and raged after my departure.

"I'm glad you were here," he had said. And so was I.

Claire and I 'sprang' him from the Nuffield the following Saturday. It was another unspeakably foul day in an unspeakably foul autumn. 'The heavens have been weeping ever since the worst was confirmed,' I wrote.

He was very weak and drawn but determined that we should stop at a pub, as I had promised on the Wednesday. We chose the London Inn at South Brent, which turned out to be the sort of pub where your shoes stick to the carpet. Chippy managed to get down a pint of Strongbow, while I had two pints of Bass, with the rain fairly lashing down on the old A38 outside. It all seemed so horribly appropriate – the storm, the tacky pub, our feeble attempts at cheerfulness, and all in the South Hams, where we were both born.

We got him settled in Claire's cottage, she moving in with me next door. He seemed to be OK, gradually gaining strength, until the following Wednesday when his wound, which had gone septic, burst horribly, horrifyingly. Claire, using the medical training which she had been given during her time with the TA, was magnificent. If it hadn't been for her, Chippy might well have died of blood poisoning.

After that we gradually nursed him back, if not to health, then at least to the sort of state in which he might be able to cope with the chemotherapy necessary to extend his life. When I say 'we', it was actually almost entirely Claire's doing, as I was out most evenings on Dartmoor, not getting back until late, having battled through yet another rainstorm.

There were one or two lighter moments. He was visited by the last love of his life, a lovely girl called Antonia, who worked with him at Wolferstans and to whom he was hopelessly, in every sense, devoted. On the evenings when I was at home, we talked of what we might do when he was in remission. One final Cat's Whiskers, perhaps, or a holiday to somewhere exotic. He said he'd like to go to Hawaii.

He did spend a couple of days with mother, but he wasn't happy being with her. I think it hurt him too much, knowing how much his condition was hurting her. So, for the most part, he just sat in Claire's sitting room, staring out across the flooded Levels into space, alone with his thoughts.

Eventually, in early December, we decided that he was well enough to cope with the journey back to Plymouth, to move back into his own home, with treatment to follow shortly. I drove him down on Saturday lunchtime, December 9, stopping at the pub at Avonwick, just off the A38. That evening, I took him to his old haunt, the Stopford Arms, to meet up with Tony Oxley.

We had to summon the doctor when we got back, to see to his wound. He looked anything but fit enough to undergo a gruelling bout of chemo, but then, I reasoned, if he didn't have it soon, it might be too late. The next day, I took him to the Butchers Arms, next to the Royal William Yard, for a final pint, before driving back to Langport, riven with guilt and foreboding.

His friends and colleagues at Wolferstans kept an eye on him during the days that followed, but the signs were not good. When I rang him from the platform at Cheshunt station on the Thursday, after a singularly fruitless meeting with Tesco, he was rambling and barely coherent. I agreed with Wolferstans' senior partner, Paul Woods, a good friend to both of us, that the best place for him was Langport.

The following day, late on another miserable afternoon, he returned, driven by one of his junior colleagues, whom I'd not met before. I watched anxiously as he was helped down the 38 steps to our cottages. He was in a bad way, barely able to put one foot in front of another, so we put him to bed, this time in my cottage, in my bed.

Mother came the next day but he wouldn't see her. I tried to cheer him with news of Brian Lara's 182 against the Australians at Adelaide. It was the last conversation we had.

Our splendid GP, crinkly-haired Dr Michael Richards, who looked as if he would be entirely at home in an episode of Dr Finlay's Casebook, gave him morphine, and he drifted into unconsciousness. Penny, the District Nurse, was also quite superb. That night and the next, Claire and I sat with him and talked of all the good times we'd had together, just in case he might be hearing without speaking.

Penny couldn't be with him on the Monday morning, so a different nurse, Janice Williams, arrived to look after him while I set off for the Bath and West Showground for the Somerset NFU Annual meeting, Digby Jones of the CBI the main speaker, to give my Regional Director's Report. I said I'd be back at lunchtime.

As I drove away from the showground at around 1 o'clock, down the A359 towards the crossroads where I turn right towards the A37 Fosse Way, I was suddenly gripped by a chill as cold as death. I didn't imagine this. It happened. That, I am sure, was the moment Chippy died.

When I got back to the cottage, the nurse was in tears. He'd died maybe half an hour earlier, unconscious but with her by his side. I was too late. I went upstairs. He looked almost skeletal in death. All of the flesh had shrunk from his features, leaving hollow cheeks and a strangely hooked nose, like the beak of a hawk. I thought how much he resembled his father,

I hated myself for not having been there when he died. What did another bloody NFU meeting matter when your brother, your best friend, your soulmate, is at death's door? But then I thought, that's probably how he would have wanted it, to die alone, not inflicting the agony of that moment on his brother, or his mother come to that.

Dr Richards arrived to certify the death, the undertakers were there within an hour or so, to carry his pitifully wasted carcase up the steps in a bodybag. I rang whoever needed to be rung, starting with mother, then Claire, then Mandy, then Paul Woods, then Richard Mac. I wasn't eating, on account of a colonoscopy due the following day, Chippy's fate and a familial tendency to cancer having set my own alarm bells ringing. But I could drink white wine and did.

Mother was driven over by Mandy in the evening for the mutual comfort and support that only families can provide at times like these.

Chippy was cremated in Taunton on the Friday after Christmas, and we held a memorial service at Sparkwell Parish Church a week later. Chippy's Wolferstans colleague and great friend, Mike Horwood, paid moving tribute. We got drunk in Chippy's honour in the village hall afterwards. His ashes weren't spread until the autumn, on the sand-hill next to the 16th tee on Saunton West, with its views to the sea and Hartland Point to the west, and over both courses to the east, after a 'Chippy Memorial Cat's Whiskers' attended by all the old faithfuls.

And the colonoscopy? The consultant surgeon, Richard Welbourne, found and removed two polyps, both with the potential to turn cancerous. But for Chippy's illness, they might not have been found until it was too late. His final gift to me in life was life itself.

21

Foot and Mouth

For all that 2000 had been a nightmare of a year, I was doing my best to be optimistic when I came to write the NFU South-West business plan for the year ahead. In the introduction I wrote as follows:

2000 was the year in which the fortunes of farming touched rock bottom. But it was also the year in which the first green shoots of recovery began to show, and in which important progress was made in developing policies, measures and structures to achieve an industry which is inherently competitive and which does not depend for its prosperity on external economic or political factors to anything like the extent it has in the past.

We even had a strategy for achieving that, called 'New Directions for South-West Farmers', built around the concept of 'making the cake bigger' by tapping sources of additional income such as the market for top quality regional food and from environmental payments.

"We should aim to make the South-West the Fortnum and Mason of British farming and food," I would exhort in my speeches. The farmers looked unconvinced.

Indeed, even in my own mind, there was an element of whistling in the dark to keep my spirits up about all of this optimism. Chippy's death hit me hard. It left me feeling stunned, almost in a state of shock. Life went on, but it felt as if I was just going through the motions. It didn't help that I had decided to give up my ten Hamlet cigars a day smoking habit. There was no evidence at all that smoking had contributed to Chippy's cancer, but it just seemed sensible to reduce the risk of my suffering the same fate. I used nicotine patches for a time and somehow managed to resist the temptation to resume a habit which I had always enjoyed – as a reward, rather than a crutch – even when crisis struck.

The first I knew that Foot and Mouth Disease had returned to Britain after an interval of nearly 19 years was when my phone started ringing early on the morning of Wednesday February 21. The BBC was reporting that a case had been identified in pigs at an abattoir in Essex. Would I care to comment? I expressed an appropriate degree of concern without, it must be said, being overly worried. I thought back to the outbreak on the Isle of Wight in 1981, when I'd been summoned from my Sunday lunch to write a feature for the Western Daily Press, nearly getting myself breathalysed in the process. That had proved to be a nine-day wonder. I suspected this might be the same.

The media, however, were soon on the case. By the time the Wiltshire County Committee meeting at Lackham College finished that afternoon, BBC Points West had asked me to give a live interview on that evening's programme, and both the Western Daily Press and the Western Morning News were after feature articles, which I wrote that evening.

As more news came through, I started to feel less sanguine. It soon became clear that the infected pigs hadn't brought the disease with them from their home farms, which would have made tracing relatively straightforward. They had caught it at the abattoir, which had presumably been infected by a previous batch of pigs. But which batch of pigs and when? The number of lorries that must have arrived at the abattoir whilst it was infected could have run into the hundreds. Did they, or their drivers, pick it up? And if so, how many other farms might they have visited subsequently, taking the disease with them?

The Government moved quickly. Exports of meat and livestock were banned almost immediately, and by Friday that week livestock movements had been halted and markets closed. Then, that evening, the news came through that the source of the outbreak had been traced – to a pig farm at Heddon-on-the-Wall in Northumberland, about as far away from the South-West as you could get. The mood that evening at the Tiverton and Cullompton NFU Dinner was one of profound relief. The outbreak would serve to remind politicians and public of the need to be on our guard against dodgy food imports, without crippling the West Country's livestock industry. Thank goodness for that!

The next morning I drove to a deserted Taunton Market to give more interviews – slightly less doom-laden this time – on what the impact of the outbreak might be. That accomplished, I went on to Bridgwater, to join a gathering of retired NFU group secretaries at Bridgwater and Albion Rugby Club, convened by John Garland, a rugby man to his boot-straps. It was a convivial occasion, the Devonians recalling how, in the 1967 outbreak, they'd been instructed by their boss, the mighty Hugh Crowle, to set up disinfectant road-blocks on the A38 where it crossed the border from Somerset, even though the disease never got any nearer than Shropshire!

Claire was away on TA duty in Canada so that evening, I walked up to Eli's for a couple of pints, cooked my supper and settled down to watch the television. It had been a wearing week, but we seemed to be through the worst of it. Then my mobile phone rang. It was Ben Bennett, the MAFF Divisional Veterinary Officer (DVO) for Devon. I guessed immediately what was coming. His exact words were: "I'm afraid we've got Foot and Mouth in Devon, Anthony, and it's as bad as it can get."

He went on to explain that one of his veterinary officers had been called out that afternoon to a farm at Highampton, near Hatherleigh in the wilds of West Devon, where cattle were showing suspicious symptoms. The disease had been confirmed. The farm was the premises of a well-known farmer and livestock dealer called Willie Cleave, who wasn't an NFU member but whom I knew vaguely by reputation.

"He's got probably eleven holdings of his own, with connections to maybe twenty or thirty others," said Ben. "We'll be checking them all out as fast as we can. There'll be a statement in the morning."

I sensed immediately that we had a major crisis on our hands. It wasn't just the prospect of slaughtered livestock, devastated farmers, plumes of smoke from burning pyres and potentially enormous economic damage and disruption, it was the inevitability that we, the South-West NFU, would be at the epicentre of the crisis and that our reputation could stand or fall on how we handled it. As I knew all too well, there were people in the organisation who would seek to use the spotlight of public and media attention to pursue their own personal or political agendas, given half a chance. We needed to show balance, realism, resolve and recognition of the interests of the many other countryside and rural interests that could be damaged by the outbreak.

After ringing everyone in the NFU who needed to know, as per our contingency plan, the last thing I did that evening before going to bed was to leave answerphone messages with the BBC and ITV newsdesks, to report the outbreak, make myself available for interview from six the next morning and to say that, until further notice, no-one other than myself was authorised to speak on behalf of the NFU in the South-West.

There was a sharp frost overnight and, as expected, the phone rang just after six and kept on ringing for most of the morning. After cooking a roast lunch for my sister Felicity and her friend, I headed off to Exeter for the first of many press conferences in the MAFF offices at Winslade Park, south of Exeter.

Ben Bennett went through what I already knew and explained about the various forms: A for a suspected outbreak, C for a confirmed outbreak and consequent slaughter, D to impose a standstill on farms thought to be at risk. An 'infected area', covering some 400 square miles of West Devon had been declared and all of the livestock on Willie Cleave's Devon holdings would be slaughtered, once valuations had been agreed, a total of some 1,100 sheep and 600 cattle. It was clearer than ever that we had a major outbreak on our hands.

Over the week that followed, that became ever more obvious, with outbreaks being reported in Cornwall, Wiltshire and, most significantly as it turned out, Gloucestershire. And, although our elected county office-holders would need to be kept informed and involved, I was determined that our response should be run from a single point of control and command, with me and my senior staff very much in the driving seat.

Mike Ellingham, our vastly experienced Regional Technical Adviser, who was brilliant with detail, would look after the technicalities of the various restrictions and keep in touch with local authorities in respect of footpath closures, which were swiftly put in place. Ian Johnson, our Regional PR officer, had the formidable task of dealing with a deluge of media inquiries for contacts, information and comment.

For the rest it was fortunate that my policy team had already been assigned to particular counties, following the latest NFU re-organisation: Robert Deane was looking after Dorset and Somerset, John Newell had Wiltshire and Gloucestershire, Peter Morris Devon and Paul Cooper, our irrepressible poultry specialist, Cornwall. Each would have the task of keeping in touch with the MAFF vets, NFU office-holders and group secretaries in their respective patches, reporting back to a team meeting every day.

Robert also took on the key responsibility of writing and issuing our 'FMD Bulletins', to keep the membership up to date with developments. Based very much on the daily bulletins we had introduced during the BSE crisis, these were faxed and, increasingly, e-mailed at least every day to a distribution list which started in the hundreds and finished in the thousands. June Harry, with 45 years of NFU service to her name, did a superb job in organising the distribution. One of very few silver linings to the FMD crisis was that it prompted the widespread adoption of computers and e-mail by the West Country farming community.

As for me, as well as co-ordinating our response and being the main contact with NFU HQ, senior MAFF staff, the RDA and, as time went on, MPS and Ministers, I soon became the front man – "that Foot and Mouth bloke off the telly", as people would say if they recognised me in the street. This happened partly by accident, but mainly by design.

There were farmers whom I trusted to act as spokesmen – the Devon NFU Chairman, David Hill, foremost amongst them. But given the intensity of the media interest, we couldn't afford to get the message wrong, and I did at least lack nothing in experience when it came to giving radio and television interviews, and I could also, of course, speak for the entire region. I also knew that at times of crisis people like to see a familiar, trusted face, someone who was telling it like it was, with a minimum of political or organisational spin.

As the West Country's 'face of Foot and Mouth Disease', I did, however, endure something of a baptism of fire. On the day after that initial press conference, I found myself being grilled – and that was the word – by Kirsty Wark on BBC 2's Newsnight.

Kirsty was not in sympathetic mode. Her angle of attack was that the FMD outbreak was symptomatic of an industry which habitually cut corners, was notorious for bad practice and treated farm animals – sheep especially – as if they were nothing more than sacks of coal. For it had by now become clear that it was sheep, being moved in their thousands from Hexham and Carlisle markets near the source of the outbreak in Northumberland, from market to market, dealer to dealer, farm to farm, as farmers geared up to claim their sheep subsidy, that were the main vectors of disease. I countered by insisting that farmers were not routinely careless of animal welfare and that, however numerous they might be, sheep movements would not have been a problem if the disease hadn't been allowed to reach Heddon-on-the Wall in imported meat products in the first place.

"If you import food from around the world, as we do, you must expect to import disease from around the world as well," I argued.

I kept my end up reasonably well, but the encounter did teach me an important lesson. The outbreak of FMD had lifted the lid on the realities of livestock trading, and what it revealed was not a pretty sight. Kirsty Wark was far from being alone in her unhappiness at the way in which sheep were being shunted around the country. That was the message from the general public, as well. Their support for the farming community in its hour of need was magnificent, but it was not unconditional. Better practice and higher welfare were their not unreasonable expectations, and that was something we needed to acknowledge.

Over that first week of the crisis the pattern of my FMD daily life gradually fell into place. It went something like this: 6.15 get up, check my phone, have breakfast and drive to Exeter to be there by 8 am. At 8.05 I would go into our little radio studio to be interviewed down the line by Vic Morgan for the BBC's Good Morning Devon programme, a fixture that endured every weekday for the next three months. After that there would maybe be a couple more interviews, the post to be seen to, a staff meeting to report on the latest situation in our various areas of responsibilities, compare notes, discuss the contents of that day's bulletin and plan for the day ahead. Then there might be a meeting at the RDA or Devon County Council, which was always a bit of a relief from the never-ending telephone calls if I was in the office.

Those telephone calls were the most stressful and emotionally draining aspect of the entire business. The calls were often from farmers or their wives in a state of despair, desperate for news of a suspected outbreak nearby, or pleading for something to be done about animals which they couldn't feed because of Form D restrictions, or, worse still, with their yards piled high with the carcases of slaughtered cattle and sheep, with no idea of when they might be removed or incinerated. We would offer what comfort we could and contact either or both the relevant DVO, the MAFF Regional Director, Mike Highman, or, if it was really serious, we would pass it up the line to the team co-ordinating the NFU's response at Head Office, who did a terrific job.

At lunchtime I would head into Exeter for a live interview at 1.10 for the ITV regional news, followed by a quick dash to BBC Radio Devon, where I would give a down-the-line TV interview for the BBC lunchtime programme. Every afternoon there was the MAFF press conference where I would both get the latest news on outbreaks and the measures being taken to control the disease, ask the questions that needed to be asked and provide comment and interpretation for the assembled journos. Then back to the office for more phone calls, help write that day's Bulletin and brief Ian.

Then, at 5.45, it was back into Exeter for the ITV evening news just after six and on to Radio Devon again, to be interviewed live down the line by Justin Leigh or Teresa Driscoll for BBC Spotlight. On Mondays I would drive to Bristol to appear live on Points West, doing my stuff for Spotlight on the unmanned camera in the newsroom. Mondays apart, when I would drive straight home, my final port of call was back at the office, to chat to whichever staff were still there and maybe write one of my newspaper columns.

"'Kin'ell, Arab," I would say out loud, as I climbed wearily into the car after one of these days for the drive home to Langport, "Kin'ell". It was one of Chippy's favourite expletives when the going was tough, and through all of this mayhem, day after day, week after week, I could feel him by my side, keeping me going but also giving me a sense of perspective. This was a farming crisis, nothing more. It would pass. Compared to losing your brother to cancer, it was just a bump in the road.

The number of outbreaks grew slowly as the crisis unfolded. West and North Devon and the Forest of Dean were the main foci of infection, although we did experience a handful of outbreaks in Cornwall, Wiltshire and, a bit later, Somerset. But it soon became clear that the process of confirming disease, slaughtering and burning the livestock and disinfecting the farms was going anything but smoothly.

MAFF's contingency plans were mostly based on experience in the 1967 outbreak, when farms were both much smaller and more self-contained. No-one had any experience of assembling the hundreds of tons of straw, coal and railway sleepers necessary to create a pyre capable of incinerating, in the case of Willie Cleave's home farm, 200 cattle and 800 sheep. To allocate this massive logistical challenge to MAFF vets with absolutely no experience of anything even remotely similar made no sense at all. Ben Bennett and his team did their best and were understandably reluctant to admit that they couldn't cope, as calls for the army to be brought in grew louder.

The suspicion was that the Blair government was reluctant to involve the army, and so by implication concede the scale of the crisis, because it might mean the General Election scheduled for May 3 having to be postponed. I'm not sure that was necessarily true. A more plausible explanation for what did indeed seem to be anything but a decisive response to a rapidly worsening crisis – bearing in mind that the situation in Cumbria was even worse than in Devon – is that MAFF fatally under-estimated the extent to which the disease had spread in the period of up to three weeks prior to the discovery of the first outbreak when it was in the sheep population without anyone realising it, because, rather as with Covid 19 and teenagers, sheep will very often carry FMD without showing any symptoms. It was only when they came into contact with cattle that the disease's presence was revealed.

At any rate, within less than fortnight, it was clear that, despite the protestations of the Minister of Agriculture, Nick Brown, at one level, and Ben Bennett at another, MAFF were fighting a losing battle; at every afternoon press conference the bags under Ben's eyes grew bigger and his demeanour more haggard. At that on March 18th I rather cruelly asked him if the disease in Devon was out of control. His weary reply was that "it is not out of control, but it is difficult to say yes or no to that. I wouldn't say it is fully controlled either."

That was enough for me. In a distinctly self-satisfied performance in the House of Commons, Nick Brown had insisted that all was well. Infuriated by his complacency, I accused him, on live television, of being "in denial" and of putting politics before people. The next evening, as I was driving up to Bristol for my Points West appearance, I took a call on my car-phone from Ben Gill. He had evidently not been impressed by my attack on the Government. He started haranguing me as I passed Cullompton and, by the time I reached Weston-super-Mare, he was still at it.

His complaint was that I was jeopardising various measures which the NFU was attempting to extract from Government; my response was that I was only reflecting the overwhelming opinion of my anxious, angry, embattled membership. There was no meeting of minds. It was only the first of several similar confrontations.

However, my anger and frustration, amplified deafeningly through the pages and editorials of the Western Morning News, whose Farming Editor, the late and much-missed Carol Trewin, and Editor, Barrie Williams, could not have been more helpful and supportive, was starting to produce some results.

A day or two later the army arrived, even if Major Belinda Forsythe and her contingent of trainee military police were anything but what the doctor ordered. Rumour had it that, as they arrived at disease control HQ at Clyst Hydon, they were booed by the veterinary staff. Whether that is true or not, they certainly did very little to improve the situation. Their role was to 'oversee' the logistical operation of slaughter, incineration and disinfection. They weren't required to get their hands dirty themselves, merely to sit in judgement on what MAFF's exhausted vets were up to. Worse still, their presence served to complicate rather than simplify the case-handling process.

Just as great a weakness as the logistics of the exercise was MAFF's communications which, apart from the daily press conferences, were non-existent. They made no attempt at all to tell the farmers on the front line what was going on or what might happen next, something which made our role in the NFU even more important and valued.

In an attempt to remedy this cardinal weakness, MAFF decided to send one of their supposedly brightest stars down to the rebellious West Country, to take over control of the response to the outbreak from the unfortunate Ben Bennett and quell the revolting natives. This was Andy Lebrecht, a career civil servant with a supercilious air who enjoyed the good things in life and reportedly didn't stint himself when it came to wining and dining in his boutique hotel in Exeter. He reminded me instantly of Simon Cadell's portrayal of the hapless 'man from Whitehall', Dundridge, in the television adaption of Tom Sharpe's novel 'Blott on the Landscape', and did about as much good.

His successor, the appropriately named Tim Render wasn't much of an improvement. In early April, when I stopped for diesel on my way back to the office after lunchtime television duties, I spotted a headline in that day's Daily Mirror: 'Phoenix, the calf that came back from the dead,' it read, over a photograph of a doe-eyed, pure white calf. I quickly deduced that the calf was a survivor from the Membury disaster, in which cattle and sheep from no fewer than 15 holdings had gone up in smoke. 'Phoenix', as it had inevitably been dubbed had somehow survived. I rang Tim Render to warn him of what was afoot.

"If you lot insist that that calf has to be slaughtered you'll be crucified," I told him.

He seemed unconcerned. "Oh well, we'll just have to leave it up to the vets," was his reply. "Rules are rules."

Entirely predictably the vets insisted that an exception could not be made for a single calf, no matter how beguiling it might appear or iconic it might have become. And the media balloon duly went up. It wasn't until Alastair Campbell became involved that a reprieve was granted. I would love to have known what he'd said when news of this entirely gratuitous cock-up reached him.

Meanwhile, the politicians were arriving in Exeter, thick and fast. On March 23 Tory party leader William Hague turned up for a series of meetings with farmers, tourism people, economists and local politicians. He was earnest, but less than inspiring. 'Sleep in his eyes, deeply unimpressive,' I recorded in a rare diary entry.

That Friday evening I think I felt more tired than at any other point in the saga. I woke the next morning with an epiglottis so swollen that I could hardly speak. By lunchtime it had begun to wear off, which is just as well, because the Prime Minister, having apparently taken personal control of managing the crisis, was in town. I met him, with one or two others, in an office at MAFF HQ in Exeter.

Alastair Campbell was with him and straight away got on the right side of me by claiming to remember me from when I had been the NFU's South-West Regional Information Officer and he was a cub reporter on the Tavistock Times. "I knew I could always rely on you for a good quote" (or words to that effect), he said. Blair looked almost as tired as Hague had done the previous day. But his commitment to getting the mess sorted out did come across, even if his motives weren't necessarily all that altruistic.

"What can we do to help?" he asked. I said that the main thing was to provide a military dimension which could actually make a difference by getting stuck into the grim work on-farm. And acting quickly was vital to minimising the risk of spread from an outbreak. The standard procedure was for the MAFF vet on the ground to ring a specialist at HQ in London, describe the symptoms and seek confirmation. But with cases multiplying across the country, there were reports of this process having taken over 12 hours.

"Why can't you trust the vet on the farm to make the diagnosis?" I asked.

Blair turned to Alastair Campbell. "Can we do that?" he asked. The great man nodded his approval. "OK then, we'll do that, and I'll see what we can do about the army as well."

There was a scrum of reporters, photographers and cameramen to be fought through as we emerged from what was no more than a half hour meeting. 'More satellite dishes in that car park than at Jodrell Bank,' I noted. I then gave probably half a dozen interviews, saying that the Prime Minister had listened to what we'd had to say and seemed genuinely concerned etc before heading gratefully back to Eli's and then home.

About a fortnight later I had just got back into the office after the MAFF press conference when my secretary called across to say she'd got a phone call for me.

"It's the Prime Minister," she said. And so it was. From platform 4 on Colchester station, waiting to catch the 16.19 to London (I could hear the station announcer in the background).

"Hello, Anthony. It's Tony Blair here. I just wanted to follow up on our meeting, to make sure that what we agreed about confirmation of diagnosis had actually been actioned."

I was able to reassure him that it had and, after a few more friendly exchanges, he was off. It struck me that, whilst this said a lot about Tony Blair's personal commitment to the cause, it said almost as much about his confidence, or lack of it, in the ability of his officials to deliver.

Tony Blair had promised that he would send Nick Brown to see us, and on the Monday the Minister of Agriculture Fisheries and Food duly appeared. He was met by a slightly random group of farmers, most of whom seemed to be from Dartmoor, where an unexplained case at Dunnabridge, miles away from any other outbreaks, had led to the slaughter of hundreds of sheep and cattle – including Anton Coaker's beloved Galloways, whose bloodlines stretched back more than a century – as 'dangerous contacts', which they almost certainly weren't.

Much of the discussion concerned stopping the disease in its tracks. In Cumbria the so-called 3 kilometre rule was being introduced, which meant that any sheep, cattle or pigs within 3 km of a confirmed outbreak would have to be slaughtered. We managed to avoid that being imposed in Devon, but the 'contiguous cull' that we got instead was almost as bad. This was introduced the following weekend, after a bewildering series of changes of policy. "Black Friday" was how I (unoriginally) characterised what was indeed a dark and chaotic day on that evening's television.

By this stage, four weeks in, it had begun to dawn on me the extent to which my broadcast appearances were being relied upon, not just in the farming community but through the wider rural population of Devon and Cornwall, for information, comfort and support. Messages of appreciation, many from people I'd never heard of, were arriving by phone and e-mail.

Some kind soul left a bottle of brandy outside the door to the Regional Office with a note which read, 'With grateful thanks – you look as though you might need this.' Then my mother rang from her home near Hemyock to say that prayers were being said for me in church on Sunday mornings. As the days went by, I found myself nominated for a medal, President of the NFU, Minister of Agriculture, Prime Minister and even (tongue in cheek by the BBC in Plymouth) canonisation! The Western Morning News devoted an entire editorial (which I couldn't bring myself actually to read for months afterwards) to me under the heading 'Hero at front line of Foot and Mouth'.

This would all have been very gratifying, were it not also distinctly alarming. If thousands of people are hanging on your every word, you have to make very sure that the words are the right ones. 'Must avoid personality cult,' I wrote in my diary. 'Beware complacency. Long way to go. You know what comes after pride ...'

Quite apart from the daunting sense of responsibility which all of this entailed, it also raised the fear that the media might get bored with me from over-exposure and would move on to spokesmen more likely to offer something controversial or extreme. So I took to thinking up a single headline phrase for each evening's television interviews: "staring into the abyss", nightmare scenario", "like Sisyphus pushing his boulder up the mountain", "the end of the beginning, not the beginning of the end" as well as that "Black Friday", which I'm told produced a ragged cheer around the BBC newsroom in Plymouth.

Rule one that I set for myself in these broadcasts was to be factual and honest. What people crave most of all at times of crisis is accurate information, even if the news is bad. Nothing is worse than uncertainty. And I was better placed than anyone to provide accurate information, not just from my contacts with the MAFF vets or NFU staff at HQ (who were now firmly embedded in the daily 'birdtables' at which all of the key agencies exchanged information), but from the farmers out there in the thick of it who were ringing in to give us whatever news there might be. I knew, for example, about the two disastrous outlying outbreaks, at Dunnabridge on Dartmoor and Membury in East Devon, before they'd even been confirmed, because I spoke to the farmers concerned myself.

Unlike MAFF spokesmen I was not constrained by politics or higher authority. I could tell it like it was, without fear or favour, even if that did get me banned twice from speaking to the national media, at the insistence of Ben Gill! There was no special pleading, and I always tried to remember that there were a lot of other rural interests at stake besides farming. So I would speak out against gratuitous and unnecessary closures of countryside activities which carried no recognisable risk of spreading the disease, like Exeter race meetings, for example.

Only once in this context was I left dumbfounded and that was when I was being interviewed by the distractingly attractive Susan Osman on BBC Points West on the Monday before the Easter weekend. I'd said something about how we were hoping that the holiday would give rural tourism a much-needed boost. Whereupon she ran a report from Clinton Rogers about a farmer who had deliberately put his cattle out on the slopes of Glastonbury Tor so as to prevent people from being able to walk there over the Easter weekend.

"No doubt he's got his reasons, but I think that's very sad," was all I could say in response.

"Be reasonable. Be balanced. Be honest. Be up-beat where you can, matter-of-fact where you can't, and don't cock it up," I would say to myself before these broadcasts and other public appearances. By and large (and there were some slip-ups) I think I managed that.

It amused Claire no end to hear me being described as "the voice of common sense", when there are indeed times when that is not my most obvious quality. But it was a label I was more than happy with. As recently as 2017 I stopped off for pint at a small brewery in what was once Wallace Day's milking parlour, just off the Tarka Trail in North Devon. There was just one other customer, besides the brewer.

"Don't I know you?" he said, looking me up and down. Then it dawned on him. "Corse I do. You'm the voice of reason!" Well, sometimes maybe.

Early April did indeed mark the end of the beginning of the crisis. But the two biggest tests of my resolve to be straightforward, rational and, as far as possible, unemotional – the contiguous cull and the debate over vaccination – were just beginning to rear their ugly heads. In the early stages of the outbreak the situation was tragic for those unfortunate enough to have their herds and flocks infected, but it was also straightforward: the animals were diseased so, according to the UK's 'stamping out' strategy for FMD, they had to be slaughtered.

But as the number of red pins – marking confirmed outbreaks – began to spread across the map of Devon, it was becoming clear that something more than a reactive slaughter policy was required to stop the disease in its tracks, especially as there was no sign of the sunnier weather which might dampen down the infection. The incessant rain of March and April only deepened the prevailing gloom, as well as making life still more difficult for the thousands of farmers under Form D movement restrictions.

In Cumbria the proactive disease-control policy took the form of the brutal 3 km slaughter zone. In Devon we got the contiguous cull. This was devised by a team of statistical modellers at Imperial College London, featuring a certain Neil Ferguson, whose doom-laden forecasts produced the Coronavirus lockdown, and Dr Cristl Donnelly, who has had a lot to do with bovine TB policy down the years.

This team, having as far as we could gather, no knowledge or experience of the nature and structure of farms in North and West Devon, had fed a lot of unrefined data into their computers and come up with the conclusion that the way to stop FMD was to slaughter pre-emptively livestock on farms which bordered a confirmed case. It made no difference if the border was a 100-yard stretch of double hedgerow a mile from the buildings in which the infected animals had been housed, against a field which had seen no sheep or cattle all winter. It was technically contiguous, so that farm's animals had to go.

When Cristl and co came to Exter in April to justify their approach, in vain did we try to point out that this made no sense. Farms in that part of Devon were not neatly ring-fenced, geometrically arranged entities. They often consisted of a base holding, around the farmhouse, onto which all sorts of bits and pieces of land had been tacked over the years. If each of the farms had been surveyed and areas at risk of contact with neighbouring infection and any stock which might have been vulnerable pin-pointed, then the policy might have made sense. But none of that was done. A shared boundary with an outbreak farm meant a death warrant. End of.

This approach was not only stupid, it was cruel: to farmers as well as their livestock. Very many of the best sort of farmers in the high-risk areas did everything in their power to prevent their livestock becoming infected, up to and including sending their families off to live with friends and relatives while they barricaded themselves in on the farm.

There were other farmers, I'm sorry to say, who were much less careful. Compensation payments for slaughtered livestock were generous – over-generous many would say. Those for whom animals were no more than a tradeable commodity – money on four legs – very often made no attempt whatsoever to prevent their stock becoming infected. In some cases, very much the reverse. One farmer in South-East Dartmoor was sent to prison for repeated attempts to try to mimic the symptoms of FMD by adding gorse and gravel to feed for his sheep.

On another occasion I was rung by one of the best farmers on northern Dartmoor to be warned that a well-known local cattle dealer had 900 bullocks in his sheds, adding that he would be very surprised if the disease didn't strike. Within days it had done, the gentleman in question no doubt happily pocketing a cheque for several hundred thousand pounds shortly afterwards.

Now, if the only loser from this sort of opportunism was the taxpayer – and the 'Welfare Slaughter Scheme' was arguably an even greater fraud on the public purse – then maybe it could be dismissed with a shrug as the sort of price one has to pay in dealing with crises where urgency must necessarily trump bureaucratic niceties. But with the contiguous cull one greedy farmer's gain might be the loss not just of one conscientious, livestock-shielding, neighbouring family farmer but often of two, three or even more.

I am not claiming that the seeking-out of infection happened on any significant scale, despite the persistent rumours of 'infected lambs' tails being available on the internet' and suchlike. I never saw any hard evidence of that, but there certainly were instances where infection was invited rather than resisted, and when that did happen, it hurt.

Four times as many farms in Devon had their livestock slaughtered in the name of the contiguous cull as had confirmed disease. Only on 20% of those 700 'contiguous' farms was disease subsequently confirmed, and they would probably have been picked up in any case by the existing 'dangerous contact' policy, which was based on common sense. NFU HQ told us to accept the contiguous cull as the necessary price of bringing the outbreak under control.

We, and that included our elected office-holders as well as senior staff, would have none of it. "Computerised carnage" was how Ian Johnson described it, a phrase I was only too ready to repeat on sundry television appearances. More to the point, we vowed to support any NFU member who was threatened by the contiguous cull and wanted to resist it. My doughty regional Legal Adviser, Alayne Addy, helped dozens of farmers keep the slaughtermen at bay for the necessary 21 days (the time it would take for any latent infection to show itself). MAFF insisted that we were risking the spread of the disease and would live to regret it.

So let it be said that in only one of the 150 cases where farmers succeeded in resisting the contiguous cull did disease subsequently develop and that took no other herds or flocks down with it because all the neighbouring herds had already been slaughtered. As an editorial in the Veterinary Record put it, the contiguous cull was 'the most bloody, tragic and disgraceful misjudgement ever committed in the name of science.'

Which brings us on to vaccination, which was, in essence, an alternative to the contiguous cull. Rather than slaughter stock at risk from a nearby outbreak, cattle at least could be vaccinated (sheep and pigs would probably still need to be slaughtered), thereby creating a clear ring to prevent disease spreading any further. The vaccines were available, and a full-scale training exercise went ahead, preparing vaccination teams to put the policy into effect.

The Dutch had used vaccination to control their outbreak, but the vaccinated animals had subsequently been slaughtered. That was not required under international animal welfare protocols but, if vaccinated animals were allowed to live, it meant that exports from that county, region or even country would be banned for a year, so there would be a commercial price to pay. Which is essentially why the NFU at national level was adamantly opposed to vaccination. "We have to kill, kill, and keep on killing until we have stamped out this terrible disease," declared Ben Gill on national television.

I was appalled. After an initial reluctant acceptance of the medieval spectacle of hundreds of dead animals burning on giant bonfires with their feet in the air, shrouding the countryside in smoke and the stench of death, the public had become sickened by slaughter. Enough was enough.

At a more practical level the sheer number of animals which were now having to be slaughtered was overwhelming MAFF and the army's capability for disposing of the carcasses. Dead animals were left piled up in farmyards sometimes for weeks on end. A huge burial site was constructed at Ashmoor at vast expense although, by the time it was available to be used, rendering capacity had been ramped up sufficiently to cope. And whilst a policy of 'vaccination to live' might not suit the livestock industry's financial interests, it could make all the difference to tourism, which was a far bigger contributor to the West Country's economy, especially as winter turned eventually to spring. If at-risk livestock were vaccinated, footpaths could be safely re-opened, Dartmoor, Exmoor and Bodmin Moor made accessible again and the entire countryside of the South-West declared open to visitors.

It was an argument that I championed enthusiastically, earning myself another ban from the national media, courtesy of Ben Gill. But the anti-vaccinators prevailed. After dithering for weeks, Tony Blair eventually came down against vaccination and against, I suspect, his better instincts. "Killer Giller", as I called him privately, may have won the battle, but in the process he had succeeded in sacrificing much of the public support for farming which had marked the early stages of the crisis. In a straight fight between money and animal welfare, money had been put first. The countryside remained largely closed until August. Thousands more cattle and sheep were slaughtered, at vast cost, completely unnecessarily.

That autumn, at a get-together of Duchy of Cornwall tenants at the Two Bridges Hotel on Dartmoor, I was hailed by the Prince of Wales, whom I'd met more than a few times previously.

"You're that chap from the NFU, aren't you?" was his opening shot. "The one who talked so much sense about vaccination and so on," he added. "Unlike that President of yours, Gill. Dreadful man!"

I couldn't disagree. From a public relations point of view, the NFU had snatched defeat from the jaws of victory.

Claire and I had decided to get married in the immediate aftermath of Chippy's death. His illness had brought us closer together, as it did the entire family. A spring wedding had seemed like a good idea, and the obvious time for it was the fourth week in May, between the Devon County and Bath and West Shows. Even in the absence of both shows, it turned out to be good timing. FMD had by no means gone away by this stage, but new cases had slowed to a trickle, likewise my television appearances.

The wedding was not a lavish affair: service at St Mary's, marquee on the lawn, nibbles and champagne, in lovely spring sunshine. I didn't have a best man. That would have been Chippy's role. I was weary, over-wrought and half-cut when I came to make my speech, and all the pent-up emotion just came gushing out, as I reduced myself and most of the guests to tears.

That apart, it was a very happy occasion! After a boozy evening in the pub, we left at some unearthly hour the next morning to drive to Penzance to catch the morning helicopter to Tresco, only to encounter thick fog which delayed take-off until the evening.

When I went into the nearest supermarket to buy a newspaper I was disconcerted to be confronted with a photograph of the pair of us, all over the front page of the Western Morning News. I spent the day visiting St Michael's Mount and the Star at Crowlas, while Claire slept off her hangover in the car. We did stay two nights in the New Inn, but the fog declined to lift, so on Monday we decided to cut our losses, catch the Scillonian back to Penzance, and onward to Plymouth, the Roscoff ferry, and Brittany, which was blissful.

When I got back to work the following Monday, it felt as if a line had been drawn. We were through the worst. Now for the recovery.

22

Aftermath

The second stage of the Foot and Mouth convulsion – the clean-up and the beginnings of recovery – was nothing like as traumatic as the outbreak itself, but almost as exhausting. My local celebrity status was already generating invitations to speak at meetings, open fêtes, chair conferences and so on, and I made a resolution to accept as many as I could, as a small way of saying thank you for all of the support and encouragement I'd received.

One of the first such commitments was to compère a concert in the theatre at Holsworthy, a town which was probably more connected to its agricultural hinterland than any other in the region and around which the outbreak had raged mercilessly. The concert was in aid of the Western Morning News' 'Green Wellie' campaign, a splendid initiative which raised more than half a million pounds to help victims of the outbreak. My joint compère was Des Shadrick, farmer, Liberal county councillor and a thoroughly decent and thoughtful man, who quite outshone me with his wit and charm.

The place was packed, there was a sense, almost of celebration as well as of relief in the air, and we enjoyed a varied programme that, like a stick of rock, had Holsworthy running all the way through it. The Holsworthy Town Band were in fine form, a quite remarkably barrel-chested girl blasted out tunes on the post horn with tremendous lung power, skill and panache, children from both the local schools did their stuff, and we even had a heartfelt rendering of 'Glorious Devon', a song that Chippy and I used to sing with father on the piano when we were children, but which I hadn't heard for years.

After that there were any number of fêtes, vintage tractor rallies, farmers' markets and flower shows to be opened, with poor Claire having to listen to much the same speech – including much the same jokes! – at all of them. However, far and away the most daunting undertakings were the public meetings. One of the first was at the village hall in Shebbear in north-west Devon. It had been organised by the local Methodist Circle (for Methodism is still strong in that part of Devon) and, as I set off from Exeter to drive there one August afternoon, I had in my mind a group of maybe 20 or 30 local people, sitting round in a circle to reflect with me on the outbreak. When I arrived (late), I was confronted with a substantial village hall, packed to the rafters with something like 200 people, all brimming with anticipation and excitement at the prospect of my inspiring words of wisdom. Not only that but, as I was being introduced by the chairman, I discovered that my brief was not to discuss what had happened in the previous four months or so but to 'look to the future'. And I had prepared absolutely nothing in the way of speaking notes. I busked my way through it somehow!

It was a similar story a few months later at Honiton, in front of an even bigger audience. I gathered that my appearance to give the 'Offwell Lecture' at the Beehive was the biggest thing to happen in the town for years. People were spilling out into the street! My heart sank within me as I looked out across that sea of expectant faces. How could anything I might say possibly match the sense of expectation that I could feel across the hall? It was a truly frightening experience.

Not all of my engagements were quite so demanding, however. In early September I was invited to be the 'guest of honour' at a wedding reception at Little Torrington, where Iris, the barmaid at the George Inn at Hatherleigh, the very epicentre of the outbreak, was marrying a local man called Jim Connell, neither of whom I'd met before. I wasn't quite required to emerge bare-chested from a giant cardboard wedding cake, but that was certainly the feel of the occasion. I probably visited Hatherleigh more often than any of the other FMD hotspots, getting to know the Mayor, Tony Hayward, a lovely man who ran a fish-and-chip shop in the town, really well.

A week after Jim and Iris's wedding I was back in Hatherleigh, to unveil a memorial to the outbreak and its impact on the town – a striking sculpture of a ram's head – and to speak in a service of thanksgiving in the cattle market afterwards, alongside Bishop Michael Langrish of Exeter, who had known very little of farming before coming to Devon but whose empathy with and concern for the rural community provided much comfort both during and after the outbreak. As bishops go, he was up there alongside Jim Thompson of Bath and Wells, another great champion of the farming community at whose farewell service in Wells Cathedral I spoke that November.

By September I was beginning to find my celebrity status distinctly wearing, not least at the two big county shows, the Devon County and the Royal Cornwall, which were moved, respectively, to August and September, and held without livestock.

Of the latter, I recorded in my diary:

I could hardly walk ten yards around the showground without someone grasping me warmly by the hand, to thank me for being 'the voice of sanity' or suchlike. One simply must respond warmly and gratefully, as they so obviously mean it, but it is wearing.

I continued, without much conviction.

I am not beginning to regret my decision to accept every invitation without questioning its significance. But I am beginning to appreciate the physical and emotional price that has to be paid. Next week promises to be absolutely brutal, to the extent that I actually turned down an invitation to speak (as a late replacement) at the Somerset County Cricket Club annual dinner.

Such is the price of fame!

You will be relieved to know that I do not intend to go through every event I opened, speech I made or presentation I received. But I will mention just three more, because they meant a lot.

The first was the South-West Food and Tourism Awards, at Barrington Court near Ilminster in November. I had seen a lot of Malcolm Bell, the boss of South-West Tourism, during the outbreak, me speaking up for farming, he for tourism, without us ever coming to verbal blows, which, considering the tensions between the two sectors, was quite an achievement on both our parts. Kim Howells, the Tourism Minister and one of the liveliest, most engaging politicians you could ever meet, was the guest speaker and gave out the awards – including one for me, for 'Services to South-West Tourism'! I don't think that any of the other awards I received gave me quite so much pleasure.

Noel Edmonds, the DJ and television presenter, who owned an estate not far from Okehampton and had been helpfully prominent in the Green Wellie campaign, had been at that awards ceremony and had said some nice things about me, and he was alongside me again on December 21, standing with the Mayor, Tony Hayward, next to the ram's head at Hatherleigh, for a live BBC 'Spotlight' special, looking back on 'the year of Foot and Mouth'.

I can't remember exactly what he said when his turn came, but it was something to the effect that, for all the misery, anguish and stress of the outbreak, not a single farmer in Devon had been driven to take his own life.

"And for that, we have this man to thank," he said, turning to me. "The common sense that he showed and the comfort that he brought genuinely helped save lives."

It is, I believe, true that there were no FMD suicides in Devon and, if I had a small part to play in that, then Heaven be praised, for there were some amongst my membership who were just itching to have a corpse or two that they could, as it were, parade in front of the media and employ in accusing Tony Blair and co of having 'blood on their hands'.

The third occasion that I remember with particular pleasure from that period was when, in the early spring of 2002, I was asked to give a 'Lenten Lecture' in Truro Cathedral. The lectures were the brainchild (I think) of the Bishop of Truro, Bill Ind, a jolly, bouncy, cricket-loving cleric, with whom I always got on well.

It was another awe-inspiring occasion. I had always (probably taking my lead from my father) looked upon Truro as the poor relation among the South-West's cathedrals. It might be an example of the very best Victorian Gothic, but Victorian Gothic it still unmistakeably was, in sharp contrast to the medieval splendour of the likes of Wells, Exeter, Salisbury and Gloucester.

However, all such architecturally snobbish thoughts went out of my head as I took my place at the lectern in the transept and looked down the length of the nave. It was full to bursting. All the Cornish gentry seemed to be there (and Cornwall has a lot of gentry!) as well as scores of my Cornish farming members. But at least this time I had a script, and not a bad one, though I say it myself.

I was asked to address 'The Role of the Cornish Farmer in the 21st Century', although my thoughts could equally well have been applied to farmers throughout the South-West. I argued that the public, as consumers and visitors to the countryside, were looking for more from the farming community than merely efficient commodity production, and that both greater prosperity and greater job satisfaction would flow from accepting that new, broader, role.

> It will not be easy, but if we can redefine the role of the farmer in the 21st century in a way which is in tune with the public mood, and which farmers themselves understand, then we will be a long way down the road to recovering self-respect and the self-confidence which goes with it. That way fulfilment lies, and ultimately that way profit lies as well.
>
> So what is the role of the farmer in 21st century Cornwall? It is to produce and market high-quality food, to provide facilities for rest, recreation and business, and to maintain and manage the countryside

which is at once such an inspiration and an economic asset, all in ways which contribute to the community and the environment.

It is not so much a new role, as an expanded one, with food production still at its core. Performing it will involve challenge and change. This is no soft option. But, for better or for worse, that is what society wants of its farming community, and that community will be more prosperous and more fulfilled if it not merely accepts its new role but embraces it.

That still, I would maintain, holds true.

The post-FMD period did inevitably have its hubristic moments. My celebrity status was understandably resented by some of my county office-holders and senior staff, who had worked just as hard, but in less prominent roles, and so hadn't enjoyed the recognition they deserved. I also – entirely predictably – failed to avoid the trap of being carried away with my own self-importance and probably deserved the label by which I was known in Cornwall NFU circles – the Regional Dictator!

While Claire and I were away on holiday in Tobago in October (much the most exotic location I've ever visited), Chris Rundle, no doubt encouraged by my old enemy Derek Mead, wrote a typically poisonous piece about me for the Western Daily Press under the headline 'Farming's fallen hero'. Shortly afterwards (as I discovered only when we got home) a delegation led by David Hill, the Devon Chairman (doubtless egged on by Richard Haddock), had gone to NFU HQ to confront Richard Macdonald, as Director General, and Roger Ward, as Director of Regions, with a litany of complaints about their over-mighty Regional Director.

"What they want as a regional director is an efficient administrator, not a superstar," Roger subsequently explained. I daresay many others thought the same, although in my own defence I should point out that, during the years I was in charge, both the Somerset county branch and the South-West region were among the top performers in terms of both subscription income and cost-effectiveness, while my staff teams were second to none.

At my appraisal the following year Roger offered me early retirement, on modestly generous terms. It was an appealing offer, especially as there had been talk the previous summer of me being offered a Lib Dem life peerage, which would have meant giving up my NFU role in any case. But nothing seemed to be coming of that and, in the wake of divorce, I needed reasonably gainful employment to pay the mortgage and keep the overdraft under control. Besides, there were still many aspects of the job

that I enjoyed, not least the FMD recovery programme and the work of
the South West Chamber of Rural Enterprise (SWCoRE), which had been
formally launched that autumn. And for every county office-holder who
resented my prominence, there was at least one other who thought it well-
deserved and helpful to the cause. So I decided to solider on.

There was plenty to keep me occupied. In February the report of the
so-called Curry Commission was published. The conclusions of Professor
Ian Mercer's inquiry into the handling of the FMD outbreak in Devon
could best be summarised in one word – 'lamentable' – while the key word
in Sir Donald Curry's conclusions about the future of British food and
farming was 'reconnection'. His 'Policy Commission', as it would be called,
had been born partly, obviously, from FMD, but also from the industry's
underlying problems, which the outbreak had served to highlight.

In his introduction to the finished report Sir Donald wrote:

> *We believe the real reason why the present situation is so dysfunctional
> is that farming has become detached from the rest of the economy
> and the environment. The key objective of public policy should be to
> reconnect our food and farming industry; to reconnect farming with
> its market; to reconnect the food chain and the countryside; and to
> reconnect consumers with what they eat and how it is produced.*

There has been some progress with this 'reconnection agenda' in the
ensuing twenty years, perhaps particularly in the interest which there now
is – at least among the more affluent consumers – in locally produced, often
organic, food and drink, from which the West Country has been a major
beneficiary (and with Taste of the West playing an important role).

As for the rest, I'm afraid that the replacement of MAFF by the Department
of Food, the Environment and Rural Affairs (Defra) and the appointment
of that singularly cold fish, Margaret Beckett, to head it, sent precisely the
wrong signals to a still economically embattled farming community about
the Blair government's intentions. They could read the writing on the wall
outside the new department's offices, and the word 'agriculture' did not
feature.

Even so, I thought that the report was fair, balanced and sensible, if
optimistic in its conclusions, and welcomed it accordingly. The suggestion
of a 'broad and shallow' scheme to reward farmers modestly for keeping
their farms in good environmental order – the Entry Level Scheme or
ELS, as it became – built on experience with ESAs, although it probably
set the bar too low. It left too wide a gap between *maintaining* landscape

and biodiversity and the payments/regimes for actually *enhancing* it, with the result that little real progress was made in improving the quality of the farmed environment over the ensuing years.

However, much the most controversial recommendation was to increase the amount of money available for environmental schemes and rural development programmes by 'modulating' – i.e. top-slicing – each farmer's support payments on crops and livestock by 10% rather than the then current rate of 4%. In a debate which has distinct echoes of the present (2021) Government's policy of diverting an ever greater proportion of farm-support payments into 'public goods', the NFU nationally said no, with Ben Gill, who never had much time for his fellow North Country farmer, the Northumbrian Donald Curry, particularly fierce in his denunciations.

But in the South-West, with our proliferation of National Parks, AONBs, ESAs, rural development ambitions and local food agenda, we were rather keen on the idea. The money released could be used to make a real difference to farming and the countryside, rather than paying for the Caribbean holidays of East Anglian barley barons. It seemed to me that the alternative to modulation was not farmers being paid their subsidies in full but farmers maybe not getting their subsidies at all. So yet again, we had an HQ versus South-West bust-up, although on this occasion my members were solidly behind me.

Meanwhile, the farming community across the West Country was beginning slowly to recover from the shock and dislocation of what was the most traumatic event to have occurred in the Devon countryside, certainly since the dreadful harvest failure of 1879, arguably since the Civil War.

I concluded my review of the year for the Western Morning News with an optimistic thought:

> *2001 may be remembered as the year in which the farming community*
> *not only went through the fire, but also started to rise from the ashes.*

It is true that the effects of the outbreak were not as long-lasting as many had feared. The RDA, with its Deputy Chairman, Jeremy Pope, of the brewing family, very much to the fore, did a fine job in administering Business Recovery Grants which helped the tourism industry get back on its feet. Farmers who had had their livestock slaughtered at least had their compensation to fall back on, while those who were closed down for months on end by Form D restrictions, and who were probably worse affected financially than outbreak farms, showed typical family farm resilience.

Five years later, when I was given the singular honour of being appointed President of the Devonshire Association, a sort of Devonian equivalent of the Royal Society, my Presidential address was entitled 'An Ill Wind – The impact of the 2001 outbreak of Foot and Mouth Disease in Devon'.

As part of my research, I circulated a questionnaire to the 179 Devon farms where disease had been confirmed and the animals slaughtered. Of the 107 who replied, only two had taken the opportunity to give up, with another 15 opting to let their land and take semi-retirement. All of the rest re-stocked, sometimes with the same numbers as before, sometimes with more livestock and in some cases with fewer, so as to allow time for a diversified enterprise or a part-time job off the farm.

When it came to how the experience had left these farmers feeling about themselves and their calling, there was a three-way split. A third said it had reinforced their determination to be a livestock farmer; a third said it had left them profoundly disillusioned; and a third said it had given them the chance to take stock and change direction. But perhaps the most interesting aspect of my mini-survey came in the section where I'd asked for any further thoughts.

"It was a total life changing experience," writes one farmer. "Not just our attitude to the way we earn our living but about the way we exist and live our lives."

"My husband's anger from it has never really gone away," writes another. While even someone who has branched out successfully in a new direction since the outbreak reports that: "My elderly parents didn't cope with it; my mother has since passed on and my father is now paralysed with a stroke."

As many people have remarked, whilst Foot and Mouth may have united the 'rural community' in the widest sense in support of the victims of the outbreak and in a readiness to make sacrifices to bring it to the earliest possible end, it was also hugely divisive within individual communities. As between, for example, those who made no particular effort to avoid infection and were rewarded with a fat compensation cheque, and those who cut themselves off from the world to keep the disease at bay and whose reward was months of restrictions and a heavy financial loss. This is reflected in the comment of one farmer: "A great big effect of FMD was the pressure on relationships with family, friends, neighbours etc. Some damage was not reparable, and left many awkward situations in our parish."

The depth of cynicism in the motives and abilities of government in its various forms that was bred by the experience is also painfully apparent, with several respondents suggesting that the outbreak was either started by the government, or deliberately mishandled, in order, as one respondent puts it ,"to do away with farmers".

But if most of the comments speak of bitterness at the way the outbreak was handled, and disillusionment at how the world of farming has not been changed for the better subsequently, there is plenty of evidence as well of optimism and resilience.

Several respondents had converted to organic farming and were enjoying it. Others are clearly proud to be able to boast of the success of their new business ventures, and there are many who say that the crisis gave them the opportunity to make changes to their businesses earlier than might otherwise be the case.

A revealing insight into the psychology of family farm relationships is provided by the farmer's wife who now feels "more included in the business" with their new herd of cows, than she did when she and her husband were milking the cows handed down from the in-laws.

But even as the farming community struggled to get back to something like normality, yet another 'reform of the Common Agricultural Policy' loomed on the horizon. This one went by the name of the 'Mid-Term Review' (given that it was five years into the intended ten-year life of the previous set of reforms), and it was radical in its ambitions.

'De-coupling' was the buzzword. The plan was that all of the pre-existing livestock subsidies and crop payments would be bundled up together and paid to farmers as a flat-rate payment per hectare, regardless of what they actually chose to do with the land. It was very similar to the 2020 'basic payment' regime, which the Government is planning to move away from, post-EU.

This seemed to me to be a pretty good idea. The fact that farm subsidies were tied to livestock and crops meant that they tended to be treated as part of the return for producing those livestock and crops, which meant that the buyers of farm outputs – supermarkets foremost among them – did not have to pay as much to be assured of a continuing supply. What was intended as a subsidy to the farmer became instead a subsidy to the retailer or the end-consumer. Under this new system, that link would be broken so that, if a livestock or arable enterprise was not profitable in its own right, not counting the subsidy, the farmer would be better off abandoning it, meaning that in time the supermarkets etc would have to pay a price representing the true cost of production.

We organised the usual programme of member meetings to explain and debate the new system. At all of those at which I spoke, and in all of the newspaper columns and television interviews I gave at the time, my message was the same: if you want de-coupling to work for you as farmers, you must treat it as a separate payment – put it into a different account – and only carry on milking cows, or rearing beef cattle and lambs or growing corn or whatever, if the enterprise is profitable in its own right. Otherwise, you might just as well endorse your single-payment cheque and post it off to Tesco.

It was maybe an over-simplification, but I remain convinced it was the right message. But not many of my farming members saw it that way. The farmers could see my point but didn't much like the idea of pocketing their cheques and producing nothing in return. It went against every instinct in their make-up.

The other big argument was over whether a farmer's single payment should be based on what he or she as an individual had been claiming in the way of subsidies in previous years, the 'historic' basis; or whether it should be an average based on the total amount paid to farmers in England in a base period, divided by the number of hectares of eligible agricultural land, the 'averaged' basis. The most intensive farmers favoured historic payments; the less intensive wanted an averaged basis. In the end we got what Mrs Beckett called her 'dynamic hybrid', under which there would be a progressive shift from historic to averaged over a period of years.

This might not have been such a bad idea if the Defra IT systems had been even remotely capable of delivering it fairly and on time. But they weren't. The whole thing became a hugely distracting and damaging shambles. It was yet another example of what the foot-and-mouth experience had taught us: that the hallmark of government in modern Britain is incompetence. Neither the handling of FMD nor the single-payment fiasco were symptoms of a conspiracy against the farming community; they were just gigantic cock-ups.

However, not even the CAP had as much influence on the fortunes of farming in these years as the pound/euro exchange rate, and in 2003 that changed for the better, as sterling weakened, so lifting farm prices and payments (set in euros) and making imports more expensive and therefore less competitive.

This meant that we could switch at least some of our attention from short-term economics to longer-term issues like growing crops for fuel –

miscanthus being a particular favourite in the South-West – and the debate over genetically modified foods (GMs), promoted by the Government under the title 'GM Nation'. The NFU was broadly in favour. I and many others had our doubts. In July 2003 I devoted one of my Western Morning News columns to the subject:

> The latest contribution to the Government's 'GM Nation' debate was conducted on Monday morning at the Devon Drivers' Centre at Westpoint, to the accompaniment of loud off-stage squeals and screeches. Happily, these turned out to emanate not from an organic lady from Totnes being strangled by the man from Monsanto, as from the Centre's skid-pan. Still, as Chairman Martin Howlett remarked, the fact that, outside, they were driving round and round in circles, making a huge amount of noise and getting precisely nowhere did seem rather appropriate.
>
> Open minds on this subject are as rare as ... well, I was going to say, as rare as hen's teeth, but who knows what may be around the corner where GM is concerned! Anyway, just about the only thing which the protagonists at Westpoint could agree upon was that the video which the Government has had made in an effort to 'inform' the debate is a load of rubbish.
>
> "It's all just opinion," declared one farmer. "What we need if we are going to form a sensible judgement is facts!"
>
> Ah yes, but which facts? The facts that support the argument that GM technology is the greatest boon to mankind since the invention of the wheel; or the facts which lend weight to the view that rogue GMs represent the greatest threat to the survival of the planet since the asteroid which wiped out the dinosaurs?

My conclusion was the unoriginal one that it ought to be left to consumers to choose whether or not to buy and eat GM foods, on the basis of clear and accurate labelling, whilst still admitting some doubts:

> But if that is my rational response to the GM issue, my visceral one is that, in the end, no good will come of it. I'm with the Roman poet Horace. "Naturam expellas furca, tamen usque recurret," he warned, over 2,000 years ago. "You can drive Nature out with a pitchfork, but she will soon find a way back."

That summer I was awarded the OBE, 'for services to the rural economy in the South-West', a citation which pleased me as it suggested that I had done a bit more than stand up for farmers during the two big crises of BSE and FMD, important though that might have been. Prince Charles sent me a telegram, although it was all the messages of congratulation from people across the region, many of whom I'd never even met, which gave me the most pleasure. That, and what it meant to my mother. At my investiture in October the Queen asked me whether the farming community was recovering from the shock of Foot and Mouth. I was able to reassure her.

The four years after the 2001 FMD outbreak did have a bit of an 'after the Lord Mayor's Show' feel about them for A Gibson. My diary is full of references to 'treading water' and 'a bittersweet year'.

We were making some headway with the 'regional' agenda, but progress was slow and the agency on which I had pinned such high hopes, South-West Food and Drink, ran into trouble almost as soon as it was launched. Other initiatives, such as the 'Rural Enterprise Gateway', which provided free advice and sign-posting to farmers looking to diversify, did make a worthwhile impact, but, as with the Objective 1 programme, we were rather better at creating delivery bodies than actually delivering the goods.

Nor did the farming agenda change much. My main day-to-day preoccupations remained milk prices, bovine TB and badgers – plus CAP reform, with all its divisiveness. The fact that legislation to ban hunting was going through Parliament and would become law in February 2005 further poisoned the political atmosphere. As I wrote at the time:

If there is one word to describe the mood of the countryside at the end of 2004, it would be 'disaffected'.

And things didn't improve much in 2005.

Within the NFU there were further ructions over the move of HQ from London to a new building on the Royal Showground at Stoneleigh in Warwickshire, and over a plan to scrap county committees, which went down like a lead balloon. The militants were still on the march as well, mostly over milk prices, although not to the extent that either Richard Haddock or Derek Mead could get themselves elected as national office-holders.

But there were some consolations. Being President of the Honiton Show in 2003 for its first show on its new showground alongside the A30 was a singular honour, even if the weather was so hot that I almost melted inside my pin-stripe suit and panama hat. Michael Hawkins, Donald Arscott and Trevor Larcombe ran the thing like clockwork.

Then there was the appointment we made in November 2001, to succeed Robert Deane, who was moving on to greener pastures after being a pillar of the NFU South-West region for the previous eight years. She was the first of five short-listed candidates, a dairy farmer's daughter from Cornwall, and my notes read:

Cool and calm and confident. Experience of Objective 1 projects could be useful. Thinking underdeveloped but quite fluent. Positive thinker, Customer focus. Outward looking. Good answers on Policy Commission and access.

Her name? Melanie Saunders, now Melanie Squires MBE. She succeeded me as Regional Director in 2006 and has been doing a great job ever since!

Closer to home, we finally succeeded, after several years of trying, in finding a house for my mother to buy in Langport. It was down by the river, with lovely views across Huish Level, just 200 yards or so from where Claire and I were living and within easy walking distance of the shops. It was being sold by Nina Cox, mother of Rupert Cox (chief Executive of the Bath and West at the time of writing), whom we had known for many years.

Mother spent the rest of her days there, playing a full part in church and community. For her and for us, it was the happiest possible final landing. She died peacefully at her home in August 2011 at the age of 87, Mandy and Claire having combined to bring her home from Musgrove Park hospital. I gave the address at her funeral, paying tribute to "a remarkable woman", which is what she was.

As for myself, I knew that it was time to move on. Nothing had come of the peerage suggestion and, although I was approached to stand for the Liberal Democrats in the West Devon constituency in the 2005 General Election, I decided that, whilst I might enjoy being what they call a 'good constituency MP', I didn't have sufficient partisan enthusiasm to immerse myself in the full panoply of Lib Dem policies, as was apparently expected.

So, when Richard Macdonald rang me on the car phone one Friday afternoon to ask me if I would be interested in becoming the NFU's Director of Communications, it seemed like the right opportunity at just the right time.

23

Water, water everywhere

The Somerset Levels and Moors has always flooded. Life for the farmers of this strange and distinctive stretch of country has always been a matter of finding a survivable accommodation with the all-pervasive water.

The worst flood of which records exist was in January 1607, when a storm surge sent the waters of the Bristol Channel crashing through the rudimentary sea defences and as far inland as Glastonbury. Thousands of acres of land were swallowed up and hundreds of people drowned, along with their livestock, with hundreds more being left homeless. The nearest thing to that in modern times was the sea flood of December 1981. The work that was done in the wake of that, on building new sea walls and otherwise shoring up the coastal defences, mean that the Environment Agency now rate a repeat of that episode as a 'one in 200 years' likelihood (although climate change may significantly shorten the odds).

But if flooding from the sea is a rare event, flooding caused by heavy rainfall on the crescent of hills which form the catchment areas for the rivers that flow through the Levels has become, or at least seems to have become, increasingly common. And as peace was gradually restored in the conflict over land drainage on the Levels, thanks to management agreements and the ESA, so the focus shifted towards flooding and what to do about it.

The first big flood in which I got involved was in 1979. That was a summer flood, in early June, and summer floods always cause a lot more damage than winter ones. This, I soon learned, was because the warmer flood water is, the less oxygen it contains and the faster inundated crops and grass will die. There's also the issue of silt deposition, which was particularly severe in that 1979 flood because so much grassland was laid up for silage and hay, just wating to be cut. Nothing ruins grassland, whether for grazing or for winter fodder, like mud, and the damage was considerable.

However, neither this episode nor the next one, in the winter of 1990, produced much in the way of a blame game. Flooding was a fact of farming life on the Levels, and a network of mostly farmer-populated 'internal drainage boards', operating under the umbrella of well-funded water authorities in the 1980s and the National Rivers Authority in the 1990s, meant that the damage-limitation infrastructure – the ditches, rhynes, flood banks, spillways, main rivers and pumping stations – was reasonably well maintained and in good working order. Or that at least was what was generally assumed.

However, any such complacency was abruptly shattered in early August 1997, when 68 mm of rain fell in two days and thousands of acres of land, in the southern Levels especially, disappeared under water at the height of summer. I visited the area shortly after the waters had receded, leaving behind a stinking, silt-encrusted mess, littered with dead fish.

On this occasion there was no philosophical acceptance of an act of God on the part of the local farming community. They were furious. In my office in Exeter the following Wednesday, I had Stuart Gothard from Stoke St Gregory shouting down the phone at me, then willow-grower Nigel Hector, then cider-maker Julian Temperley, then Langport farmer Peter Maltby, and on it went. Nigel's comments may be taken as representative of the general mood. "It's a complete farce," he told me. "Sheer incompetence."

'It' was the response of the recently created (1995) Environment Agency when the scale of the flood risk had become clear. The rain had fallen over the weekend of August 2-3. By Tuesday water levels in the rivers were rising fast, and a major flood looked inevitable. It was time to switch on the pumps, to get floodwater out of the moors before the rivers rose so high that pumping would simply be a matter of pointless water recycling. But two of the most crucial pumping stations promptly ground to a halt, making the flooding far worse than it would otherwise have been.

The grim details were revealed at a meeting in Bridgwater a week later. First of all, the severity of the rainfall had not been predicted by the Met Office so the EA were not geared up for a flood emergency. Then, when the extent of the threat became clear and engineers went to put the pumps on, the Curry Moor pumps became clogged with weed and, by the time that was cleared, the river level was too high for pumping to be worthwhile, while the new electric pumps at West Sedgemoor broke down within 15 minutes of being switched on, with the result that 24 hours of pumping was lost between the Tuesday evening and late on Wednesday. We were promised an internal inquiry, with the finger of blame being already pointed at the EA's contractors and Government penny-pinching. MAFF was proposing to cut flood defence spending by £10 million, we were warned.

The farmers who had lost thousands of pounds worth of grazing, maize and cereals, on Curry Moor especially, wanted us to sue the EA for damages, using the NFU's Legal Assistance Scheme. But when the lawyers looked at it, they discovered that the EA could only be sued successfully for sins of commission, not omission. Had the Agency done something – lowered a flood bank, for example, or decommissioned a pumping station – then they could be held responsible for the damage caused as a result. But simply neglecting to keep flood-banks and spillways at design height, or merely assuming that pumps were in full working order without testing them, was not actionable. So there was nothing to be done.

Despite the EA's internal inquiry – which did indeed blame their contractors – there were no signs of any obvious improvements and, when the next test of the EA's flood readiness arrived in the winter of 1999/2000, the story was much the same. That was a wretchedly wet winter. I was living at Langport by now, my cottage looking out across the river Parrett to Huish Level and the moors stretching away towards Muchelney and beyond, so I had a front-row seat for the six flood events that unfolded that winter and spring.

The worst of them was in April. The river went over the spillways on the night before Good Friday, April 15, and by later that day I was writing in my diary of the 'brown, wave-tossed sea which Huish Level has again become'. Given that spring was by now well-advanced, the grass growing and the flood-water warming, it was essential that the floods should be pumped away just as soon as the water level in the river allowed. But yet again, as I wrote at the time, 'The breakdowns and the cock-ups which have accompanied just about every flood event on the Levels for the past two years began to set in.'

Two of the three antiquated pumps at Long Load on the river Yeo, where the worst of the flooding was concentrated, broke down as soon as they were turned on, while some bright spark decided to turn the third pump off at night, so that the sleep of the local residents was not disturbed. The result was that the water was pumped off too slowly, its temperature rose, de-oxygenation set in and the grass died.

David Hubbart, a pipe-smoking, hard-driving, no-nonsense, slurry-under-his-fingernails dairy farmer, who had moved to Somerset from Derbyshire and was milking cows at Knowle near Long Sutton, lost 40 acres of his silage ground, costing him, he reckoned, at least £8,000. More to the point, as far as the conservation bodies were concerned, the nests and eggs of hundreds of pairs of ground-nesting birds had been swept away in the flood.

This time, the issue reached the House of Commons, thanks to David Heath, the Lib Dem MP for Somerton and Frome, whose constituency included the worst affected areas and who would go on to become a very effective Defra Minister in the Cameron-Clegg coalition. In a measured, balanced and eloquent exposition of the problem, he pointed out that Somerset Council Tax payers already paid more per head towards flood defence than those in any other part of the country. Yet the £6 million which this raised was not enough to maintain flood defences even in their current, dilapidated condition. And anyway, he argued, why should the burden of protecting an area of international importance for wildlife – which was damaged just as much by flooding as the farming interest – fall exclusively on Somerset?

Elliot Morley, the rather lugubrious, ineffectual Minister responsible, with whom I crossed swords on several occasions, responded sympathetically, without promising anything worthwhile, unless and until "local people come together and agree a long-term management plan, which is based on the river catchment".

Well, Somerset was ahead of him there. The increase in the frequency and severity of flood events on the Levels wasn't solely down to a mixture of Government cuts and Environment Agency cock-ups. The third and arguably equally important element in the equation was a steady increase in the speed at which heavy rainfall was coming off the upper catchment and into rivers like the Parrett, Tone and Brue.

The older generation of Levels farmers would tell me that, 'back in the old days', by which they probably meant the 1930s and 40s, the water level in the Parrett at Langport wouldn't start to respond to heavy rain in the upper catchment until maybe 48 hours after the event. By the later 1990s, that had come down to around 24 hours, and today it is barely more than 15. The result was that the peak of the flood, looked at in profile, was much sharper and higher than it had been, which meant either raising the flood banks to meet the new challenge, which was expensive and environmentally dubious, or accepting more flooding.

But there was a third way available to meet this situation, and that was to slow the rate at which rainfall came off the upper catchment, so that the hills around the Levels acted more like a sponge and less like a sloping roof. This was not an original approach. The theory had been around for years, but in

Somerset a farmer and prominent Lib Dem county councillor Humphrey Temperley decided that the time had come to put it into practice.

Now Humphrey was perceived, especially in the farming community, as a bit of an upper-class maverick, what with his Eton education, his Liberal politics and, not least, his getting himself thrown out of that famous Tom King meeting at Burrowbridge for arguing forcefully for SSSIs. He also made national headlines in 1997 for leading a raid on the buffet supper of a German twinning delegation in the Bridgwater Arts Centre, having accused them of pinching the food laid on for the group of Czechs that he was hosting in a neighbouring room. It developed into a food fight, dubbed by the Bridgwater Mercury as 'the battle of the drumsticks'.

But like all of his family (father Professor Neville Temperley the mathematician, brother Julian Temperley the cider-maker, niece Alice Temperley the fashion designer), he had a fierce intelligence allied to a sometimes quixotic determination to get things done. He now makes wine in France with his second wife, Baroness Sue Miller, but in those days he was farming alongside the Parrett at Thorney so knew all about the flooding issues at first hand.

In March 2000 Humphrey had launched something called the 'Parrett Catchment Project' with the tag-line on its logo of 'A future when it rains ...'. It brought together all the main players in flood defence, conservation, farming and so on, plus the local authorities and the RDA. I went to the launch and offered the NFU's financial as well as moral support, to the tune of £1,000. Whilst the PCP had 12 distinct components, the concept essentially was a trade-off: farmers would do what they could through changes to land management in the upper catchment, creating flood storage areas, planting trees and so on to reduce the speed and volume of run-off, in return for the EA doing more to keep the rivers, pumps and flood banks in good order. The issue was being tackled from both sides, with the farmers reducing the threat and the EA minimising the impact.

The other great beauty of the approach was that, apart from the tidal barrage downstream from Bridgwater which was proposed and which was always, as we shall see, a fairly distant prospect, it didn't involve any expensive flood defence engineering. The flood risk would be reduced using almost entirely natural processes; working with the grain of the landscape and river systems rather than trying to impose solutions upon them.

Apart from wishing the project well and writing enthusiastically about it in the Western Daily Press and elsewhere, I didn't get involved until the summer of 2003 when, out of the blue, Humphrey rang me up to say that he was standing down as Chairman of the Management Committee, and would I like to take over from him? Viewing this as something of a vote of confidence in my impartial commitment to finding solutions that served all of the interests in the Levels, I accepted and took over at the AGM that September.

I think it would be fair to say that the PCP had rather run out of its initial steam by this stage and needed a bit of a shot in the arm. In that context I was very fortunate that a lady called Sarah Diacono had just joined Somerset County Council and that amongst her responsibilities was the PCP and the EU programme which underpinned much of its finance, the 'Joint Approach to Flooding', or JAF programme, in which Dutch and German projects were also involved. Sarah proved to be a godsend. She took the project by the scruff of the neck, identified what needed doing and by whom and soon had the whole thing back on track.

A lot of good work was done. The Somerset Farming and Wildlife Advisory Group (FWAG), which I'd helped get off the ground back in the 1980s, took on the advisory work with farmers in the upper catchment and, under the leadership of Ben Thorne, very well they did it too. FWAG was an organisation which had been set up by farmers for farmers and thus enjoyed a degree of trust and credibility to which an organisation like English Nature (as it was then) could not aspire.

Through farm visits, farmer meetings and individual advice they succeeded in changing the way that land was being farmed across thousands of acres. Using a mixture of encouragement and financial incentives, they persuaded farmers to do things like switching from arable to pasture on sloping ground, ploughing along the contours rather than across them, planting cover crops on bare land in the autumn and steering clear of crops likely to cause soil erosion or accelerated run-off in vulnerable areas, maize chief amongst them.

Further down the catchment the plan was to create temporary flood storage areas and what were called 'new wetland habitats' – mainly ponds – so as to siphon off some of the water, hold it for a time and then let it go once the peak of the flood had passed. We did actually create one such temporary flood storage area, on Robert Vaux's farm at Chiselborough, and we would have had another, in the Isle valley west of Curry Rivel, until we discovered that, under the Reservoirs Act, it would be subject to a horribly expensive inspection regime, even though the water would be held for no more than a few days, and the works involved were just a few earth banks.

The other thing that we were good at in the PCP was what we called 'public engagement' – explaining what we were trying to do and why, to the local people especially, who have always had a healthy suspicion of well-meaning outsiders trying to interfere with how they live their lives. So we had walk-in sessions in village halls, we organised 'PCP in practice' days with coach trips for people to visit our various sites, we issued regular newsletters and we held three very successful 'River Festivals', at Langport, Taunton and Bridgwater, until the money ran out.

Money, as always, was the problem. We were financially supported by the main partners, the conservation and farming bodies as well as local authorities, the EA and the water companies, but the really big money – £650,00 over three years, plus matched funding – came from the EU, and we knew that, when that came to an end in April 2006, our ability to deliver, as opposed merely to aspire, which had been so important to our credibility, would very largely disappear.

We carried on for another year or so after the money ran out but, when what was almost a parallel body, the Levels and Moors Partnership (LAMP), folded in 2007, the sensible thing to do seemed to be to combine the two partnerships. LAMP was much more to do with community than with flood prevention, but the two have always been closely intertwined on the Levels, so it made sense in those terms as well.

The outcome was the Somerset Water Management Partnership, which I also chaired until it was taken over by Somerset County Council in 2013. It was a useful talking shop, which maintained the shared commitment which was such an important element in the two previous partnerships, but I would be hard pressed to identify any real difference it made on the ground.

So did the PCP make any real difference? Jonathan Porritt's outfit, Forum for the Future, certainly thought so. They carried out a 'sustainability appraisal' of the project and concluded that it had had:

> *a considerable impact on catchment-wide sustainability ... River water and soil quality are improving as a result and, although not directly targeted, landscape quality is being enhanced.*

They also commended the overall approach of the project, as deserving:

> *national acknowledgement as a forerunner of the type of partnerships the Environment Agency is now working to establish to progress catchment management and River Basin Management Plans for implementing the European Union's Water Framework Directive by 2015. The evidence shows that the PCP is still well ahead of the game.*

We won international recognition as well. In September 2007 the EU Agriculture Commissioner, Mariann Fischer Boel, a singularly imposing Danish lady and the most powerful person in European agriculture, took time out to visit Patrick Palmer's flood attenuation pond, hard by the A303 at Bower Hinton. The PCP was, she said, an example to the rest of Europe of co-operation in natural water management.

Sadly whatever difference the PCP was able to make in reducing the flood risk by slowing the flow has long since been overtaken by events. Water (and soil) now comes off the upper catchment faster than ever, thanks mainly to the vast area of maize now being grown, much of it to feed heavily subsidised anaerobic digester (AD) plants.

I am still involved in catchment management, as Chair of the Somerset Catchment Partnership, which has more to do with water quality in the rivers than flood prevention but which is grappling with the same issues in the upper catchment as the PCP but with much less success. The Government insists that it is committed to what is called 'the catchment-based approach'. But when it comes to putting its money where its mouth is, the only change has been for the worse. Our Defra funding amounts to the princely sum of £15,000 a year – which is roughly the same amount of money which, indirectly, it pays out to a farmer growing 50 hectares of maize for an AD plant.

However, we are getting ahead of ourselves. The one major element in the PCP's work programme which we did not achieve was item 9: 'building a tidal sluice or barrier downstream of Bridgwater'. This had long been both a personal and professional ambition of mine. The Parrett is the only one of the rivers which run through the Levels which does not have a tidal sluice, or clyse as they're called in these parts, at its mouth to prevent the high tides of the Bristol channel pushing up river to meet floodwater coming down, and so create what is called 'tide-lock'.

All the EA modelling I have ever seen has shown that a tidal exclusion sluice would greatly reduce the risk of flooding, not only in Bridgwater but in several of the moors upstream. It would also, of course, mean that the Parrett inland of the sluice would be a very different river. Instead of those banks of slimy mud, embellished with discarded shopping trolleys, which so disfigure the river as it runs through Bridgwater, you would have a penned stretch of clean river, around which the Bridgwater riverside, and arguably the entire town centre, could be regenerated. When I chaired the local regeneration partnership, the aptly-named Bridgwater Challenge, from 2008 to 2011, we spent a lot of time asking local people what they thought would make the greatest positive difference to the town. Far and away the most popular choice was a tidal sluice and with it a better river.

One of the first things I did after taking over the chair of the PCP was to form another partnership, the Parrett Sluice Partnership, committed to making the thing happen at last. We had support from the EA, the County Council, the RDA, Sedgemoor District Council and, most of all, from the people of Bridgwater. Yes, it would cost a lot of money to build a sluice, anything up to £40 million, but then a report which we had commissioned from the consultants WS Atkins had put the potential economic gain at £370 million, so the cost-benefit ratio was spectacular!

The principle of building a sluice was eventually approved. Sedgemoor District Council, concerned to protect the 11,400 homes that were said to be at risk from a tidal flood, started collecting a levy from developers to pay for it. But the conservation bodies were not happy. Those banks of slimy mud were an important habitat for a rare(ish) mud snail. Besides, the EU's various directives took a very dim view of altering the natural characteristics of 'water bodies' like the Parrett. A Thames Barrier-style surge barrier, only to be used when particularly high tides were threatened, might be acceptable; a tidal exclusion sluice, changing the nature of the river through Bridgwater and acting as a focus for regeneration, would not.

So, frightened off, Sedgemoor caved. A surge barrier it is eventually to be, at a cost of goodness knows how many hundreds of millions of pounds, as an insurance against what, even if the climate change predictions are correct, cannot be much more than a 'one in 50 year' risk and with no wider benefits. It makes me angry every time I think about it.

Meanwhile in the Environment Agency an agenda which, if not exactly secret, was certainly not advertised was beginning to unfold. My first inkling of what was afoot came at a meeting in Taunton involving Tony Owens, a very capable senior executive in the EA's Wessex region. We were talking about the PCP's objective to 'dredge and maintain river channels' and I said something which I have often said during my association with the Levels, which is that you will only get what you want from the area if you manage the water to achieve it, assuming that that almost went without saying.

"I shouldn't be too sure about that," said Tony. "There is a growing school of thought in the Agency that a more sustainable solution would simply be to let nature take its course, allow the flood banks to deteriorate, abandon the pumping stations, allow the rivers to silt up and leave the Levels to revert to one gigantic swamp."

I took what he'd said seriously. Even so, I was taken aback by a conversation I had with his ultimate boss, the EA's Chief Executive, Barbara (now Baroness) Young, a few months later. It was at an EA reception at Woodbury Park. We were introduced, and I explained that, as well as being the NFU's Regional Director, I was also Chairman of the PCP.

"Huh," she snorted derisively. "If I had my way, we'd attached a limpet mine to every pumping station in Somerset and blow them all to kingdom come." I took the precaution of noting down her exact words in my diary, and it's an exchange that I have often recalled in subsequent years.

In the event, she decided not to go quite that far. Instead, the EA embarked on a policy that might best be described as one of 'benign neglect'. Hiding behind studies – commissioned by themselves – which purported to show that dredging and other forms of river maintenance were a waste of time and money (and no doubt with the underlying thought that if the rivers flooded more frequently and the land became wetter, well then so much the better), dredging was discontinued. The fact that this also saved money was an added bonus. It would be another seven years or so before the chickens thus released came home to roost.

The summer of 2012 was one of the wettest of recent years. In June, the moors south of Langport and Currymoor flooded. That might have happened even if the rivers had been dredged. But it was the time it took for the river levels to fall low enough to allow pumping to start – which dredging certainly would have reduced – which was the real killer. At the height of summer, it only took a few days for the floodwater on the moors to become so de-oxygenated and polluting that the EA dare not pump it back into the rivers without treating it first with what seemed like the UK's entire supply of hydrogen peroxide. Wildlife sites on which millions on pounds had been spent were reduced to a stinking, slimy mess.

Yet even after that, the 'swampists', as I called them, held out. At a conference at the Bath and West the following year, the EA's Martin Weiler declined to offer any assurance that the rivers would be dredged, instead offering a 'robust debate'.

Well, we certainly got that the following winter, when the floodwater went over the spillways and out into the moors in the week before Christmas and stayed there for the next three months. On January 5 I noted in my diary:

The moors are full, the south bank of the river has almost disappeared, the water level in the garden is the highest I've ever seen it, and the rain is lashing down. The swampists will say that it shows there is no point in dredging the rivers and that we might just as well abandon the moors to flood storage. Everyone else will say that it shows why the main rivers simply must be put back in good working order. Not sure if this bout of flooding, which promises to be even worse than last winter's, is a blessing in disguise or the worst thing that could have happened.

In the event, it turned out to be a bit of both. For the residents of villages like Muchelney, Thorney, Moorland and Northmoor Green, either cut off or flooded out as they were, it was indeed a nightmare, which brought the world's media rushing to Somerset – where they made the excellent King Alfred at Burrowbridge their unofficial headquarters.

Langport escaped being flooded by about six inches, which was just as well because the town is below the level of the river and the ancient pump that saved Langport back in 1960 is no longer even theoretically functional. When my mother had moved into her house on the riverbank back in 2002 and was alarmed to find the land on the far side of the river under several feet of water, I'd reassured her that the height of the respective banks meant that the moors to the south of the river would have to fill up with floodwater to a depth of ten feet for as far as the eye could see before her side of the river flooded. In the winter of 2014 that happened, but fortunately only just.

But it did, as I'd hoped, serve to focus attention – most of it critical – on the state of the rivers. I'd bumped into the government minister responsible, Owen Paterson, at the Oxford Farming Conference, and lobbied him hard about dredging. Not long afterwards I spotted the junior minister responsible, Dan Rogerson, at a cider reception in the House of Commons and rather spoilt his enjoyment of a glass of Sheppy's by having a good go at him as well, following up with a letter in my capacity as Chairman of the SWMP which was released to the press and earned me an interview on national television.

The following day I had a call from Edwin White who, as Chairman of the Bath and West, had been leading a Somerset Levels Relief Fund to raise money to pay for essential dredging, in the absence of Government funding. He said that he'd been in touch with his friend Christopher Booker, the Sunday Telegraph journalist and one-time 'Muckspreader' in Private Eye, on the subject of dredging and that Booker had in turn been in touch with his friend, Owen Paterson. The outcome was that Owen Paterson would be coming to Bridgwater on the following evening, Sunday January 26, to put a 'proposal' to a group of the main players, myself included.

Paterson was late and in a bad mood, and the meeting was fairly chaotic. A puffed-up Ian Liddell-Grainger, the local MP, was there, together with Alan Lovell, Chairman of the EA's Regional Flood Defence Committee and a thoroughly sensible man, Ray Adlam, who farms at Westhay and has been involved in Levels drainage and politics for even longer than I have, Kerry Rickards, the Sedgemoor Chief Executive, who had taken the bold step of declaring a 'major incident' the previous week, Nick Gupta, the local boss of the EA, and Edwin White. (Note: no-one from the County Council – noses seriously out of joint!)

After a great deal of inconsequential toing and froing, Owen Paterson offered us a deal: serious money for dredging and the green light for a Somerset Rivers Authority, in return for a locally organised and funded all-embracing plan designed to prevent a recurrence of the present situation. We shook hands.

I was involved in the drafting of the plan and all of the politicking which surrounded it. Through my contacts at the Duchy of Cornwall, I was able to get a briefing paper to the Prince of Wales when he visited Muchelney and the other flooded villages in early February. Judging by the conversation I had with him at Stoke St Gregory village hall, he'd taken it all in!

I also met the Prime Minister, David Cameron, when he paid us a visit, pleading with him to allow Somerset to raise a special rate so as to fund the new authority that was proposed. He took the point, and all sorts of promises have been made subsequently, but the issue of long-term funding remains unresolved. Still we did eventually get a Twenty Year Flood Action Plan, and the Somerset Rivers Authority and the rivers were indeed dredged. There hasn't, touch wood, been a serious flood since.

Apart from my Chairmanship of the SWMP, my other locus in all this was as chairman of something called the Levels and Moors Task Force. This had come out of the work of the SWMP, consisted of representatives of all the relevant agencies and interests, and was charged with producing a 'Twenty Year Vision' for the future of the area.

We had the blessing of the Defra Minister concerned, Richard Benyon, plus a modest amount of financial support to pay for a secretariat. It was something I was happy to do, not least because I believed passionately in the cause. Our meetings were amicable and constructive. I could sense the underlying tension between the 'let nature take its course' brigade and those, like me, who believed that intelligent management was the key, but the timing was propitious. The floods of 2012-14 had given everyone the chance to see what a largely unmanaged outcome would look like, and it hadn't been a pretty sight from any perspective.

I was determined that our 'vision' should not be seen as one dreamt up by a bunch of outsiders, seeking to impose their own agendas on the area. So when we'd agreed a draft, I sent it out by email to every Parish Council on the Levels and Moors, asking either for their comments or, preferably, endorsement. I can't say that we had a huge response. What I can say – and this is hugely important in the context of the various attempts that have subsequently been made to revisit or re-imagine the 'vision' (invariably from the perspective of a sectional interest) – is that it does have the buy-in of the people who matter most, the people who actually live and work in the Levels and Moors, through their elected representatives. It is also, I am happy to say, embedded in the Twenty Year Action Plan.

The other thing I was determined about was that it should be as jargon-free as possible and should not extend to more than a single sheet of A4 paper. We adopted it unanimously at a meeting at the Environment Agency in Bridgwater. I had a stinking cold and was feeling lousy, but I went home that day in high spirits. It wasn't entirely as I would have written it (I would have added an objective of excluding wind turbines, solar panels, new pylons and other landscape-damaging hardware!), but it seemed to me to represent a fair consensus to which everyone concerned can work.

I'll include it in full in an appendix. Suffice to say here that it is indeed based on land and water management to achieve the outcomes that we want. What must always be remembered in considering the Levels and Moors is that this is almost entirely a man-made landscape. It has acquired its rich and distinctive landscape and biodiversity because of the way it has been farmed over the centuries. It is thus, perhaps to a greater extent than anywhere else in Britain, a *cultural* landscape, as opposed to a natural one, and must be managed accordingly to protect this rare and special quality.

There is, of course, room for nature reserves, like those on West Sedgemoor, Ham Wall and the Avalon Lakes, and very wonderful they are too. There is room as well for what you might call high-water-level farming, such as was encouraged under the ESA Tier 3 and, more recently, with Higher Level Stewardship. But for the vast majority of the area, the objective must be for it to be farmed, but farmed in the right way – in the ways that helped create all that supposedly 'natural' interest in the first place.

That, of course, was what the ESA sought to achieve, with a fair degree of success. Since it was scrapped in 2006 we have been going backwards. As I look out of my study window across Huish Level, I see weed-infested pastures, over-grown, un-pollarded willows and choked ditches. The Red Ruby Devon cattle which were once finished long and slow on the Levels' rich pastures in their thousands are long gone, driven off by the 'thirty-month rule'. Back in the early 2000s I did try to interest our local meat-processing plant in marketing what I was going to call 'Slow Beef' – native-bred bullocks like Devons, Herefords and Angus, fattened off grass for two winters and three summers in traditional Levels fashion. It would be some of the finest beef in the world and might bring back to the Levels the numbers of cattle that the area so desperately needs. But nothing came of it.

Mind you, we're better off here than in some part of the Levels. Large areas of the peatland in the Brue Valley are now given over to maize which, with its associated herbicide regime and damage to soil structure, is just about the most environmentally unfriendly crop known to man. Under the ESA, the farmers – many of them older, and semi-retired – were quite happy to pocket their modest payments and let the grass out for seasonal grazing. Now that option has gone, they can hardly be blamed for taking the money on offer for a bit of maize ground, linked to an AD plant.

I wish I could say that all of this is going to be changed for the better under the Government's new Environmental Land Management Scheme (ELMS), but I very much doubt if it will. So-called renewable energy trumps landscape protection every time, and all the environmental groups seem to be interested in are lavish projects designed to 'enhance' or 're-create', which involve piling large amounts of money on small areas of land, usually to no worthwhile effect.

When it comes to environmental schemes, the old saying applies: "Money is like muck – no good unless it be spread." I daresay that if the new scheme were to include an incentive for pollarding the willows, there would be an outcry. It seems that no-one dares cut down a single tree these days, for fear of falling foul of the green brigade, with the result that the countryside is becoming horribly overgrown, the Levels and Moors included.

It would be wrong to conclude from all of this that nothing has been achieved in the last twenty years. The rivers are a lot cleaner than they were, and the key stretches have been dredged. The Somerset Rivers Authority has also done a good job in increasing the capacity of the Sowy River, to take pressure off the Parrett. And run-off and soil erosion in the upper catchment would certainly be even worse but for the work done by the PCP and which is now continuing under the aegis of Defra's Catchment Sensitive Farming initiative and FWAG. Numbers of breeding waders are beginning to recover, albeit mostly in the various nature reserves, and the re-introduction of species like the cranes and bustards has been a great success.

But as I sit here and look out across the Parrett to the moors beyond, I honestly could not say that the Levels are in a better state from any perspective than they were twenty years ago. The classic Levels landscape of the green gridiron of fields and ditches, accentuated with pollarded willows, is becoming scruffy and overgrown. The fields have a splashier, rushier, scrubbier look to them than they once had. In the wetter areas, the grazed marsh is reverting to ungrazed swamp.

Our Vision for the Levels and Moors in 2030, of 'a thriving, nature-rich wetland landscape, with grassland farming taking place on the majority of the land' is a long way from becoming reality.

24

Dartmoor

Dartmoor was a looming presence – the backdrop to my life – throughout childhood. Sparkwell is just outside the National Park, but it was only a short walk up the hill to the china clay works on Smallhanger Down, and there were regular trips to Harford Moor or Cadover Bridge. My father was always promising to take us to the fabled spot called Hawns and Dendles, but we never quite made it. I've still never been there.

When we lived at Derriford on the edge of Plymouth, we only had to walk a few hundred yards up the Tavistock road, and a view opened up of a great swathe of southern Dartmoor, from the moor above Shaugh Prior, with Sheepstor beyond, westward to the two tors topped with masts, Sharpitor (its radio mast long gone now) and North Hessary Tor. I have already recalled the train journeys which Chippy and I would take up the old Southern region main line to Bridestowe and so out onto the moor, and there were bus trips as well, sometimes on the Western National number 83, to Grenofen Bridge, where we would swim in the river Walkham.

Proximity to Dartmoor was the main attraction of the move to Dousland after my parents' divorce in 1964. I'm sure that my mother would have preferred somewhere nearer Plympton, where she was teaching in the grammar school, but the pair of us – for Chippy enjoyed the moor almost as much as I did – talked her into it. Our bungalow was just one field away from Yennadon Down and less than a mile from Burrator reservoir.

Mother was great friends with Elizabeth Hopson, a famed election agent for the Liberal party, who lived at Sheepstor with husband Bill and children Sybil and Stephen. Chippy and I would meet up with Steve and go in search of mortar bomb cases (as we imagined them to be) and other military litter left behind by the soldiers who used the moor and conifer plantations around Burrator for training.

We once came across a cache of at least 50 rounds of live .303 ammunition, which we bore triumphantly home, much to my mother's horror. On other days we would walk to the Devonport Leat under Leather Tor and spend hours having what we called 'boat races' – Pooh Sticks, as they tend to be known these days – using carefully selected twigs of bracken as our craft. Crazywell Pool was another favourite destination, although we could never quite bring ourselves to swim in its fabled, murky depths.

If Chippy was otherwise occupied, I was quite happy going for walks on my own, with just our mongrel dog Penny for company. We might go up the old railway line to the granite quarries at King Tor, or out past Sheepstor to the abandoned farmhouse at Ditsworthy Warren and the long stone rows stretching out across the moor at Drizzlecombe. There were ruined farmhouses around Burrator as well, presumably abandoned when the valley was flooded to create the reservoir in the 1890s. They could be just a little bit frightening.

The longest walk I went on by myself was from Okehampton, which I reached by the early train, back home to Dousland, via Yes Tor and High Willhays (Dartmoor's highest point), Cranmere Pool, Two Bridges, Princetown and Walkhampton common. I always felt slightly apprehensive on the night before a long walk on the moor, but once I was out there I revelled in the freedom and aloneness and that sweet moorland smell, never sweeter than in a thick Dartmoor drizzle.

We only had one bad experience with the dreaded Dartmoor fogs, and that was when we were out on the Southern blanket bog, trying to find the Abbot's Way, somewhere near Crane Hill. It is a bleak, boggy, featureless stretch of moorland, which we didn't know at all well. When the fog came down we could see barely ten yards ahead of us, but we remembered the advice of the greatest of all Dartmoor walkers, William Crossing, whose 'Guide to Dartmoor' was our bible, on what to do in a dense fog: find a stream and follow it in the direction it is flowing; sooner or later you will get off the moor. We found a stream sure enough, hoping that it was the beginnings of the river Plym which would take us in more or less the right direction for home. It wasn't. It was a tributary of the Erme and, when we finally emerged from the murk, we found ourselves somewhere near Piles Copse, far from home and miles off course. It was a weary trudge back to the phone box at Cornwood, from where we were eventually rescued by our worried mother.

In my NFU career I didn't really get involved with Dartmoor until we were regionalised in 1989 and I started to take meetings of the Dartmoor Hill Farming Committee and attend the Dartmoor Commoners' Council meetings as an observer. John Hodge, whose farm above Okehampton I had first visited in the wake of the 1978 blizzard, was the main man in both

– delegate to HQ Hill Farming Committee and Chairman of the Council. He was – still is, I'm glad to say – one of the best farmers on the moor, with a particularly fine flock of Scotch Blackface sheep, but in those days he had the reputation of being shrewd, perhaps even a little bit cunning, politically astute and single-minded, all qualities that come in very handy if you're trying to navigate a course between the whirlpools and reefs of Dartmoor farming politics!

On Dartmoor there hadn't been anything like the conflict that had been seen on Exmoor during the 1970s. The scope for reclamation was much more limited, and most of what could be ploughed up and put down to grass, mainly around Princetown, had been. The big bone of contention on Dartmoor was common rights. Historically the number of grazing rights a commoner could exercise was based on 'levancy and couchancy', that is to say the number of animals he or she could pasture and/or feed and house on the home farm during the winter months.

In the run up to the 1965 Commons Registration Act the NFU recommended one livestock unit (one cow or five sheep) per acre of 'in-bye land' (enclosed fields, usually around the farm), which was generous to be sure but not unreasonable. In practice, however, the commissioners appointed to oversee the registration process simply accepted the numbers that were claimed, unless someone objected, which only rarely happened. This led to absurd situations such as that on one of the Widecombe Commons, Jordan Manor, where the number of registered rights worked out at over seven livestock units per hectare. That is roughly 30 times what would be a realistic carrying capacity.

The sharper, larger graziers soon twigged what was going on and claimed every right they could, very often registering an already inflated number of rights on several different commons. These 'robber barons', as I tended to think of them, were much the most difficult group to deal with when it came to the ESA negotiations.

There was supposed to have been a second piece of commons legislation, which would have regulated how the rights which had been registered could be exercised. But for various reasons that never materialised, with the result that the commoners who had been honest had lost out, and those who had simply thought of a number and doubled it were prospering mightily. In order to bring some order to this unsatisfactory state of affairs, the NFU and the commoners, with considerable support from the MP for Totnes, Anthony Steen, decided that what was needed was a Dartmoor Commoners Council, set up by Act of Parliament, to give it real teeth. In 1985, after encountering all sorts of difficulties along the way, that eventually materialised.

I always enjoyed the meetings of the Commoners Council, although it did seem singularly ineffective when it came to controlling the regular offenders, who would graze more animals than they were entitled to or allow them to stray onto someone else's patch. The fact that the custom on Dartmoor was for the commoners to be expected to 'defend their common' from strays, didn't help matters. John Hodge, as Chairman, with Russell Woolcock, a well-known Tavistock auctioneer as his Secretary, did their best, but not always to much effect. A typical exchange might go something like this:

> *Commoner from the floor: "Mr Chairman, I'm sorry to say that, despite what we agreed at the last meeting, Mr So-and-So's ewes are still on our common, where they've no right to be. This has been going on for years. What are you going to do about it?"*
>
> *Chairman: "Russell, did you write a letter?"*
>
> *Secretary: "Mr Chairman, I did."*
>
> *Chairman: "Well, Russell, you'd better write them another letter."*

And so it would go on.

In 1994 Dartmoor was given Environmentally Sensitive Area (ESA) status. The farmers were wary after their battles with Dartmoor conservationists like Lady Sayer in the past, but take-up on the 'in-bye' land gradually picked up. The biggest environmental problem was reckoned to be over-stocking, driven by a system of headage payments which meant that the more sheep and cattle a farmer grazed, the more subsidy he received.

An individual farmer might decide that the ESA payment was sufficient to compensate him for cutting back. But what about the commons, which occupy some two thirds of Dartmoor's total area, and on each of which scores of commoners might enjoy the right to graze? Most, if not all, would need either to reduce stock numbers or not to graze at all. How on earth were agreements to be negotiated on that basis, given the rivalries and blood feuds that existed on virtually every common?

Loving Dartmoor as I do, and relishing a challenge, I made up my mind that, if anyone should ever ask me to become involved in facilitating an ESA for a Dartmoor common, I would at least have a crack at it. Besides, there was big money at stake. The Forest of Dartmoor and the surrounding 'Commons of Devon', as they are known, cover some 36,000 hectares. At a compensation rate which, including various top-ups, could be as high as

£85 per hectare, that meant that there was a potential £3 million a year available to help the farmers of Dartmoor, many of whom were struggling. And, we assumed, it would be good for the environment of the moor as well.

Sure enough, about three years later, I was asked to facilitate an agreement for Easdon, a small common not far from Moretonhampstead. The commission proved every bit as challenging as I had anticipated. We held various meetings, from which anything but a consensus emerged. The small graziers mistrusted the larger ones, the non-graziers resented the graziers (and vice versa), everyone mistrusted the owners, and they didn't much take to me!

At the heart of my problems was the fact that even though a commoner might be perfectly happy with what he as an individual was being offered, if someone else was getting more than he was reckoned to deserve, the deal was off, even if that meant that no-one would get any money – which in the end was precisely what happened on Easdon!

My next commission, at Gidleigh in 1997, had a happier outcome. In the course of it we developed an approach that became a model for many other commons across the moor. At the heart of it was a balance: between compensating the minority of farmers who were required to de-stock the common (because without their consent there could be no agreement) and rewarding the majority of non-graziers, because without their forbearance in not stocking the moor an ESA could never even have been contemplated.

The process went something like this. After being invited by the Chairman of the relevant Commons Association to get involved, we would call an initial meeting of all commoners, at which I would explain how an agreement would be constructed: a flat-rate payment for each paid-up but not used grazing right; 10% to the commons owners (who were the Duchy of Cornwall for the Forest of Dartmoor but mostly private landlords for the peripheral 'manor commons'); a payment per livestock unit for stock removal, plus something for shepherding, administration and maybe ponies. Most of the money went, quite rightly, towards stock removal, each payment being based on the difference between the numbers which had been grazed on the common in the year prior to the ESA agreement and the reduced numbers allowed.

I would then arrange to meet all of the active graziers individually on their farms, to agree past and future numbers of livestock, and would construct a draft agreement on the basis of that, and then put it to a further meeting of the commoners to seek their approval. Sounds straightforward, doesn't it? I can assure you that it was anything but. With some commons – Brent stands out, and Widecombe and, most of all, the 11,000-hectare Forest, with its hundreds of graziers – one needed the skin of a rhinoceros, the patience of a saint and the negotiating skills that George Mitchell displayed in the Northern Ireland peace talks to achieve the necessary consensus.

It took the average Dartmoor farmer about a nanosecond to realise that the bigger the difference between past and future stocking levels he (and they were usually, but not always, male) could show, the bigger the cheque he would get. Obviously he wanted to be able to graze as many sheep and cattle as possible under the ESA so the tendency was to inflate previous numbers. I, of course, had no way of knowing how accurate the figures were that I was being given. But the other graziers did, and they didn't hold back when it came to saying so. It would usually take several meetings and umpteen telephone calls to arrive at a workable plan, and even then there were always second thoughts and grumbles.

I would always finish what I took to be the final meeting of the Commons Association by saying something like: "Right now. You know what your stocking was and will be, and you know what every other grazier's is. So if you're not happy, say so now, or forever hold your peace." An uncomfortable silence and much shuffling of feet would ensue, after which we would repair to the pub for a much-needed pint.

But you could be quite certain that, the next morning, I would have one or more of the graziers on the phone saying something like "You know those figures old Reg was claiming;? Well, they'm a complete fiction. Didn't like to say so at the time."

Much the biggest challenge was the Forest of Dartmoor, all 11,000 hectares of it. It had never in at least the previous 2,000 years been a 'forest' in the sense of being covered in trees but was the last remnant of the royal hunting forest which the whole of Dartmoor (and much of Devon) had been back in Saxon and Norman times and it was still effectively owned by the crown, through the Duchy of Cornwall.

Historically commons neighbouring the Forest could pay to exercise what were called 'venville' rights on the Forest, alongside the tenants of the Duchy farms. The Dartmoor Commoners Council, in its wisdom, had decided to convert these venville rights into registered grazing rights by doubling the rights on the home common so that, if a commoner had, for example, 500 rights on Okehampton common, he or she would be awarded

500 rights on the Forest. This, despite the fact that historically a grazier's rights, based on his home farm, could be exercised either on the home common or the Forest, but not on both simultaneously.

The fact that, through an accident of history in 1505, when for whatever reason, the commoners of Ugborough, Harford and Brent had failed to pay for their venville rights and had been excluded ever since, only compounded the unsatisfactory nature of the position. Anyway, the result was that thousands of rights were registered on the Forest by hundreds of graziers and non-graziers alike and would have to be taken into account in the ESA process. This was hideously complicated, sometimes bad-tempered, to the extent that two graziers came to blows in a pub car park and, if it hadn't have been for Anton Coaker, Mike Spry and their colleagues on the Forest of Dartmoor Commoners' Association Committee, we would never have got there. But with £1.1 million a year up for grabs, all the effort was worth it.

Still, I enjoyed the challenge and, being reasonably numerate, I enjoyed working out who would get what, how many sheep and cattle they could graze and when. The experience, both at the meetings and especially on the farms, also gave me a much deeper insight into what it means to be a farmer on Dartmoor. I was struck by the simplicity of farmhouses, farmhouse kitchens, farmyards, farming systems, as much as by anything, and by some of the eccentricities which a lonely life on the moor tends to breed. I think of the two brothers who hadn't spoken to each other for twenty years and who would only address each other using me as an intermediary.

"Mr Gibson, I would be grateful if you could tell my brother" (standing in the opposite corner of the village hall) "that the stock numbers he's claiming are a load of rubbish."

"Mr Gibson," the other brother would reply, "you can tell my brother that it's him that's talking rubbish."

Then there was the millionaire farmer (who purported to despise the ESA and everything to do with it) whom I found living in dusty squalor. We discussed the finer points of his stocking regime, and the deadly feud he was engaged in with his uncle, surrounded by piles of decades-old Farmers Weeklies, wearing Barbour jackets as it was freezing cold and he hadn't bothered with any heating.

One quite substantial common, with over £100,000 at stake, had only four active graziers, each of whom cordially loathed all the others. I spent a grim winter's afternoon with them in a cold village hall. One conversed only in grunts. Two of the others were from families that had been at war with each other since the sixteenth century, and neither was giving an inch. After about two hours I thought I'd almost got there, when the younger of the two protagonists, who we'll call Ronald, remembered something.

"Oh, Mr Gibson," he said. "I almost forgot. There's those 100 or so Scotch yaws (Dartmoor for ewes) that I graze up beyond Whitelake. We'll have to count they."

"Scotch yaws above Whitelake!?" exclaimed the other grazier, who we'll call Arthur, disbelievingly. "I was up Whitelake the other day and I surenuff didn't see any Scotch yaws. So where be they now?" he added with a note of challenge in his voice.

A shadow seemed to pass over Ronald's brow. Then his eyes lit up.

"I couldn't rightly say where they be now, Arthur. But I can tell 'e one thing – they'll be back!"

All told, between 1997 and 2004, I helped to negotiate 19 ESA agreements for Dartmoor Commons, worth a total of £2.3 million a year to the commoners, or £23 million over the ten-year life span of the agreements. That is not to say that these agreements would not have been concluded without my efforts; I've no doubt that the local land agency fraternity would have been only too happy to step into the breach and would have charged accordingly. I did it for nothing more than the job satisfaction it provided, and the outcomes usually were satisfying, even if the process could be tortuous and frustrating.

I saw myself as an honest broker, doing my best for NFU members and non-members alike, and for the greater good of Dartmoor itself. Whether the hundreds of hours that I devoted to it really represented a worthwhile use of my time, it would be for others to judge. In my defence I would point out that the vast majority of the meetings were in the evenings. There were months on end – the autumn of 2000, for example, when my brother was dying of cancer – when I would be on Dartmoor three evenings a week, trying to knock heads together in some remote village hall, and it is a long way back from Cornwood to Langport at 10 o'clock at night, especially if your carefully crafted agreement has just been torn to pieces and it's back to the drawing board.

I don't doubt that the commoners were grateful for the compensation cheques, and that £23 million over ten years must have made at least a small difference for the better to the Dartmoor economy, even if the net benefit, after allowing for the impact of de-stocking, must have been substantially less. Whether the ESA was good for Dartmoor is another matter altogether.

We in the NFU had always said that the ESA stocking levels, based as they were on research in the Lake District, were too low, and that they risked the commons becoming overgrown with bracken, gorse and scrub. And so it proved, particularly on the relatively favoured commons on the south of the moor.

Historically, before the import of hardy Scotch sheep and Galloway cattle in the nineteenth century, Dartmoor would be almost empty of stock during the winter. The farms on the edge of the common might turn out a few Whiteface sheep or South Devon cattle for some exercise and a bit of grazing between November and April, but that would be about it. In the summer, by contrast, the moor would be thick with cattle and sheep. Up until that 1965 Act, farmers in every parish in Devon, barring Totnes and Barnstaple, enjoyed the right to turn animals out onto the moor during the summer. And in dry summers, when Dartmoor was the greenest place in Devon, cattle would be driven from as far afield as Kent and Sussex to take advantage of the 'free' grazing available on the moor, helping to keep the gorse, bracken and Molinia grass down in the process and creating the Dartmoor eco-system that the ESA was supposed to restore.

But I'm afraid that the old pattern of grazing – light in the winter, heavy in the summer – is not replicable. It suits the moorland farmers to keep their herds and flocks much the same size all the year round. And farmers off the moor have lost the right to graze, even if it was a realistic proposition under present rules and regulations to drive or truck cattle and sheep many miles to be let out on a Dartmoor common, which it certainly is not. Maybe something intelligent and effective will come of the Government's new Environmental Land Management Scheme (ELMS). But then again, maybe not.

I still love Dartmoor and still walk there whenever I can, seeking out the wilder, more remote stretches of moorland, where you're less likely to encounter other walkers, as, for me, solitude is such an important part of the experience. The family connection to the moor has been maintained, as well. My elder daughter, Joanna, now lives at Ilsington, just below Haytor, with her husband Phil and daughters Hermione and Darcy. They all love the moor as well. There's nowhere quite like it.

25

Why farming matters

I wasn't entirely surprised when Richard Macdonald asked me to "stand in" as Director of Communications, and I did rather enjoy the irony of being asked to help steady the ship after all the times that Richard had advised me to "steady on, Ant" when I'd been in 'wild man of the west' mode. The possibility had been mooted several times before, and in the early 1980s, when Richard Maslen had decided he'd had enough, I did actually apply for the job, only to be beaten by Warren Newman, who knew plenty about corporate PR but nothing about farming and who didn't last long.

I got my revenge on Warren Newman by regaling my Western Daily Press readers with the story of how he'd spent thousands of pounds on an NFU hot air balloon to take to the skies over the Royal Show. He had been disappointed by the lack of response and perked up when a red-faced farmer arrived on the NFU stand and asked, "Is that balloon your doing?" Well, yes it is, replied Warren, with all due modesty. "In that case you can expect to hear from my lawyers," exploded the farmer. "It's spooked a bunch of my heifers, and they've gone crashing through a barbed wire fence and cut themselves to ribbons." It nearly got me the sack, but it was worth it!

That apart, I hadn't found the prospect particularly appealing. As Regional Director I was reasonably well-paid, and the salary on offer for moving to HQ was never enough to cover the cost of renting a flat in London to live in during the week, as there was certainly no way I was going to move permanently away from my beloved West Country.

This time it was different. I would be working from Stoneleigh, not London, and a flat in Kenilworth or Warwick would be affordable. Besides, after nearly 14 highly eventful and demanding years as Regional Director, a change might be as good as a rest. I told Richard I would think about it, but confided to my diary that 'the more I think about it, the more appealing a prospect it seems. I am growing stale and weary in my present job and the prospect of Haddock as regional chairman is appalling. I could probably do the job reasonably well, and if I can't, I can always retire.'

The existing Director of Communications, whom it seemed I might supplant, was Rachel Oliver, a forthright, feisty character, who had twice come close to winning Totnes for the Liberal Democrats, earning herself some ageist-related national headlines when she described her Tory opponent, Anthony Steen, as a "white-haired, burnt-out, old man". I knew her a bit, not least because she had been given the task of 'coaching' me for my aborted Lib Dem candidacy, but she was more a friend of my mother's. Anyway, she was (is) bright, articulate, opinionated and outspoken, and she went at her job with the NFU like a bull at a gate.

Fatally, however, she over-estimated the capacity of the NFU hierarchy for accepting uncomfortable truths, as well as their willingness to focus on getting the message right for opinion-formers and the general public, even if it might not go down too well with the membership.

She wasn't helped by the fact that her appointment coincided with the NFU's move from London to Stoneleigh, involving the loss of many experienced members of staff. Her team was therefore almost entirely new and had little or no experience of working for a complicated and demanding membership organisation like the NFU, in which the default reaction, whenever farming got a bad press – and we were getting a lot of bad press at around that time – was to blame the Public Affairs department. Nor was her front man as President, an intelligent but unassuming first-generation livestock farmer from South Wales, Tim Bennett, the most charismatic leader that the NFU had ever had. Anyway, I gathered that, rightly or wrongly, Rachel was on her way out and that, if I took the job, I would be inheriting a fairly dispirited team who had a lot to learn about the ways of the NFU.

It is probably worth saying at this stage that, as with all things I've done in my life, I had never had any training or obtained any qualifications in PR. A history degree trains you for nothing but equips you for just about anything. So, from the time when I was made Deputy Press Officer in Knightsbridge in 1974, I'd just picked it up as I'd gone along, learning from the people around me and often from my own mistakes.

I have always been reasonably good with words and have always got on well with the journalists I've come into contact with. My two golden rules were: always try to be helpful, and never say 'no comment'. Ironically the other useful asset that I enjoyed was my lack of any significant farming background. It meant that I could see farmers as others see them, and shape the message accordingly, always with at least half an eye on how it would go down with the membership because, if you lost them, you wouldn't last long. So I developed a technique in which the substance of the message took care of the first part of that aspiration, while the tone looked after the second.

If Rachel was unlucky in the Presidential material with which she had to work, then I was the complete opposite. The coming man in the upper reaches of the NFU was Peter Kendall, a 45-year-old, hard-driving, fast-talking, hyperactive arable farmer from Bedfordshire. I bumped into him in early January 2006 as he was bouncing down the High during the Oxford Farming Conference , which I went to every year, mainly so I could stay in the guest room at Queen's. "I gather you're coming to sort out our PR," he said breezily. "Look forward to working with you." And with that, he was gone.

At that stage, neither his ascendancy to the Presidency nor mine to Director of Comms had been nailed down. But he duly got the better of Tim Bennett in the elections and, after a distinctly informal 'interview' in the Fleece at Cirencester, in which I made it quite clear that I was not looking to be any sort of front man, I duly got the job.

I arrived at the NFU's smart new HQ on the morning of Monday March 20, weary after a largely sleepless night and long journey, and distinctly apprehensive. But there was to be no gentle induction phase. I was straight in at the deep end:

> *Richard (Macdonald, the Director General) appeared, to whisk me into the Heads of Department meeting, followed by a sugar meeting, followed by an office-holders' meeting, interspersed with meetings with Sarah Whitelock (my right-hand woman). It was a case of – one minute new boy at school; the next, in the eye of the storm.*

A couple of weeks later, as I was just about to take Claire out to supper to celebrate moving into my spacious but rather soulless flat in Kenilworth, my mobile phone rang. It was Richard, to inform me that the H5N1 strain of bird 'flu, which had been causing concern in eastern Europe and Asia, had arrived in Britain, in the shape of a dead Scottish swan. There was evidence that humans might contract the disease, possibly sparking a pandemic. The media would be all over the story like a rash.

I had my first major crisis on my hands. Animal disease seemed to be stalking my career like Banquo's ghost. By the time we reached the restaurant, the story had broken. I spent 45 minutes on my phone in the street outside, lining up poultry farming interviewees for ITV News at Ten and the BBC's Newsnight. It was the start of a hectic few days, but by the end of the week I was able to conclude that 'the week's events may not have been a triumph for the NFU's new Director of Comms, but nor have they been a disaster either.'

However, if truth be told, the first few months in my new job were anything but happy ones. I seemed to be spending far too much time correcting mistakes in spelling and grammar in the stuff we were putting out, even to the extent of having to re-write entire press releases. Our website needed a lot of work and in the meantime, despite Helen Cotterell's best efforts, was generating a constant, irritating litany of complaints, and I could sense the resentment amongst my team at being taught old tricks by an old dog up from the sticks.

Worse still, I didn't feel I had the confidence of the President. I suspected that, like many a President before him, he was looking for a flashier, whizzier, more Madison Avenue-style Director of Comms than dyed-in-the-NFU-wool Gibbo. Sure enough, a couple of months in, Richard Mac confided in me that "Peter's looking to bring in some big names from outside on the policy side."

Guy Smith, the abrasive Essex farmer who chaired the NFU's 'Communications Group' (and would go on to be a very effective Deputy President), didn't seem to think much of me either. And, just to put the tin lid on things, I was becoming an insomniac, not just on Sunday nights but during the week as well. By the end of May I had decided that I hated being away from my team in the South-West, hated weekly commuting, hated my flat in Kenilworth and hated my job.

After that low point things gradually improved. At the start of 2006 both farming and the NFU were at a low ebb. Farm incomes were recovering only slowly, particularly on livestock and dairy farms, the introduction of the 'single payment scheme' had been a fiasco, milk prices were on the way down and the TB situation was so bad that the Government was on the point of introducing pre-movement cattle testing. And then on top of that came bird 'flu. Margaret Beckett didn't much like the NFU and had shown no real enthusiasm for her job at Defra, and her replacement, that June, by David Miliband, who knew nothing about farming, suggested that the Defra Secretary of State-ship was just being used as sort of railway siding, where politicians on the way up could be parked for a time whilst awaiting a better opportunity.

At the Treasury Gordon Brown was making no secret of his hostility to the CAP and his belief that there was little point in supporting domestic agriculture when food could be imported cheaply from around the world. Food production was increasingly being seen as merely a rather inconvenient by-product of an industry that ought to be focused on environmental management. Not a week would go past without one or other of the broadcasters or newspapers unearthing yet another health scare linked to food. Morale among farmers and in the NFU was at rock bottom.

The great consolation of all this was that the only way was up! The advent of a dynamic, personable, articulate, up-beat President in Peter Kendall seemed to me to point the way forward. "What we need is a proper strategy," Guy Smith kept insisting. So I devised one. It would be based on re-establishing the economic and environmental case for a thriving, productive farming and food sector; explaining to the chattering classes who seemed to have written British agriculture off why the industry still had a vital role to play in our national life; in other words, 'Why Farming Matters'.

We would not, as so often in the past, be holding out the begging bowl for an industry in distress. We would be making the case not from the farmer's perspective but from that of the national interest. A successful campaign on this basis would, it seemed to me, provide the all-important under-pinning rationale for politicians to be helpful, as well as another reason for consumers to buy British food.

The original concept was for the campaign to be broken down into a series of themes: 'why farming matters to the economy', for example, or 'why farming matters to the countryside'. But when I presented my ideas to a management meeting on July 14, Malcolm Thomas, Director of NFU Wales, a gruff-voiced boyo who looked as if he might have played flanker for Neath, stood up to say: "You're over-complicating things. Keep it simple. It should be just 'Why Farming Matters'."

I saw immediately that he was right, and that is what the campaign became. He also said that, since I had taken over, the standard of NFU communications had improved beyond all knowledge. What with that, and the fact the June meeting of the NFU's ruling Council had, for the first time in years, passed without anyone criticising the Public Affairs Department, I felt that I was finally earning some credibility in my new role. In September my appointment was made permanent, on generous terms, and I moved into a snug little barn conversion, out in the country near Rowington.

'Why Farming Matters' was not exactly the sort of sexy theme that Peter Kendall had doubtless had in mind when thinking about our communications strategy. It was old-school NFU, and it was carried through in old-school ways: leaflets, posters, car-stickers, even beer mats, as well as an authoritative report for the consumption of MPs and opinion-formers. I had run much the same sort of thing as South-West Regional Information Officer back in 1980 with 'Farming, the Heart of the West Country'.

But it was a clear, simple and above-all outward looking message, and it did its job. In that, I had much to thank Peter Kendall for. Like all NFU leaders down the years, his natural instinct when things weren't going well was to blame the Government (or Europe) and ask for more money and support. But we knew from the opinion sampling that had been done in Rachel Oliver's time and previously, that whingeing played badly with a British public who had plenty of problems of their own to contend with (and would have many more, come the 2008 banking crash). So my advice to Peter was to be "relentlessly positive" and, for most of the time, he was.

Peter Kendall was, at once, an inspiring man to work with and a difficult one. He delivered our messages – about the value of productive farming, or the potential of 'sustainable intensification', or the role that farmers could play in renewable energy production – with energy and conviction. He was the ideal front man at a time when British agriculture and the NFU were trying to pick themselves up off the floor and convince Government and country that the industry had a bright future. He was about as far from the "'idn no future in farming, we'm all buggered" school of thought that I was used to encountering at NFU branch meetings in the West Country as could be imagined.

Besides his energy, which appeared to be boundless, he also had a lively, fertile mind, and the combination of the two could make life challenging. He liked to get up at 5.30 in the morning and get stuck into his e-mails. By 8 o'clock he would be on the road – and on the car-phone to me. He had usually had about six bright ideas overnight, as to what we should be doing or who we should be talking to in order to get our message across. Over time I learned to say that I would consider and consult and get back to him a bit later. By the time he came striding into the office (which wasn't that often, in any case) he had usually forgotten about all but maybe one of his bright ideas, so we would get to work on that.

The directors' and office-holders' suite, on the ground floor of our spacious and stylish new headquarters in its parkland setting, had something of the atmosphere of a rugby club about it. Martin Haworth, our insouciant Director of Policy, had played in the centre for Oxford, Richard Macdonald claimed to have played a starring role for Richmond, Meurig Raymond, the Deputy President and a lovely man, was a dedicated follower of Welsh rugby while our President was still occasionally turning out for his local veterans side. Office-holder meetings always had a distinct whiff of testosterone about them.

Peter was also a great swearer, regardless of who his audience might be, something I wasn't at all used to, especially in front of female members of staff. On one occasion he reduced a joint NFU/RSPB conference to an embarrassed silence when he told a joke about the little girl who had asked her farmer father if she could dispatch a magpie caught in a Larsen trap. When he gave his assent, she did just that, with a cry of "Take that, you fucker!"

But the office-holder secretarial team didn't seem to mind all the effing and blinding too much. They were a lovely bunch of ladies, who worked opposite the door to my office and who rather took me under their collective wing. Nicky Edwards (now Sawdon) looked after the President as best she could, Gill Thompson ministered to Meurig and the Vice-President Paul Temple, Kate Sargeson (now Walters) was Richard Mac's PA, while Jeanette Clarke, a wonderfully calm and efficient presence, looked after me superbly well.

The NFU had rented an office conveniently next door to Defra in London after the bulk of the operation had moved to Stoneleigh, which is where most of the top brass spent much of their time, leaving just me and Ken Sutherland, the Finance Director, to hold the fort in Warwickshire. This meant that, whenever someone rang in, wanting to have a go at the President or whoever, they got put through to me, for conversations in which the patience I'd learned in all those years in the South-West stood me in good stead.

Much the two biggest stories of my two and a bit years at Stoneleigh were the summer floods of 2007 and the outbreak of foot-and-mouth disease that August. Other than organising a press visit to some of the flooded farms in the Severn Valley, and surviving a nightmare journey home on July 22, when it seemed that around every corner on the A429 across the Cotswolds there might be a lake to swallow up my Saab, the floods did not add much to my usual burdens. The FMD outbreak was a different matter.

I'd got news of it from Richard Mac on the last evening of my holiday with Claire in Braunton, where we were staying, as usual, for Saunton week. We had just got back from a visit to the world's best fish-and-chip shop,

Squires, followed by a pint or two at the Black Horse when I picked up the message.

An outbreak of Foot and Mouth, in cattle, in Surrey, in August? It was hard to believe. The explanation was not long in emerging. There had been a leak of virus from the Government Animal Health laboratory at Pirbright. The worst-affected farmers were Roger Pride and his family who, under huge pressure from the media, agreed to give a press conference, but they were nervous and unsure what to say. Could the NFU help out? The next day I was despatched to Guildford, leaving Sarah Whitelock in charge of coping with all the press enquiries we were getting at Stoneleigh, which she did very well.

The most difficult part of what followed was getting the text of the statement agreed with the family, who were understandably anxious to get the wording just right. That having been achieved, it was left to me to read it out and then answer questions from the 20 or 30 reporters who crowded into the press conference. The BBC's 24-hour television news service carried the whole thing live. I did OK. After that, I headed off to Pirbright, where another clutch of satellite television vans were encamped. I gave a series of interviews, hypothesising that the most likely cause of the outbreak was a leak from a pipe carrying waste water from the laboratories to a treatment plant, which turned out to have been pretty much the case.

The week that followed was hectic but not remotely as traumatic as the first week of the 2001 outbreak. Gordon Brown, who had succeeded Tony Blair as Prime Minister only six weeks or so previously, was determined to show that, this time, the Government was on the ball, imposing (unnecessarily as it turned out) a nationwide ban on livestock movements and cutting short his holiday and returning to Downing Street to take personal charge of the damage limitation exercise. Peter Kendall was swiftly summoned to meet him, which made for more of the right sort of coverage.

Surrey in August is not West Devon in February, and the outbreak was swiftly snuffed out. Or at least we thought it had been, until September 14, when news of a second outbreak came through, this time in a flock of sheep at Egham. I was with all of the great and the good of the farming world at a reception at Highgrove House, complete with HRH, for the launch of one of Sir Donald Curry's ideas – a 'Year of Food and Farming' in 2008.

I was struck by the incongruity of the two events: a planned 'celebration' of British agriculture just when the industry seemed threatened by another major crisis. In the event, neither the outbreak nor the 'Year' came to anything very much.

Later that autumn I met Gordon Brown for the first and only time. He and Peter Kendall had obviously got on pretty well, as the PM had offered a room in 10 Downing St for the launch of our 'Why Beef and Sheep Farming Matters' campaign – livestock farming was once again going through a rough patch – in November. What is more, he was there in person to give his blessing to our less than earth-shattering event.

At first I was quite impressed. He was less dour than I'd been expecting and seemed to be quite enjoying himself, shaking hands and chatting with all and sundry. But when it came to the photographs, I noticed that he was standing awkwardly on tiptoe, leaning forward, with a rather silly grin on his face. He had obviously been told that this was the way to present himself to the camera to best advantage. And this in a politician whom we'd been given to understand would offer substance rather than style. I was not impressed.

By this time I had decided that the time was fast approaching to call it a day. It was the largely sleepless Sunday nights that finished me off; that and the seemingly endless running sore of badgers and bovine TB. Mary Tudor famously said that when she died, the word 'Calais' (which she had lost to the French) would be found written on her heart; on mine you will find 'badgers'.

My impending retirement, the following May, was announced in October. When I told my team, the announcement was greeted with a stunned silence. They seemed genuinely shocked and sad. I consoled them with the thought that, whoever took over would be in the happy position of building on success, rather than stopping the rot. The good ship NFU was firmly back on course.

I was determined not to be a lame-duck Director of Comms in the remaining months of my tenure, and I did succeed in setting the wheels turning for a re-branding of the NFU (to coincide with our centenary year in 2008), something which came to fruition – inexpensively, it should be said – shortly after I'd departed.

I did manage to go out on a high, as well. In early 2008 the press was full of stories about the increase in the world's population and the question mark over future food supplies. Food production was suddenly back in fashion. At the various meetings at which I bade my farewells, I was fond of saying that I had joined the NFU at the end of the last period of sustained agricultural prosperity and was leaving it at the start of the next such era.

It maybe hasn't quite worked out like that but, since my departure, we've certainly seen nothing like the BSE crisis or the dreadful recession which followed it.

I said my farewells to friends and colleagues in the South-West NFU at what was in all respects, save my overlong and rambling speech, a lovely occasion at Dillington House that April. Unforgivably I failed to mention the most senior and distinguished farmer in the room, dear old Fred Elliott, with whom I'd worked so closely over West Sedgemoor, when he was Chairman of HQ Parliamentary Committee in the 1980s and from whom I'd had nothing but kindness and support throughout my career.

I did get the chance to make some amends when, a few years later, he asked me if I could turn his memoirs, which he had dictated as a sort of stream of consciousness to an amanuensis, into an autobiography. The result was 'From Wiveliscombe to Whitehall – A Farmer's Life'. We launched it at a splendid gathering of Fred's friends, relations and NFU colleagues at Wiveliscombe Rugby Club, with Fred presiding genially, by now into his nineties. The occasion felt a bit like a cross between a memorial service and a wake, but with the main man still being very much alive to hear and enjoy the tributes.

A tearful farewell on a sunny Friday in May 2008 wasn't quite the end of my NFU career. Over the course of the next three years, three Directors of Comms came and went, leaving the department once again in a bit of a pickle. In 2011 I was asked if I would like to come back for six months as 'Strategic Communications Consultant', working with Martin Haworth who had taken over as an interim Director of Comms, alongside his role as Director of Policy. I had often dreamt of precisely such an eventuality (and occasionally still do), just as I'm sure many other recent retirees do. So I said yes, with some misgivings (those sleepless Sunday nights again). Once again, I think I helped steady the ship and get her back on course but wasn't tempted when I was offered a second six months.

It was time for new leadership, which has since been provided most effectively, from what I can gather, by Fran Barnes. In the end I did indeed succeed in leaving the NFU's communications in good hands.

26

The voice of Somerset cricket

I had three objectives immediately in mind when I retired from the NFU in May 2008. The first was to buy a campervan or motorhome, in which to travel on my own down the Celtic coast of Europe from Cape Wrath to Cabo Sao Vicente. My account of that journey, my 'Celtic Odyssey', was published, to modest acclaim, and copies are still available!

The second of my goals was to select, contextualise and have published a representative selection of my father's cricket writing for The Times. This had been greatly enjoyed at the time by very many people, and not just cricketing people, and deserved, I was sure, to have its memorial. My first approach was to the newspaper itself, but the reply I got was that it wasn't sufficiently commercial.

However, Marcus Williams, one of the very few survivors from my father's day, got back to me to say that he'd met up with a cricket publisher, who'd had precisely the same idea, and suggested I got in touch. So I did. The publisher turned out to be Stephen Chalke. We hit it off straight away, and he's been publishing my books ever since, poor chap, none of them, it should be said, more successfully than 'Of Didcot and the Demon – The Cricketing Times of Alan Gibson'.

Much to my surprise, given the strength of the competition, it won the MCC/Cricket Society award for 'Cricket Book of the Year' for 2010. One of the other books on the shortlist was 'Golden Boy', the biography of Australian cricketer Kim Hughes by Christian Ryan, which was subsequently voted 'best cricket book of all time' by readers of Wisden Cricket Monthly, which is a useful form line!

I was presented with my certificate at a very grand dinner in the Long Room at Lord's. I made a little speech, in which I said that, for all my father's disdain for Lord's and the cricketing establishment, he would secretly have been very proud, which I think was true, then had my photograph taken with Scyld Berry and John Barclay (who had been one of my father's favourite cricketers) and went off to sign copies at the bookstall which Stephen had set up in an ante-room.

To think that I had done justice to my father, and to myself, made it one of the happiest and proudest moments of my life. I flew back to Langport on wings of exultation.

Stephen rang me the next morning to reflect on the evening, and we offered each other mutual congratulations.

"The cheque will come in handy, I daresay," he suggested.

"Cheque?!" I replied. "What cheque?"

"The cheque for £3,000 that you get for winning the thing," he explained. "Don't say you've left it behind!"

Indeed I had. I'd no idea that there was any money attached to the award and had been more than happy simply with the honour of winning. Frantic phone calls to Lord's ensued, and eventually the cheque was retrieved from a rubbish bin, still in the envelope from which I'd pulled out my certificate. All was well. Claire and I set off for a celebratory lunch at the Hive café on the beach at Burton Bradstock.

And my third ambition? Well, that was to resume my cricket commentary career: not in the summer of 2008, as that was taken up by my Celtic adventures, but in 2009, provided I could find someone to employ me. So, in the spring of 2009, I e-mailed Geoff Twentyman, legendary Bristol Rovers footballer, who had been Sports Editor at BBC Radio Bristol since I'd last worked for the station in 2005.

"Of course, we'd be delighted if you could do some commentary," he replied. "It'll be great to have you back." My spirits soared.

The next I heard was when I was in my room in the Nuffield Hospital in Taunton, enjoying my habitual post-colonoscopy meal of coffee and a bacon sandwich, heavily seasoned with relief. I took a call from Dan Albert on the Radio Bristol sports desk.

"Geoff wonders if you could do Somerset's game against Warwickshire in the Friends Provident on April 19," he enquired. You bet I could.

I hadn't actually watched any Somerset cricket in the previous three seasons, what with working in Warwickshire and the Celtic trip, so I took myself off to the County Ground in Taunton for the first day of Somerset's championship game with Warwickshire, immediately prior to the Edgbaston fixture, to familiarise myself with both sides.

It turned out to be a typical – for that era – Taunton run-fest. I watched Ian Bell laying the foundations of a century and Jonathan Trott removed by Ben Phillips for a duck. But, in truth, I chose the wrong day. Had I been there on the third and fourth days I would have seen James Hildreth score an unbeaten 303, the earliest triple-hundred in an English summer, and Craig Kieswetter make his maiden century for Somerset.

I was nervous about the resumption of my commentary career and slept poorly on the Saturday night, driving up to Birmingham first thing on Sunday morning. It was a beautiful sunny spring morning, and, at 55 overs a side, I knew that Phil Tottle and I, sharing commentary, would be in for a long day. But any apprehension that I might have been feeling was soon forgotten once play got under way. Cricket commentary is not something you forget how to do, and after a few overs it felt like I had never been away, especially with the reassuring presence of Tots, whom I'd worked with many times before.

We took it in turns to commentate and summarise, five overs at a time. I was much happier with the commentary than the summarising, something that still holds good! It was an exciting game of cricket as well, Ian Bell contributing another classy century to set Somerset a target of 272, which was chased down stylishly thanks mainly to an unbroken stand of 188 between Kieswetter, who finished with 138*, and Zander de Bruyn, 73*. I felt reasonably content with my own efforts and distinctly encouraged by Somerset's, as I drove back down the M5.

That season turned out to be the first of all too many in which Somerset promised much but ended up winning nothing, despite seeming to have all the ingredients for success, in the one-day competitions especially. The batting order of Marcus Trescothick, Arul Suppiah, Justin Langer, James Hildreth, Zander de Bruyn, Craig Kieswetter and Peter Trego was probably as strong as any since the palmy days of Rose, Denning, Richards and Botham.

I wasn't called up for T20 Finals day, when Somerset were well beaten in the final by Sussex, but I was at Taunton, alongside Phil Tottle and our expert summariser Mark Davis, for what was effectively the final of the Pro 40 league, with Somerset only needing to beat Durham to win the title. The County Ground was packed, the cider was flowing and hopes were high. But, for once, the batting didn't really fire, and a total of 242 looked maybe 30 runs short on another belter of a pitch. The game was settled in the first seven overs of Durham's innings, off which Phil Mustard and returning Taunton hero Ian Blackwell (sacked by Justin Langer for being too fat) thrashed 79 runs.

That loss to Durham was the first of four losing finals, two in the 40-over competition and two in T20, as well as coming second in the county championship in six of the next 11 seasons (counting the Bob Willis Trophy).

I missed two of the cruellest disappointments, both in 2010, when Somerset would have beaten Hampshire in the final, had Marcus Trescothick had the wit to run out Dan Christian – batting with a runner but out of his ground – off the final ball, and at Chester-le-Street when Somerset would have won a first County Championship had they beaten Durham.

But I was there for all the others, invariably with an initially optimistic, then progressively downcast Mark Davis by my side. I enjoy working with Mark. I'd watched him come flying in from the River End at Taunton, blond hair streaming in the wind, to bowl fast left-arm in that great Somerset team of the mid-1980s, and subsequently he'd helped produce any number of good cricketers as a highly respected coach at Millfield School. I haven't come across many more astute analysers of a game of cricket than Mark, and he combines that with a good voice and a genial manner, rarely if ever falling into the trap which claims so many ex-player summarisers of becoming too technical. We knew our roles: mine to describe what is happening out on the field of play, Mark's to explain it.

The two Lord's finals, against Warwickshire in the CB40 in 2010 and against Surrey in the YB40 a year later, were disappointing in more than just the outcome. Sadly there was nothing like the sense of occasion that we'd enjoyed with all of those Lord's finals back in the 60s, 70s and 80s.

A combination of a 3 pm start and the fact that the two finalists had been confirmed only a week earlier meant that Lord's was barely even half-full in 2010. The ECB had, belatedly, paid for some coaches to transport the Somerset faithful to Lord's (given that the last train to Taunton would have left Paddington before the scheduled finish of the game), but the surge of cider-fuelled passion which had been such a feature of all of Somerset's triumphs over the years was missing. We were well-beaten in both games despite the best efforts of James Hildreth against Warwickshire and Jos Buttler and Steve Kirby in the Surrey game.

There was no lack of excitement at Edgbaston for T20 Finals Day in 2011 and, yet again, Somerset were warm favourites. The semi-final against Hampshire was almost a repeat of the previous year's final, finishing in a tie after Somerset had seemed to have it won, and Alfonso Thomas's skill in the super-over seeing us through. We went on to lose the final, of course, to a Leicestershire side inspired by the ultra-competitive Paul Nixon, who took a quite stunning catch to dismiss Keiron Pollard, on whom so many

Somerset hopes were pinned. However, another ultimately disappointing season did have one saving grace, and that was being able to commentate on a world record, when Arul Suppiah took six wickets for five runs with his slow left-arm against Glamorgan on a dark, dank, Cardiff evening, watched by the usual two boyos and a sheepdog. He is another to have been coached by Mark, who was as astounded as I was by this unlikely feat.

That was it for finals, for another eight years. We did come a very creditable second in the Championship in 2012, in a season dogged by injury and rain, and reached Finals Day for the third year running, this time at Cardiff, losing feebly against Hampshire. For me, apart from the dreadful weather, the 2012 season was notable mainly for the emergence of a new generation of hugely talented young Somerset cricketers: Lewis Gregory (whom I'd first seen and been impressed by when as a 17-year-old he'd taken four wickets in a friendly against Pakistan), the Overton twins Craig and Jamie, Jack Leach and Craig Meschede.

Word also reached the county ground of the exploits of a young man called Tom Abell, who appeared to be breaking every Taunton School batting record in the book. He made seven centuries in 11 innings, scoring 1,156 runs at an average of 192 and was anointed Wisden's Schoolboy Cricketer of the Year! Even though a deeply frustrated Brian Rose called it a day at the end of the season as Director of Cricket, the future of Somerset cricket was looking bright.

The season of 2013 was the first in which the BBC, subsidised by the ECB, offered ball-by-ball commentary on every match in the County Championship. Only on the BBC website, to be sure, with Five Live Sports Extra dipping in from time to time on the more significant games, but the listenership grew steadily and our efforts seemed to be appreciated, particularly by the more dedicated county cricket followers, of whom there are many more than you might imagine.

Prior to this arrangement, Radio Bristol had not usually provided commentary on the County Championship, so I had never attempted ball-by-ball commentary on a four-day match before. I suspected that it would be more of a challenge than limited-overs cricket, where there is almost always something happening. Maintaining interest through an over consisting of four balls left alone outside the off-stump and the other two pushed defensively back down the pitch, was obviously going to be a challenge, especially on a fourth day with the game petering out into a tame draw.

Having scored for John Arlott, Brian Johnston, Christopher Martin-Jenkins, Henry Blofeld and my father, my commentary style was – is – inevitably fairly old school. I do try to see the funny side of whatever is happening on or off the pitch, but I'm not a great 'josher', in the manner, say, of Phil Tufnell. I'd rather chat about games and players from the past, or maybe the buildings and landmarks we can see from the commentary box – that famous view of the Quantocks from the County Ground at Taunton being the most obvious example. It helps that most of my fellow commentators know their county clubs inside and out and are broadcasters with a broad range of interests, so that only rarely have I felt that what is essentially a conversation around, as well as about, a game of cricket has been running out of steam.

I also learned from my co-commentators the importance of homework. Before every game I will compile a dossier on both sides, including all the latest stats. I am fortunate as well in having my 'personal statistician', as I like to call him, in Steve Pittard, joint landlord with his two sisters, Maureen and Trish, of my local, the splendid Rose and Crown at Huish Episcopi just outside Langport, better known to all and sundry as Eli's. Steve is a cricket nut and digs out all sorts of obscure facts and figures for me before every Championship game – perfect for enlivening a quiet period of play.

This may be a case of the wish being father to the thought, but it has struck me how well-suited so many of my fellow commentators are to their counties: the impeccably courteous, super-confident Mark Church, is the epitome of the best sort of Surrey boy; there is unmistakeably something of the 'Shire' about the now retired Bob Hunt in Gloucestershire; Dave Bradbury is as calm and as flowing in his commentary as the River Severn as it sweeps through Worcester; the ever-enthusiastic Kevin Hand brings a patrician metropolitanism to his commentaries, even when he's not at Lord's; and there is more than a touch of Sussex by the sea about breezy Adrian Harms. I'm not sure to what extent I typify Somerset, but I do enjoy a drop of cider!

I'm afraid I can't stretch the analogy to include another relatively recent feature of the cricket broadcasting scene, the women commentators, as they are all 'third voices', who travel around the country, providing what is often some much-needed balance between the inevitably slightly biased judgements of the county men. But Izzy Westbury, Isabelle Duncan and Lizzie Ammon have brought a very welcome new dimension to the commentary box, reflecting the long overdue rise in prominence of the women's game in recent years.

Another saving grace of modern cricket commentary is social media. Twitter, in particular, gives listeners the chance to say what they think either about what's happening on the field of play or the commentary (it's usually polite!). It serves to broaden the conversation to include the listeners, as well as providing a steady stream of good material.

My first game in that ground-breaking 2013 season was at Chester-le-Street. My car thermometer showed 3° C as I drove into the ground on the morning of April 10! However, Martin Emmerson, the 'home commentator' and a son of Durham if ever there was one, could not have been more welcoming or better company; he impressed me immediately with the way he was able to combine commentary with a constant stream of tweets, a skill that I have never quite mastered. The weather was damp, as well as cold, but I was grateful for the breaks in play for rain and bad light, as I was discovering that six hours of commentary a day, with just a 40-minute break for lunch and 20 minutes for tea, was hard work. By the time I came to drive the 330 miles back to Somerset on the last day, I was as weary as I can ever remember.

It was a game that rather set the tone for the season for both clubs. Somerset bounced back after a dismal first-innings effort with the bat to bowl Durham out second time around for 116, leaving themselves a stiff but by no means impossible target of 235 to win. They were going well at 130/2, and then collapsed, losing their last eight wickets for 56 runs as Chris Rushworth and Graham Onions ran amok. Durham would go on to win the County Championship; Somerset would struggle to avoid relegation.

That was a particularly miserable season for Somerset's captain, Marcus Trescothick. An ankle injury, sustained at Trent Bridge, kept him out for much of the season and, when he did return, the runs dried up. It wasn't a particularly happy dressing room either, dominated as it was by the wicket-keeping rivalry between Kieswetter and Buttler.

The England selectors had asked Somerset to give Buttler the gloves for the white-ball games, with Kieswetter keeping in the Championship. But neither Kieswetter nor the new Director of Cricket, his fellow South African Dave Nosworthy, were happy with that, so Kieswetter continued to keep in all forms. That left Buttler with little option but to move on if he wanted to progress his England career, and he joined Lancashire at the end of the season.

It was more than sad. Jos is a Somerset man through and through, born and bred at Wedmore, school at King's College Taunton, playing for the Somerset age-group teams since he was in short trousers. It was also, according to Brian Rose, unnecessary. When I was helping him with his autobiography, 'Rosey', he told me that if he had still been in charge, he would have given Buttler the gloves and made Kieswetter the captain, batting him at number four. That, he reckons, would have kept the pair of them happy. I still cling to the hope that, one day, perhaps in the evening of his career, Jos will come back to play for the county that I know he loves. All of Somerset would rejoice.

While all this was going on, I had been hard at work on 'Gentlemen, Gypsies and Jesters – the Wonderful World of Wandering Cricket'. This had been the brainchild of Simon Dyson, a fine cricketer with all the right connections at Lord's and elsewhere in the cricket establishment and a thoroughly good bloke. His idea was to publish a compendium of the more famous of the wandering clubs – the I Zingaris, Free Foresters and Somerset Stragglers of this world – to raise funds for Chance to Shine, the charity which does such a splendid job introducing children in the state school sector to the joys of cricket.

All costs were covered by sponsorship, so all the proceeds from sales would go to the charity and, thanks to a golfing connection, I was asked to do most of the writing and editing, substantially assisted by Stephen Chalke, who published the book and was a major factor in its success. The members of the wandering clubs proved to be a fertile market, and we sold every last copy, raising £50,000. As for me, whose previous experience of wandering cricket amounted to one game against the Free Foresters, I learned a lot about one of the more exotic corners of the world of cricket.

For the last eight seasons, I have covered most of Somerset's one-day games and roughly half of those in the Championship, where I share commentary with the excellent Stephen Lamb. There have been some memorable moments, of both pleasure and pain. One which was a bit of both was the remarkable century that James Hildreth scored, on one leg, after having his right ankle broken by a Jake Ball yorker in the final game of the 2016 season against Notts. It put Somerset in pole position for that elusive first County Championship. Either Middlesex or Yorkshire would need to win their game at Lord's to deny us.

Somerset having completed a comfortable win on the third day, we gathered at the ground on what would have been the fourth day to follow proceedings at Lord's on the television. The omens were not encouraging.

It seemed almost too convenient that late-order resistance had enabled Yorkshire to claim the fourth batting point they needed to keep them in with a chance of the title, were they to win the game.

On a slow Lord's pitch, they would have stood every chance of being able to bat out for a draw on the final day. As it was, there was the inevitable contrived finish, a deal having been struck in which Yorkshire had agreed to keep swinging even if they lost wickets. Somerset hopes, never high, died when Toby Roland-Jones removed Tim Bresnan, precipitating a Yorkshire capitulation and a Middlesex championship. Andy Nash, the Somerset Chairman, and Chris Rogers, the captain, put a brave face on things, but it did feel as if we'd been done out of a Championship for the second time in seven seasons.

We had our revenge – of sorts – at the end of the following season, by beating Middlesex in the final game at Taunton, so consigning them to Division 2 and saving our own Division 1 bacon in the process. End-of-season Taunton pitches had by this stage become notorious for the amount of help they granted the Somerset spinners Jack Leach and Dom Bess. But with Somerset needing a win to avoid the relegation that had seemed certain only three games previously, Simon Lee, the Head Groundsman, was evidently leaving nothing to chance.

The Middlesex Director of Cricket, Gus Fraser, doing his very best Eeyore impression with added swear words, insisted that the pitch had been raked at one end. The fact that the Middlesex left-arm spinner Ravi Patel took seven wickets in Somerset's first innings and Jack Leach four in Middlesex's did nothing whatever to improve his mood. It took James Hildreth to put things in perspective and maybe save Somerset from a relegation-consigning points penalty. His masterful second-innings century emphatically gave the lie to suggestions that the pitch was unplayable.

I am ashamed to say that when the final Middlesex wicket fell – Steven Finn lbw to Leach – I got completely carried away with excitement and relief at Somerset's 'great escape', entirely forgetting to offer commiserations to Middlesex. When one is broadcasting to both sets of supporters, there is an obligation to be as even-handed as possible.

Just less than a year later, the Taunton pitch was in the spotlight again, eventually to provide me with the rarest outcome in first-class cricket. Somerset were playing Lancashire in early September, still with an outside chance of overtaking the Championship leaders, Surrey. Sure enough, the pitch was another raging turner. A combination of Lewis Gregory's aggressive second innings 64 and Jack Leach's career-best 7/74 in the Lancashire second innings left Somerset needing just 88 to win.

But, after Graham Onions had made the initial breakthrough, wickets fell with alarming regularity, mostly to Lancashire's accomplished South African left-arm spinner, Keshav Maharaj. Even so, Somerset were hot favourites when a lusty blow from Jamie Overton brought the scores level, with two wickets still standing.

I was on commentary now, in anticipation of a Somerset win. Bess, going for glory, charged down the pitch and was stumped, bringing Leach to the crease. Overton then played out a maiden from Onions, to leave Leach on strike against Maharaj. For three balls he defended. But with the fourth his patience snapped. He went for a leg-side slog, didn't time it, and mid-wicket was waiting to take the catch. At that very moment, my co-commentator, Scott Read, had to put down his mic to file a report for BBC Manchester at the back of the box. He just had time to say "Bailey" as he passed me.

"It's a tie," I shouted, with something approaching glee, for once setting partisan disappointment aside. "Tom Bailey takes the catch! What a quite remarkable end to an extraordinary game of cricket."

Thank you, Scott. I might have got Tom Bailey right, but in all the tension and excitement I wouldn't have counted on it.

It was the first tie in the County Championship since 2003 and the first involving Somerset since 1939, which was before the BBC offered commentary on county cricket. So I am fairly sure that I am the only person to have commentated on a Somerset tie in first-class cricket.

What else stands out? Well, with my fellow commentators in mind, there was the County Championship game at Taunton in June 2017 when I was working with dear, departed Dave Callaghan, 'Cally' as he was known to his legion of admirers. I enjoy working with all of the other commentators on the circuit, but Cally stood apart, not only for his deep knowledge of Yorkshire cricket and for his kindness and consideration to me but for his sheer professionalism.

Between the tea interval and close of play on each day of Championship cricket, he was expected to provide live reports, not just for his 'home' station of BBC Radio Leeds but for every one of the BBC's myriad of Yorkshire stations, either on his mobile phone or during commentary. He did it perfectly, exactly to time, every salient detail included, and he did it without noticeably breaking his commentary stride.

My last game with him was at Scarborough in 2017 when Somerset won on a fast, bouncy pitch, and didn't we have some fun, during and after each day's play. He died suddenly and much too young of a heart attack the following winter, deeply mourned by everyone who knew him, a master of his art.

That Yorkshire game at Taunton in 2017 was one of the closest I've seen in the Championship. It was evenly balanced all the way through, Somerset eventually needing 262 for the win on an unresponsive pitch. They were going well on 231/6, but then lost three quick wickets so that when Jack Leach was lbw to Sidebottom, 12 were still required. But Jamie Overton was still there, and he was on strike at the start of 86th over, to be bowled by Adam Lyth with his part-time slow left-arm, and just four needed.

It was anyone's game, and it was Cally's turn to commentate (we were doing alternate ends). Typically of this generous man, he invited me to do the honours and call Somerset home. Off Lyth's third ball, big Jamie decided that the moment had come. He would belt it over mid-wicket for the winning boundary. Except that he didn't belt it, he chipped it, straight into the grateful hands of Carl Carver at short mid-wicket. Yorkshire had won by three runs.

I've described two ties in 50-over cricket, against Notts and Essex, and two hat-tricks, on successive days at Trent Bridge in the last game of the 2018 season, Tom Abell's on the third evening, Craig Overton's the next morning, all three of his victims being taken at second slip by Trescothick, another cricketing rarity.

Thinking of Trescothick, there was that sad day at Guildford in June 2019 when, after struggling for form all season, he was given out caught behind off his thigh-pad (the umpire later apologised) and trudged back to the pavilion shaking his head – "Quite possibly for the last time," I suggested on commentary, a forecast that proved all too accurate.

But that was a rare moment of sadness in a season that, right from the outset, seemed to offer Somerset their best chance of this or any other era of claiming that elusive first County Championship. So confident was I that this would indeed be Somerset's year that, from the outset, I wrote a diary of all of their games, thinking how well it might sell if they triumphed. And how close they came to vindicating my faith in them!

With their seam attack on fire in the summer of 2019, Somerset won more matches in the Championship than ever before and were going so strongly by early September that I was on standby to travel to Southampton for what was, by rights, my colleague Stephen Lamb's match. A good win there would make the championship safe, even before the final game against Essex.

It wasn't, of course, to be. After twice being in a winning position, Somerset were ultimately as poor at the Ageas Bowl against the South African seamer Kyle Abbott as they had been against Maharaj (again) at Headingley in July. Those two defeats meant that we needed a win in the final game against Essex, an imperative that was to have lasting consequences.

It rained, of course. We were beaten by the weather. Despite the excitement of that final afternoon when Tom Abell forfeited Somerset's second innings to allow one final tilt at glory, it was overall a deeply depressing four days. That imperative was a result pitch, which cost Somerset a vindictive, under all the circumstances, 12-point penalty.

I still published my diary, calling it 'Somerset's Summer', and we sold all 200 copies. But for the wretched weather, that might have been 2,000!

Much the most poignant memory of that season came just after the moment of triumph at Lord's, in the Royal London Cup final win over Hampshire, Somerset's first Trophy for 14 years. I was on the outfield, looking to button-hole a few of Somerset's heroes for interview when I spotted Charles Clark, the Somerset Chairman and a friend for over 25 years, in his wheel-chair.

We knew that he was in the grip of cancer and that he didn't have long to go. At the halfway stage I'd visited him and Rebecca (Pow, his wife) in their box, and he was looking pale and ill. But now his features, puffy from chemo, were lit up by a broad grin and happy, shining eyes.

"I've lived to see us lift a trophy," he said, triumphantly. "But the people I'm happiest for are our wonderful supporters. They're like having an extra man in the team. The best supporters in the country."

It was just so wonderfully typical of Charles that, at this moment, which must have been emotionally overwhelming for him, he should be thinking of others. A fine man of Somerset, greatly missed, who loved his cricket dearly.

My other unreservedly happy memory of 2019 was the publication of 'Rosey', the autobiography that I'd helped Brian Rose to write during the preceding 12 months. It was a commission that I'd been delighted to undertake, having followed Brian's career both on the field and off it since he'd made his Somerset debut in 1969. No-one has given Somerset County Cricket greater service over the years, as player, captain, cricket chairman, scout, coach, Director of Cricket and now President.

Brian has a deceptively diffident manner – 'Dozey Rosey', as he was christened by his mentor Brian Close. But that belies a fierce intelligence and a steely resolve, which not only made him the most successful captain in Somerset's cricketing history but which has helped him survive any amount of ill-fortune, from the blow to the eye which ended his England career onwards.

We tended to meet in the bar of the Royal Hotel on the seafront of his home town, Weston-super-Mare, me armed with my recording machine, Brian with his memories. He sometimes took a bit of getting started but, once he'd got going, the stories, the opinions and the insights came pouring out. Mind you, transcribing them wasn't that easy, because Brian has a quiet voice, which was sometimes difficult to pick out above the clack of the balls on the pool-table, the sports commentary on the television and the barmaid chatting to her favourite customers.

To have been able to get to know so well one of my all-time cricketing heroes, and to hear first hand about the exploits, off as well as on the field, of that greatest of Somerset teams, was a wonderful pleasure and privilege. All of the speech-writing I'd done in my NFU career stood me in good stead when it came to relating Brian's life in Brian's voice.

The 2020 season was, inevitably, a strange affair. 'Bittersweet' was how I described it at its end: bitter, in that it started four months late, with no spectators, Somerset missing out on the Bob Willis Trophy at Lord's when they could only draw with Essex and failing by the narrowest (and eminently avoidable) margin to qualify for finals day in the T20; sweet, in that we did actually get some cricket, Somerset bowling and fielding brilliantly in the Bob Willis, and the coming generation of batsmen breaking through spectacularly, Tom Lammonby in particular a revelation. Tom Abell was an inspirational captain. Craig Overton led the attack superbly.

I missed only one day's play in the entire two months of cricket and felt suitably privileged to have been amongst only a handful of people who were able to watch any live cricket at all, let alone as much as I did.

Commentary without spectators is more of a challenge in that you can't rely on the crowd to provide the atmosphere and underscore the excitement; you have to generate and maintain it yourself, albeit with plenty of help from the players. Somerset's cricket in the Bob Willis matches never lacked for intensity (unlike one or two other counties). or indeed for volubility. and was one of the main reasons why they were, indisputably, the best team in the competition. The only real disappointment was that five-day match at Lord's. The weather was cold, the pitch was turgid, a crucial toss was lost, the commentary position was poor and, once Essex had got the first innings lead they needed to win the Trophy in the event of a draw, a draw was what they settled for.

As I drove back to Langport that evening, I took to contemplating what the future might hold. For Somerset, nothing but good, I would hope. To go with the experience of Steve Davies, James Hildreth and Jack Brooks, they have an outstanding crop of youngsters, with Tom Abell and Craig Overton of an age to bridge the gap between the two generations. Despite the occasional T20 aberration, Jason Kerr is a remarkably effective coach.

For cricket on the BBC, and therefore for my prospects as a commentator, it is hard to be so confident. The advent of the 'live streams' – unmanned webcams beaming live video via the county websites to the viewing faithful – has undoubtedly been a blessing, and never more so than in the behind-closed-doors 2020 season.

Somerset's, master-minded by the ever-helpful Ben Warren, was one of the earliest and remains probably the best. Up until this season it has carried our BBC commentary. But for the T20 matches in 2020 Somerset found sponsors for the live stream, and the sponsors, understandably, wanted their money's worth, which meant advertisements with which the BBC was, equally understandably, not prepared to be associated, leaving Somerset to hire their own commentary team. It is a dilemma which I profoundly hope will be satisfactorily resolved.

As for me I would love to carry on for a few more years, always provided that the vital connection between eyes and mouth is still fully functional. I have enjoyed my second coming as a cricket commentator. I count myself hugely privileged to been able to watch and describe some great players in what has arguably been a longer period of sustained success in all formats than any other in Somerset's history.

I think immediately of Marcus Trescothick's languid power as another seemingly effortless off-drive skims through the covers. What a great day it was when he passed Harold Gimblett's record for the most first-class centuries for Somerset with his 50th against Warwickshire in May 2017, Peter Trego ribbing him afterwards by suggesting that he'd asked his team-mates to refer to him as 'Harold'. Or maybe James Hildreth, so shamefully snubbed by the England selectors, making batting look the easiest thing in the world, even against top-class spinners on a turning pitch, while Jos

Buttler's power-hitting was a sight to behold, from the moment he came into the side at the age of 18.

Among the bowlers, Alfonso Thomas, an adopted son of Somerset if ever there was one, is an abiding memory, gliding in at the death of a one-day game to deliver a series of piercing yorkers. He always reminded me a bit of Shakespeare's Cassius, with that 'mean and hungry look', exuding menace. And then there is Peter Trego, the very personification of the swashbuckling spirit of Somerset cricket, heaving another massive pull into the car park, triggering memories of that day in September 2010 when he sent a straight drive crashing through the next-door commentary box window, to lay out BBC Wales' Eddie Bevan.

Among the current generation I have cherished the raw-boned muscularity of the Overtons, the power-hitting and deadly yorkers of handsome Lewis Gregory, the craft and humour of Jack Leach, the flowing cover drives of Steve Davies, the insouciant brilliance of Tom Banton and the unquenchable boyish enthusiasm of tousle-haired, freckle-faced, almost painfully honest Tom Abell.

I thank them all, not just for the way they've played their cricket but for their patience and eloquence in the often enjoyable, occasionally painful interviews which I record after each day's play. Trego was always the man to go to if Somerset had had a really bad day, as he would be honest but upbeat and often very funny. No matter how desperate a situation Somerset might have found themselves in, good old Pete would always construct a scenario leading on to victory.

The perfect climax to my commentary career would, of course, be to commentate on a first County Championship for Somerset. As to that, we live in hope, although as a Somerset cricket follower who has lived through so many Championship near-misses in the last sixty years, I'm not raising my hopes too high!

27

The greatest cider show on earth

My first Bath and West Show was at Plymouth in 1958. It was staged in the city's Central Park, towards the end of the show's time as a peripatetic event and, with a claimed attendance over the four days of over 100,000, was one of the more successful of that era. My memories of the occasion are sketchy, but I do remember enjoying the sheep shearing, which I now know was won by one of the best and kindest farmers it has been my privilege to meet: Albert Cook, from South Molton, who died in January 2020 at the age of 94. He was President of the Devon County Show in 2010, when he was 85, and could still shear a sheep in a little over three minutes. Given that family background, it is hardly surprising that Albert's great-nephew, a certain Sir Alastair Cook, has turned out to be as keen on farming sheep as he is on scoring runs!

I must have enjoyed my day at the show because when I was sent away to Monkton Combe I joined the school Young Farmers Club specifically because it had an annual outing to the Bath and West, which by then (1965) had moved to its permanent showground just south of Shepton Mallet. I remember being impressed by the cattle, but I was equally fascinated by the kitchen-knife salesmen who were, and indeed still are, such a feature of the trade-stand avenues. I was even talked into buying a small but very sharp vegetable knife, with which I inadvertently stabbed my friend Dave Godby in the arm, something which is not quite such a happy memory.

It would be another 11 years before I was back at the show, this time as NFU South-West Regional Information Officer, for the press preview on a baking hot day at the end of May 1976. From then on, I went to every Royal Bath and West, as the show became in 1977, for the next 31 years. It wasn't always an entirely frictionless association. The show was being much criticised during most of those years for no longer being "a proper agricultural show", as the farmers liked to put it.

"It's become a town show," they would complain. "All kitchen knives and candy floss. You don't see half the farm machinery there that you do at the Royal Cornwall," they would add, rubbing salt into the wound.

The cause of restoring the show's agricultural credentials was one that I championed in my Western Daily Press columns throughout the 1980s, somewhat to the irritation, it should be said, of successive Bath and West chief executives and chairmen, who were doing their level best to increase and improve the agricultural content but who were swimming against a tide which is still flowing strongly today. Farmers and their families may like to see row upon row of gleaming farm machinery when they visit one of the big shows, but they don't tend to buy much of it any more. Which means that it's not worth the while of the machinery manufacturers and dealers to go to the very considerable expense of taking a stand at a show like the Bath and West, which in turn means less machinery, more farmer complaints and so on it goes in a downward spiral.

This situation is by no means unique to the Bath and West. From 2009 to 2018, in my role as part of the Devon County Show's PR team, I made it my mission to restore, if not the reality, then certainly the perception of that show's farming content with, I would immodestly suggest, some success. But the Bath and West has always been first in the firing line because in the old days it used to travel around the larger towns and cities of the south of England, which inevitably gave it something of an urban focus, while its permanent home at Shepton Mallet makes it very convenient as a day-out destination for the people of Bristol and Bath. They do indeed, on the Saturday in particular, give it much more of the atmosphere of a gigantic street fair than of a serious-minded agricultural show for rural folk.

I would argue – indeed have argued, for many years – that this is as much a strength as a liability because it allows the show to act as a gigantic shop window to an audience of customers who, in most other contexts, are becoming increasingly disconnected from the people and businesses who produce their food. If they go away happy and contented after a day at the Bath and West, ideally laden down with local food and drink, they'll be much more likely to be supportive when it comes to their attitudes and buying choices than if the show did not exist.

And all of the opinion research indicates that the biggest appeal of shows like the Bath and West is that they are primarily *agricultural*. That's what makes them different and special. It's their USP – unique selling point, in the language of the marketeers. Which means that somehow or other, show organisers have to keep that distinctive agricultural flavour, even if they have to pay for it. This is already happening with farm machinery. Livestock exhibitors will almost certainly have to be similarly incentivised to bring their animals to a show like the Bath and West if that absolutely vital element of the appeal isn't to fade away.

Anyway, you will gather from all of the above that I have always been a great supporter of agricultural shows of all sorts. So, when Jane Guise, the then Chief Executive of the Bath and West asked me in 2009, after I'd retired from the NFU, whether I would be interested in becoming a Trustee of the Royal Bath and West of England Society, I said yes straightaway.

I found out that I was joining an interesting bunch of committed, intelligent people, all of whom give their time completely free of charge because they, like me, believe in the cause. We may not be diverse, in terms of ethnicity, but we are, I believe, a pretty fair representation of what you might call the Bath and West's constituency, and we do include several high-powered women.

We provide strategic direction for the Society and its shows (which include the hugely successful Dairy Show, as well as the main Bath and West), taking advice from the Society's Council, which consists to a large degree of the volunteers who make the shows happen, and working with the Chief Executive, to keep the whole operation solvent and successful, which isn't always as easy as it might sound. Without the out-of-show events on the showground which bring in income all the year round, we couldn't afford to run the main show or fulfil our wider charitable objectives.

Initially my main concern was with the farming content, both of the main show and the Society's wider activities, although, since the days of 'A Taste of Somerset' back in the 80s, I've always been a keen advocate that shows like the Bath and West should make a major selling point of top quality and, above all, local food and drink.

My other great interest was the Bath and West's heritage, which stretches back as far as 1777, when an entrepreneur from Norfolk, Edmund Rack, brought together a group of like-minded gentlemen in Bath to form what would become the Bath and West of England Society 'for the encouragement of agriculture, arts, manufactures and commerce'.

The Society didn't stage its first show until 1852, at Taunton, and that was seen very much as a way to achieve its mission of agricultural improvement, as opposed to being an end in itself. As a history graduate I perhaps appreciated the importance and the value of the Society's heritage more than most so was very happy to take on the chairmanship of the committee which looks after its library, held by the University of Bath, and its archives, in the care of Bath City Council, when my friend from French apple war days, Arthur Davies, retired.

However, given my background as a cider campaigner with Camra, it was the Bath and West's links with the world of cider that interested me as much as anything. This too had a long and proud history. Not long after the Society was founded, cider-making in the West of England went into a long and steep decline. That remarkable Victorian polymath, the Rev Sabine Baring-Gould, who took a great interest in cider among his many other enthusiasms, dated this to the imposition of excise duty on cider in 1763. Instead of producing top-quality apples for skilled artisan cider-makers, the farmers made cider only for the use of themselves and their workers.

Baring-Gould wrote as follows in the 1890s:

> *The workman likes a rough beverage, one that almost cut his throat as it passed down; and this produced the evil effect that the farmers, who were bound by their leases to keep up their orchards, planted only the coarsest sort of apples and the higher quality fruit was allowed to die out. The orchards fell into and in most cases remain still in a deplorable state of neglect.*

The Bath and West played an important role in rescuing West Country cider from this sorry state of affairs. A man called Robert Neville-Grenville, who owned an estate at Butleigh in the heart of Somerset cider country and was a big wheel in the Society, led the way. He began collecting apple trees to plant in his orchards at Butleigh Court and writing articles for the Bath and West Journal. With a bacteriologist called Frederick Lloyd and the sponsorship of the Bath and West, he set up a laboratory on his estate in which to carry out experiments, testing and comparing different apple varieties and techniques. This would eventually become the National Fruit and Cider Institute at Long Ashton near Bristol. Founded in 1903, it did much good work for the cider industry until it was, short-sightedly, wound up almost exactly a century later.

Enter the Bath and West again. Towards the end of the Research Station's life one of its most prominent retired scientists, Ray Williams, got together with a West Dorset apple grower and Bath and West stalwart, Rupert Best (son of Rear Admiral Tom), and other apple and cider enthusiasts to put together the 'Orchards and Cider' exhibition at the Royal Bath and West Show.

After a break of some 25 years competitive cider classes had been revived, albeit only in a corner of the Bees and Honey tent. But with interest in cider growing rapidly, thanks not least to the hugely successful advertising campaigns run by the Irish company Magners (even if their claimed cider-orchards were about as substantial as Irish mist), the scope for something more ambitious was obvious.

top: Wedding day with Claire

below: Après golf: three Cat's Whiskers stalwarts – John Knight, Chippy and Miles Elder – in the clubhouse at Royal North Devon

𝔚estern 𝔐orning 𝔑ews

● *Voice of the Westcountry* ●

● **'A long dark shadow has been lifted. The plague has passed. We are free. Let's celebrate'**
— Anthony Gibson

Devon foot and mouth free

● **PRAISED:** Farmers' leader Anthony Gibson yesterday

CAROL TREWIN
FARMING EDITOR

THE nine-month-long shadow of foot and mouth disease has finally been lifted from the Westcountry, with Devon awarded foot and mouth-free status last night.

The rural community was celebrating the official end of a nightmare which saw 173 confirmed cases in Devon and thousands of farms suffering under crippling restrictions.

There were also eight cases in Somerset and four in Cornwall.

Devon National Farmers' Union chairman David Hill said it was the end of a very long and bitter battle. "All the heartache, frustration and sacrifices have been rewarded with foot and mouth-free status," he said.

"It has been a long journey but we are here at last, and Devon will no longer be seen as a pariah."

The first case was confirmed in the Westcountry at Burdon Farm, Highampton, West Devon, on February 24. The last

was on June 17 near Wellington, in Somerset.

More than 900 farms lost their livestock as part of the controversial contiguous cull or because they were believed to be "dangerous contacts".

More than 4,000 were affected by crippling restrictions

REACTION TO DECISION
– Pages 4 & 5

and 412,353 cattle, sheep, pigs and goats were slaughtered.

But the granting of foot and mouth-free status is far from the end of the massive problems caused by the epidemic for both farmers and rural businesses.

Lib-Dem MP John Burnett, whose West Devon and Torridge constituency was the worst hit by the outbreak, said: "It is not the

end of the story by any means for those farm, tourism and other rural businesses hit by foot and mouth. There will be difficult times and I don't believe the Government has learnt the lessons of the disaster."

Farmers who have been under crippling restrictions imposed to stop the spread of the disease face a terrible winter.

Mr Hill said: "There are still 4,000 farms that were on D Notices that have suffered grievous financial damage to the point of disaster, Lord Haskins recommended compensation, but where is it?"

The change to foot and mouth-free status brings Devon in line with Cornwall, Somerset and Dorset, and means livestock can be traded outside the county for the first time in nine months

Two weeks ago, the European Union agreed that lamb exports from FMD-free counties could resume. That will also now include Devon lamb.

Delight of Anthony, the man hailed a hero by farmers

THE Westcountry's hero of the foot and mouth crisis was celebrating last night as Devon's foot and mouth free status was officially declared at midnight.

South West National Farmers' Union director Anthony Gibson said: "A long dark shadow has been lifted from the countryside. The plague has passed and we are free. Let's celebrate."

Mr Gibson received praise throughout the region's farmers.

His incisive weekly column in the WMN

was avidly read by thousands and isolated farmers also tuned in to his TV and radio reports.

Dartmoor farmer Leyland Branfield, who lost his livestock as part of the contiguous cull, said Mr Gibson had been a "keystone through the dark days of the crisis".

"He was always accessible and approachable and kept everyone informed. He was impartial and accurate. He acted as a channel of communication, telling farmers what was happening out there."

◆ **VORACIOUS PREDATOR FROM THE TROPICS IS FOUND IN WESTCOUNTRY WATERS** ◆ SEE PAGE 3

top left: Not pulling any punches (verbal ones, at any rate) with Leader of the Opposition William Hague at the height of the Foot and Mouth crisis

middle left: With the Prince of Wales and Diane Lethbridge after the crisis is over

bottom left: An honorary degree from the University of Exeter, 2007, with Claire, my mother and Dame Floella Benjamin, the Chancellor

above: With my OBE at Buckingham Palace

top: The engine room at NFU headquarters at Stoneleigh:
(from left) Jeanette Clarke, Kate Walters, Gill Thompson, Nicky Sawdon

bottom: With Somerset Chairmen past and present, 2008: *(front)* Fred Elliott (1980), *(first row)* Patrick Palmer (1979), Mary James (1991), Brian Rowe (1982), *(middle)* Ian Ham (1995), Maurice Adams (1987), Michael Vearncombe (1988), *(rear)* Alan Bartlett (1996), David House (1985), John Hebditch (2008), Dick Pearce (1981)

top: The 2013-14 floods: the view from home across the Parrett to Huish Level, with Muchelney beyond

above: Orchards and Cider's Rupert Best *(left)* receives his Silver Medal for best orchard 2019, with chief steward Bob Chaplin and key sponsor Martin Thatcher

right: Presenting the Bath and West's Gold Medal to the late John Hecks, one of the great men of Somerset cider

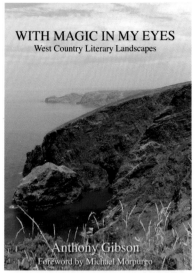

WITH MAGIC IN MY EYES
West Country Literary Landscapes

Anthony Gibson
Foreword by Michael Morpurgo

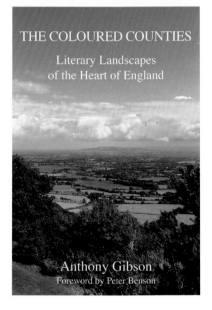

THE COLOURED COUNTIES

Literary Landscapes
of the Heart of England

Anthony Gibson
Foreword by Peter Benson

top: Taking a breather at Cranmere Pool on the way to the Ted Hughes stone

middle: Found it! On the Ted Hughes stone on Dartmoor

bottom: Claire on the Cat's Back

top: Favourite job, favourite ground – Taunton

middle left: Celebrating a Somerset victory with the club chairman, the late Charles Clark, his wife Rebecca Pow and the two Toms, Banton *(left)* and Abell

middle right: With Vic Marks *(left)* and Jack Davey at the launch of 'Of Didcot and the Demon' at The Star, High Littleton

bottom: With John Barclay after winning the MCC/Cricket Society Book of the Year award at Lord's, 2010

All the family

top (left to right):
Pippa with Grace, Joanna with Darcy, Nick, Becky with William, George with Arthur, Mandy, Claire, Phil with Hermione

middle:
Isabella, Joel, Amanda, brother Adam

bottom:
Murray, Matthew, sister Felicity, Dave

The new venture would take the cider competition up several gears, as well as giving visitors an insight into everything that goes into the creation of the West County's most characteristic drink. Within the first few years of the Orchards and Cider marquee, entries in the cider classes went from a few dozen to several hundred and the 'cider tent', as it was colloquially known, became one of the show's biggest attractions.

A feature of the judging of the cider classes was the inclusion, in the final stages, of a 'celebrity judge' to add a bit of PR gloss. In recent years this role has been filled by, among others, the chef Tom Parker-Bowles, the musician Chris Jagger and the interior designer of Grand Designs fame Kevin McCloud. In 2007 (when I suspect a genuine celebrity must have let them down!) I was asked if I might be interested. It took me all of a millisecond to say yes.

The prospect didn't seem quite so enticing when I found myself confronted with what seemed like an endless line of wine-glasses half full of cider – at 8.30 of a Thursday morning! There were, in fact, about 30, but that was only the drys and the mediums. By the time I'd swirled, sniffed, slurped and spat my way through the sweets, the sparkling, the bottled, the branded and the perries, I must have tasted the best part of 100 ciders, and all before lunch!

I did my very best to follow the admirably restrained example set by my fellow judge, the deeply knowledgeable Nick Bradstock, and swallow either the barest minimum or not at all. But when each of the fields had been narrowed down to the final half dozen, and with so much pride and prestige resting on the result for the cider makers who had entered, I felt I really had to imbibe at least a mouthful of each if I was to make a properly informed judgement. And the longer the morning went on, the stronger that feeling became!

By the time we came to the Championship class, I was swaying – or so my wife Claire insisted – like a big old poplar in a fresh breeze. It was a close-run thing, but we gave it to a single-orchard cider made as his own venture by Gaymers' chief cider-maker Bob Chaplin (who also happened to be the Orchards and Cider Chief Steward). It was a beautiful reddish-gold, almost auburn, in colour; dry, appley, but without the slightest hint of acid or vinegar. If one could bottle a balmy Somerset October day, then this is what it would taste like. The runner-up, a characteristically bitter-sharp Devon cider, made by another Orchards and Cider stalwart, Chris Coles of Green Valley Cyder at Topsham, was barely a half point behind. Both were examples of the new wave of West Country ciders – well-made, clean-tasting and allowing the true apple flavours to come through.

As I tottered off in the direction of lunch, I felt thoroughly satisfied, on three counts: first, that we had made the right decisions; second, that the overall standard of the entries had been so high; and third, that I was still upright!

Claire looks after communications for Sedgemoor District Council and was waiting at the Council's stand for me to take her on to lunch. Just at that moment they were entertaining their local MP, one Ian Liddell-Grainger, with whom I had never seen eye to eye. Not realising the connection, he pronounced to all and sundry as I was approaching: "Oh look, here comes that plonker Gibson."

"Yes," said Claire, as cool as you like. "He's my husband. He's been judging the cider, and he's taking me to lunch in the Council tent."

Collapse of pompous little Member of Parliament, although I mustn't be too rude about him as he is the Chair of the All-Party Parliamentary Cider Group, whose receptions in the House of Commons I attend twice a year.

My judging efforts, and the speech I made subsequently – of which more in due course – obviously didn't do me too much harm, however, because, when Rupert Best decided that it was time to call it a day as Chairman of Orchards and Cider after 13 years of growth and success, I was asked to take his place and again was only too happy to oblige.

By the time I took over, at the beginning of 2014, the cider competition was attracting well over 500 entries, making it probably the biggest in Europe. So I decided that it needed a re-branding to match its status and success, and from the 2014 show onwards it has been the British Cider Championships, one of two national championships now staged as part of the show, the other being the British Cheese Awards

It would be good to be able to write that, since then, West Country cider-making, the British Cider Championships and the Royal Bath and West Show have all gone from strength to strength, but it would be only partly true. The small-scale, artisan sector of the industry has certainly been growing vigorously. In 2018, at Bob Chaplin's suggestion, we introduced a 'newcomers' competition, which attracted over 50 entries in its first year. But, even before the coronavirus, the wider cider industry was struggling, with consumption falling, orchards being grubbed up – in Herefordshire in particular – and thousands of tonnes of cider apples being left to rot.

There are all sorts of reasons for this. So called 'fruit ciders' must take much of the blame. Most of them are just flavoured fermented glucose, with hardly even a passing acquaintance with any sort of apple, let alone a cider apple. But they have captured a big share of the market, at the expense of more traditional, apple-based products (even if a lot of the apple in the big national brands does come from imported apple concentrate as opposed to home-grown fruit). It's also true that rather too many hectares of orchards have been planted on the strength of the 'Magners boom', which has fizzled out since the parent company decided to focus on other products in other markets. It may be true that, even after all of those recent orchard plantings, we only grow a fraction of the cider apples that on the face of it would be needed to produce the UK's annual output of around 180 million gallons of cider. But production in a good year is still more than the real market, as opposed to the theoretical one, can absorb.

But for all that, there has indeed been a renaissance in interest and enthusiasm for what we might call 'genuine' cider. In 1980, you may recall, I could identify no more than around 50 commercial cider-makers when it came to inviting them to sell their wares at the Great British Beer Festival. I do not know what the exact number is as I write in late 2020, but Alan Stone, who has taken over from Bob Chaplin as Chief Steward of Orchards and Cider and has produced several invaluable county handbooks on cider-makers, reckons that there could be as many as 650, of whom three-quarters have started up in the last ten years.

Nor is this new breed of cider-makers by any means confined to the traditional cider-making areas. Good cider is now being made in every part of the UK. The runner-up in the 2016 British Cider Championships was a dry cider made by Andrew Boyd of Kilmegan Cider in Dundrum, County Antrim, Northern Ireland. Two years later, the reserve champion came from Stourbridge in the West Midlands, and there are thriving cider-making scenes as far afield as Nottinghamshire, Yorkshire, Cheshire and Scotland.

If the great names of West Country cider-making – Temperley, Perry, Hecks, Chaplin, Sheppy, Poole – still appear frequently on the lists of class and championship winners, so do much less familiar names. The 2015 Champion British Cider was made by a husband-and-wife team, Victoria and Simon Baxter, from Longburton near Sherborne, with only six years' cider-making experience behind them, and the 2019 winner, Rob Whale from Shepton Montague, was another comparative novice. On a rather more commercial scale, but still relative newcomers, Harry's Cider, at Long

Sutton, just up the road from where I live in Langport, are, for my money, making some of the best ciders in Somerset and carried off the top prize with their superb single variety Dabinett in 2018. We maybe don't get as many ciders and perries entered from Herefordshire as we would like (they reckon – wrongly – that our judges favour the South-Western ciders), but the brilliant Tom Oliver has been inspiring an equally exciting revival in that great cider county and is always well represented in our classes.

Perhaps the most striking difference between the ciders entered for the competitions now, as compared with, say, 15 years ago, is the extent to which the overall quality has improved. Back when I did my judging stint in 2007, the first thing that the judges did was to eliminate, often with a single sniff, any cider that was obviously 'off', usually because of a fungal problem called 'mousiness'. That hardly ever happens now.

For that, as well as the skill and enthusiasm of the cider-makers, we have a company called Vigo to thank. Set up by Alex Hill in the 1980s, it has revolutionised the equipment – mills, presses, fermentation vats, yeasts – available to the smaller cider-maker. They have been loyal sponsors of Orchards and Cider in what is a classically symbiotic relationship. And talking of sponsors, I mustn't forget the livery companies – the Fruiterers, the Coopers and the Pewterers – who have been great supporters over the years.

So, yes, the artisan cider scene is vibrant, exciting and growing. But it is also still very definitely a niche market. And that I'm afraid is how it is likely to stay. In that speech I made back in 2007, I just about managed to repeat what I consider to be the pre-conditions for genuine cider to make the sort of breakthrough that real ale has done: a workable definition, based on the use of predominantly cider varieties of apple and traditional methods, and an excise duty regime which doesn't just exempt the smallest makers from tax but which doesn't discourage them from growing, by introducing the sort of sliding scale of duty which has done so much to fuel the explosion in new small breweries. On the former there is no agreement, and with the latter the big cider-makers are opposed. So I'll not be holding my breath on either account.

However, there is still much to celebrate and enjoy about cider in Britain today, and celebrate and enjoy good cider and perry is precisely what we do each year in Orchards and Cider at the Royal Bath and West – the 'Greatest Cider Show on Earth', as we like to think of it. If there is a cloud hanging over the future, it is more to do with the Show itself than with the cider tent. In common with every major agricultural show, the Bath and West has been hit very hard by the coronavirus pandemic. I would like to think that the response from the show-going public, when events like the Bath and West can be held again, will be the same as it was in 2001 after Foot and Mouth – a realisation of how much has been lost, followed by a surge of relief and support at being able to get it back again, on the theme of 'you don't know what you've got till it's gone'.

But the future for the big shows, with their hefty overheads in staff and permanent buildings, the difficulty of attracting trade stands when so much business is now being done on the internet, the expense for a shrinking and over-worked farming community of taking their animals to a show for three days and the number of competing attractions, such as food fairs, was already looking uncertain. Despite all of our best efforts to increase attendance and attract new trade stands, from the world of food and drink especially, numbers coming through the gate seem to have reached a ceiling, even when the sun is shining. What might happen in a really wet year hardly bears thinking about.

By contrast, the one-day shows, like the Honiton Show, the Mid-Somerset, Shaftesbury and Gillingham and the lovely Melplash, are thriving. It is much easier to spare a day for a show, whether you're a farmer, a livestock exhibitor, a local business, an organisation like the NFU or a local good cause, than it is to give up the best part of a week. Overheads are low, which means ticket prices can be kept competitive and attendance can be concentrated on a single day rather than being spread over three. A one-day show may not have the scale of the Bath and West, the Devon County or the Royal Cornwall, but I'm not sure how much sheer size is a draw these days. The demise of the Royal Show in 2009 stands as a warning to all of the big shows, even if that was mostly the product of avoidable mismanagement.

I am not predicting the demise of the Bath and West, or of the Devon County or the Royal Cornwall, for that matter. The loyalty and dedication of the volunteers who keep their show on the road is such that I am confident that even the huge loss of income from the coronavirus pandemic will be survived. But it won't be easy and will require a willingness to adapt without ever losing the essence of each show's particular character and ethos. The world of West Country cider is managing to graft new methods and styles onto the fundamental principles of the cider-maker's art. The world of West Country agricultural shows will need to take a similar approach: tradition on the one hand, innovation on the other.

28

Literary landscapes

It was while I was travelling down the West coast of Ireland on my 'Celtic Odyssey' that I hit upon the idea of writing a book about the links between writers about the countryside and the landscapes that had inspired them. I had just bought a copy of JM Synge's 'Aran Islands', knowing that it would add colour and interest to a visit there, and was wondering what I might profitably do to make use of Carmen, as my motorhome is called, once the Celtic trip was over. Then it struck me: why not travel around England the following summer, writing about ... oh yes, I know what we can call them, 'literary landscapes'?

It wasn't as if the concept was entirely new to me. Back in the 1970s, when Mandy and I spent several lovely holidays at La Sablonnerie on Little Sark, I'd bought Mervyn Peake's 'Mr Pye', which was set on the island, and cycled or walked to the various locations that he had employed, to bring both place and words to life. La Coupee, the narrow causeway which links Little Sark to the main island, was one of them:

> *Ahead of him, the high, dangerously narrow track of La Coupee, curled through the night like a white ribbon. It seemed to be suspended in the air. The iron railings on either side shone balefully.*

It was a similar story with our holidays to North Devon. I never went without something by Henry Williamson or RD Blackmore. Reading the books where they'd been set just added so much enjoyment and depth to the whole experience.

Like young Henry, when he had first arrived at Braunton in the summer of 1914, I would stop at one of the gateways on the top road from Braunton to Georgeham, and gaze out across

> *an immortal tract of sea and land and sky, more infinite than anything my eyes had seen. A tract of sandhills and white lines of breakers, a lighthouse like a bleached rabbit's bone, a narrow estuary like the tail of a skate, widening into the sea. All that blue length of land ended at Hartland Point, and beyond under the westering sun the sea stretched without landfall to the coast of America.*

The lighthouse may be long gone, but in other respects the prospect is still exactly as Henry Williamson saw it, and it still takes the breath away.

However, the more I thought about the idea, the more obvious it became that the whole of England was rather too ambitious a canvas. So I settled instead for the four most south-westerly counties which, thanks to their many glorious and distinctive landscapes, have inspired more than their fair share of novelists and poets. The result was 'With Magic in my Eyes – West Country Literary Landscapes'*, published by Stephen Chalke's Fairfield Books in 2011 and a modest success. A few years later, I decided on a follow-up, this time charting the literature and landscape link-ups of the counties stretching from Wiltshire in the south to Shropshire in the north, taking in Gloucestershire, Oxfordshire, Worcestershire, Warwickshire and Herefordshire along the way. The outcome of that was 'The Coloured Counties – Literary Landscapes of the Heart of England'*, published, again by Stephen, in 2017 to rather less acclaim, even though I reckon it is the better of the two books. Copies of both are still available!

I enjoyed writing them both immensely, visiting any number of beautiful places, many of which, especially for 'The Coloured Counties', I had never been to before. I also stayed in any number of hospitable campsites in often glorious settings. And I darkened the door of many a splendid pub! For this book I will pick out just a selection of those in which the connection between landscape and literature seemed most intense.

The first, and perhaps the most obvious, was the walk that I went on from Nether Stowey to the Valley of the Rocks, in the footsteps of Coleridge and Wordsworth, in the course of which they hit upon the idea of writing 'The Ancient Mariner'. They made that particular journey in November, setting off in mid-afternoon and staying the night at Watchet after crossing the Quantocks. I did the walk in May, staying overnight in the Ship at Porlock (where another poet of that era, Robert Southey, had also stayed, writing a sonnet called simply 'Porlock' as he sat by the 'alehouse fire').

My way took me up the hill past Walford's Gibbet, named for a sad tale which Martin Hesp has brought to life in 'The Last Broomsquire', over the iron age fort of Dowsborough, where Coleridge and Dorothy Wordsworth lay in the sunshine and thought great and possibly wistful thoughts, along the track known as the Great Road, from where the two poets must have

---

* 'With Magic in my Eyes' is a line from Thomas Hardy's 'When I Set Out for Lyonnesse', 'The Coloured Counties from AE Housman's 'On Bredon Hill'

looked out across the murky waters of the Bristol Channel, prompting Coleridge to recall a dream of a skeletal ship and Wordsworth to remember a passage in Shevlocke's Voyages about giant albatrosses in the South Seas. By the time they reached the Bell in Watchet, where they stayed the night, they had fixed upon the idea of jointly writing a poem about a mariner who kills an albatross and pays for his sin. They even started writing it that evening, although Wordsworth soon lost interest and left it all to Coleridge. I contented myself with a pint and a pasty for my lunch.

So onwards to Porlock, taking the train from Watchet to Dunster (this was before the coastal path along this stretch was completed), and up over Grabbist Hill, which had been the inspiration for Mrs Cecil Alexander's 'purple-headed mountain' in 'All Things Bright and Beautiful' which she wrote whilst staying in Dunster in 1848. On this walk there is a literary connection around every corner!

After staying the night at the Ship, I made the steep climb up from Porlock Weir to Culbone and took photographs of Ash Farm, looking still much as it must have done when Coleridge was hospitalised there with dysentery and had the dream, under the influence of laudanum, which produced 'Kubla Khan'. From there I followed the coastal path along that awe-inspiring stretch of coastline where Exmoor meets the sea, to Lynmouth, Lynton and journey's end in the Valley of the Rocks, surely one of the most dramatic landscapes in all England. One of my few regrets in life is that I've never played cricket on the ground in the valley bottom. What a walk that is, and how much to think about, as well as to marvel at, along the way! And what poetry we have to thank it for!

Moving west into Cornwall (and ideally visiting Blackmore's Doone Valley en route) one is spoilt for choice: think of Launceston and Charles Causley, Morwenstow and Hawker, Betjeman and St Enodoc, Daphne du Maurier, AL Rowse and Jack Clemo and St Austell Bay, D H Lawrence and Zennor, or Virginia Woolf and St Ives.

But if I had to choose the Cornish location where the connection between landscape and writer is strongest, it would be Thomas Hardy and the towering cliffs of the North Cornwall coast east of Boscastle. The tiny village of St Juliot was where Hardy met the girl who would become his first wife, Emma Lavinia Gifford. She was the rector's sister-in-law, he the budding architect tasked with 'restoring' St Juliot's crumbling Saxon church.

Hardy set his third novel, 'A Pair of Blue Eyes' here. Elements of it are autobiographical, although not including the famous scene where Elfride, the heroine, strips to her smalls so as to use her voluminous petticoats as a rope to rescue her would-be lover Henry Knight who is clinging desperately to the cliff-top.

The young couple were happy enough roaming through the countryside together, but the marriage was not a particularly happy one. It was only when Emma died in 1912 that Hardy realised what he had lost and how much he had loved her in those early days together. The result was his 'Poems of 1912-13', which are some of the finest and most emotional he wrote.

There is 'Lyonesse' which gave my book its title, but the poem that perhaps evokes most vividly their early love and that majestic coastline is 'Beeny Cliff', from which I will quote the last two stanzas to give you the flavour:

Still in all its chasmal beauty bulks old Beeny to the sky,
And shall she and I not go there once again now March is nigh,
And the sweet things said in that March say anew there by and by?

What if still in chasmal beauty looms that wild weird western shore,
The woman now is – elsewhere – whom the ambling pony bore,
And nor knows nor cares for Beeny, and will laugh there nevermore."

Devon is richer in novelists than in poets. Henry Williamson, we have mentioned. And whatever one may think of his politics, he does bring the North Devon countryside and its people to life quite brilliantly, not only in 'Tarka the Otter' but in all his voluminous writings. The walk which I've called 'the Williamson walk', from his cottage by the church at Georgeham to the 'great, golden, tiger shaped beast, striped with dark hedgebanks' of Baggy Point, then Croyde, over Saunton Down, across and around Braunton Burrows and so to Velator, Braunton and over the top back to Georgeham, is one of the finest in Devon, especially if, like me, you're a Tarka fan.

Dartmoor has Sir Arthur Conan Doyle, Eden Philpotts and Baring-Gould, Bideford and Westward Ho! inspired Charles Kingsley to write the novel after which the seaside resort is named, Agatha Christie set two of her whodunnits on Burgh Island off the South Devon coast and the jungle of the Undercliff between Axmouth and Lyme Regis is where John Fowles set his 'French Lieutenant's Woman'.

But the moment that gave me the greatest satisfaction when I was researching the Devon chapters of 'With Magic' was finding the Ted Hughes stone in the wilds of Northern Dartmoor. The fact that it was a lovely late summer's day and there didn't seem to be soul in sight for miles around made it all the more special.

Not that Ted Hughes was particularly inspired by Dartmoor. His 'Moortown Diary' poems are based on the farm that he and his second wife Carol bought for her father Jack Orchard several miles to the north of the moor. But what he memorably called the 'grey sea-shape' of the moor forms the backdrop to those poems.

Mention of Ted Hughes brings me on to his great friend Michael Morpurgo, who lives not far away from Moortown Farm, at Iddesleigh, with his wife Clare, and whom I have known for over 20 years. It was back in the late 1990s that he had telephoned to invite me to Nethercott, to see for myself the work he and Clare were doing – with the enthusiastic support of Ted and Carol Hughes – to give inner-city children the experience of working on a farm for a week.

'Farms for City Children', the enterprise was, and is, called and I was hugely impressed with it. What I liked most about it was that this was not an attempt to 'educate' children about what a hard life farmers have and how they deserve to be better understood and more loved. Instead, it is all about the children, and how the experience of a week's hard work on a farm can broaden their horizons, build their self-worth and bring them into contact with the natural world.

Michael and Clare asked me if I would be interested in becoming a trustee, to create a link between FFCC and what might be called the farming establishment. I said that I would be delighted to and served as a trustee for 19 years, making many friends, not just at Nethercott but at the charity's two other farms: Wick Court in the Severn Vale and Treginnis Isaf on the coast beyond St David's. It was, and remains, the worthiest of causes.

Michael very kindly agreed to write the foreword for 'With Magic', something I've been feeling distinctly guilty about ever since, because, other than a passing reference to his children's novel 'The White Horse of Zennor', his name is otherwise conspicuous by its absence from the book. My excuse, and it is a feeble one, is that 'War Horse', which was inspired by a conversation in the splendid Duke of York at Iddesleigh and in which the 'home' scenes are set so firmly in the North Devon countryside, had yet to emerge from its relative obscurity. However, in writing that foreword, he was, in a way, returning a compliment, as I had written a preamble to his very moving novel, 'Out of the Ashes', set during the Foot and Mouth epidemic. We had launched the book at the NFU Headquarters in Covent Garden – Ben Gill conspicuous by his absence, a slight for which I never did forgive him.

But back to literary landscapes, and over the border into Dorset. Thomas Hardy and Wessex is probably the most obvious author-landscape connection of them all. We have already paid tribute to that great novelist and poet in Cornwall so let us turn instead to William Barnes, most famous for his dialect poetry but who was a remarkable man in many respects: brilliant teacher, gifted violinist, wood-block engraver to a professional standard, a linguist who could speak or understand some 17 different languages and, of course, poet, all entirely self-taught. He was born at Bagber, a mile or so west of Sturminster Newton, the son of a smallholder who worked on the local farms to earn some extra cash. He spent much of his childhood at Pentridge Farm by the river Stour, with his father's sister and her husband and their nine children. He was obviously deeply happy there, in that sleepy, pastoral, verdant countryside through which the river winds its leisurely way, something that comes bursting out of poems like 'Uncle an' Aunt' and 'By the River at Pentridge Farm'.

As a linguist he became strangely obsessed with the way in which, in his opinion, the 'pure English' spoken by the Anglo-Saxons of Wessex had been corrupted by 'borrowed terms' from Latin, Greek and French, and his dialect poems certainly began as almost a propaganda exercise in demonstrating the superiority of the old language. He did write in modern English as well but, strangely, it is the dialect poems, for all the forced quaintness of their language, which have much the greater poetic impact. One of my favourites is 'The Geate a-Vallen to':

In the zunshine ov our zummers
With the hay time now a-come,
How busy wer we out a-vield
Wi vew a-left at hwome,
When wagons rumbled out ov yard
Red wheeled, wi body blue
As back behind 'em loudly slamm'd
The geate a-vallen to.

The circular walk which I describe in 'With Magic', from Bagber Common via Cutt Mill to Stur and back again, is a joy, and Barnes' final resting-place, in the churchyard of Winterborne Came, from which the sun, suddenly catching the brass plate on Barnes' coffin, flashed 'The Last Signal' to Hardy, is not to be missed either.

We will return to Somerset in due course. For the moment, let us head northwards into Wiltshire and the country of 'The Coloured Counties'. For evocations of that great diarist Francis Kilvert, Langley Burrell, just north of Chippenham, is the place to go. It was where he was curate from 1872 to 1876 and, in a happy coincidence, given that I was actually reading his diaries at the time, it was where I was based when I first moved back to the West Country in 1975. But surely the most famous, and most influential, Wiltshire link between writer and landscape is to be found on the downs south of Swindon, the country of Richard Jefferies.

Jefferies wasn't just inspired by the countryside around him, he was spiritually subsumed by it. From his home next to the reservoir at Coate – a most beautiful spot in its own right, the setting for the 'Bevis' children's adventure books, the farmhouse where he grew up a Jefferies museum – he would make his way to the top of the Downs and either lie there for hours, soaking up the 'ancient sunlight' to arrive at an elevated consciousness, or march for miles across the downland landscape, billowing as it does like the rolling sea. The mysticism of his relationship with that country was a seminal influence on Henry Williamson.

Despite suffering from all sorts of ailments, Jefferies wrote prolifically on agriculture, wildlife, game-keeping, the parlous condition of the farm-worker in late-nineteenth-century England, as well as the Bevis books and a number of uneven novels of which 'Amaryllis at the Fair' is probably the best known. But the book of which he was most proud was his autobiography, 'The Story of my Heart', which explains, at more length than clarity, the mysterious communion that he felt with the natural world around him. Take a copy and read extracts while you are lying on the grassy ramparts of Liddington Camp, high above Swindon, the M4 and the North Wiltshire countryside, and you will feel maybe just an inkling of what Jefferies was driving at.

From here we can walk east along the Ridgeway to the village and its surrounding countryside which was my favourite Oxfordshire location, Uffington. The village itself was home from 1933 to 1945 to John Betjeman and his wife Penelope Chetwode. He was happier there than she was, and the village inspired his poem 'Uffington'.

A century earlier Thomas Hughes had grown up in the village. It is from Uffington that Tom Brown departs on being sent away to Rugby School, a connection now celebrated by the 'Tom Brown's School Museum', in what was indeed the village school in Hughes' day. Uffington also boasts the 'Blowing Stone', set modestly on the roadside outside what was once the Blowing Stone Inn.

Legend has it that King Alfred himself applied his mouth to one of the holes in the boulder to summon his troops for the Battle of Ashdown against the marauding Danes. Sadly, so far from the 'grewsome sound between a moan and a roar' which Thomas Hughes describes in his 'Scouring of the White Horse' my best efforts produced not a squeak.

But that mention of King Alfred and the Battle of Ashdown does lead us to the downland above the village, which is as rich in literary connections as Uffington itself. A mile of so west along the Ridgway at the top of the downs is Wayland's Smithy, a huge Neolithic barrow, which features in Sir Walter Scott's 'Kenilworth', so called for the invisible blacksmith – possibly the Devil – who would shoe a horse overnight if a silver coin had been left on the stone lintel over the barrow's entrance.

Then there is the White Horse itself, one of the most ancient and distinctive in all of southern England, overlooking Dragon's Hill, where St George killed the dragon. Besides Hughes' descriptions of the seven-yearly 'scourings' and associated merry-making, GK Chesterton found inspiration here for his poem 'The Ballad of the White Horse', celebrating the victory of the Christian Saxons over the pagan Danes.

To Chesterton's patriotic eye, the White Horse stands for Britain and British values:

Before the gods that made the gods
Had seen their sunrise pass,
The White Horse of the White Horse Vale
Was cut out of the grass.

Before the gods that made the gods
Had drunk at dawn their fill,
The White Horse of the White Horse Vale
Was hoary on the hill.

Age beyond age on British land,
Aeons on aeons gone,
Was peace and war in western hills,
And the White Horse looked on.

For the White Horse knew England
When there was none to know;
He saw the first oar break or bend,
He saw heaven fall and the world end,
O God, how long ago.

The poem may be over-long and patchy in quality, but it was cherished by British troops in the trenches of the First World War, as well as offering up two apposite quotations used in Times editorials during the second such conflict: 'I tell you naught for your comfort' for the fall of Crete and '"The high tide!" King Alfred cried. "The high tide and the turn!"' after the battle of El Alamein and Churchill's 'end of the beginning' speech.

An Oxfordshire location not to be missed is Boar's Hill, south of Oxford, with its associations with two Poets Laureate in John Masefield and Robert Bridges, two poets of the First World War in Robert Graves and Edmund Blunden, and Matthew Arnold, who wrote of the 'Signal Tree', which is still there and from where he looked down upon 'that sweet city with her dreaming spires'. What was once a golf course is now in the care of the Oxford Preservation Trust and offers both fine views over the city and lovely walks.

Warwickshire is Shakespeare country, and even though he set most of his plays (the history ones apart) in unlikely foreign parts his countryman's instincts and agricultural knowledge do sometimes break through, although it's hard to trace any linkage on the ground. Tolkein was, of course, a Brummie and quite possibly got the inspiration for the clash of cultures in 'The Lord of the Rings' from the contrast between the Lickey Hills, where he loved to walk – the Shire – and the dark, smoky city spread out below – Mordor.

The Warwickshire literary connection that I most enjoyed was that between George Eliot and her native Nuneaton. The town itself has not a great deal to offer, other than a fine statue of the novelist, but just to the south, next to a huge roundabout, is Griff House, now an undistinguished pub but once the big farmhouse where the young Mary Ann Evans was brought up by her mother and father, who managed a big local estate. Just up a lane is a bridge over a canal and, if you follow the towpath north, you will come to a sign for 'Griff Hollows', which is unmistakeably the original for 'Red Deeps' where Maggie Tulliver has her fateful romantic encounter with Philip Waken in 'The Mill on the Floss'. It is strange to be in so wild and seemingly remote a spot, so close to the town and its hustle and bustle.

If you are looking for remoteness, then you will find it in the south Shropshire hills. This was a new landscape to me, but I spent a happy and energetic few days in early 2016, walking on Long Mynd in the snow and making the acquaintance of the Stiperstones and the Devil's Chair.

This is Mary Webb country, the 'loam and lovechild' novelist whose genre was so brilliantly mocked by Stella Gibbons in 'Cold Comfort Farm'. Rather like Eden Phillpotts and Dartmoor she seemed to construct the plots of her novels to fit the landscape, rather than the other way around. With the possible exception of 'Precious Bane', they are not particularly distinguished works of literature but, if you are visiting this beautiful and still largely undiscovered corner of England, be sure to take a Mary Webb novel with you.

There are any number of walks that will take you to Mary Webb's most celebrated locations. My favourite was from the little village of Bridges, up the hill past Coates Farm to the Long Mynd and then back through Ratlinghope (pronounced ratchup) to the excellent Horseshoe Inn. And, talking of pubs, the Anchor, a lonely roadside inn almost into Wales to the west of Clun – the 'Mermaid's Rest' as it is in Mary Webb's 'Seven for a Secret' – is also worth a visit, if you can find it open.

AE Houseman we will come to when we reach Worcestershire. Suffice to say that Wenlock Edge (the place not the poem) I found a bit of a disappointment because, as with so many of these locations, the trees and undergrowth have been allowed to run riot, blocking out the views. It is possibly best appreciated from the summit of the Wrekin, which also overlooks the remarkably well-preserved Roman fort of Viroconium (Wroxeter), which features in 'On Wenlock Edge' as well as inspiring an early poem by Wilfred Owen.

The outer reaches of Herefordshire, along the Welsh border, where Bruce Chatwin's novel 'On the Black Hill' is set, were similarly undiscovered country to me. I decided we would make a a weekend of it for a visit, staying in Hay-on-Wye, just over the border into Wales, as a special treat for Claire on her birthday!

The landscapes here are mean, moody and magnificent. The weather was just mean and moody. This is not the Herefordshire of one's imagination: the orchards, the meadows, the rich loamy soils, the beautiful white-faced cattle, or even the polytunnels. Under the louring bulk of the Black Mountains, the fields are small, the land is poor and people are few. I have been nowhere in England that feels quite so remote.

All of which makes it the perfect setting for Chatwin's novel, or maybe saga would be a better word, about the entwined lives of a pair of unworldly farming brothers, Lewis and Benjamin Jones. The action centres around two farms, The Rock, whose owners, the Watkins family, are locked in a vicious feud with the Jones', and The Vision, home to the brothers.

Claire and I found the Rock easily enough, looking every bit as tattered and run-down as it is described in the novel, complete with rusting coach, a half-finished shed, a chilly-looking slate-roofed farmhouse with a punctured horsebox keeled over outside, all in the lee of a towering slab of mountain.

However, there is no exact equivalent for The Vision, which Chatwin has straddling the English-Welsh border. The best match we could find was Black Hill Farm, not exactly on the border but with views both west to Wales and east to England, the abandoned tractors, the piles of rusty machinery, the grimy windows and peeling paintwork suggesting exactly the sort of no-frills slavery to the land which the novel depicts.

We passed it as we drove up the steep lane to the car park below the Cat's Back, and there could be no more appropriately descriptive name for the razor-edge escarpment to which one eventually climbs. I walked north along the narrow path, the slopes on either side falling almost precipitously to the Olchthon Brook in Wales and the river Monnow in England, determined to reach the Black Hill itself. Claire took one look from the summit and scrambled back down to the car. In the sort of weather we endured that day, it is a frightening as well as an awe-inspiring landscape. But as a context for Chatwin's atmospheric book? Perfect.

The next day we headed south to a very different literary landscape, the Leadon Valley in north Gloucestershire, which for a few years a century previously had been home to not one but five poets: Lascelles Abercrombie, Wilfrid Gibson, Robert Frost, Edward Thomas and John Drinkwater, with a sixth, Rupert Brooke, a regular visitor.

This was my second visit to the country of the 'Dymock poets', timed to coincide with the flowering of the wild daffodils for which this stretch of countryside is renowned. I had been disappointed with my first visit the previous summer. Yes, the poets' various habitations were still there – Frost's and Thomas's cottages scarcely more than a field apart, and Gloucestershire County Council had done its best to encourage literary pilgrimages by signposting a series of 'poets' paths'. But I'm afraid that if any of the poets were to see this countryside now they would be heartbroken. Most of the apple, pear, plum and cherry orchards have been grubbed up, the meadows ploughed and planted with heavily sprayed oilseed rape and wheat, hardly a Hereford cow in sight, and several of the paths had been allowed to become so overgrown as to be impassable. But at least the pub, the Beauchamp Arms, is excellent.

From almost anywhere in the Leadon Valley, you can see May Hill, surmounted by its copse of Scots pines. It dominates the southern horizon and seemed an obvious next port of call, especially because of its links with one of the most celebrated of the Dymock poets, Edward Thomas. His most famous poem is, of course, 'Adlestrop' but I'm afraid that unremarkable village hardly merits a visit, given that British Rail, in a quite extraordinary act of cultural vandalism, demolished the station at which Thomas's train stopped 'unwontedly' on that hot summer's afternoon in 1914.

May Hill is a much better bet for lovers of Thomas' poetry, for it was on the slopes of this hill that he wrote one of his best-known poems, 'Words' , whilst on a visit to his friend, Jack Haines in June 1915.

> *Will you choose*
> *Sometimes –*
> *As the winds use*
> *A crack in a wall*
> *Or a drain,*
> *Their joy or their pain*
> *To whistle through –*
> *Choose me,*
> *You English words?*
>
> *I know you:*
> *You are light as dreams,*
> *Tough as oak,*
> *Precious as gold,*
> *As poppies and corn,*
> *Or an old cloak:*

The views from May Hill are stunning in every direction except to the north-east, where they have been blocked off by an unlovely larch plantation. But it is one of the most rewarding of all literary destinations, with its echoes of John Masefield, Ivor Gurney and Winifred Foley, as well as Edward Thomas.

I am conscious that this chapter is running away with me, so I will mention just a few more places were the walks are lovely and the literary associations are strong. Let us start with the Malverns, that magnificent range of mini-mountains that erupt from the flood-plain of the river Severn. Think of the Malverns and you probably think of music and Sir Edward Elgar more than you would think of literature. But WH Auden lived near here in the 1930s, and walked and wrote on these spectacular hills. And it was falling asleep and dreaming on the slopes of Herefordshire Beacon on a May morning in the fourteenth century that was the inspiration for William Langland's 'Piers Plowman'. Walking there, and looking east, one can see immediately what he meant by his 'fair field full of folk'.

Almost anywhere in and around the city of Gloucester will have echoes of the brilliant but tragic composer and poet, Ivor Gurney. Crickley Hill with its country park is the most obvious, although I found the walk from the Boat at Ashleworth to Burrrow Hill the most rewarding. If you want to link Gurney with his great friend and fellow Gloucestershire poet, Will Harvey, then head for Framilode and the Arlingham Horseshoe

> to see how Ashleworth nestles by the river
> Where eyes and heart and soul may drink their fill

Not far to the East, on the other side of the Cotswold escarpment, is Gloucestershire's, if not the entire West Country's, most visited literary landscape, the Slad Valley, home not just to Laurie Lee and the setting for 'Cider with Rosie', but also to his friend, a less heralded writer but arguably almost as good a poet, Frank Mansell. The Gloucestershire Wildlife Trust has created a 'Laurie Lee Wildlife Trail' which includes all the most evocative 'Cider with Rosie' locations and runs through some beautiful countryside, even if, as so often, the landscape has been allowed to become rather too overgrown for my taste. I spent a blissful summer's day walking through the Slad Valley, finishing at the Woolpack, which was Laurie Lee's local. It has a bar dedicated to his memory and is just an apple's throw from his grave in the lower churchyard.

But, beguiling though the Slad Valley undoubtedly is, my favourite literary landscape destinations are almost all in high places, from which you can look out and reflect on yourself and the world around you, just as William Langland did from the Malverns all those centuries ago. And no high place has more literary associations than the great bulk of Bredon Hill, on the Gloucestershie-Worcestershire border, looking west to where the Avon joins the Severn with the Malverns beyond, north to the great Midland plain, east to Broadway and south to the Cotswold ridge.

AE Housman's poem 'On Bredon Hill' provided me with the title for 'The Coloured Counties', and Bredon Hill could fairly be described as the fulcrum of the book. Yet whilst it is probable that Housman may have walked on the hill, given that it is more or less on the way from his home at Fockbury just outside Bromsgrove, to his godmother's house at Woodchester in the Cotswolds, where he loved to visit, there is no evidence that he did so.

Rather, as with his 'blue remembered hills' of Shropshire, it was the views of Bredon Hill from the hill at Worm's Ash above his home, rather than the views from Bredon Hill that stirred his muse. That would also account for the fact that 'On Bredon Hill' is included in 'A Shropshire Lad', even though it is nowhere near that county. Still, it bothers me not at all whether he visited

Bredon Hill or not, any more than does the fact that his Shropshire locations were in most cases imagined rather than real. The emotions that the poems convey are real enough, and the poetry in which they are expressed is lyrical enough. Housman, a crotchety, rather stuck-up repressed homosexual, may have been a hard man to love, but he, or maybe his alter ego, wrote some very fine poetry which is redolent of the English countryside.

My first visit to Bredon Hill, back in the 1980s, had been to enjoy the cider in the pub at Elmley Castle. When I returned in the summer of 2015, I camped near Ashton-under-Hill, where Fred Archer farmed and, when he was asked to give a talk to his local Townswomen's Guild, discovered he had a talent for story-telling. The result was over 20 books recounting rustic tales of farming, the countryside, his friends and neighbours and, of course, of Bredon Hill. Not great literature perhaps, but good reading nonetheless.

I started my walk over Bredon Hill from the churchyard of St Barbara's, opposite Fred's farm and where he is buried. As I climbed higher up the eastern flank, my thoughts turned to Housman and then to Shakespeare as I looked out north beyond Evesham towards Stratford and then to the man who argued cogently that Shakespeare may himself once have walked here, John Moore. A Tewkesbury man, he was a prolific journalist, a campaigning countryman, a joint founder of the Cheltenham literary festival and a vivid and amusing story-teller, most famously in his 'Brensham Trilogy' – 'Portrait of Elmbury' (set in Tewkesbury), 'Brensham Village' (set in the village of Bredon) and 'The Blue Field' (set on Bredon Hill). The books are funny, brimful of local colour, and he has a wonderful cast of characters, so much so that the books were adapted for a BBC television series in the 1960s.

From 'Parson's Folly', as Banbury Stone Tower on the summit is popularly known, Moore claimed that one could see twelve counties, four cathedrals and sixteen abbeys. That may be a slight exaggeration, but on the day I was there, I certainly counted Worcestershire, Gloucestershire, Herefordshire, Warwickshire, Shropshire, Staffordshire, Monmouthshire, Glamorgan and Somerset among the counties, and Gloucester and Worcester among the cathedrals. There are few finer prospects in the entire West of England than the view from this summit. Next time your journey takes you up or down the M5, make time for a detour to Bredon, with its elegant church spire, and a walk up the hill to Parson's Folly. You will not be disappointed.

And so back home to Somerset, and to my very own literary landscape, spread out before me as I write: the Somerset Levels with the hills on the

Dorset border beyond. The poet CS Sisson lived just up the hill from here and mined the Levels landscape for metaphors. The river Parrett, which flows past the bottom of my garden, has been celebrated in verse by my friend James Crowden. Burrow Hill, topped by its lone sycamore, makes me think of Peter Benson, whose debut novel 'The Levels' was set in the countryside around the hill and who, as a novelist who uses landscape in his books as powerfully as anyone, was kind enough to write the foreword to 'The Coloured Counties'.

Then there is Ham Hill, reputedly the largest Iron Age fort in southern England, where the eccentric John Cowper Powys set his Hardy-esque novel, 'Wood and Stone', and thinking of John Cowper from that remarkable Powys family puts me in mind as well of his brother Llewellyn and his wonderful West Country essays. On a clear day, I can just about make out the 'Thyrsus-shaped' tower on St Michael's Hill, above Montacute, the village that was home to the farm-worker poet Thomas Shoel, and where the Rev Francis Powys fathered his brood of 11 extraordinarily talented children.

And if I make my way up the steps to the top of Langport's 'Hill' and look west, there are the Quantocks, hovered over, it almost seems, by the spirits of Samuel Taylor Coleridge and William and Dorothy Wordsworth.

One way or another it is not a bad vantage point for someone with an interest in writers and the countryside!

Writing the two literary landscapes books was a labour of love. I hadn't really expected to make any money out of them and didn't! But the process of researching and writing them was a joy. Many of the writers had previously just been names. Finding out all about poets like William Barnes and AE Housman, or novelists like John Cowper Powys and Bruce Chatwin, and being able to walk in their footsteps, writing the book as I went along, was a deeply enriching experience.

My research also brought me into contact with a group of people I had never really encountered before – the members of the literary appreciation societies dedicated to my various authors, any one of whom would probably know more about their hero or heroine than I did. As very much an enthusiastic amateur, submitting my text for their approval was sometimes distinctly daunting. Mostly they were kind and corrected my mistakes and misjudgements gently, although I did get a frightful telling off from a Cornish expert on the blind poet Jack Clemo for getting his (distinctly complex) poetic inspiration entirely wrong, and very glad of it I was when I discovered the error of my ways.

Researching Ted Hughes was a particular challenge, knowing his widow Carol and how jealously she guards his reputation. We had a meeting, kindly facilitated by the novelist Jane Feaver, with whom I worked at Farms for City Children, in which she put me on the right track, and, after a great many drafts had gone to and fro, the text was finally agreed. Carol even very kindly loaned me a photograph of Ted and her father, Jack Orchard, having a drink together at Hatherleigh Market. All seemed just fine, until Stephen Chalke decided to edit Jack out of the picture, me having failed to explain who he was. Carol did eventually speak to me again, but it took some time!

Launching the books was fun, as well. For 'Magic' we chose Culmstock Village Hall, the village in the Blackdowns where RD Blackmore had been curate and where he'd set his novel, 'Perlycross'. Michael Morpurgo was there, alongside the novelist Peter Benson and the poet James Crowden, all of whom gave readings, plus a strong representation from the various literary societies, including a chap from the William Barnes Society who gave an extempore (and largely impenetrable) reading in Barnes' version of the Dorset dialect. Colleagues from the NFU turned up as well, Rebecca Pow was there, and Vic Marks, with his wife Anna, made a special guest appearance, much to the delight of Peter Benson, who seemed positively star-struck at his presence. A Taste of the West buffet was washed down with Bolhayes Cider, and a good time was had by all. It was if all of the threads of my career had been woven together in one event.

Appearances followed at various literary festivals, including the very posh 'Ways With Words' event at Dartington Hall. It was a new and slightly frightening experience to know less about my subject than most of my audience, but the saving grace was always the West Country itself.

Our literary associations are one of this region's greatest treasures, and with one or two notable exceptions – like the ubiquitous Tarka – we don't make enough of them. My only regret is that my mother, who taught English all her working life and knew far more about my authors than I did, had died just a few months before 'Magic' was published. How much she would have enjoyed meeting all those kindred spirits at the festivals – and putting me right if I got anything wrong!

29

In conclusion

I suppose I should start this brief retrospective with regrets, such as they are. I might have followed a different career, as a history don, perhaps, had Plymouth City Council given me a grant to study for a DPhil, or maybe as a television presenter or full-time journalist. But I doubt if I have ever been enough of an intellectual for the former, or sufficiently pushy and enquiring for the latter. Besides, as far as a media career was concerned, actually getting on and doing things has provided me with far more job satisfaction than I could ever have had from solely reporting on or criticising what other people might have been doing.

In terms of changing things for the better, I might perhaps have achieved more had I gone into full-time politics with the Liberals, or the Liberal Democrats as the party became. There would have been three problems with that. The first is my personal political philosophy. I am no fan of socialism and to vote Tory would be unconscionable. My liberalism is of an old-fashioned, Gladstonian brand. I am no nannying social democrat, so that I've never really fitted comfortably into the modern Liberal Democrat mould. The second is that, while I am fairly sure I would have been a good constituency MP, I am equally sure that I would have been for ever falling out with the party managers, given that, by nature, I am anything but a conformist. And the third? Getting elected!

I regret spiting my father by insisting on rowing in my second year at Monkton Combe, rather than sticking with cricket and learning how to bat properly. I regret not trying harder to persuade my brother to have his 'pain in the guts' properly explored and dealt with until it was too late. And, in my professional life, I regret that I couldn't quite get a tidal exclusion sluice on the Parrett over the line, and so paved the way for the regeneration of Bridgwater. But that's about it.

As for achievements, it would be fair to say that my fifty years and more of honest endeavour in various fields will scarcely have created even the slightest ripple on the great ocean of world history. But I hope that I have helped a lot of good people weather various storms, like milk quotas, BSE and Foot and Mouth, as well as playing a useful role in good causes like real ale, local food, intelligent water management and good cider. The fact that I was able to play a part in finding a workable accommodation between farming and conservation in places that I love, like Dartmoor, Exmoor and the Somerset Levels, gives me particular satisfaction, even if so little has been done to build on the progress that was made back in the 70s and 80s. It is gratifying as well that my writing and broadcasting about cricket seems to be enjoyed. I could never aspire to the standards set by my father in either, but I do feel as if I've made the best of what talent I was blessed with.

And talking of blessings reminds me of my sister Felicity, and the play she wrote called 'Kurt Cobain in my Wardrobe', which was performed some years ago at the Tobacco Factory in Bristol to considerable critical acclaim. Faced with a series of familial difficulties and crises of confidence, the hero is fortunate enough to be able to take advice from the ghost of the Nirvana lead singer, whom he encounters in his wardrobe. It concludes with Kurt reminding him of what is really the dominant message of the entire piece – that we should count our blessings. And how right that is!

So here goes. I was unquestionably blessed in my genes, which provided a good helping of intelligence, a streak of competitiveness, a strong work ethic and a smidgeon of ball-playing ability. I was also blessed in my parents. My father may have been a difficult man to live with but, both directly through his encouragement and indirectly through the examples he set, both the good to aspire to and the bad to avoid, he has been my biggest single influence. However, it was thanks to my mother that both Chippy and I were able to come safely through what could have been very difficult childhoods. She was there for us throughout our adult lives as well, sometimes chiding, sometimes disappointed, sometimes proud of us but always loving, and to my wives and family as much as to me.

My family is my greatest blessing, It seems to have grown quite remarkably since that nuclear family of four, back in the 1950s, of which I am the only survivor. Even with the loss of Chippy, there are now 22 of us, counting wives, children and their husbands and wives, siblings and their families and my five grandchildren.

Mandy and Claire have both had a lot to put up with, I'm ashamed to say, Mandy especially, but I would never have achieved half of what I have done without their love and support. Claire was a tower of strength both during Chippy's illness and after his death.

Credit for the way my three children have turned out belongs almost entirely to Mandy. They and my five grandchildren are a very special blessing: Joanna, married to Phil Limb, living on Dartmoor with their two bright and beautiful daughters, Hermione and Darcy; Rebecca, married to Nick Kearns, living on Guernsey with their two handsome sons, William and Arthur; and George, married to Pippa (Frayne as was) living just down the road at Shepton Beauchamp, with their daughter Grace, who is an absolute poppet. Joanna and Phil have the Riverford organic vegetable box franchise for North Devon, so a farming link there. Becky and Nick are both in finance. George works for the Met Office while Pippa is with the National Trust. I'm very proud of them all.

My brother Chippy I have written about. He was a blessing, even if it may not have seemed that way when as boys we were fighting like cat and dog. I keep a small glass jar of his ashes on the window-shelf in front of my desk and think of him every day.

My other brother Adam is away in Abu Dhabi, where he is Headmaster of Cranleigh Preparatory School, with his wife Amanda and daughter Isabella. Like George, Adam is an alarmingly fit triathlete, something that he gets from his father, who was a considerable cross-country runner in his youth, and which George certainly didn't get from his! Adam's son Joel, my nephew, is a bright, athletic and personable chip off the old block.

My sister Felicity is probably the most creative of the three of us and has novels in her as well as plays, although for the moment she has her hands full with her two boys, Matthew and Murray, and special needs teaching. She and husband Dave live with the boys and nine cats at High Littleton, just up the road from where Felicity grew up in the Old Market Tavern.

I have been hugely fortunate in my NFU colleagues down the years, be they in the Somerset County Branch or the Regional Office in Exeter or in the Public Affairs department at Stoneleigh. It is hard to think of one's erstwhile boss as a blessing, but I do owe Richard Macdonald a special debt of gratitude for the way he stuck by me, sometimes a bit wearily, when calls for my head were being made at regular intervals from the various bigwigs or ministers I had upset.

Then there were the secretaries and PAs who looked after me so well, saved me from so many disasters, put up with my foibles and kept me sane down the years. In chronological order: Joan Townsend, Kendall Noyes, Kay Mayberry, Angela Nation, Helen Robinson, Julie Archer, Lucy

Farmiloe and Jeanette Clarke, with a special mention as well for dear June Harry. I was blessed in every one of them.

It is a fact that I don't have any really close friends. My best friend was always Chippy. Stephen Hopson would be my oldest friend, with John Knight not far behind, but they live on Dartmoor and at Sherston respectively, so we don't see each other that often. What I am blessed with, however, are the many very good friends that I have made from my time working in the farming community, in cricket, in journalism, at the Bath and West, in Langport and in golf.

And not the least of my blessings is where I have been able to live for most of my life: Totnes, Sparkwell, Derriford, Dousland, Oxford, Sparkwell again, Sherston, Clayhidon and Langport. Apart from three and a half years spent in London in the early 70s I have been fortunate enough to have lived in the South-West for all of my time on earth, and I would not have had it any other way. Claire and I now live in adjacent but not adjoining cottages, on Langport's hill looking south across the Levels towards Muchelney, so we each have our personal space – and I can assure you that that is a blessing as well, especially for Claire!

As for what the future may hold, who knows? I am just very grateful to have got this far.

Appendix

A vision for the Somerset Levels and Moors in 2030

We see the Somerset Levels and Moors in 2030 as a thriving, nature-rich wetland landscape, with grassland farming taking place on the majority of the land. The impact of extreme weather events is being reduced by land and water management in both the upper catchments and the flood plain and by greater community resilience.

- The landscape remains one of open pasture land divided by a matrix of ditches and rhynes, often bordered by willow trees. Extensively managed wet grassland dominates the scene with the majority of the area in agriculture in 2010 still being farmed in 2030.

- The floodplains are managed to accommodate winter flooding whilst reducing flood risk elsewhere. These flood events are widely recognised as part of the special character of the Levels and Moors.

- The frequency and duration of severe flooding has been reduced, with a commensurate reduction in the flood risk to homes, businesses and major roads in the area.

- During the summer months there is an adequate supply and circulation of high quality irrigation water to meet the needs of the farmers and wildlife in the wetlands. On the low-lying peat moors, water levels have been adopted which conserve peat soils and avoid the loss of carbon to the atmosphere. Water quality has improved and meets all EU requirements.

- The Levels and Moors are regarded as one of the great natural spectacles in the UK and Europe with a mix of diverse and valuable habitats. Previously fragmented habitats such as fen and flower-rich meadows have been re-connected and are widely distributed. In the north of the area over 1,600 hectares are managed as reed-bed, open water and bog. Elsewhere the populations of breeding waders exceed 800 pairs. Each winter the wetlands attract large numbers of wintering wildfowl and waders regularly exceeding 130,000 birds. Wetland species such as Crane, Bittern and pollinator populations flourish.

- Optimum use is being made of the agricultural potential of the Levels and Moors, particularly on the higher land, whilst unsustainable farming practices have been adapted or replaced to secure a robust, sustainable base to the local economy
- New businesses, including those based on 'green tourism', have developed, meeting the needs of local people and visitors alike, while brands based on the area's special qualities are helping farmers to add value to the meat, milk and other goods and services that they produce.
- The internationally important archaeological and historic heritage of the area is protected from threats to its survival and is justly celebrated, providing a draw to visitors and a source of pride and identity to local communities.
- Farmers and landowners are rewarded financially for the public benefits and ecosystem services they provide by their land management including flood risk management, coastal management, carbon storage and the natural environment.

Somerset Levels and Moors Task Force January 31 2014

INDEX

(for reasons of space, close family and some incidental names are omitted)